B. H. HAGGIN began in 1923 to contribute articles and reviews to *The Nation* and other magazines. He was music critic of the Brooklyn *Daily Eagle* from 1934 to 1937. In 1936 he became record critic, and from 1939 to 1957 he was music critic of *The Nation*. From 1946 to 1949 he wrote the column "Music on the Radio" for the Sunday New York *Herald Tribune;* he reviewed records in *The New Republic* from 1957 to 1966; and he reviewed music and ballet in *The Hudson Review* from 1958 through 1972. He now reviews records in *The Yale Review* and writes on music for *The New Republic*. His previous books include *Music on Records, Music for the Man Who Enjoys "Hamlet," Music in The Nation, Conversations with Toscanini, Music Observed* now in print as *35 Years of Music, The Toscanini Musicians Knew, Ballet Chronicle and A Decade of Music.*

D1211406

This edition contains a supplement with additional new recordings since 1970.

BOOKS BY B. H. HAGGIN

B. H. HAGGIN

THE NEW
LISTENER'S COMPANION
AND RECORD GUIDE

FIFTH EDITION

HORIZON PRESS • NEW YORK

OCT. 28/79

Best Wishes On Your 26th,

Love

Sheila

FOREWORD TO
THE NEW LISTENER'S COMPANION
AND RECORD GUIDE

As against the writing that encourages the reader to find the meaning of a piece of music in its historical background, this book begins by encouraging him to find it in the internal operation of the piece. Thus it asks him to do as a listener what E. M. Forster once prescribed for the critic: to consider the work as an object, an entity, and discover the life in it. And two chapters on musical procedures and forms, in which the author describes the life, the internal operation he perceives in certain pieces of music, will help the reader to do this for himself with the other music discussed in the book.

What the reader discovers in this music from his own listening will provide him with the means of testing the evaluations in the survey of the literature of music that follows the introductory chapters. This survey offers a reasoned exercise of judgment and taste by the author, which—since it is reasoned —is not dogmatic, and in fact induces a similar exercise of judgment and taste by the reader. And this is true also of the chapters on performance of music, on jazz, on the critical writing that has been done on music; and of the new sections dealing with recorded performances of the music discussed in the book.

CONTENTS

PART ONE

PART ONE

1

INTRODUCTION: THE READER
AND THE CRITIC

The first chapters of this book are what I have thought would be helpful to someone who has just begun to be interested in music—interested, for one thing, in discovering whether he gets from music anything like what he gets from a novel, a play, a poem, a painting. They include a description of musical procedures and forms from which he should not be deterred by the quotations in musical notation: all he is asked to do is to try letting his eye follow as he listens—something he will, I think, find not only possible, but helpful in impressing what he hears on his mind. The knowledge of the procedures and forms will be helpful in the same way; and an additional benefit from this material will be detailed acquaintance with several great pieces of music. But he can, if he prefers, skip Chapters 3 and 4.

After these first chapters the book offers a critical survey of the literature of music, addressed not only to the newly interested reader but to anyone—whatever his musical experience and understanding—whose interest in music gives him a further interest in what critical perception may reveal in it. I have written in the expectation that he is going to do his own listening and reach his own conclusions about what he hears; and that I will merely be pointing out things for him to listen to and evaluate. Which is to say that I will be performing the function of the critic; and I think it would be good for me to state at the outset what I understand this function to be.

The critic is a music-lover and listener like his readers: he is the expert and professional listener, who is assumed to have greater powers of perception and judgment than the amateur, and therefore to be able to make his readers aware of things in the music which they mightn't notice by themselves. He functions as a sort of guidepost, saying in effect: "I hear this happening at this point"—after which his reader listens and may say: "Yes, I hear it too." But he also may say: "No, I hear *this*." That is, the critic uses his powers to animate those of his reader—but only to animate, not to dictate: what he says about a piece of music is true for the reader only if it is confirmed by the reader's own ears. And each critic writes for the group of people who have found his perceptions and evaluations sufficiently confirmed by their own experience.

Underlying what I have just said is the fact that criticism does not, as some people think it must, offer the one possible and correct opinion, arrived at by measuring the piece of music with a set of established caliper-like esthetic principles for determining the good and the beautiful. The piece of music is a special kind of communication; the critic reports the effect of that communication on a mind operating not with impersonal esthetic principles but with personal sensitiveness, perception and taste; and the communication may impress different minds differently. The critic, then, reports not what is true, but what is true for him, and what becomes true also for the reader who finds it to be so when he listens to the piece.

All this to prepare the reader for the discovery in this book that I too have, as a critic, done my own listening and evaluating—the discovery, that is, of opinions which occasionally differ from those of other critics and even from that awesome authority, accepted opinion. Accepted opinion finds greatness in every note set down on paper by a great composer like

4

Bach or Mozart; I hear in some works—and must report hearing—dull products of a routine exercise of expert craftsmanship. Accepted opinion holds some symphonies and concertos of Brahms to be works of tremendous profundity, and there was a time when they impressed me that way; but today I hear in them only the pretension to profundity. And on the other hand I esteem Tchaikovsky, to whom accepted opinion condescends.

There would be no need of preparing the reader for such dissents in a book about literature. But anyone conditioned by the announcements of music on the radio, the notes on record envelopes, the program notes at concerts, the reviews of these concerts in newspapers, needs to be prepared for the shock of a questioning of the accepted valuation of a theoretic exercise by Bach, a potboiler by Mozart, an imitation of Beethoven by Brahms, a piece of slick trash by Puccini or Ravel.

In sum: I am bound to report what I hear; and the reader then is free to find what I say to be true or not true for him. That is our relation in this book.

I should perhaps mention that if I take more space for Berlioz than for Haydn it isn't because I consider Berlioz greater than Haydn: the space in each instance is what is required by what I think needs to be said about each composer. And the same for differences in treatment of the composers—e.g. the inclusion of detailed analysis of particular works, or of quotations in musical notation, in one instance and not in another.

And I should, finally, speak of the difficulties in writing about music—primarily the difficulty in using words about a means of communicating what words cannot communicate. I operate on the assumption that it is legitimate to speak of the *Benedictus* of Beethoven's *Missa Solemnis* being about the blessedness at the heart of things, even though precisely what Beethoven "says" about this blessedness is something to be learned only from the music.

5

2

THE MEANING OF MUSIC

I said that a piece of music is a communication. And if you are one of those to whom a Beethoven symphony is a lot of meaningless noises, you may say: "Tell me what it communicates"—meaning of course "Tell me in words." But the simple inescapable fact of the situation is that what Beethoven says in those sounds cannot be told in words.

Someone observed once that art is not superfluous—by which he meant that the artist produces it to communicate something he can't communicate in any other way. You can see this most clearly in poetry: the particular images and overtones of sense and feeling from the lines

> When to the Sessions of sweet silent thought
> I summon up remembrance of things past

are communicated only by this particular assemblage of words; and you won't get them from a statement in other words like "When in hours of meditation I recall the past."

So with painting. In one of his finest essays, *Music at Night*, Aldous Huxley writes about two paintings of the Virgin, one by Piero della Francesca, the other by Tura—about how they observe the same current symbolical conventions but differ "in the forms and their arrangement, in the disposition of the lines and planes and masses," and how as a result of this pictorial difference they "say" different things. Huxley describes what he thinks those different things are; but the point of his essay

6

is that words cannot really tell us what the two paintings "say," and that we can learn this only from the paintings—from Piero's "welding together of smooth and beautifully balanced solidities," from Tura's intricate lines and writing surfaces—themselves.

This is true also of the grave, powerful, massive emotions to which, says Roger Fry, we are compelled by a Cézanne still-life—by the way a few apples and pears, commonplace objects entirely without emotional associations, are "reduced to pure elements of space and volume" and "coordinated and organized by the artist's sensual intelligence." That is, Fry can describe those emotions as grave, powerful and massive; but we can discover what they really are only from that organization of elements of space and volume on the canvas.

So with the piece of music, an organization of sounds which don't, like words, refer to external objects, but do have internal coherences that are meaningful to an ear sensitized to them. Huxley's example in his essay is the *Benedictus* of Beethoven's *Missa Solemnis;* and he says correctly that it is a statement about the blessedness at the heart of things, but that no words can give us any knowledge of what Beethoven felt this blessedness to be—that we can learn this only from the music.

Actually, Cézanne compels us to those grave, powerful, massive emotions not just with one painting of apples and pears but with many; and the state of inner illumination and superearthly exaltation that Beethoven attained in his last years is communicated to us not just in one piano sonata or string quartet but in a number of works. And from this you may understand that our interest in a work of art is an interest not just in its meaning but in this meaning as embodied, made explicit in the organized detail of the work of art, and as newly and differently embodied and made explicit in the organized detail of each work of art. We are interested in those grave, powerful, massive emotions as they are communicated by each different painting of apples and pears by

Cézanne; in that state of inner illumination and superearthly exaltation as it is communicated by each different piano sonata or string quartet of Beethoven.

If then you don't understand what Beethoven "says" it is because the sounds he uses are not a meaningful language for you; and the thing to do is to learn this language as you would any other. If you enjoy the music of Kern and Rodgers that is because its musical language is the one you do understand— the one you learned, as you did English, by hearing it from earliest childhood. Probably, if you had heard Beethoven as early, as much, and as long as Kern and Rodgers you would understand him as well; and if you want to acquire an understanding of Beethoven's vocabulary and ideas (for actually his language is the basic one of all Western music, popular and serious) you will have to live with them and get to know them as well as those of Kern and Rodgers.

Which is to say that you will have to listen to Beethoven's music, and keep listening. That, fortunately, is all you will have to do: music is easier than French in this respect. With French you have to learn the things the words refer to, and the grammar that organizes them in statements; but the meaning of a statement by Beethoven is an internal coherence of the sounds that you will apprehend directly from them by listening to them, or not at all.

And so try the experiment of listening to the beginning of the third movement of Beethoven's Trio Op. 97 (*Archduke*)— just the two statements of the piano that are echoed by the violin and cello, no more; and just once. Listen to it once again the next night, and every night for a week or two or as long as you care to continue the experiment. The passage may say as little to you after a month as it did the first night— in which case you will have to accept the fact that Beethoven and you are not for each other. But on the other hand it may, one of those nights, suddenly come alive for you and begin to make a definite though indefinable sense; and this will be the beginning of an understanding of music, the opening up of a new world of artistic experience as rich and stimulating as that of literature or painting. One thing is certain, however: if you don't get the meaning of Beethoven's statement from the statement, you won't get it from anything else.

There are some whose disappointing experiences with music lead them to argue that a piece of music must have within itself the evidence of its having been produced by a certain human being in a certain time and place, and to conclude from this that if they were told something about the composer and his period they would be better able to understand his music. And there are books which "treat music in the terms of the men who created it." Now certainly the Cézanne painting of a few apples and pears was not produced by a disembodied ability to put paint on canvas: each of the countless decisions to choose *this* bit of paint and place it in *that* relation to the other bits on the canvas was a decision by the whole man, involving all his experience, thought, emotion, insight, and involving also the ideas about painting, the general ideas, and all the other things that had influenced him as a human being and artist. And certainly this was true of the Shakespeare sonnet from which I quoted a couple of lines. But the result in the end was an organization of elements of space and volume on the canvas, an organization of words on the page; and to know what was involved in the process is not the same thing as to experience the effect of the painting or the sonnet that resulted from the process; nor is it necessary or helpful in experiencing that effect. The effect is produced on one's mind by the organization of pictorial elements on the canvas, the organization of words on the page, and by nothing else; and one experiences it solely by looking at the one and reading the other. Similarly, whatever the biographical and historical influences involved in the process that produced the opening statement in the third movement of Beethoven's *Archduke* Trio, the result of the process was an organization of sounds with an effect which you can experience not by reading about the biographical

and historical influences but only by listening to the organization of sounds in the statement.

To repeat: just as the way to understand a poem is to read
it, and the way to understand a painting is to look at it, so
the way—the only way—to understand a piece of music is to
listen to it, and to keep listening.

This is also the way to deal with the difficulty that arises
when you listen beyond the opening statement in a piece of
music. A poem lies before you on the page; and you can
read each line as slowly and as many times as you need for
the rhythmed sound, the images, the overtones of sense and
feeling to register on your mind. A painting hangs before you
on the wall; and you can look at it as long as you need to
take in all the details and their organization and be affected
by them. But the sounds of a piece of music succeed each
other in time—too quickly for your ear to catch some of the
details or your mind to grasp them fully and relate them to
others; with the result that instead of a coherent succession
you may hear only a number of unconnected fragments. And
the remedy for this is again to keep listening.

One way is to listen to the entire piece: with each hearing
you will catch more of the details you missed and fit them
into their places in what will become an increasingly coherent
succession. Another way is to listen to the opening statement—
of, for example, that third movement of the Beethoven trio—
and then to a little more, repeatedly, until this additional
passage is familiar and makes sense not only by itself but in
relation to the first part; and to keep adding a little at a time
to what you already know, until you know the entire piece.

If you want help—the help that will point out the details
your ear may have missed, the large formal design you may
not have been aware of—and if you want this help from a
book, then you will have to do something that will cost more
effort. For you will come up against a major difficulty for
both the writer and the reader of a book about music—the
difficulty of correlating printed word with living sound.

A statement about a passage of music which the reader hasn't heard can have no more real meaning for him than a statement about a line of poetry he hasn't read or a detail of a painting he hasn't seen. But whereas the writer can quote the line of poetry or reproduce the detail of the painting, he cannot provide the sound of the passage in the symphony. The only thing he can do is to help the reader to find it on a phonograph record, giving the passage in musical notation to make it easier to recognize and grasp. This isn't easy for the writer even when it is possible; and it calls for effort by the reader. But if the effort isn't made the statement is just words, which the reader can repeat, but without really knowing what he is talking about.

And so if you want to know more than you can discover by your own listening, you can read the next two chapters; but then you will have to make the effort involved in hearing as you read. If that effort is more than the additional knowledge is worth, you can skip the next two chapters.

3

MUSICAL PROCEDURES
AND THE FORMS THEY PRODUCE

"What she wants other people to know," Edmund Wilson wrote once about a novelist, "she imparts to them by creating an object, the self-developing organism of a work of prose." What a composer wants other people to know he too imparts to them by creating an object, this one the self-developing organism of a work of musical sound. What kind of object and organism, created out of what substance and by what procedures, you can discover by listening to examples; and two good ones to begin with are Bach's *Passacaglia* and the Prelude to Wagner's music-drama *Tristan und Isolde*.

You can, if you wish, merely listen to them in the ways I described in the last chapter—all the way through repeatedly, or a little at a time—and become increasingly aware of what happens in the course of each piece. Or you may want me to point out what happens—in which case you will have to do a little more than just listen: you will have to gear your listening with my statements, and for this purpose have your eye follow musical notation as your ear follows the sound, the more easily to grasp the musical detail and fix it in your mind.

Even if you intend to follow the second course of action it is a good thing to begin by listening straight through the two pieces to get an idea of certain general characteristics. For one thing, that the object is made of sound which progresses in time (hence the term *movement* of a symphony), and which conveys meaning of the indefinable kind I discussed earlier. Hence that the progression in time reveals gradually not only a developing form in sound but a developing meaning—a train of musical thought. And that the object in the end has a size and weight commensurate with the magnitude of the thought it embodies.

The next step is to listen to detail and observe by what operations the object is produced and the thought proceeds. Listening again to Bach's *Passacaglia* you can this time hear that the grave opening statement

is repeated—and not just once but a second time, a third, a fourth (stop here for the moment). And you discover from this that musical thought, unlike the thought of prose, proceeds by repeating itself—in some instances by repeating itself exactly.

Having said this I must add a qualification. The opening statement of the *Passacaglia* is repeated without change; but each time you hear something new with it, which makes the repetition a *variation*—the same thing said in a different way. Here are the repeated statement and different accompanying material of the first four variations:

Variation 1

theme marked by asterisks

This progression in terms of a melodic figure is *figuration*.

Variation 2. Continuation of the figuration of Variation 1.

13

Variation 3

Variation 4

The *Passacaglia*, then, is produced by the operation of the variation procedure, and is one of the *variation forms*—the one with a continuous succession of variations on a brief repeated theme called the *ground-bass* (though it doesn't stay in the bass).

Another thing you discover from these first variations is that music, unlike prose, can say more than one thing at a time, and that what you hear most often is not a line of sound but a texture. When there are several clearly defined lines or *voices* moving at the same time, as in these variations, you have *counterpoint*, and the texture is *contrapuntal*. And at any point in the progression if you read vertically instead of horizontally the combination of sounds at that point is a *chord*, and the succession of chords is *harmony*.

Still another thing to observe in these first variations is that while the theme maintains its unvarying form and pace, the varying accompanying material becomes increasingly animated, and its texture increasingly dense and complex, with a resulting effect of increasing momentum and intensity. The cumulative impact of the repeated ground-bass, the crescendo of intensity in the accompanying material—these together produce the effect of the passacaglia form.

When now you listen further in Bach's *Passacaglia* you discover that the intensity doesn't increase in one single unbroken crescendo—that it is alternately built up and lessened, until it is eventually carried to a concluding maximum.

In Variation 5 it is lessened:

theme itself varied

Also the figuration is carried into the ground-bass itself; and thus you discover that the theme itself can be varied.

But in Variation 6 the ground-bass is unvaried again, and the flowing accompanying material begins to build up the intensity that is further increased by the denser textures of Variations 7 and 8.

In Variation 9:

theme itself varied

the figuration is again carried into the ground-bass itself; and the momentarily lessened intensity builds up to the force of Variation 10.

In Variation 11 you hear the ground-bass transferred for the first time to an upper voice, with a single line of flowing accompanying material down below. Additional voices create a denser texture and greater urgency in Variation 12; but there is sudden quiet in Variation 13:

in which the intricate texture varies, envelopes, and obscures the ground-bass.

In Variation 14:

the quiet continues, the figuration in which the ground-bass is involved is simpler.

In Variation 15:

the quiet becomes hushed, the figuration even simpler.

16

The hush is broken by Variation 16:

in which the ground-bass is unvaried and forceful below the explosive figuration. The intensity is maintained in Variation 17, with its brilliant accompanying figuration, and further in Variation 18:

Then, in Variation 19:

the intensity begins to increase; and in Variation 20, with its denser textures, the crescendo of intensity builds up to its maximum point in the powerful conclusion.

When the thunderous final chord of the *Passacaglia* breaks off you hear the first half of the ground-bass once more. Over it Bach has written in the score *Thema fugatum*, which tells you that the theme, after having been subjected to the procedure of variation in a passacaglia, is now to be subjected to the procedure of *fugue* in a fugue. That procedure is to discuss a theme in several lines of thought that proceed simultaneously —which means that fugue is a contrapuntal procedure, and the fugue a contrapuntal form. The theme discussed is the *subject;* the lines of thought are *voices;* and a fugue is in two or three or four or more voices.

17

The fugue which follows Bach's *Passacaglia* is in four voices; and the discussion begins with an *exposition* in which one by one the voices enter with a statement of the subject. Usually the first voice enters alone; then, when the second enters with the subject, the first continues with the *countersubject;* then, when the third enters with the subject, the second continues with the countersubject, and the first with material that fits in with both; and so on. In the present example the subject is stated even the first time with the countersubject; and each time the voice that had the subject continues with the countersubject, while the voice that had the countersubject continues with a second countersubject.

Here is the sequence of entries in the exposition of this fugue of Bach:

You will have noticed how again, with the increasing animation and density of the contrapuntal texture as the voices enter, there is increasing intensity. And in the further course of the discussion you will hear the alternate building up and lessening of intensity that you hear in the *Passacaglia*.

Something else to notice is the momentary digression, here called an *episode*, after the second statement of the subject, which delays the third statement and adds to its effect when it arrives. This effect of the return to what was departed from is an important one in music, as you now discover when you listen to the further course of the discussion in Bach's fugue— i.e. to the further statements of the subject separated by episodes—and hear the increasing impact of the return to the subject after each longer and weightier episode, and the climactic effect of the last return to a statement of the subject which develops into a great concluding summation, or *coda*.

19

And now let us consider the other piece from which you were to discover how music operates and what the operations produce. The Prelude to *Tristan und Isolde* is the musical equivalent of a prologue spoken before the curtain rises to inform and prepare you for the drama that is to come—which is to say, a preliminary statement and discussion of several musical themes that will figure prominently in the course of the music-drama. Two of these themes are heard in the opening statement of the Prelude:

There is a pause; then the statement is repeated—not exactly, like the theme of Bach's *Passacaglia*, but with a change—at a higher level of pitch:

The effect of this change is to qualify the original meaning of the statement, to develop it, to carry the musical thought further—as against the variation's saying the same thing in a different way.

Again there is a pause; then another, distended, more forceful repetition at a still higher level of pitch, developing the thought further:

Another pause; then [2] of the last statement is repeated:

then only its concluding two notes—first by the violins:

then by the flutes:

and finally, very emphatically, by the entire orchestra, which carries the line of thought to a momentary conclusion:

Out of the opening statement, then, there has been elaborated, by the procedure of repetition with modification, a musical paragraph—the beginning of an organism which now extends itself by the same procedure as new ideas enter and are developed.

Thus, with the conclusion of the first paragraph this idea:

is developed:

and then is qualified by a new idea and its development:

to the point where another idea enters and is developed:

and continues with this:

And now [3] returns (oboe, clarinets, horn) with increasing sonority and intensity, to bring this second line of thought to its momentary conclusion.

There is a pause in which [3] is reflected on:

These reflections increase in urgency and are carried to an emphatic conclusion; at which point [4] re-enters (oboe, English horn) to set the progression of thought in motion again.

As before, [4] continues with [5] (flute, oboe, English horn, clarinet), whose developments, increasing in intensity, again lead to the re-entrance of [3] (violins, cellos), which also increases in intensity, to the point where the intensity lessens as a new idea enters:

Its developments bring references to [2] (horn, English horn), and work up to the impassioned re-entrance once more of [3] (strings), which now in turn works up to increasingly powerful proclamations of [1] (horns) and [2] (trumpets). This is the climax of the discussion; and from the point of maximum intensity it subsides into quiet recollections of the opening statements, which eventually lead to a hushed transitional passage (cellos and basses) and a pause for the rise of the curtain.

In this piece you have heard one idea stated and repeated with modification to the point where another idea was stated and repeated with modification to the point where still another was so stated and repeated, and so on in the progression of the self-developing organism. Also, you have heard again, as in the Bach fugue, ideas returned to after being departed from, and the end, after the climax, return full circle to the quiet statements of the beginning. These are things you will hear in most of the music you will encounter. But usually with this difference: that the circular deployment of the material of the organism will have a more clearly defined schematic pattern—the pattern of one or another of the forms we shall examine in the next chapter, which may be called *cyclical* forms (in accordance with the dictionary definition of *cycle*).

The Prelude to *Tristan* has demonstrated that there is form in music that is purely organic, like the form of prose. But the pieces you will hear in the next chapter will demonstrate that there are also the forms of music that are schematic, like the forms of poetry.

The schematic patterns are something for you to be aware of, as you are aware of the pattern of a sonnet. But there is a danger of thinking of form in music as being only schematic pattern. And I had you listen to the Prelude to *Tristan* to make you aware of form as something organic, and to impress upon you the necessity—when you are listening to a piece that is in a schematic form—of taking in all the organically related substance that deploys itself within the schematic pattern, as you take in all the organically related substance that deploys itself within the pattern of the sonnet.

And there is one other thing to impress upon you. Someone told me once how at college he had found the first quarter-inch of a number of records almost destroyed by all the students who had played that much and no more in preparation for theme identification in their music appreciation courses. A few themes were all that these students got to know of those pieces of music, and all they thought there was to know about any piece of music; and other people have got the same idea from books like the one that offered the themes of a number of symphonies as "just what the listener wants to know, and all that he, lay or expert, *needs* to know: the stuff of which symphonies are made." What your guided tour through the Bach *Passacaglia* and the Prelude to *Tristan* should have made clear is that you must hear not only the themes but what is elaborated out of them and what happens between them.

4

MUSICAL FORMS—II

The simplest cyclical form is one with only one cycle—one departure and return. It can be expressed as *A B A;* and it is called *ternary form* or *three-part song form.* If you listen straight through the second movement of Schubert's String Quintet Op. 163 you will hear a succession of three large sections: the first slow and quietly sustained, the second agitated and vehement, but quieting down at the end for the repetition of— which is to say, the return to—the first.

Something else to notice is that there is also a cycle of keys: the first section is in E major; * the second in F minor; and when it quiets down it maneuvers a return to E major in the third section. Because there is this organization of—and by—keys in the cyclical forms, they are also *harmonic forms.*

And now when you listen the second time give your attention entirely to the substance that deploys itself within the cyclical pattern—the substance that makes the movement one

---

* C major:

C minor:

The two series of sounds thus related in the major and minor scales can begin with D or E or any other note.

of the most sublime and most affecting utterances in all music. As the movement begins:

notice the dense and rich texture, which is extraordinary and possibly unique (I can't at the moment recall anything like it); and notice also how this texture works—how, as the sustained melody and harmony of the second violin, viola and first cello progress, their meaning is amplified and intensified by the brief expressive figures of the first violin, the plucked notes of the second cello. And when, after the vehement middle section, there is the return to the opening section:

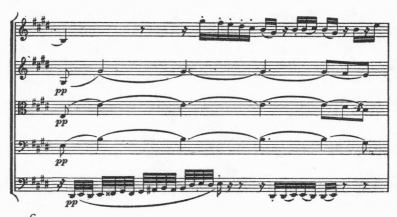

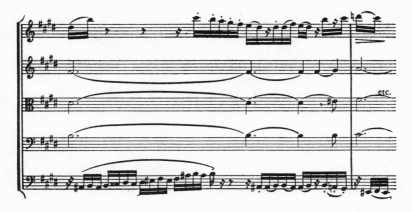

notice that the first violin and the second cello now play intensifying variations of their original parts, which transform the brief figures of the one into passages of the utmost poignancy, and the plucked notes of the other into passages of great dramatic force. Eventually the variations subside into the original figures and plucked notes for the conclusion of the movement.

And so from this piece you learn that the variation procedure is sometimes applied to the repetitions in cyclical forms.

Our next piece of music, the third movement of Mozart's *Eine kleine Nachtmusik*, illustrates one of the ways the cyclical pattern we have just considered can be less simple: each section of the large cycle *A B A* is itself a smaller cycle; and the pattern of the movement can be expressed as

$$A \quad B \quad A$$
$$a\ b\ a \quad c\ d\ c \quad a\ b\ a$$

More exactly, the movement is a *minuet with trio* (accept the term *trio* without the historical reason for it); and with the cycle of keys, and the traditional repetitions of the smaller

27

sections in the performances you will hear, the pattern becomes

minuet	trio	minuet
(G major)	(D major)	(G major)
a a b a b a	c c d c d c	a b a

As you listen, then, you hear first *a:*

which is repeated; then *b:*

leads back to *a;* after which *b* is repeated, and again leads back to *a*.

Now the trio, in which *c:*

is repeated; then *d:*

leads back to *c;* after which *d* is repeated, and again leads back to *c*.

And now the minuet again, without repetitions.

I have used this simple, small-scale example because it exhibits the pattern so clearly and can be given in full detail. Now listen to the third movement of Schubert's String Quartet Op. 29, a more expansive and elaborate example—elaborate, among other things, in the wonderful shifts, or *modulations*, of key that are characteristic of Schubert. Because it is more elaborate I can give you only the beginning of each section and let your ear go on from there to complete it.

This is how *a* of the minuet begins, in A minor:

a is repeated; then *b:*

builds up to a climax and pause for the return to *a*. But when [1] is heard from the cello this time, it is with the D changed to D sharp, which brings the breathtaking surprise of C sharp minor instead of the original A minor for [2], after which there is a shift back to A minor. *b* is repeated, and again returns to *a*.

Now *c* of the trio, beginning in A major:

29

c is repeated; then *d:*

1st violin   etc.

which after several shifts of key returns to the A major of *c*, though not to its opening statement. *d* is repeated, and again returns to the A major of *c*.

And now the minuet again, completing the large cycle.

Our next piece of music, Mozart's Rondo K.511 for piano, illustrates another way in which the cyclical pattern can be less simple: the piece comprises not one cycle but two; and the pattern can be expressed as *A B A C A*, with *A* each time in the key of A minor, *B* in the key of F major, and *C* in the key of A major. Each of these sections, moreover, is itself a smaller cycle; and a coda sums up at the end. The complete scheme, then, is

$$A \qquad B \qquad A \qquad C \qquad A \qquad \text{Coda}$$

a b a   *c d c*   only *a*   *e f e*   *a b a*

And you hear first *a* stating the exquisitely contoured and poignant melody which the piece keeps departing from and coming around back to (hence the term *rondo*):

p   cresc.   etc.

Then *b* develops the thought in C major:

mf   etc.

returning to *a* and A minor—but to an *a* with its contours elaborated and its poignancy intensified by the variation procedure:

and this is the point at which to mention that the return is made each time to a new variation of the original *a*.

Now *B*:

which ranges extensively through its cycle of substance and keys before returning to another variation of *a*.

And now *C*:

which ranges even more extensively through its cycle of substance and keys before returning to still another variation of *a*. And the successive variations of *a* that you hear in this last cycle of *A* reach a maximum of impassioned intensity in this final one:

After which you hear last references to *a* in the coda's concluding summation.

Our next piece of music is the first movement of Mozart's *Eine kleine Nachtmusik*, to illustrate another way in which the single large cycle may be less simple than the one we began with.

In the first section of the cycle you hear a sequence of ideas and their developments. First an opening fanfare:

31

which claims attention for

which pauses expectantly for

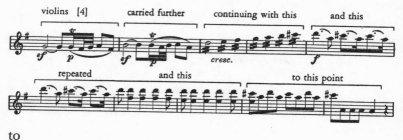

which is broken into by this transition:

to

which leads to

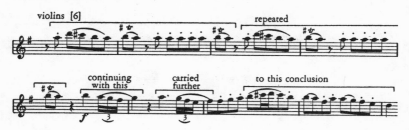

which is repeated and extended:

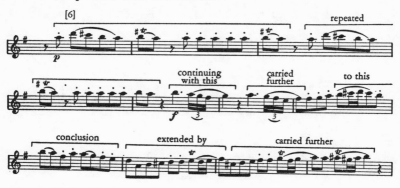

after which this:

concludes the sequence, which may be repeated in its entirety, but usually is not in performances nowadays.

In the second section of the cycle some of the ideas of the first, taken out of their original context, yield new developments which combine with new ideas to form a new sequence of organically related substance. Thus the opening fanfare:

now claims attention for

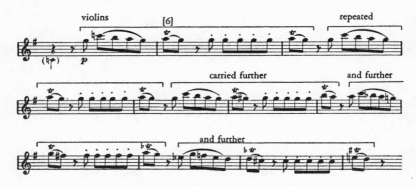

and then

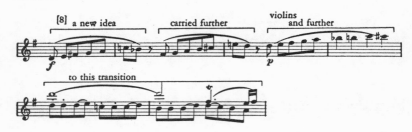

prepares you for the return to

which begins the restatement, with slight modifications, of the sequence of ideas and their developments in the first section.

At the end of this restatement [7] is changed and extended:

and leads to a little concluding flourish:

In this cycle the section in which the ideas are first stated and developed is the *exposition;* the section in which some of them are further developed is the *development;* the section which restates the ideas and developments of the exposition is the *recapitulation;* and the extension of [7] at the end of the recapitulation is the beginning of a little coda.

It is the middle section, with its development of ideas from the first section, that provides one difference from the simple cycle we considered first. And another difference is the cycle of keys: the exposition, beginning in G major, modulates to the *dominant* key, D major (the point of modulation being the C sharp in the transition from [4] to [5]); the development modulates further—to C major, A minor, G minor—until in its last two measures the dominant of G major (the chord on the fifth step of the scale) prepares you for the return of that key with the recapitulation; and the movement now remains in G major to its conclusion.

As before, I have used the simple, small-scale example from *Eine kleine Nachtmusik* because it exhibits the pattern so clearly and can be given in full detail. Now listen to the first movement of Schubert's Piano Sonata Op. 78, in which the cycle, by virtue of its scale and expressive content, is in effect a dramatic narrative, with the exposition presenting the elements of the drama, the development presenting their dramatic involvements, the recapitulation of the original substance of the exposition having the effect of a resolution of those involvements, and the coda providing final conclusions.

The implications of the tranquilly, spaciously meditative opening statement, in G major:

35

are developed for some time; then a more animated statement, in D major:

is developed with increasing liveliness to moments of force, which break off for quiet statements again:

and the meditative tranquility of the exposition is established with seeming finality by the references to [1]:

which bring it to a close.

We are, therefore, entirely unprepared for what we hear now in the development: the meditative opening statement with the iron-like power it acquires from being hammered out fortissimo in G minor, the tensions this creates in its rhythm, the tensions in the imitations of this rhythm by bare octaves in the bass, the eruptions of these octaves that carry the passage up to a proclamation tremendous in its sonority and distentions. The tension is relaxed momentarily in a quiet development of [2], only to be built up as before to a similar climax, and to be relaxed again in a similar quiet interlude. Then treble and bass octaves in imitation hammer out that development of [2] with increasing intensity, which suddenly relaxes in another quiet and poignant development of [2]; and this eventually brings the return to [1] for the recapitulation

36

of the original substance of the exposition, now entirely in G major, and the more affecting for the dramatic involvements that have intervened. The sequence ends, as before, with [4]; after which the brief coda builds up last references to [1] into a powerful concluding summation.

This three-part cycle is the distinguishing feature of the grouping of movements which achieved definition at the hands of Haydn and Mozart, and which was given different names in accordance with the instruments it was written for: *sonata*, when it was written for one instrument or two; *trio*, when it was written for three; *quartet*, when it was written for four; *symphony*, for the then newly standardized symphonic orchestra that we know; *concerto*, for a solo instrument and orchestra. The cycle is therefore referred to as *sonata form;* but since it is the normally prescribed form for the first movement, it is also referred to as *first-movement form;* and since the first movement is normally in quick tempo, for which the Italian direction *allegro* is used, it is also referred to as *sonata-allegro form*. The terminology is inaccurate and confusing, since sonata form is not the form of the entire sonata or symphony but only the normal form of its first movement; since it may also occur in other movements; and since one of these may be the slow movement of the work. And there is further confusion in the fact that the sonata, symphony, trio, quartet and the rest constitute *the sonata forms*.

In one of *the sonata forms* of Mozart or Haydn we find three or four movements—that is, separate and complete organisms, unrelated in substance (the carrying over of themes from one movement to another is begun by Beethoven), diverse in character, yet bound together in one way that we shall see in a moment, and intended to complement each other and produce the effect of a single artistic experience. The diversity is in part one of tempo: normally the first movement is fast, though sometimes preceded by a slow introduction; the second is slow; the last is again fast; and when there are four

37

movements a minuet with trio—later a faster *scherzo with trio*—precedes the last movement, though sometimes it precedes the slow movement. What binds the movements together is key: in addition to the unifying cycle of keys in each movement there is a unifying cycle of keys in the group of movements. Thus, the first movement of *Eine kleine Nachtmusik* is a cycle which begins and ends in G major; the second movement is in the same way in C major; the minuet movement is again in G major; and so is the finale. In Schubert's Piano Sonata Op. 78 the cycle of keys is G major, D major, B minor and G major; in his Quartet Op. 29 it is A minor, C major, A minor and A major (a work in a minor key sometimes ends in major).

The forms used in the movements are for the most part the cyclical forms we have been examining in this chapter. The distinguishing feature of the sonata forms is the cyclical first-movement form, or sonata form, or sonata-allegro form normally prescribed for the first movement; and prescribed for the minuet or scherzo movement is the cyclical minuet or scherzo with trio. The other movements have more latitude: in the slow movement we find sometimes simple ternary form, sometimes first-movement form; in the finale sometimes a rondo, sometimes first-movement form. Moreover, cyclical forms are not the only ones that are used: sometimes we find a slow movement or finale in variation form.

The only variation form we have examined is the passacaglia; and of this one there is only one example in the literature of the sonata forms: the finale of Brahms's Symphony No. 4. It has one interesting feature: the return of the theme after Variation 15; the return of Variations 1, 2 and 3 after Variation 23; and the return of the theme a second time at the beginning of the coda—all of which introduce a cyclical element into the variation form.

The variation form that you will encounter more frequently in the sonata forms is the one called *theme and variations,* in which the theme that is varied is not a single brief statement but a longer sequence of statements. The third movement of Beethoven's *Archduke* Trio, the first piece of music I suggested you listen to, provides an example.

The theme, as usual, is in two parts, the second of which answers and completes the first. The first is played by the piano:

and repeated by the violin and cello. Then the second is played by the piano:

with only its conclusion repeated by the strings. And there are similar repetitions of the two parts in each of the variations which elaborate the theme in different figurations.

Here is the beginning of Variation 1:

Then Variation 2:

Then Variation 3:

Then Variation 4:

And now there is a return to the theme, with the effect such a return has after intervening involvements. But as the theme proceeds this time it is altered by the change of the original F sharp to F natural:

and by further changes in the second part, which expands into an extensive, wide-ranging coda with implications of summation that reach sublime conclusions.

This is an example of the introduction of the cyclical element into a variation form by the return to the theme at the end. And another example of this that you might listen to is the concluding variation movement of Beethoven's Piano Sonata Op. 109, in which the last variation—extraordinary in the increasing momentum of its increasingly rapid figuration that finally effloresces into trills—subsides into a simple restatement of the sublime theme.

Beethoven also provides impressive examples of the combination of variation and cyclical form in which the theme and its variations alternate with a recurring statement or section that remains unvaried. One of these examples is the exalted third movement of the Ninth Symphony.

After a couple of introductory measures you hear

which is the first in a sequence of statements that constitute the theme. Its conclusion leads to

which in turn leads back to a variation of the theme:

Again [2], unchanged except that it is in G major instead of D major. When it ends you expect the second variation of the theme; what comes instead is a fugal discussion of [1a], which ranges widely before it finally leads to the variation you expected:

And this time the conclusion of the variation leads to this solemn call:

which introduces the extensive final summation of the coda.

You have just had an example of a fugal episode occurring in a movement of one of the sonata forms; and you will find other such episodes in the second movement of Beethoven's Seventh Symphony, the second and last movements of his *Eroica* Symphony. And not only episodes but entire movements: his Piano Sonatas Op. 106 (*Hammerklavier*) and Op. 110 end with fugues; his Quartet Op. 131 begins with one.

In addition, the second and last movements of the *Eroica* provide extraordinarily impressive demonstrations of something that has been evident in the other pieces of music I have presented—in the occurrence of the cyclical element in the fugue, of the variation procedure in cyclical forms. That something is the freedom with which the organism operates within the schematic pattern.

Strictly speaking, the second movement of the *Eroica* is in ternary form; but it is ternary form that is considerably more than *A B A*—the more being what happens after *B*. You hear, then, a gigantic opening section (*A*), beginning, in C minor, with

continuing with

and ending with

then the middle section (*B*), in C major:

and a return to [1], which leads not to [2] and [3] but to this powerful fugal episode:

which builds up a tremendous climax that breaks off for a momentary reference to [1]. This too is broken into by another forceful outburst, which eventually quiets down into a poignant accompanying figure for [1]:

which this time does continue with [2] and [3]—the ternary pattern being completed at last. And the end of [3] brings

43

the beginning of a sequence of affecting details in an unusually extensive coda.

And so with the last movement. After a boisterous introductory passage you hear a two-part theme:

followed by several variations. Then the theme is combined with a new two-part melody:

which leads to a fugal discussion of a subject derived from the theme:

44

This reaches a climax which breaks off for the return of [2], which then is varied. The variation builds up to a vigorous statement of [1] in combination with a new tune:

This is developed and brought to a conclusion; then you hear [2] again, leading to another fugal discussion—this time of [1] inverted:

It is carried to a climax and a conclusion; then, after a pause, comes a melody which you recognize as [2] made solemn and sublime by the slow tempo and poignant harmonization. It is repeated in grandly proclamatory style; then there is a quiet transition to

another variation of [2], which builds up to a climax that breaks off for the hush before the joyous outburst that brings this extraordinary movement to an end.

To these two examples I add one more: the great concluding variation movement of Beethoven's Piano Sonata Op. 111. After the wonderful theme:

you hear a series of variations which eventually build up to a halt on a sustained trill with references to [a]:

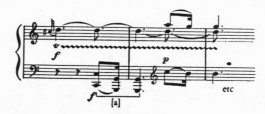

This is the beginning of a wide-ranging digression—concerned with [a], then with [b]—which eventually ends in a return to the theme, heard now over fast-moving figuration, and gradually building up in intensity to a joyous and exalted climax that breaks off for another sustained trill—this one creating a dazzling ethereal radiance for a last superearthly statement of the theme.

These last three examples should impress on you the necessity I spoke of at the end of Chapter 3—of following attentively the detail of the organically related substance that deploys itself within the schematic pattern. It is this that makes each rondo or first movement *that* rondo or first movement and no other—or, to put it more generally, makes each piece of music unique. And your concern, in listening to music, is with the unique series of events in each particular piece of music.

5

BEETHOVEN

The pieces of music I presented in the preceding chapters are some of the greatest works in our musical literature. And remembering how indiscriminately the word *great* is tossed about—how anything and everything presented on the radio is "great music"—I think it advisable to establish what I mean by the word when I apply it to those pieces by Beethoven and Schubert.

In his book on Beethoven, which I recommend as collateral reading, J. W. N. Sullivan discusses Beethoven's music as an expression, in successive works, of a developing personal vision of life—that is, of developing states of consciousness that were generated in him by his external experience, conditioned by his spiritual nature, and made explicit in the terms of his art. "In his capacity to express this content," says Sullivan, "Beethoven reveals himself as a great musical genius, and the content itself reveals him as a great spirit." And concerning this he observes further that "perhaps even Shakespeare never reached that final stage of illumination that is expressed in some of Beethoven's late music."

This tells us not only what makes Beethoven's music great, but what makes the *Eroica* a greater piece of music than the First Symphony, and the Piano Sonata Op. 111 even greater than the *Eroica*. As against the First Symphony—the work of a young man confident, exuberant and untroubled in the exercise of his rich gifts—the *Eroica* is the work of one who

47

has come to know catastrophe and suffering, and who in the blackest moments of his life has found in the resources of his own spiritual nature and creative powers the courage and strength to resist, to survive, to triumph (the heroism which the *Eroica* is concerned with is, then, as Sullivan points out, Beethoven's own). But as against this man for whom suffering is something to assert oneself against, the composer of the concluding movement of the Sonata Op. 111 is one who has come to the final realization of suffering as something to accept, in Sullivan's words, "as one of the great structural lines of human life," and who has attained "that unearthly state where the struggle ends and pain dissolves away."

Sullivan warns against a possible misinterpretation of what he says: Beethoven's music is not to be listened to as a sort of diary of daily events in his life. It tells us not his experience, but his attitude toward his experience; and not his immediate response to any and every happening of the day, but states of consciousness representing a lifetime of continuing perception and response to perception: the joyous exuberance and humor embodied in the Eighth Symphony, the exaltation communicated by the Sonata Op. 111, were not responses to the petty turmoil and wretchedness that filled Beethoven's daily existence at these times. Moreover, to Sullivan's warning I will add a reminder that we are concerned not with the joyous exuberance or the mystical exaltation itself, but with this as it is made explicit and communicated in the organized detail of the piece of music—and not just the detail of one piece of music but the constantly new and unique detail of each of a number of pieces.

The greatest Beethoven—greatest in what he says and in his use of his art to say it—is, then, heard in his last works: the last symphony, the last string quartets, the last sonatas and other pieces for piano, the *Missa Solemnis*. And we are concerned with the superearthly exaltation of his last years as it is embodied not only in the concluding movement of the Sonata Op. 111 but in the concluding movement of the Sonata Op. 109, the third movement of the Ninth Symphony. And not only these but the slow movements of the last quartets: on the one hand the expansively elaborating variation movements of Opp. 132 and 127; on the other hand the *Cavatina* of Op. 130 and the third movement of Op. 135, which exhibit the concentrated brevity of some of Beethoven's late writing (other examples of this brevity are the quietly reflective opening movement of the Sonata Op. 109, and some of the Bagatelles Opp. 119 and 126 for piano). Also the *Kyrie*, *Benedictus* and *Agnus Dei* of the *Missa Solemnis*. And other sections of the *Missa* in which, as in the final choral movement of the Ninth Symphony, the exaltation is carried to ever higher points of jubilant ecstasy.

We are concerned also with what lay behind the final illumination. For one thing, what is communicated by the *Arioso dolente* movement of the Piano Sonata Op. 110, the slow movement—tremendous in poignant expressive implications as in size—of the Piano Sonata Op. 106 (*Hammerklavier*). And for another thing, what is communicated by the grim opening movements of the Ninth Symphony, the *Hammerklavier* Sonata, and—in more concentrated fashion again—the Sonata Op. 111.

And we are, finally, concerned with those "strange seas of thought" in which—Sullivan says of the last quartets—Beethoven discovers "unsuspected islands and even continents," as we come to know them not only from some of the movements of the quartets but from the mystically introspective introduction to the *Benedictus* of the *Missa Solemnis*. And above all from passages in the *Diabelli Variations* for piano—Variation 20:

and the suddenly still and distant chords:

that follow the vehement fugue of Variation 32 and lead to the
final apotheosis of Variation 33. These passages in the *Diabelli
Variations* are perhaps the remotest points Beethoven's mind
attained in the regions Sullivan speaks of.

In all these his mind can be followed without difficulty;
but the *Great Fugue* Op. 133 and the concluding fugue of the
Hammerklavier Sonata most listeners find obscure and formidable.

A great spirit and great musical genius is heard also in
those two tremendous movements of the *Eroica* Symphony
that were presented in Chapter 4, and in its opening movement, a dramatic progression no less tremendous in its urgency, tensions and climaxes, its developing structure, and
their cumulative power. And if that great spirit moves us
with the range and force of the expressive content of the
works of this period, the great musician amazes us with the
profusion of musical forms embodying this content, their
variety, and on occasion their innovations.

Thus, what is expressed in the successive movements of the
Eroica is expressed again in the Fifth Symphony, but with differences. The dramatic first movement is more grimly concentrated; and in later movements expressive content dictates

an innovation in structure: the dramatically hushed conclusion of the scherzo movement leads in unprecedented fashion into the opening triumphant proclamation of the finale; and later in the finale the development breaks off at its height for a recapitulation of the hushed transition to the opening proclamation.

Unprecedented too are some of the things that happen in the Piano Concerto No. 4. The audience assembled in Prince Lobkowitz's house in March 1807 for the first performance (with Beethoven himself at the piano) expected to hear first the usual orchestral introduction that would secure attention for the eventual entrance of the solo piano—instead of which it was the piano itself that claimed attention immediately with its spaciously meditative opening G major statement, this surprise being followed by the surprise of the strings' B major answer. And later came the extraordinary and unprecedented dialogue of orchestra and piano in the slow movement, leading to the piano's soliloquy, and to concluding hushed recollections of the opening dialogue—all of which make this brief movement one of Beethoven's most affecting utterances.

There is then the externally imposing, monumental Beethoven of the *Eroica* and Fifth Symphonies, who is heard also in the joyous Symphonies Nos. 4, 7 and 8; the breathtakingly energetic finale of the Quartet Op. 59 No. 3; the grandiose Piano Concerto No. 5 (referred to as the *Emperor*); the dramatic Piano Sonatas Opp. 53 (*Waldstein*), 57 (*Appassionata*), and 90, Violin Sonata Op. 47 (*Kreutzer*), Quartets Op. 59 No. 2 and Op. 95. And there is the lyrical, meditative Beethoven of the Piano Concerto No. 4, who is heard also in the Symphony No. 6 (*Pastoral*); the Piano Sonatas Opp. 54, 78 and 81a (*Les Adieux*); the Quartets Op. 59 No. 1 and Op. 74 (*Harp*); the song-cycle *An die ferne Geliebte*.

In addition there is the playful Beethoven who contrives little surprises and jokes. For example the opening theme of the finale of the Symphony No. 8 coasting along *pp* until it collides with the *ff* C sharp; the unexpected play with that C sharp in the coda, ending with the unexpected change of key; the two places where the full orchestra breaks off, and first the flutes and strings *p*, then the bassoon and kettledrum *pp* go chortling on. Or in the finale of the Piano Concerto No. 5 the episode in the development in which the piano takes off grandly with the imposing principal theme, but gets into a sort of tailspin of faster and faster passage-work that collapses into decisively final statements of the full orchestra—whereupon the horns enter quietly with a new key in which the piano takes off with the principal theme again, only to get into the same tailspin of fast passage-work that collapses into the same final statements of the orchestra—whereupon the oboe and bassoon enter quietly with still another key in which the piano takes off a third time, only to end up in the same way.

I mentioned earlier—as against the expansiveness of the *Eroica* Symphony—the concentration in the first movement of the Fifth; and other examples are the powerfully concise *Coriolan* and *Egmont* Overtures, the fiercely concise opening movement of the Quartet Op. 95. The slow movement of the Piano Concerto No. 4 is a more unusual and striking example of this concentration and brevity; another is the slow movement of the *Waldstein* Sonata, in which the opening statement returns with an added figure in the bass that builds up tremendous tension and power (if, that is, it is played that way). But there are also remarkable examples of expansiveness to take note of: the endlessly and delightfully inventive second movement of the Quartet Op. 59 No. 1; the second movement of the Quartet Op. 59 No. 3, with a strangeness in its poignancy that leads Sullivan to speak of its "remote and frozen anguish."

The first movement of Op. 59 No. 3 begins in fact with a slow introduction, mysterious and remote, which could introduce one of the last quartets. And this brings us to several other works in which there are intimations of what is to be heard in the music of Beethoven's last years: the *Archduke* Trio, whose wonderful slow movement you are already acquainted with; the Piano Sonata Op. 101 with its tranquil and lovely opening movement and profoundly reflective slow movement; the Violin Sonata Op. 96 with its similarly tranquil and lovely but rather strange first movement and the powerful slow variation in the finale; the Cello Sonata Op. 102 No. 1 with its wonderful slow introductions to the two movements; the Cello Sonata Op. 102 No. 2 with its great slow movement—especially the middle section, and the return of the opening section with the cello's comments on the piano's statements.

Interesting in this connection is the Mass in C, with startlingly beautiful and expressive passages and powerful dramatic strokes, all on the small scale of an early try at something which when attempted again years later would come out with the sustained intensity, grandeur and exaltation of the *Missa Solemnis*.

And finally Beethoven's only opera, *Fidelio*, which in this country (but not in Europe) is generally considered one of his failures, but actually has some of the greatest and most effective dramatic music after Mozart's. Not only Leonore's famous *Abscheulicher! wo eilst du hin?* introducing her noble aria *Komm, Hoffnung*, but the wonderful quartet *Mir ist so wunderbar*, the *Prisoners' Chorus*, the affecting duet *Wir müssen gleich zu Werke*, the tremendous orchestral introduction to the dungeon scene and Florestan's *Gott! welch' Dunkel hier*, the affecting duet and trio and the dramatic quartet that follow, and the sublime *O Gott! welch' ein Augenblick!* at the end.

Of the four overtures Beethoven wrote for the opera the *Leonore* No. 3, one of the most popular pieces in the orchestral repertory, has generally been thought of as the final perfected achievement of which the *Leonore* No. 2 is an earlier, imperfect version; but actually No. 2 uses much the same thematic substance in a completely achieved work that is in its own different ways fully as impressive as No. 3, with some details even more impressive. One of these is the prolonged

activity of the cellos and basses at the end of the slow introduction—their progression, in the last two measures, from B
natural to D flat, then back to B natural, and only then at
last to the expected C of the beginning of the Allegro portion
of the overture. Another is the more extensive development
in this portion that reaches its climax in the off-stage trumpet-
calls. And another is the omission of the recapitulation after
the trumpet-calls, in accordance with a dramatic logic which
the *Leonore* No. 3 sacrifices in completing the formal scheme.

As for Beethoven's early works, they begin with his attempts to write in the style and forms established and left to
him by his illustrious predecessors. These attempts produced
on the one hand fluent, characterless imitations like the Piano
Trio Op. 11 and the Piano Quartet or Quintet Op. 16, but
on the other hand works like the Serenade Op. 8 for string
trio in which the eighteenth-century delicacy, grace, loveliness and charm appear to represent something genuinely
felt by Beethoven himself. And also a long series of works in
which his own voice makes itself heard with increasing insistence, authority and impressiveness.

That voice is heard in the imposing slow introduction to
the Cello Sonata Op. 5 No. 2; in the vehement outbursts of
the fast movements of the Symphony No. 1; in the introspective slow movement of the Piano Concerto No. 1; in the dramatic outbursts, contrasts and silences of the first movement
of the Symphony No. 2, the elevation of its slow movement,
the explosive exuberance of its scherzo and finale. And similarly in other works—some of the piano sonatas, some of the
chamber music. In particular the String Quartets Op. 18,
with their pages of engaging writing in eighteenth-century
style, but also their pages in which Beethoven's individuality
asserts itself: the affecting slow movement of No. 1; the graceful opening of No. 3 and its lovely slow movement; the impassioned opening of No. 4, its delightful Andante scherzoso
in place of the usual slow movement, the engaging trio of its

minuet movement, its bustling finale; the lilting first movement of No. 5, its charming minuet and fine trio, its energetic
finale; and above all the humorous first movement, fine slow
movement, intricately cross-rhythmed scherzo, and lovely
slow introduction to the engaging finale, that make No. 6 one
of the best of these early works.

And only Beethoven's voice is heard in several outstandingly fine works that we encounter at the end of this early
period. The Piano Concerto No. 3, for example, is pure Beethoven in its powerfully dramatic first movement (e.g. the
piano's first entrance: its three upward-rushing scales ending
with the impact of cannon shots, which lead to its forceful
proclamation of the principal theme of the movement), the
expansively introspective slow movement, the dramatically
eventful finale (e.g. the episode near the end of the development, in which the orchestra's fugato breaks off for the surprise of the piano's hushed A-flat octaves, which lead to the
further surprise of the E-major statement of the principal
theme—all in preparation for the piano's last return to the
principal theme in its original key of C minor).

So with the Piano Sonata Op. 31 No. 2, characteristic in
its imposingly dramatic first movement, poignantly lyrical
slow movement, and dramatically eventful concluding perpetuum mobile. Also the Violin Sonata Op. 30 No. 3, equally
characteristic in its energetic fast movements and gracefully
wistful middle movement.

And so with the Piano Sonata Op. 31 No. 3, characteristic
of the genially relaxed and lyrical Beethoven in its grace,
warmth, good humor and bubbling high spirits. Also the
Piano Sonata Op. 28, sometimes called *Pastoral* because of its
quiet mood throughout, and much of it—especially the first
and last movements—very lovely. And the String Quintet Op.
29, of which every movement is an astonishing manifestation
of Beethoven's matured powers.

6

SCHUBERT

What Sullivan says of Beethoven I would say of Schubert: his music reveals him as a great spirit and great musical genius. I am aware of the generally held opinion that credits Schubert with lovely and affecting writing, but the writing of a lyricist without the powers of large-scale content and construction revealed in Beethoven's music—a lyricist whose large-scale works, then, are mere garrulously repetitive, structurally diffuse successions of lovely melodies. But in this instance, as in some others, I would say generally held opinion rests on nothing more authoritative than the unperceptive listening that started it and the inattentive listening that has kept it going—as you have discovered if you listened attentively to what actually happens in the Schubert pieces that were presented in Chapter 4.

In the minuet movement of the Quartet Op. 29, for example, there is not only some characteristically beautiful writing, but—in that unexpected shift to C sharp minor—one of those miraculously achieved intensities of loveliness and expressive force that are characteristic also of Mozart and Berlioz. They are to be heard in breathtaking succession in the last quiet passage just before the end of Mozart's G-minor Symphony, and after the first two simple phrases of the English horn's serenade in the third movement of Berlioz's *Harold in Italy;* and they occur in similar succession in the scherzo movement of Schubert's posthumous Piano Sonata in B flat, in the de-

56

velopment section of the first movement, in the development of the first movement of the posthumous Sonata in A. And they are manifestations of powers that place Schubert with Mozart and Berlioz as one of the greatest of musical geniuses.

Similarly, the first movement of the Sonata Op. 78 offers not only, in the exposition, a characteristic example of Schubert's expansively meditative writing, but, in the development, an impressive example of the dramatic power that is no less characteristic—an example, in fact, of the iron-like power arising out of tranquil meditation that is so remarkable in Schubert. One of the most remarkable examples of this occurs in the slow movement of the posthumous Sonata in A: the recitative-like middle section that takes off quietly in a declamatory crescendo to a hair-raising climax. I can recall nothing like it anywhere in music.

And in the slow movement of the Quintet Op. 163 we hear the sublimity of other writing of Schubert's last year—most notably the opening pages of the posthumous Sonata in B flat, which communicate a final illumination such as we hear in Beethoven's last sonatas.

It is true that the first movement of the B-flat Sonata descends from the sublimity of its opening pages. But it rises again to the wonderful concluding reflections of the exposition, and to the later sublimities of the development which lead to those of the recapitulation of the opening pages. And the English critic Tovey is right in finding the weaknesses in works like this sonata to be "relaxations of their powers," and in contending that "neither Shakespeare nor Schubert will ever be understood by any critic or artist who regards their weaknesses and inequalities as proof that they are artists of less than the highest rank"; that "the highest qualities attained in important parts of a great work are as indestructible by weaknesses elsewhere as if the weaknesses were the accidents of physical ruin"; and that Schubert must be regarded, "on the strength of his important works, as a definitely sublime composer. It does not matter when, where,

57

and how he lapses therefrom: the quality is there, and nothing in its neighborhood can make it ridiculous."

That is the way to view the redundancies and diffuseness of works like the beautiful Quartet Op. 161, Piano Trio Op. 100 and Piano Sonata Op. 42. But on the other hand there are works in addition to the Quintet Op. 163 and Sonata Op. 78—works like the *Death and the Maiden* Quartet, the Piano Trio Op. 99, the posthumous Piano Sonata in C minor and Sonatas Opp. 53 and 143, the last two symphonies—which do not demand such indulgence. What they do require is the realization that Schubert's mind operates expansively, and this at all times—whether in an extended progression of thought or a single statement, and whether the utterance is tranquilly meditative or powerfully dramatic. And the further realization that this expansiveness is not slackness—that on the contrary it most frequently operates with tension, and that the result then is highly effective large-scale construction of Schubert's special kind.

Consider for example the best known of Schubert's instrumental works, the first movement of the *Unfinished Symphony*, in which generally held opinion may have caused you to hear only the occurrences of its famous melodies. I have said Schubert's mind operates expansively; all the more remarkable therefore is the fact that the single hushed opening statement of cellos and basses is enough to achieve the purpose of the extensive slow introduction of Haydn and Beethoven. The statement appears to have only that introductory purpose, for it is heard no more in the exposition: we hear next the melody of oboe and clarinet; and noteworthy at this point is how, with the unhurried pace and calm of the sustained melody, there is the movement, the momentum, the urgency that Schubert creates with the figuration and plucked notes of the strings. Noteworthy also is the fact that while the melody itself is expansive its treatment is concise, carrying it directly and quickly to a climax which breaks off for the sustained note of bassoons and horns that is the pivot for one of Schubert's extraordinary shifts of key. And noteworthy again is how, with the quiet flow now of the famous melody of the cellos, there is the added movement and tension that Schubert creates with the syncopated accompaniment of clarinets and violas. Again the melody is expansive, its treatment concise, carrying it quickly to a climax which breaks off for last quiet reflections that bring the exposition to its close. And here we come to another demonstration of mastery: after an exposition concerned entirely with the woodwind and cello melodies it is the hushed opening statement of cellos and basses that returns now to be elaborated with increasing tension into a development of tremendous dramatic power; and noteworthy here is the way one of the climaxes breaks off repeatedly to recall the syncopated accompaniment of the cello melody. The recapitulation brings a return to the comparative calm of the woodwind and cello melodies, which has the effect of a resolution of the great dramatic conflict in the development; then the hushed opening statement of cellos and basses returns once more, to be elaborated this time into a powerful coda.

I cannot imagine anything further removed from the diffuseness and slackness generally attributed to Schubert than what is actually heard in this piece of music: the economy of its three themes, the conciseness of their treatment, the skill of their deployment in the formal design, the sustained tension from first note to last in this design—all of which adds up to one of the most remarkably compact and effective pieces of large-scale construction in the symphonic literature.

Nor is it diffuseness and slackness that we hear in the gigantic first movement of the Symphony No. 9, but rather an enormous energy, manifesting itself in an increased expansiveness of the themes and their treatment, a sustained momentum and tension—first in the solemn introduction, then in the animated exposition with its great pronouncement of the trombones over the unceasingly driving movement of the second theme, then in the development in which this driving movement builds up to tremendous climactic references to the trombone pronouncement, and finally, after the recapitulation, in the coda in which group after group of the orchestra joins the huge upward rush to exalted heights. Grandeur is what the expansiveness, momentum and tension produce; and grandeur continues to be the outstanding characteristic of the subsequent movements—above all the extraordinary whirling finale. We hear something like it in the finales of the Quartets Op. 161 and *Death and the Maiden;* but in the symphony the energy and momentum are breathtaking, and the reiterated opening notes of the expansive second theme over the unceasing whirl build up to tremendous pronouncements in the exposition, development and recapitulation, and to final sublimities in one of the greatest of codas.

I have been talking until now about the greatest of Schubert's large-scale instrumental works. In addition there are large works of lesser stature which have beautiful pages—like the Fantasia Op. 159 for violin and piano, the Octet Op. 166 for strings and winds, the Quintet Op. 114 (*Trout*) for piano and strings. And there are engaging minor works like the early Sonata Op. 162 for violin and piano. Also there are the smaller-scale and more intimate examples of his mature writing for the piano, the *Moments musicaux* and Impromptus, most of them as affecting in their loveliness and melancholy as anything Schubert ever wrote. Affecting in the same way is the *Andantino varié* Op. 84 No. 1 for piano four hands; and other fine pieces in this category are the Fantasie Op. 103 and Grand Duo Op. 140.

And there are, finally, the songs. At a time when the instrumental works of Mozart and Beethoven were eliciting from the seventeen-year-old Schubert only inconsequential imitations, a poem of Goethe could elicit such evidence of astonishingly matured imaginative and musical powers as *Gretchen am Spinnrade.* And this susceptibility to poetic stimuli, activating constantly more matured powers, resulted in a steady flow of songs throughout his life. It was a flow which included, inevitably, many that were less impressive than

Gretchen: Conceding that "in his six hundred songs there is, no doubt, as Brahms said, something to be learnt from each one," Tovey points out that "*Erlkönig* and *Gretchen am Spinnrade* stand alone in four volumes of early work," and observes that "even in the later years there are songs . . . from which Brahms could have learned little but the fact that Schubert was always keeping his pen in practice, whether or not he had anything in his head at the moment." But the flow also gave us some of our most treasurable pieces of music—single songs like *Nacht und Träume, Du bist die Ruh', Der Doppelgänger, Der Tod und das Mädchen, Geheimes, Der Jüngling an der Quelle, Das Lied im Grünen,* and the great song-cycles *Die schöne Müllerin* and *Die Winterreise.*

7

MOZART

From the towering and expansive immensities of Beethoven and Schubert we turn to music one of whose outstanding characteristics is its subtlety in the expression of powerful meanings. We hear in Mozart's music a melancholy, passion and intensity that some of his contemporaries found disturbing, but these powerful emotions expressed with an economy and conciseness analogous to what the mathematician calls elegance—manifestations of a keenness and precision of mind which only Berlioz exhibits in comparable manner and degree. And the English critic W. J. Turner considered Mozart to be the supreme classical artist precisely because in his music intensity and passion are crystallized in the clearest, the most beautifully balanced and proportioned, and altogether flawless musical forms.

Nobody has written with anything like Turner's wonderfully illuminating insight about the special qualities of Mozart's music and the ambiguities they create. For example about the "still, unplumbed melancholy underlying even his brightest and most vivacious moments." Or about the vital energy in which Turner doubts Mozart was exceeded by any other composer: the finale of Beethoven's Seventh Symphony, he contends, produces a bigger volume of noise, but not the quick, tense rush of Mozart's Overture to *The Marriage of Figaro*—the one being like the rumble of thunder, the other like the flash of lightning. "Its effect upon the mind," Turner

says of the overture, "is out of all proportion to its impingement on the senses"—something that is true of all of Mozart's
music.

It may not be true for some listeners accustomed to the
luxuriance and vehemence of Wagner and Strauss; but for
others—after that luxuriance—the effect of Mozart's music is
the greater for its economy and subtlety. For these listeners
there is no need of waiting for Wagner and Strauss: they find
Mozart completely adequate for every demand of the drama
he is setting. They find this so when they listen to the orchestra's comments in Leporello's *Catalogue Aria* in *Don Giovanni:*
to the discreetly mischievous detached notes of the violins,
answered by cellos and basses, at the beginning; the eruptions of the violins and woodwinds, like bursts of laughter, a
moment later; still later the suave phrase with which the
violins punctuate *son già mille e tre;* after this the quiet ascending scale of cellos and basses, answered by the descending
scale of violins, both like repressed laughter over *In Italia sei
cento e quaranta;* and so on. Or the grandly impassioned and
lamenting phrases of Donna Anna's *Fuggi, crudele,* the abrupt,
energetic and bold phrases of orchestra and singer in Donna
Elvira's *Ah chi mi dice mai:* what more modern music could
place each character on the stage more effectively? Or Don
Giovanni's *Là ci darem la mano:* could Wagner or Strauss have
achieved anything as elegantly seductive? Or the solemn D-
minor chords with which the overture begins; then the ominous dotted rhythm of the strings over which sustained woodwind chords lead to the poignant figure developed by the
violins and interrupted by the vehement outbursts of the entire orchestra; then the powerful ascending scale passages,
again over the ominous dotted rhythm that continues through
the final measures which—first forceful, then quiet—lead to
the Allegro portion of the overture: the Prelude to *Tristan
und Isolde* does not establish the atmosphere for the drama to
come, does not take possession of the listener's mind and emotions, more quickly and completely.

63

There are comparable things in *Così fan Tutte:* in the first act the quintet *Di scrivermi ogni giorno!*, the trio *Soave sia il vento*, the aria *Come scoglio;* in the second act the duets *Secondate, aurette amiche* and *Il core vi dono*, the aria *Per pietà*, the duet *Fra gli amplessi*. And in *The Magic Flute:* the ensembles involving the Three Ladies, the ones involving the Three Boys, the arias of the Queen of the Night, Tamino's *Dies Bildnis ist bezaubernd schön*, Pamina's *Ach, ich fühl's*, the trio *Soll ich dich, Teurer, nicht mehr seh'n?*, the fugato of Tamino and the Two Armed Men, Tamino's and Pamina's *Pamina/Tamino mein! O welch' ein Glück!*

But wonderful as all these are, they are surpassed by what is heard in *The Marriage of Figaro:* the three-hour outpouring of incandescent invention—miraculous in its varied loveliness, expressiveness, characterization, dramatic point and wit— that is one of the supreme wonders achieved on this earth by human powers. Nor do I mean only the vocal invention: *Figaro* surpasses the other operas in orchestral writing of the kind I have described in the *Catalogue Aria*—with its three-hour running fire of comment that creates the atmosphere of comedy in which even the serious things happen. And in this connection I will mention Tovey's observation that in the G-minor Symphony Mozart's musical language is, as it is in fact everywhere else, that of operatic comedy—by which Tovey doesn't mean that what is said in this language is humorous: one often, he says, finds the language of comedy the only dignified expression for the deepest feelings. It is in this manner that they are often expressed by Mozart—the result being the ambiguity that is one of his outstanding characteristics, and of which an outstanding example is *Così fan Tutte*, with its apparently farcical action for which Mozart wrote some of his most poignant and sublime music, and with things like the aria *Come scoglio*, whose apparent grand style sometimes invites the suspicion that it is parodying itself.

Nor—to get back to *Figaro*—do I mean only the vocal and instrumental invention of the arias. The work rises to its greatest incandescence in the climactic ensembles—the comparatively brief *Cosa sento!* trio of Act 1 and sextet of Act 3, the extended finales of Acts 2 and 4, of which the one of Act 2 is the supreme achievement of its kind, and incidentally the supreme demonstration of the adequacy I spoke of a moment ago. Nothing could be simpler than

and nothing more modern and complex could express more effectively the Count's and the Countess's amazement at seeing Susanna step out from the cabinet. So with what follows: the bland irony of Susanna's *Signore! cos' è quel stupore?.;* the atmosphere of wonder created by the orchestra for the Count's *Che scola!*, the Countess's *Che storia è mai questa*, Susanna's amused *Confusa han la testa;* a moment later the atmosphere of high comedy created by the orchestra for the Count's entreaties, the women's severe *Le vostre follie non mertan pietà;* still later the elaborate and menacing politeness of the Count's *Conoscete, signor Figaro, questo foglio chi vergo?* and the violins' impudent amusement behind Figaro's *Nol conosco;* the stolid stupidity in a state of excitement conveyed by the gardener's *Dal balcone che guarda in giardino*, burlesqued by Figaro's *Via piangione, sta zitto una volta;* and finally the suspense created for the Count's sparring with Figaro by the orchestra's long development of the figure

which swells to triumph for Figaro's *è l'usanza di porvi il suggello.*

The finale of Act 4 is another such succession, for whose conclusion—and the climax of the entire work—Mozart holds in reserve a last marvel. Its overwhelming effect, like that of anything else, comes partly from its context—where it is placed, what it follows. Three hours have been filled with the sorrow of the neglected Countess's *Porgi amor* and *Dove sono;* the agitated awakening emotions of Cherubino's *Non so più cosa son;* the enchanting playfulness of Susanna's *Venite, inginocchiatevi;* the longing of her *Deh vieni, non tardar;* the irony and menace of Figaro's *Se vuol ballare;* the mockery of his *Non più andrai;* the bitterness of his *Aprite un po' quegl' occhi;* the pompous malice of Bartolo's *La vendetta;* the ear-ravishing loveliness of the *Letter Duet;* the wit of Susanna's duets with Figaro, Marcellina, the Count; the comedy of the first-act trio, the third-act sextet, the great finale of Act 2, the finale of Act 4. Three hours have been filled with the orchestra's running fire of comment, which has continued to the last to create the atmosphere of comedy for even the serious happenings: even in the hush of amazement and wonder produced by the Countess's entrance the violins have softly chattered their amusement. But now at last there is an end to all this— a moment's silence; and when the Count begins his *Contessa, perdono* we hear music which speaks of the sublimity of human forgiveness—music which, after what has come before, is overwhelming. It becomes even more overwhelming when it is taken up by the entire group, and when it is carried to a point of superearthly exaltation. Then, in the silence which follows, solemn octaves of the strings gently ease us down to earth again—and to the bustle and fanfares of the final curtain of the operatic comedy. The passage lasts only a few minutes; but those three or four minutes, coming after the three hours, create the most wonderful moment I can recall in opera.

From the comedies of the last years of Mozart's short life (he died at thirty-five) we turn back to the *opera seria* he wrote at twenty-five—to *Idomeneo,* in which, says E. J. Dent in his illuminating book on Mozart's operas, we "see the young Mozart at his greatest heights." Dent speaks of the

work's nobility and dignity of conception, its intense serious-
ness, the "monumental strength and . . . white heat of passion
that we find in this early work of Mozart's and shall never
find again"; and this turns out to be an accurate description
of what we hear: the grandly impassioned gestures with
which the overture begins, the continuing urgency of its so-
called second subject in A minor, the breathtaking shift to C
major; the powerfully expressive detail with which the orchestra points up the recitatives; the noble style of the beautiful
arias; the dramatic use of coloratura style—most notably the
descending staccato scale in Electra's final aria that suggests
the laughter of a demented creature; the power of the great
quartet, and of the chorus *O voto tremendo!*

For the rest there are two more comedies to take note of.
One, the full-length *The Abduction From the Seraglio*, composed
a year or two after *Idomeneo*, has some lovely and charming
music in addition to the great bravura aria *Martern aller Arten*.
The other, the one-act *The Impresario*, composed the same
year as *Figaro*, has a delightful overture and superb vocal
writing in its two arias and trio.

I have called Dent's book illuminating; and nothing in it
is more so than his observation that "the theater is the sphere
in which Mozart is most completely himself; his concert
works—concertos, symphonies, quartets and sonatas—are all
fundamentally evocations of the theater." The truth of this
statement is most evident in the concertos: the special circumstances which produced them made them the most ex-
plicitly dramatic in character of Mozart's instrumental works.
And those circumstances also made them the most elaborately
contrived, the richest in substance, the most complex in form,
the most fascinating and exciting and in all ways impressive
to listen to.

Mozart produced most of his greatest concertos for the occasions at which he presented himself to the public as the
greatest musician of his time—exhibiting the capacities of the

greatest performer, in music that exhibited the capacities of the greatest composer. He wrote a concerto as an actor might write a play for himself to appear in; and the form he produced was in effect the musical equivalent of a play. Listening to the opening movement of one of the piano concertos we first hear the orchestra perform with increasing suspense in anticipation of the moment when it bows itself from the center of the stage, so to speak, and the piano makes its first entrance, to hold attention for a while with graceful, lovely melodies, dazzling passage-work, exchanges with the orchestra, and eventually to work up to a brilliant exit, at which point the orchestra prepares for the piano's next entrance, and so on—the piano's last such entrance being made for the *cadenza* that exhibits the pianist's powers of improvisation, after which the orchestra brings the curtain down on the movement. And we hear similar dramatic alternation of orchestra and piano in the slow movement that presents the piano in Mozartian sustained vocal melody, the finale that often presents it in Mozartian high spirits.

(Parenthetically, for those who read Chapters 3 and 4, I add a more detailed description of the form of the Mozart concerto which other readers can skip. The first movement is an adaptation of the procedure of the earlier ritornello concerto originated by Italian composers and taken over by Bach. In the first movement of Bach's *Brandenburg Concerto* No. 2 or his D-minor Concerto for clavier or violin, we hear an opening statement by the orchestra that keeps returning after alternating passages for the solo instruments—this constantly returning statement of the orchestra being the *ritornello*. What Mozart does is to have the alternation of ritornello and solo passages take place within the succession of exposition, development, recapitulation and coda in the first movement of the symphony: the exposition begins with the orchestra's opening ritornello and is completed by the first solo section; the recurrence of the ritornello brings the second entrance of the piano for the development and the recapitulation; the next recurrence of the ritornello, interrupted by the solo cadenza, provides the coda. You will note that in this scheme of Mozart's there are fewer alternations of ritornello and solo passages that are more extensive and elaborate than in the Bach concerto; and another thing to note is that this heightens the dramatic effect of the course of events in the symphony movement, makes it more externally explicit. That is, the more extensive and elaborate opening ritornello delays the entrance of the solo instrument, and in so doing builds up suspense in anticipation of this entrance—very much as the minor characters in a play may create suspense in anticipation of the first entrance of the principal character. And so with the later recurrences of the ritornello. Interesting in addition is the distribution of substance between orchestra and piano, the changes in distribution in the recapitulation as against the exposition. In the exposition some, but not all, of the ideas stated in the ritornello are repeated by the piano, which introduces additional ideas that were not stated in the ritornello. In the abbreviated recapitulation some of the ideas of the exposition are restated and some are not; and an idea originally stated by the orchestra may now be restated by the piano, possibly in a different order and context, and with modifications of the idea itself. All this was contrived by Mozart for sharp-eared listeners who were expected to remember the original progression of material in the exposition and to appreciate the changes and surprises in the recapitulation.)

The purpose of the form being to impress the listener, its fascination is, first, in what Mozart contrives for this purpose. But there is in addition a special fascination in the sense it gives of the immediacy of Mozart's presence: in the piano's every phrase of melody, every passage of brilliant figuration, every trill, every ornament, we are aware, almost as his own listeners were, of Mozart himself—showing everything he is capable of, attempting to impress, to dazzle, to overwhelm, and succeeding with an apparently inexhaustible flow of the

69

unique poignant loveliness, the gaiety, and on occasion the power. These are the fascination of any one example of the form; but what is fascinating in one after another of the marvelous works is the seemingly unending variety of the invention with which Mozart fills out the same established scheme, goes through the same established series of steps in a way that is newly interesting and impressive each time, and on occasion—writing for an audience familiar with the established scheme—plays with this audience a little game of now doing what it expects and now surprising it with what it does not expect.

Thus we get the extraordinary first entrance of the solo violin in the Concerto K.219 (Mozart was also an accomplished violinist): the orchestra finishes its introduction; we expect the violin to enter at the same lively pace; and instead it begins a breathtakingly beautiful and poignant slow melody which progresses through a half-dozen measures to a conclusion and a pause; after which violin and orchestra break the spell by resuming the original lively course of the movement. And on the other hand, at the beginning of the Piano Concerto K.271 we get the surprises that represent Mozart's love of fun: the orchestra begins imposingly, but before it can finish the piano jumps in to complete the statement; again the orchestra tries, and again the piano interrupts, after which the orchestra is allowed to proceed without further interruption to the final flourish, the final bow of its ritornello; but while it is still bowing the piano bursts onto the scene with a brilliant trill that leads into its opening statement.

The Violin Concerto K.219, which Mozart wrote at nineteen, the Piano Concerto K.271, which he wrote at twenty-one, are among the first great examples of the form; and from these and other early examples we learn that the difference between Mozart at twenty and Mozart at thirty is not, as we might suppose, the difference between Mozart immature and Mozart mature. In the Violin Concertos K.218 and 219, with their characteristic mingling of high spirits and poignant loveliness; in the Violin Concerto K.216, with its especially delightful first movement, its Andante movement whose long flow of sustained melody leaves one spellbound; in the Piano Concerto K.271, with another especially delightful first movement, one of Mozart's deeply affecting C-minor slow movements, and an exuberantly gay finale whose "rush" leaves one breathless—in these early works we hear the essential Mozart expressive content and Mozart form completely and astoundingly matured. What time brings is enrichment, elaboration, subtilization, which rise on occasion to sheer incandescence; that is the difference between the first movements of K.216 (1775) and K.271 (1777), and the first movement of the Piano Concerto K.453 (1784); between the slow movement of K.271, and the C-minor slow movement of the Sinfonie Concertante K.364 for violin and viola (1779); between the slow movement of K.216, and the Andante movement of the Piano Concerto K.467 (1785); between the finale of K.271, and the finales of K.466 (1785) and 488 (1786).

Enrichment, elaboration, subtilization, then, give us the later great examples of the form—the Piano Concertos K.450, 453, 456 and 459 (1784), K.466, 467 and 482 (1785), K.488, 491 and 503 (1786), and K.595 (1791). And incandescence gives us the individual movements and entire works, among those great examples, that are some of Mozart's supreme utterances in instrumental music.

Thus K.453 has a first movement that is one of the supreme examples of Mozartian instrumental high comedy—though one in which characteristically the gaiety is mingled with Mozartian poignancy. They are mingled right from the start, in the opening violin theme that begins with grace and elegance, continues with a poignancy the more intense for the exquisite contour of the embodying phrase, and is punctuated by mocking flutters of the woodwinds. A moment later the bassoon chortles on comically after the flourishes of the full orchestra stop, leading to another exquisitely contoured and poignant statement of the violins (at this point in the recapitulation Mozart contrives a couple of his little surprises and jokes: when the orchestra's flourishes stop it is not the chortling bassoon but the piano that continues them, leading not to that statement of the violins but to a sharply contoured theme which the piano itself stated in the exposition). And such alternations continue throughout the movement.

This first movement of comedy is followed by one of Mozart's most affecting and most extraordinarily organized slow movements. A poignant opening statement recurs several times, pausing each time before a long sequence of thought takes off from it; overlaid on this pattern of arrangement are alternations of orchestra and piano, and a cycle of keys; and after the piano's cadenza the woodwinds' last enunciation of the opening statement is completed, with sublime implications, by the piano. Then the finale: a genial theme and several variations, one of them suddenly hushed and ominous with its minor mode and syncopations; and a coda made breathtaking by the tempo, style, surprises and jokes of a Mozartian operatic-comedy finale.

In the seldom-played K.456 it is the Andante movement that is outstanding, with an extraordinarily beautiful and poignant theme in G minor that is elaborated in several impressive examples of Mozartian variation-writing.

K.466, one of the most frequently played, begins with what is perhaps the most powerful of Mozart's instrumental movements. The power of the hushed D-minor opening passage is an example of effect on the mind out of all proportion to the impingement on the senses: it is achieved by nothing more than the agitated syncopations of violins and violas, the quiet eruptions of cellos and basses, with not even one of the kettledrum-strokes that punctuate those eruptions in the orchestral outburst a moment later (not only kettledrums but trumpets are added to the orchestra in this work). In the second movement it is the interlude of sustained melody for the solo piano that is noteworthy—more so even than the stormy G-minor episode later in the movement. And then comes one of Mo-

zart's incandescent perpetuum mobile finales, similar to the
one in K.271, but its momentum this time unbroken by a
minuet, and with a last-minute surprise in the coda: the
theme

heard twice before in the movement, is now changed, extended, and unexpectedly answered by the horns' and trumpets'

which becomes increasingly insistent in the crescendo that
brings the movement to a close.

Trumpets and kettledrums contribute to the festive brilliance
of the first movement of K.467, the gaiety of its finale; but
they play no part in the extraordinary Andante inbetween.
In this movement the orchestra makes a long opening statement of a succession of ideas, on which the piano then dis-
courses in several sequences of thought that get to be excitingly eventful in the way that is so extraordinary: up above
there is the calm of the melody as it proceeds with developing
tensions and involvements; while down below there is the
agitation of faster-moving accompanying violins and violas,
the power of plucked bass-notes; and occasionally there are
intensifying comments by the woodwinds. All these, working
together, build up tension and impact that make this movement, for all its quiet, one of Mozart's most powerful utterances; and indeed with this power achieved in quiet it is one
of the most extraordinary pieces of music he ever wrote.

In the first movement of K.482 festive opening proclamations claim attention for a rich flow of exquisite melodic invention; there is a similar flow of loveliness and humor in the
finale; and inbetween is another of Mozart's most affecting
and extraordinarily organized slow movements. Muted violins

73

play a long and poignant melody in C minor; when the piano enters it is to play an elaborating and intensifying variation on this melody, reinforced at climactic moments by the orchestra's strings; the winds then enter with an engaging interlude in E flat major; the piano makes a second entrance with another variation on the opening melody, again reinforced momentarily by the strings; in a second interlude, this time in C major, the flute and bassoon, accompanied by strings, carry on a gracefully ornate dialogue; then the piano engages in a powerful dialogue with the full orchestra in another variation on the opening melody; after which orchestra and piano alternate in a coda that ends with a master-stroke: the concluding phrase of the first interlude, with the intense poignancy it acquires from being now in C minor.

In K.488 there is a return to an orchestra without trumpets and kettledrums for the flow of some of Mozart's most ear-ravishing and heart-piercing melodic invention in the first movement, another of his affecting slow movements in minor mode, and the supreme example of his incandescent perpetuum-mobile finale—the most breathtaking in its profusion of ideas, its momentum, its strokes of surprise and humor. The effect of these strokes comes, again, from their context; and Mozart expects us to remember how

proceeded and ended the first time, when he brings it back later in the movement and makes it proceed and end differently—i.e. prolongs it with changes of harmony that create increasing suspense before it suddenly leaps triumphantly into the clear with

Similarly he expects our recollection of the previous two appearances of this blandly, suavely mocking statement:

etc.

to enable us to appreciate the effect of its unexpected last appearance near the end of the movement.

The large orchestra is heard again in K.491, contributing to the magnificence that is one of the outstanding characteristics of its first movement, another being its dramatic power—the power, for example, of the hushed C-minor opening passage of strings and bassoons and its forceful restatement by the entire orchestra a moment later; or of the forceful statements and the hushed concluding passage, again in C minor, after the cadenza. This movement towers above the engaging slow movement and the richly elaborated variation finale.

In K.503 too the first movement towers above the others by virtue of a grandeur and majesty that set it apart from other first movements. Thus it begins not with one of their immediately appealing opening themes, but, in the words of Tovey, "with a majestic assertion of . . . C major by the whole orchestra, with mysterious soft shadows that give a solemn depth to the tone." And these mysterious soft shadows of delicate woodwind textures after the initial radiance of the entire orchestra—the second time with a wonderful shift to C minor—are subtleties contrived for the eighteenth-century ear that may escape some listeners of today. Another such subtlety is created with a reiterated rhythmic figure, which in the opening ritornello is carried to a point where it is trumpeted forth on the note G and leads to C minor: when the orchestra trumpets forth those G's again at the beginning of the development, they are answered breathtakingly by the piano's reiteration of the figure on B, in a sudden shift to E minor that is the first of a series of such bold modulations.

Trumpets and drums are not suitable for the first move-

ment of K.595, which also stands apart from the other concertos, and in fact from everything else, in its late-in-life calm
(e.g. the opening statement of the violins, punctuated by the
strange calls of the winds), with which it conveys intimations
of agony that preceded calm (e.g. the poignantly altered
repetition of the violins'

a few moments later)—so that as a piece of late writing by
Mozart it has something like the character of a late work of
Beethoven, or Schubert's Piano Sonata in B flat. Something
of this character is heard also in the opening and closing sections of the Larghetto, which has inbetween an eventful, and
in the end impassioned, interlude of sustained melody for the
piano—one of the events being a breathtaking shift in key.
But not in the finale, in which there is only lilting good
humor, with moments of high spirits and fun.

And not, I will add, in another product of the last year of
Mozart's life, the lovely Clarinet Concerto K.622—though
the Mozartian poignancy makes itself heard in the lyricism
and gaiety.

Writing about Schubert I referred to the last quiet passage
just before the end of the finale of Mozart's Symphony in G
minor K.550—a series of textures of sounds with miraculously
achieved intensities of loveliness and expressive force. Hardly
less wonderful is the analogous quiet passage soon after the
beginning of that finale; and there is another series of such
miracles about halfway through the first movement—the passage that leads to the return of the impassioned opening statement. These are incandescent moments in one of the most
extraordinary examples of what Turner spoke about—one in
which the utmost in passion and intensity is crystallized in
the most exquisite of clear, beautifully balanced and propor-

tioned musical forms. Its expressive content and form, in fact, not only set the G-minor apart from Mozart's other symphonies but make it another of the supreme wonders achieved by human powers.

The G-minor is the second of the last great group of three symphonies Mozart composed in approximately two months of the summer of 1788. Its intense melancholy may seem at first to be related to the desperate circumstances of Mozart's life at that time; but the loveliness of K.543—even though it pierces the heart as it ravishes the ear—and the festive majesty of K.551 that has caused it to be given the name *Jupiter* teach us not to attempt such correlations of works of art with the immediate circumstances of the artist's life.

There are flashing miracles again in the finale of K.543—e.g. the series of subtly altered statements of

that lead to the return of the opening statement of the violins. And in the finale of K.551 there is another of those extraordinary rushes of vital energy, expressing itself this time in contrapuntal manipulation of the several themes which Mozart carries to a jubilantly triumphant conclusion.

Of the same stature is the less frequently heard Symphony K.504 (*Prague*) (1786), with the grand opening gestures of a slow introduction that becomes powerfully dramatic before pausing for the brilliant Allegro; with an Andante rich in thematic ideas whose development is made eventful by bold shifts of key; and with a delightful concluding Presto.

Smaller in scale are the earlier movements of the seldom-played K.425 (*Linz*) (1783)—the imposing introduction leading to the brilliant Allegro, the lovely slow movement, the minuet movement. Unexpected, therefore, is the large scale of the finale, its richness of substance and elaboration.

The frequently heard K.385 (*Haffner*) (1782) has a powerful first movement elaborated almost entirely out of its opening statement, followed by a lovely and poignant Andante, a fine minuet movement, and another delightful concluding Presto.

The power of these later symphonies is something we don't find in the earlier K.338 (1780) and K.297 (*Paris*) (1778); but we do find a poignantly lovely Andantino in K.297, an especially lovely Andante di molto in K.338, framed by delightfully high-spirited opening movements and rushing finales.

And like the concertos the symphonies include early small-scale works, K.200 and 201 (1773-4) in which we hear the essential Mozart expressive content and form astoundingly matured: in K.200 the gaiety of the opening movement and rushing finale, the poignancy of the exquisitely contoured muted-violin melodies in the Andante, the pensiveness tinged with sadness in much of the minuet movement; and in K.201 the grace and wistfulness of the opening movement, the poignant loveliness of the Andante, the gaiety of the minuet (e.g.

the comical punctuating flourishes of the winds) alternating with the exquisite poignancy of the trio; the high spirits of another rushing finale.

In Mozart's operas, concertos and symphonies we have heard the exquisite textures in which he combines the sounds of strings, of winds, of both strings and winds, of instruments and voices. You will find nothing to equal them (though Berlioz and Debussy will offer something comparable); and since string-quartet-writing is an art of texture you will hear in no other quartets the ear-ravishing use of the medium that you hear in the famous six—K.387, 421, 428, 458 (*Hunt*), 464 and 465—that Mozart dedicated to Haydn, and in K.499, which is of the same period (1782-6). Nor do they, of course, merely delight the ear: their expressive content, as always, touches the heart. And outstanding in these respects are the somberly powerful K.421, the now amusingly high-spirited, now deeply affecting K.458, the less frequently heard K.428 with its grave opening movement, its rich-textured Andante and comedy finale, and K.499 with its richly elaborated opening movement and slow movement, its lovely minuet, and another comedy finale.

But of greatest stature among the works of this category are two of the string quintets, K.515 and 516 (1787). The additional viola, by increasing the sonority and the richness of texture, contributes to the extraordinary power of the first movement of K.515; by darkening the instrumental color it contributes to the somber strangeness of the minuet and first part of the trio, the intensity of the middle part of the trio, the poignancy of the Andante. And the darkened instrumental coloring contributes, as does the key of G minor, to the effect of K.516, one of the best-known of these works, and unique in its expressive content: in no other work of Mozart do we hear such unrelieved melancholy as in the first movement, such poignancy in a minuet, this poignancy carried to such agonized intensity as in the slow movement; and nowhere does Mozart permit himself to speak with the anguish of the slow introduction to a finale whose apparent light-heartedness at first—incongruous after what has preceded it—is qualified as it continues.

Of the great string quintets that are heard less frequently than they should be, K.593 (1790) is especially notable for its deeply affecting slow movement and bustling comedy finale; K.614 (1791) for the unexpected high spirits of its delightful opening movement and finale; K.406 (1787) for its powerful opening movement and contrapuntal minuet movement in C minor, its poignant Andante.

K.406 is an arrangement of the earlier Serenade K.388 for winds, which has less expressive effect than the string quintet version but offers some of Mozart's beautiful writing for wind instruments, both solo and in combination. We hear more of this writing in the Serenade K.361, which has a very fine slow introduction, Adagio, and variation movement; and the brilliant Serenade K.375, which has wonderful details. Beautiful writing for strings and horns is to be heard in the charming Divertimentos K.287 and 334—the first with an extraordinary Adagio in the style of a great vocal aria, the second with some wonderful details in the variation movement. And beautiful writing for three strings in the Divertimento K.563, with its fine slow movement and extraordinary theme and variations.

We hear writing for the oboe that is breathtaking in its vocal style and expressive intensity in the brief Adagio that is framed by charming Allegros in the Quartet K.370 for oboe and strings. And the larger-scale Quintet K.581 for clarinet and strings offers a flow of lyricism, characteristic in its poignant loveliness, that makes it one of Mozart's most beautiful works.

Concerning the Quintet K.452 for piano and winds I am in the awkward position of disagreeing with Mozart, who in a letter to his father pronounced it "the best I have ever written"; since the opening Allegro, to my ears, is inane. But twice even in this movement—near the end of the exposition

and the recapitulation—there is a succession of scale passages
rushing up to sustained notes which create a texture with
wonderful harmonic progressions; there are impressive episodes also in the slow movement; and there are of course
wonderful textures of sounds of winds throughout.

The piano is heard with clarinet and viola in the fine Trio
K.498; it is heard with strings in the piano trios and quartets,
of which the Trio K.496 is the best, and the Trios K.502 and
548 have beautiful slow movements. It is heard also in the
sonatas for piano and violin, of which an early group includes
the charming K.296, 301, 305 and 306, the impassioned
K.304, the lovely K.378; and later ones include the powerful
K.379, K.380 with its poignant slow movement, K.454 and
481 with their very beautiful slow movements, and K.526,
the finest of the series, with one of the most charming of first
movements, a grave, richly elaborated Andante that becomes
wonderfully beautiful and deeply affecting, and one of the
most brilliant and breathtaking of perpetuum-mobile finales.

For piano solo one of Mozart's finest pieces is the Rondo
K.511 that I presented in Chapter 4. And other late works
of the same stature are the powerful Fantasia K.475 and
Sonata K.457, which are sometimes played, as they were published, together; the Sonata K.576, with some of Mozart's
most developed, most complex writing for the instrument; the
fine Sonata K.570; the Sonata K.533 and 494, with its remarkable and startling harmonic progressions; the rhythmically intricate Gigue K.574. A little earlier are the powerful
Fantasia K.396; the Suite K.399, with its interesting and engaging Mozartian transformations of the styles of the movements of a Handel suite. And still earlier are the fine Sonatas
K.333 (with a startling development in the Andante), 332,
311, 310; the engaging K.283; and K.282, with its astonishing Adagio first movement. Of the best-known Sonata K.331
I find the minuet movement more estimable than the opening
theme and variations and concluding *Rondo à la turca*.

In addition there are the fine Sonata K.448 for two pianos; the engaging Sonatas K.381, 358 and 357 for piano four hands.

Most of Mozart's church music, finally, was written in his youth while he was in the service of the Archbishop of Salzburg; and an outstanding work of this period is the Mass K.317, written when he was twenty-three. It has several sections—the *Kyrie*, *Gloria*, *Benedictus* and *Agnus Dei*—which are very beautiful; but most impressive is the *Credo*, with an Allegro opening section that acquires tremendous power from its ostinato instrumental figuration, then a change to Adagio for wonderful passages on the words *Et incarnatus est* and *Crucifixus etiam* and *passus et sepultus est*, and then a return to the Allegro with a lovely episode on *Et in spiritum sanctum*.

Once out of the service of the Archbishop he was kept busy by the instrumental works and operas with which he had to earn a living—too busy to be able to complete the *Mass in C Minor* that he began in 1782. But in its incomplete form it includes a magnificently powerful *Kyrie* with a lovely episode for solo soprano, and the wonderfully beautiful *Et incarnatus est.*

And death cut short his work on the *Requiem*, which was completed in accordance with his sketches and directions by his pupil Süssmayr. This work too has magnificently powerful sections like the *Kyrie* (with affecting passages for solo soprano), *Tuba mirum* and *Rex tremendae;* lovely ones like the *Recordare*, *Hostias*, *Benedictus* and *Agnus Dei;* and a *Lacrymosa* which takes its place with things like the Andante of the Piano Concerto K.467—what is extraordinary this time being the way the unceasing two-note violin figure builds up cumulative expressive force behind the affecting vocal parts.

Even this long discussion of Mozart's music leaves undiscussed a large part of his enormous output that I have never heard, and some works, among those I have heard, that a busily engaged eighteenth-century musical craftsman turned out occasionally without inspiration or interest, and with no more inspiration or interest for us than for him. But the works I have dealt with—their use of the medium, and what they express through this use—make that busily engaged craftsman the most extraordinary musical artist who ever lived.

8

HAYDN

Toscanini, excited once about a Haydn symphony he was going to play, exclaimed that he found Haydn more wonderful even than Mozart ("except of course," he added, "the G-minor—and the concertos"). What caused his face to register delight as he listened to a recording of the symphony was the method so well described by Tovey's statements that "the essential character of Haydn's form is dramatic surprise at the moment" and "nothing in Haydn is difficult to follow, but almost everything is unexpected." It is a surprise achieved by variety—a moment-to-moment, point-to-point varying of melodic and harmonic direction, length of phrase, rhythmic grouping and accentuation, volume, orchestral activity, which calls for attentive point-to-point listening.

Here, for example, is the opening statement of the Quartet Op. 76 No. 2:

And here is how the repetition of this statement unexpectedly prolongs its third measure and does a little fooling around in the fifth and sixth before coming to a new conclusion in the seventh and eighth:

For an example of this sort of thing in rich profusion and in a tempo that makes it easy to observe, listen to the introduction to the Symphony No. 104:

Listen, that is, to the dramatic surprise—after the radiantly
sonorous opening call and answer—of the hushed statement
of strings and bassoon in measures 3 and 4. Then the effect—
after the C sharps at [a]—of the C natural at [b], and of what
this C natural brings: the shift in key from D minor into F
major. Then the effect—after the radiantly sonorous call and
answer—of the changed hushed answer in measure 9. Then
the effect—after the development of the first-violin figure with
increasing intensity in measures 9, 10 and 11—of the sudden
taking over of that figure by the cellos in measure 12 below
sustained notes of the upper strings and flute, with increasing
harmonic complexity that is resolved in measure 13. And then
the startling effects—after the radiantly sonorous call, back
in the key of D once more—of the hushed answer, of the note

87

G instead of the expected A at [c], of the addition of the remote chord at [d], creating suspense that changes, with the harmonic progressions and the oboe comments in measure 16, to expectancy for the beginning of the Allegro portion of the movement.

This example of the packing in of detail to hold attention from one moment to the next illustrates Tovey's statement that Haydn is a great master working on a very small scale. And it illustrates another of Tovey's perceptive observations— that Haydn's forms become more subtle as his spirits rise. For what we hear in Haydn's instrumental music is a constant playing with the medium and with the listener's mind; and sometimes we hear this process raised to incandescence by his exuberance in the use of his powers for that purpose: on every page we get details which it amused him to contrive on Wednesday to startle his listeners, or hold them spellbound, or make them laugh, on Saturday. Thus the little surprises in the first two movements of the Quartet Op. 76 No. 2 leave us unprepared for the bomb that Haydn explodes in the minuet movement: a canon, with violins leading and lower strings following that make us laugh first with the unexpectedness of the procedure and then with some of the details of the progression. Or, in the Symphony No. 104, when the beautiful Andante movement has completed its formal cycle and we think it is about to end, it goes off on a wonderful wide-ranging digression. And a more obvious bit of musical fooling occurs at the end of the minuet: the silence when we are expecting another trill; and then a soft trill when we expect a loud one. Listening to such mischievously contrived details we are aware of the mind that is operating behind them—which is to say that the course of events in a Haydn symphony or quartet gives us the same fascinating sense of the immediacy of Haydn's presence and activity as we get of Mozart's from one of his concertos.

These are some of the fascinations of any one of the works; but to listen to one after another of the great last symphonies—

the final group, Nos. 93 to 104, that Haydn wrote for his two visits to London, and some that preceded them—is to be astounded by the profusion and variety of invention from this inexhaustibly fertile mind. And astounding in the same way are an even larger number of the string quartets—the many fine works, the works with outstanding individual movements, and the incandescent examples like Op. 20 Nos. 4 and 5, Op. 33 No. 3, Op. 54 Nos. 1 and 2, Op. 64 Nos. 3 and 4, Op. 74 No. 2, Op. 77 No. 2.

Moreover, the symphonies and quartets are only the best-known of Haydn's instrumental works. Recordings have recently begun to make it possible to discover the similar stature and fascination of others that are almost never played in concerts—some of the trios for piano, violin and cello; some of the piano sonatas. Pianists, a notoriously unadventurous species, are content to go on playing the extraordinarily beautiful and often amazing *Andante and Variations* in F minor, and at most the Sonatas in E flat and D.

So with the choral works. We used to hear *The Creation*, with its introductory representation of chaos that is amazing in its daring and power, its other passages that are wonderfully beautiful, and still others that charm us with their innocence and sweetness. And once in a great while there would be a performance of *The Seasons*, with its many lovely and charming pages, and some powerful ones in the *Winter* section. Now, through recordings, we know the *Nelson Mass*, the *Theresienmesse*, the *St. Cecilia Mass*, the *Missa in tempore belli*, all impressive and often superb products of Haydn's fully matured powers.

9

BERLIOZ

By the criteria I applied to Mozart—use of the medium, and what is expressed through this use—Berlioz is another of the greatest musical artists. This estimate is not the generally accepted one you will find in the histories of music and appreciation manuals; it is however what I have discovered to be true from my listening to the music; and I propose to let readers of this book make the same discovery in the same way.

I suggest, then, listening to the song *Au Cimetière* from *Les Nuits d'été*—a setting of this poem by Gautier:

> Connaissez-vous la blanche tombe
> Où flotte avec un son plaintif
>   L'ombre d'un if?
> Sur l'if, une pâle colombe,
> Triste et seule, au soleil couchant
>   Chante son chant;
>
> Un air maladivement tendre,
> A la fois charmant et fatal,
>   Qui vous fait mal,
> Et qu'on voudrait toujours entendre,
> Un air comme en soupire aux cieux
>   L'ange amoureux.
>
> On dirait que l'âme éveillée
> Pleure sous terre à l'unison
>   De la chanson,

Et du malheur d'être oubliée
Se plaint dans un roucoulement
    Bien doucement.

Sur les aîles de la musique
On sent lentement revenir
    Un souvenir;
Une ombre de forme angélique
Passe dans un rayon tremblant,
    En voile blanc.

Les belles de nuit, demi-closes,
Jettent leur parfum faible et doux
    Autour de vous,
Et le fantôme aux molles poses
Murmure en vous tendant les bras:
    Tu reviendras?

Oh! jamais plus, près de la tombe,
Je n'irai, quand descend le soir
    Au manteau noir,
Ecouter la pâle colombe
Chanter sur la branche de l'if
    Son chant plaintif!

Listen to the first three vocal statements to the words

Connaissez-vous la blanche tombe
Où flotte avec un son plaintif/L'ombre d'un if?
Sur l'if, une pâle colombe,/Triste et seule, au
    soleil couchant/Chante son chant;

Immediately striking is the exquisiteness of the vocal melody, of the underlying harmony (e.g. the changes beginning at *tombe*), of the instrumental color. And striking too is the freedom with which the melody moves, grows, takes form—freedom in relation to bar-line and meter; freedom in shape and length of phrase; freedom, then, from the conventional and expected regularities and symmetries. Even in the first statement the deployment of the four measures of vocal melody is irregular in relation to the bar-line (at *la*) and asymmetrical to the seven measures of instrumental accompaniment. In the next statement the melody is repeated, but with elaborating changes: not only the change in rhythm and contour (*un son*) and the exquisite change of F sharp to F natural (on the syllable *plain*), but the additional clause (*L'ombre d'un if*) that makes this statement asymmetrical in shape and length to the first. And in the third statement there are not only further elaborating changes in melody and rhythm but an additional clause that makes this statement asymmetrical to the second.

Clearly this is a progression in which nothing has been set down mechanically or perfunctorily; in which everything, on the contrary, exhibits the operation of a mind unceasingly attentive, active, creative—excitingly so in the placing of the occasional plucked bass-notes, which produce an effect out of proportion to their impingement on the senses. And about this there are two things to say. One is that this mind unceasingly active, which makes Berlioz fascinating to listen to, gives us music that can be described by Tovey's statement about Haydn: "Nothing is difficult to follow, but everything is unexpected." At one point after another the music moves in an unexpected direction, continues with something unforeseen, which turns out to be logical and right; and you will discover that Berlioz is in fact one of the great originals in music, whose thought, language and style are like no one else's before or after him. And the other thing to say is that in each decision to change this note in the melody or that chord in the harmony, to extend this note over the bar-line here or place that plucked bass-note there, we hear evidence that this active mind, as it fills in the musical canvas, so to speak, operates with an ear, a taste, a melodic gift, a harmonic sense, a magic with the orchestra—in short with musical powers—of a most unusual and distinguished sort.

We continue to hear the freedom and freshness of invention in the song's further statements. The melody (*Un air maladivement tendre*) repeats a figure of four quarter-notes against the three-quarter time marked excitingly by the plucked bass; then (*A la fois charmant et fatal*) it takes off, expanding freely over the bar-lines to a high point (*fatal*) from which it descends with exquisite inflections (*Qui vous fait mal* and *Et qui voudrait toujours entendre*); then (*Un air comme en soupire aux cieux*) it is quietly sustained as it rises to an exquisite inflection (*soupir aux cieux*) and conclusion (*L'ange amoureux*).

Now a new section begins (*On dirait que l'âme éveillée/Pleure sous terre à l'unison/De la chanson*): over more agitated eighth-notes in the strings the melody's groups of repeated A's are punctuated in exciting fashion by an irregularly placed and intensely poignant two-note chromatic figure of the wood-winds. This continues, with the addition only of an occasional plucked bass-note (*Et du malheur d'être oubliée/Se plaint dans un roucoulement*); but the conclusion (*Bien doucement*) is made suddenly exciting by quick repetition of the woodwind figure over plucked bass-notes. With increased agitation in the strings the melody (*Sur les aîles de la musique/On sent lentement revenir/Un souvenir*) rises with expansive freedom to a high point of intensity at which there are brilliant woodwind flourishes. Then (*Une ombre, une forme angélique/Passe dans un rayon tremblant*) the melody subsides, with the woodwinds continuing their poignant figure, and with the violins adding gleaming harmonics (at *tremblant*) which continue until the pause before the return of the opening section—this time to the words

Les belles de nuit demi-closes
Jettent leur parfum faible et doux/Autour de vous,
Et le fantôme aux molles poses/Murmure en vous tendant les bras: "Tu
  reviendras!"
Oh! jamais plus, près de la tombe/Je n'irai, quand descend le soir/Au
  manteau noir,

It is here, at the beginning of the repetition of the opening statement, that we hear the most extraordinary manifestation of the powers I have mentioned. As the voice, below syncopated woodwind chords, begins its melody, violins and violas add a descending four-note comment, modified at each repetition with overwhelming expressive effect:

I doubt that anyone has ever produced a greater effect on the mind with so little impingement on the senses.

For the rest the opening statements are repeated with only slight changes until *Oh! jamais plus* etc., when the melody's four-quarter figure is repeated over one of Berlioz's enlivening pizzicato oscillations in the cellos, and an ostinato figure in the basses. And the melody itself changes at *Au manteau noir* for new concluding statements to the words

> *Ecouter la pâle colombe/Chanter sur la pointe de l'if*
> *Son chant plaintif!*

with the orchestra speaking poignantly before *Son chant plaintif*, with it, and after it.

If one were given nothing but this song to judge from one would have to say the man who wrote it was one of the greatest masters. Any of the other songs of *Les Nuits d'été* would compel the same judgment; but I suggest listening further to *Sur les lagunes*—a setting of this poem by Gautier:

> Ma belle amie est morte:
> Je pleurerai toujours;
> Sous la tombe elle emporte
> Mon âme et mes amours.

Dans le ciel, sans m'attendre,
Elle s'en retourna;
L'ange qui l'emmena
Ne voulut pas me prendre.
Que mon sort est amer!
Ah! sans amour, s'en aller sur la mer!

La blanche créature
Est couchée au cercueil.
Comme dans la nature
Tout me paraît en deuil!
La colombe oubliée
Pleure et songe à l'absent;
Mon âme pleure et sent
Qu'elle est dépareillée.
Que mon sort est amer!
Ah! sans amour, s'en aller sur la mer!

Sur moi la nuit immense
S'étend comme un linceul;
Je chante ma romance
Que le ciel entend seul.
Ah! comme elle était belle
Et comme je l'aimais!
Je n'aimerai jamais
Une femme autant qu'elle.
Que mon sort est amer!
Ah! sans amour, s'en aller sur la mer!

We shall see later on that one of Berlioz's most remarkable procedures is the repetition at intervals of an unchanged figure or note in the constantly changing context of the developing musical thought; and he does something of the kind in *Sur les lagunes:* the orchestra's powerfully somber three-note figure (in F minor) that establishes the atmosphere of the song in the very first measure recurs at intervals, punctuating the grief-laden vocal statements to the words

Ma belle amie est morte:
Je pleurerai toujours;
Sous la tombe elle emporte/Mon âme et mes amours.
Dans le ciel, sans m'attendre,/Elle s'en retourna;
L'ange qui l'emmena/Ne voulut pas me prendre.

In this opening section we hear again the unceasing creativeness producing the freedom and variety of melodic rhythm, shape and length, the unexpected shifts in direction caused, sometimes, by progressions in the harmony (e.g. before *Sous la tombe*). And the section ends with two statements that will recur as a refrain: the plaintive *Que mon sort est amer!*, followed by the passionate *Ah! sans amour s'en aller sur la mer!*

Now a shift to B flat major brings a momentary brightness in a new section which begins (*La blanche créature*) with tranquilly sustained loveliness, but continues with increasing intensity and poignancy (*Est couchée au cercueil;/Comme dans la nature*) that becomes heavy, dark grief (*Tout me paraît en deuil*). The momentum increases with the orchestra's activity: with the violin arpeggio that introduces *La colombe oubliée*, the two-note woodwind figures and plucked bass-notes that reinforce *Pleure, pleure et songe à l'absent*, in the crescendo of intensity that continues with *Mon âme pleure et sent/Qu'elle est dépareillée.* Suddenly there is a moment's silence; then again the refrain *Que mon sort est amer!/Ah! sans amour s'en aller sur la mer!* And again the somber three-note figure, which leads again to the opening musical statement—this time to the words *Sur moi la nuit immense.* The statement is again punctuated by the three-note figure, which leads now to one of the most wonderful passages in the song. The final C of the figure descends to C flat, which is repeated by the voice in the hushed *S'étend comme un linceul* over harmonic progressions on which it pivots to start the wonderfully beautiful and moving *Je chante ma romance/Que le ciel entend seul.* This leads to the climactic statements of the song:

Ah! comme elle était belle/Et comme je l'aimais!
Je n'aimerai jamais/Une femme autant qu'elle.

Again the three-note figure, which leads to the refrain. And then a last master-stroke: the three-note figure, previously heard only from the orchestra, is heard now from the voice.

After listening to these two songs you are in a position to understand my lack of awe for accepted opinion. For accepted opinion on Berlioz—in the music histories and appreciation manuals—credits him only with a gift for orchestral color and effect, and has it that he used gigantic orchestras to conceal the poverty and banality of his melody and harmony. Writing of "the musicians of the last century, from Berlioz to Strauss," one excessively esteemed historian spoke once of "orchestral scores which when dispossessed of their tremendous orchestral ornaments show an astonishingly meager invention and vague construction." And another wrote that the full orchestra was Berlioz's principal medium because of his preoccupation "with extreme and gigantic aims"; that he used "huge choral masses" for the same reason; that "he forged anew the poetry of *Faust* and *Romeo and Juliet* to his own ends, and monstrous works came forth, half oratorio, half symphony, half lyrical and half dramatic, all blazing with color"; that he similarly used liturgical texts, in the *Requiem* and *Te Deum*, for "a colossal musical exhibition and show of power."

The composer of *Au Cimetière* and *Sur les lagunes* and the other songs of *Les Nuits d'été* doesn't seem to me to be preoccupied with extreme and gigantic aims or to be using dazzling orchestral effects to conceal meager invention; but what of the works that do use large orchestral and vocal forces? The answer happens to be given in one of Turner's critical articles that I encountered recently, written after his first hearing of the rarely performed *Requiem*. This is the work that is usually pointed to as the example of Berlioz's use of huge forces for extreme and gigantic aims; and Turner writes: "It is true that his Mass calls for sixteen kettledrums; it is true that he asks for four brass bands to be played north, south, east and west of the general body of chorus and orchestra. All these

97

things in the hands of anyone but Berlioz would have resulted in incredible vulgarity; but Berlioz could not be vulgar." When the brass bands in the *Tuba mirum* "burst out into their antiphonal blazing coruscations," says Turner, "it is as though a thousand rockets had gone up over our heads and were bursting into flames"; but this, he adds, is only their first effect: "we soon discover that these extraordinary exhilarating pyrotechnics are charged with meaning, the flames are not mere flames but *expressive, imaginative,* full of poetic significance."

It is good to have this answer to the idea of large means being connected with extreme and gigantic aims. That idea is true of some artists, but not of all; it is true of some painters, for example, but not of every painter who chooses to apply oil paints to a large canvas rather than a pencil to a small sheet of paper; it is equally not true of every composer who chooses to write for an orchestra rather than a string quartet; and, as Turner testifies, it isn't necessarily true even of a composer who elects to write for an orchestra with sixteen kettle-drums and four additional brass bands: when that composer is a Berlioz he uses such large forces with the same precision and for as legitimate artistic ends, as small ones. The impression of the *Requiem* given by the histories and music appreciation manuals is of the additional four brass bands blaring away uninterruptedly and blatantly for two hours; whereas actually they are used in only a few sections, and where they do play with full power, as in the *Tuba mirum*, they do not merely blare away but operate with imaginative purpose and effect; in addition to which—and this is something Turner doesn't speak of—they don't always play with full power. Indeed the most impressive evidence of Berlioz's integrity in the matter is the discretion and taste with which he uses them in the *Lacrymosa*.

Introduced and accompanied by an explosively agitated orchestral figuration the tenors begin a beautiful melodic passage in nine-eighth time which moves with Berlioz's characteristic freedom of rhythm, shape and direction; when the sopranos and altos repeat the passage the tenors continue with a counterpoint that is similarly free; and the next repetition by the basses is enriched and given exciting momentum by similar counterpoints of women and tenors, reaching a climax that subsides into a new and quiet section. In this, altos and tenors sing a brief figure that is commented on by the basses—the figure and comment being derived from the opening section. They continue and develop with increasing intensity to a conclusion; then comes a section (*Pie Jesu, Domine, donna eis requiem*) of tranquilly sustained melodic loveliness and exquisite harmonic progressions. From this there is suddenly a return to the explosive orchestral figuration and the tenors' nine-eighth melody of the opening; and it is here that Berlioz begins to use the four additional brass bands: in each nine-eighth measure the third group of three eighths is reinforced by a note or chord from one after another of the four bands—the effect of these cries of the brass being indescribable. And in the repetitions of the melody that effect is heightened: with the repetition by sopranos and altos the brass chords from one after another of the bands are fuller and are intensified by kettledrum-rolls; with the repetition by the basses each reinforcing chord is played by all four bands together with thunderous rolls of kettledrums and bass drums. The momentum and excitement are tremendous; and again the climax subsides into the quiet discussion of figures derived from the opening section, carried on this time in three vocal parts instead of two, hence with greater intricacy of rhythm and texture, and with wonderful comments from the woodwinds. And this time the section ends with a crescendo to a climax in which the additional brass bands join in a tremendous unison proclamation of the nine-eighth melody by chorus and orchestra.

As precisely—and on occasion as exquisitely—wrought are the sections that do not employ the additional brass bands: the radiant *Sanctus;* the *Hostias,* which uses, in addition to strings, only flutes and trombones, but these with astounding originality and impressiveness; the *Quaerens me*, for chorus without any orchestra at all. And of these the most remarkable is the *Offertorium*.

This is one of the great examples—great in scale and effect—of the procedure Berlioz used in *Sur les lagunes:* the repetition at intervals of an unchanged figure or note in the constantly changing context of the developing musical thought. The orchestral part is a fugal development of the long opening statement—a development made increasingly rich and exciting by the constantly fresh and unusual elaborating ideas and figurations that are heard with the successive entries of the statement, but also by the episodes into which the fugal progression digresses: the expansive melody to which the progression rises twice; the poignant quiet melodic passage of the violins that follows this expansive melody the second time, dying out gradually for the next fugal entry; the climax to which this entry rises almost immediately. And throughout all these developments and episodes the chorus repeats at intervals its plaintive

Until the end, when the fugal progression gradually dies out and the orchestra becomes silent, the chorus continues alone with its plaintive figure and also stops, and then something breathtakingly unexpected and beautiful happens: a succession of entries of the chorus's figure, wonderfully changed from minor to major, and accompanied by sustained notes of the winds, create an expanding ethereally radiant texture for the final words; after which the chorus's figure is the *Amen*.

Another remarkable example of the same procedure is the second movement of the symphony *Harold in Italy*—the *March of Pilgrims Singing Their Evening Prayer*. Over a marching bass we hear one of Berlioz's exfoliating melodic progressions with exquisite inflections and unexpected turns that pivot on, and are enriched by, equally unexpected and exquisite moves in the underlying harmony, and are further enriched by the subtly contrived instrumental colors. In this instance the progression is a succession of developing statements, alternately from violins and violas, each taking off from the same beginning but moving unpredictably each time to a different concluding note that is answered by a magical note of the horn with exquisite murmurings of the woodwinds—the magic of the horn note being that it seems to be a different note each time but actually is the same note sounding wonderfully different in the different contexts (something not to be achieved without the powers Berlioz is alleged not to have possessed).

After the fourth such statement the further development of the melodic idea is carried on by cellos, basses and bassoons in alternation with violins and woodwinds, while the solo viola plays the melody it plays in each movement. All this produces a texture with great rhythmic intricacy and increasing intensity, in a crescendo to the point where the opening series of statements begins again, proceeding for a time as before, but then, after the third statement, moving unexpectedly to new conclusions, each punctuated by the magical horn note. Then—over the continuing march of the basses, and with accompanying arpeggios from the solo viola—comes the *canto religioso;* after which the march returns briefly and dies out in the distance.

The other movements are no less remarkable in their different ways. In the third, *Serenade of a Mountaineer of the Abruzzi to His Mistress,* we hear first some preliminary pastoral pipings; then the English horn begins the serenade with two statements of a simple tune that don't prepare us for the sudden succession ear-ravishing melodic inflections, harmonic progressions and instrumental colorings. And in the finale, *Orgy of Brigands,* we hear an activating play with dynamics, orchestral sonority and rhythmic grouping and accentuation that is like a tossing about of thunderbolts.

Those titles of the movements of *Harold in Italy* make the work a piece of *program music*—which I would define as music whose generalized expressive meaning is linked to specific visual images, ideas or incidents. A march, with a middle section in a style with religious connotations to our ears, is made a *March of Pilgrims Singing Their Evening Prayer;* music with pastoral connotations, and a lilting tune, are made a *Serenade of a Mountaineer of the Abruzzi to His Mistress;* exciting play with dynamics, orchestral sonority and rhythmic grouping and accentuation is made an *Orgy of Brigands.*

As in the case of music with only generalized expressive meaning, the interest of program music is not in the images or ideas or incidents themselves but in their musical embodiment. And not only the interest but the value: Berlioz's *Harold,* his *Symphonie Fantastique,* his *Romeo and Juliet*—like Mozart's *Figaro* and Schubert's *Nacht und Träume*—are as good as the music he put into them; and that music, like Mozart's and Schubert's, is not less good for its connection with the literary meanings that stimulated Berlioz's musical imagination and enlarge our musical experience.

The stimulation of Shakespeare's poetry gives us, in Berlioz's *Romeo and Juliet,* a work whose central sections are the supreme, the incandescent achievements of his powers. These sections follow a number of preliminaries: first an instrumental *Introduction,* an Allegro fugato depicting *Strife—Tumult* and breaking off for imposing pronouncements of trombones and bass tuba that constitute the *Intervention of the Prince;* then the *Prologue,* in which a small mixed chorus tells the story that will be told in the later sections of the symphony—of the quarrel between the two families, of the Capulets' ball (the orchestra breaks in with a little of the brilliant ball music that we will hear later), of Romeo in the Capulet garden, Juliet on her balcony, their avowals of their love (the orchestra plays a little of the impassioned music of the *Love Scene* that we will hear later); then *Strophes,* a fervent comment sung by the solo contralto, followed by the chorus's description of the dreamy Romeo being chaffed by his friends, including Mercutio, whose exquisite *Queen Mab* Scherzetto is sung by the solo tenor and chorus (note the characteristic writing for woodwinds); after which the chorus (to music we will hear later in *Juliet's Funeral Procession*) tells of death and the reconciliation of the two families.

This brings us to the first of the sections of the symphony proper that I spoke of a moment ago. Melancholy statements of the violins represent *Romeo Alone*, and lead to one of the great Berlioz melodies: a poignant two-measure statement by oboe and clarinet that is repeated, each time with changes in harmony, orchestration and texture that increase its intensity, to the point where violins and woodwinds take off on one of those Berlioz progressions in constantly unexpected directions and with heart-piercingly exquisite inflections. The sharp rhythm of the ball music, heard as though from a great distance, breaks in for a moment but dies out for the lovely oboe melody of Romeo's *Melancholy*. Then the sharp rhythm breaks in again in a transition to the rhythmically activated orchestral brilliance of *Concert and Ball—Great Festivity at the Capulets'*.

And now comes one of those supreme, incandescent sections, the *Love Scene*, which Toscanini once characterized as the most beautiful piece of music in the world, for reasons that are evident from the start. Strings *pppp* and flutes *pp* create the enchantment of *Capulet's Garden Still and Deserted*, leading to breathtaking distant notes of a horn *pp* and last exquisite comments by the violins; then we hear the young Capulets, on their way home, singing reminiscences of the ball music over a wonderfully beautiful comment of the strings. Their singing dies out in the distance; and the music concerned with the balcony scene begins: murmurings of muted lower strings over which are heard sighs of the English horn and clarinet, and, later, exclamations of the unmuted violins which increase in intensity, then subside and break off for agitated figures of the strings that introduce the mournfully impassioned melody of the muted cellos (reinforced by a horn):

In this melody one hears, unquestionably, the voice of Romeo; and concerning it there is a comment to make which applies to everything that follows. The expressive content of the section is unmistakable: declarations, avowals, the *premiers transports, premiers aveux, premiers serments* described in the *Prologue;* and these are conveyed in musical terms of the most exquisite delicacy which not only characterize the emotions of the young lovers but reveal the delicacy of feeling of Berlioz himself. One can say of this section what Turner said of the *Requiem*—that it provided an opportunity for vulgarity, but Berlioz could not be vulgar.

The murmurings of muted strings, sighs of English horn and clarinet, exclamations of violins are heard again, and lead to a more intensely impassioned statement of the cellos' melody. This subsides into the woodwinds' agitated

which is interrupted twice by declarations of the cellos:

And these, the second time, lead to another exquisitely inflected and heart-piercing melody:

and to this statement:

which keeps returning after numerous episodes, some impassioned, some quiet and lovely, like

and (much later)

Eventually there is a last impassioned reference to the cello melody; this is followed by an agitated passage that works up to a point of great intensity at which it breaks off abruptly: the enchanted night has reached gray dawn, and the last halting, fragmentary references to [1] and last sighing exclamations with which the piece ends.

The *Love Scene* is followed by the orchestral magic of the *Queen Mab* Scherzo—the magic which at once evokes the world of the subtitle *The Fairy of Dreams* with the play of alternating woodwinds and muted strings leading to a rush of muted violins. The rush subsides; the preliminaries are repeated; and eventually the rush becomes the theme of a continuing section, with woodwinds first contributing mere glints of light and later alternating with the strings in the rush and chatter. This first section ends on a sustained trill of the violins, which continues in the next section as an accompaniment to the melody of flute and English horn—an accompaniment to which are added gleaming violin harmonics and, a few measures later, the exciting darting about of the violas in references to the rushing theme of the first section. That first section returns, but only briefly; then distant horns are heard in a new section, their statements punctuated by comments of strings and woodwinds. There is a hush, in which kettledrum-beats begin a crescendo that leads to a blazing up of the entire orchestra; this breaks off for a tremolo of violas *ff*, which drops to *pp* for evocative chords of muted strings and woodwinds; then another section begins: an ostinato of the clarinet over gleaming notes of the harp, which gradually draws additional instruments into a crescendo to a point of breath-taking orchestral splendor. This breaks off for a brief return to the first section; then, suddenly, there is a slowing down, a dying out of the exciting activity, the beginning of the end of the dream: a passage of wonderfully evocative hushed chords of muted strings, then of strings alternating with woodwinds, then string chords punctuated by silvery notes of antique cymbals, leading to staccatos of woodwinds, of plucked strings, of harps and strings, and a pause on a sustained note of the cellos; and then a last rush that brings the extraordinary piece to an end.

No less extraordinary in its own way is the section that follows, *Juliet's Funeral Procession*, which is another great example of the procedure we observed in the *Offertorium* of the *Requiem*, with the chorus repeating its plaintive *Jetez des fleurs!* on the reiterated note E at intervals during the fugal march and the melodic episode played by the orchestra, and then the violins repeating the plaintive E's at intervals as the fugal passage and melodic episode are sung by the chorus.

Extraordinary too is the next section, *Romeo in the Vault of the Capulets:* the opening Allegro agitato e disperato, the sudden silence and solemn antiphonal chords of brass, woodwinds and strings; then, over lamenting figures of muted violas and cellos punctuated by heavy accents of basses, the grandly sustained melody of Romeo's *Invocation*, dying out for a passage in which tentative phrases of the clarinet, recalling the sighs of the beginning of the *Love Scene*, alternate with increasingly agitated exclamations of the low strings in *Juliet's Awakening*, leading to the orchestral outburst of *Delirious Joy, Despair*, which breaks off for the tearing, shattering details of *Last Agonies and Death of the Two Lovers*.

Astonishing, therefore, after all this creativeness and originality, is the conventional grandiloquence of the finale.

Romeo and Juliet is only the greatest of the works of Berlioz that we owe to the susceptibility of his powers to the stimulation of poetry. At the age of twenty-six he produced *Eight Scenes from Faust*—including the beautiful *Easter Hymn* and *Peasants' Chorus*, the striking *Rat Song* and *Flea Song*, the hauntingly lovely *King of Thule Ballad* and *Romance of Marguerite*. These were retained in *The Damnation of Faust* seventeen years later, with the additional music including things as beautiful and impressive as the opening scene, the choral scene introduced by Mephistopheles's *Voici des fleurs* (note, among other details in the exquisite orchestral writing of the concluding *Dance of the Sylphs*, the activity of the harps), Mephistopheles's *Invocation* and *Serenade*, the *Minuet of the Will-o'-the-Wisps*, the trio.

Still later his love of Virgil resulted in the opera *The Trojans*, which has never been performed here by a major opera company, but of which the second part, *The Trojans at Carthage*, is available on records. Throughout there is the quietly beautiful vocal writing characteristic of Berlioz's later years; but neither this nor the lovely ballet music early in Act 2 prepares us for the incandescent septet *Tout n'est que paix* and duet *Nuit d'ivresse* later in the act, the wonderful passage with Mercure's repeated *Italie!* that ends the act, and the *Royal Hunt and Storm* that follows, with its lovely opening section and the marvelously altered repetition of this section at the end.

Another work of this period is the oratorio *L'Enfance du Christ*, with suitably quiet writing for a small orchestra, chorus and vocal soloists. Much of Part 1 is in a mellifluous nine-teenth-century oratorio style; but we begin to hear the Berlioz mind in fascinating operation in the Overture of Part 2, and in the music it introduces: the lovely *Shepherds' Farewell to the Holy Family* and the wonderfully beautiful *Repose of the Holy Family*. And there are moving and beautiful passages in Part 3: the Narrator's description of the journey to Saïs, Joseph's appeals for refuge, the trio for flutes and harp, the concluding vocal passage.

Of Berlioz's last opera, *Beatrice and Benedict*, only the delight-ful overture is played here occasionally. The most frequently heard of the overtures is the brilliant *Roman Carnival;* played less often is the brilliant overture of the earlier opera *Benvenuto Cellini;* and only rarely are there performances of the *King Lear* and *Corsair* Overtures, whose relation to their titles is ob-scure and less important than the working of the Berlioz mind that is intensely interesting in each, especially in their opening sections.

Certainly, in Berlioz's case as in every other composer's, it is possible for someone to know and understand the music and decide that he doesn't care for it. But the actual situation is that many have listened to the music in the expectation of hearing the poverty of invention they have read about, and as a result have heard only what they expected to hear; and that others have listened without such preconceptions, but with habit, and have found it difficult to gear their minds to music so different in every way from the music they were accustomed to. That situation calls for additional listening with ears and mind open to the particular distinctive and unusual things Berlioz has to say. And such listening will, I think, lead most people to the conclusion that his music is some of the most beautiful and moving that has come down to us.

10

BACH

At this point I would like to turn back to Bach, whose *Passacaglia* I presented in detail in Chapter 3; but before I speak of other great works of his I will make a general observation about his entire output. Or rather—having recently found my point formulated very effectively in one of Turner's articles—I will let him make it for me.

Quoting Terry's description of the fifty-three cantatas Bach composed between 1736 and 1744 as an "unflagging cataract of inspiration in which masterpiece followed masterpiece with the monotonous periodicity of a Sunday sermon," Turner calls it nonsense and contends that "this 'monotonous periodicity' was exactly what was wrong with a great deal of Bach's music." Bach, he says, "had arrived at the point of being able to sit down at any minute of any day and compose what had all the superficial appearance of being a masterpiece. It is possible that even Bach himself did not know which was a masterpiece and which was not, and it is abundantly clear to me that in all his large-sized works there are huge chunks of stuff to which inspiration is the last word that one could apply." What makes it difficult to evaluate the music correctly, says Turner, is Bach's virtuosity; but while the prodigious technical skill may interest and amaze the academic musician "with the score in his hands and his soul long defunct," for Turner it is valueless "unless . . . it is as expressive as it is accomplished."

This seems to me an excellent description of the essential fact about Bach—that one hears always the operation of prodigious powers of invention and construction, but frequently an operation that is not as expressive as it is accomplished.

The occasion for Turner's remarks was a performance of the *B-Minor Mass*, which is generally regarded as a towering masterpiece from first note to last, but in which I have, like Turner, come to hear only in certain portions what he describes as "those really creative moments which are popularly called 'inspired.'" For me they are the second *Kyrie*, the *Gratias agimus*, *Qui tollis* and *Cum sancto spiritu* of the *Gloria*, the *Et incarnatus est* and *Crucifixus est* of the *Credo*, the *Sanctus*, and the *Dona nobis pacem*, all for chorus; and only one aria, the *Et in spiritum sanctum* for bass. But you may find other portions genuinely expressive and moving that Turner and I do not.

Similarly you may be moved by more than what I find moving in the *St. Matthew Passion:* chiefly the chorales, the big opening and closing choruses, the great chorale-fantasia *O Mensch, bewein' dein' Sünde gross* that ends Part I ; also some of the accompanied recitatives of the soloists, but only very few of their arias—the tenor's *Ich will bei meinem Jesu wachen*, the soprano's *Aus Liebe will mein Heiland sterben*, and the alto's great *Erbarme dich*, one of Bach's most inspired moments. Or the *St. John Passion:* again the chorales, the magnificent opening chorus, some of the recitatives and ariosos, and the alto's aria *Es ist vollbracht*.

So with the smaller choral works. The Cantata No. 4, *Christ lag in Todesbanden*, is for me one of Bach's great utterances; but in some of the other cantatas, the *Magnificat*, the *Christmas Oratorio*, the *Easter Oratorio*, it is almost entirely the choral portions, and particularly the chorales, that I find beautiful and moving, rarely one of the arias; and most of these smaller works that I have heard I have, like Turner, found to be mechanical exercises of Bach's technical skill. But here again you may discover more than Turner and I.

And so with the instrumental works—in particular the ones that result from Bach's setting himself gigantic tasks and problems on which to exercise his skill. One of these is the *Clavierübung*, a collection of keyboard music comprising the six partitas, four duets, *Italian Concerto, French Overture,* and *Goldberg Variations* for harpsichord or clavichord, and the Prelude in E flat, a number of chorale-preludes and the Fugue in E flat for organ. In his notes for a recording of the entire collection Ralph Kirkpatrick contends that the "keyboard practice" of the title is to be taken "in the sense of an exercise, an activity of the spirit," and cites Bach's own statement that the various pieces have been composed "to delight the spirit of music-lovers." But Bach's way of exercising the spirit was to exercise his craftsmanship; and some of the results offer more to delight an interest in the skillful use of technique than to delight the spirit.

All six partitas are no doubt fascinating to anyone interested in their "astonishing assimilation of French, Italian and German keyboard styles"; but as a mere music-lover I find only No. 1 in B flat, and to a lesser degree No. 3 in A minor, interesting to listen to simply as music. Similarly, the *Italian Concerto* and *French Overture* may excite some listeners with Bach's "[appropriation] to the harpsichord [of] prevailing French and Italian orchestral styles of the preceding fifty years"; but listening to the music I am excited only by the slow movement of the concerto. Again, the organ pieces may interest some people with the elaborately organized "mathematical and symbolic structure" that Bach erects out of the chorales to illustrate the basic tenets of Lutheran doctrine; but what interests me as music is the magnificent opening prelude and only a few of the longer chorale-preludes—the closing fugue being impressive as a piece of fugal construction. The four duets may be "the most highly concentrated two-voice music that Bach ever wrote"; but I find them dull. And while everything in the *Goldberg Variations* may sound like "unsurpassable invention" to some ears, I hear examples of mechanical use of the variation procedure as well as things as wonderful as the three slow variations in minor mode.

Similarly, the *Well-Tempered Clavier*, with its forty-eight preludes and fugues in the twenty-four major and minor keys, includes pieces as charming as the Prelude No. 3 of Book 1, the Prelude No. 12 and Prelude and Fugue No. 15 of Book 2; as quietly poignant as the Preludes Nos. 12, 16 and 23 of Book 1 and No. 14 of Book 2; as impressive and affecting as the Prelude No. 8, Fugue No. 12 and Preludes and Fugues Nos. 4 and 22 of Book 1, the Fugue No. 9 of Book 2. But it also includes many examples of competent construction that are, for me, not interesting pieces of music.

Again, *The Art of Fugue*—Bach's last work, which he left uncompleted—contains some of his most magnificent music (which I suggest your hearing a fugue or two at a time). But of the collection of contrapuntal exercises on a theme of Frederick the Great entitled *The Musical Offering* I find only a few of the canons and the concluding six-voiced ricercare similarly impressive.

Listening to the six sonatas or partitas for unaccompanied violin, the six sonatas or suites for unaccompanied cello, one is aware of Bach's success with the difficult problem he set himself, of contriving for the instrument a melody that would imply its underlying harmonic progressions between the occasional chords. But one is aware also that solving this problem was not equivalent to writing great or even enjoyable music. Or at any rate it is what I am aware of: I hear an operation that is genuinely creative and expressive only in the great *Chaconne* of the Violin Sonata No. 4 (Partita No. 2) in D minor and the superb Prelude of the Violin Sonata No. 6 (Partita No. 3) in E; elsewhere I hear only Bach's craftsmanship going through the motions of creation and producing the external appearances of expressiveness. And I suspect that it is the name of Bach that awes listeners into accepting the appearance as reality, into hearing an expressive content which isn't there, and into believing that if the content is difficult to hear, this is only because it is especially profound—because it is "the passionate, yet untroubled meditation of a great mind" that lies beyond "the composition's formidable technical frontiers."

I might add that the formidable technical frontiers this writer refers to are the difficulties for the present-day violinist or cellist caused by the fact that the pieces were written for performance on an instrument with a flat bridge and finger-board on which the notes of a chord could be produced on the several strings simultaneously, as they cannot be on the present-day instrument with curved bridge and finger-board. The present-day violinist or cellist has to break or arpeggiate the chord, and to distend the melodic phrase to fit the ar-peggiated chord in; and the sonatas are among the accepted test-pieces with which he demonstrates his technical and mu-sical powers to the public—the powers that in this case enable him to create continuity in the distended phrases, to do this with an appearance of ease, and—if he is a Casals or a Szigeti—with an eloquence in the playing that listeners mis-take for eloquence in the music.

Among the six sonatas for violin and clavier No. 3 in E major is, for me, one of Bach's finest instrumental works; and there are interesting movements in No. 1 in B minor, No. 2 in A major, and No. 5 in F minor. But the sonatas for flute and clavier and sonatas for gamba and clavier I find unin-teresting.

An outstanding work for solo clavier is the Toccata in C minor; and other good ones are the Toccatas in D major and E minor, the Fantasy of the *Chromatic Fantasy and Fugue*. The French Suite No. 5 in G major and English Suite No. 3 in G minor have several moderately enjoyable movements; the others I find uninteresting.

Of the *Brandenburg Concertos* No. 3 in G major is for me the most impressive; Nos. 2 in F and 4 in G are also enjoyable; No. 1 in F has an impressive slow movement; No. 5 in D is only moderately interesting; No. 6 in B flat is completely boring. And of the four suites for orchestra the best-known No. 2 in B minor has charming dance movements; No. 3 in D major has some others, and in addition the famous melody known as *Air for G String;* No. 4 in D has a fugal section in the opening movement and a Bourrée that are fine; No. 1 in C is for me another boring piece.

Of the concertos for one or more solo instruments the D minor for clavier (or violin) is one of Bach's greatest instrumental works. In the two fast movements the seemingly inexhaustible flow of inspired invention becomes breathtaking; and in the wonderful slow movement a grave opening statement by the orchestra is repeated in different keys as a sort of ground-bass that provides structural coherence for the ornate and wide-ranging melody of the solo instrument.

Another great work is the Concerto in D minor for two violins, with an endless progression of melody in the slow movement that makes it possibly the loveliest piece of music Bach wrote. And the Concerto in A minor and the slow movement of the Concerto in E for violin are also fine.

The other concertos, to my ears, are uninteresting.

That leaves the important category of works for organ— important because the organ was Bach's most immediately personal medium, through which he expressed what was strongest in him: his religious feeling and his feeling for musical architectonics. These give us the great *Passacaglia* that I presented in Chapter 3; they give us also the great preludes and fugues—the Toccata, Adagio and Fugue in C, the Toccata and Fugue in D minor, the Fantasia and Fugue in G minor, the Preludes and Fugues in E flat, A minor, E minor (Leipzig), B minor, C minor (Weimar), among others. And inevitably they give us works that are impressive as large-scale construction but not as music.

We get also the chorale-preludes, which include such wonderful meditations on the texts and melodies of the Lutheran chorales as *O Mensch, bewein' dein' Sünde gross* and *Ich ruf' zu dir, Herr Jesu Christ* of the *Orgelbüchlein (Little Organ Book)*;

Herzlich tut mich verlangen and *An Wasserflüssen Babylon* of the *Miscellaneous Chorale-Preludes; Komm' Gott Schöpfer, heiliger Geist, An Wasserflüssen Babylon* and *Jesus Christus, unser Heiland* of the last *Eighteen Chorale-Preludes.* And supreme utterances like *Nun komm' der Heiden Heiland* and *Schmücke dich, o liebe Seele* of the *Eighteen.*

With Bach's music, finally, we come to the matter of transcription. Since Bach himself made some of his clavier concertos into violin concertos, or a concerto movement into a choral movement of a cantata, there would seem to be no reason against merely orchestrating one of his organ works. And good reasons can be offered for it: the desirability of making the work known to many people who would not hear it played on the organ; the advantage of having the strands of the contrapuntal texture stand out more clearly by means of different orchestral colors than they can be made to do by organ registration. But those good reasons don't include a reason that has been offered in recent years: the orchestral transcription isn't needed to fulfill completely a conception only partly fulfilled in the original organ version. The notion that the composer of two hundred years ago—or even three or four hundred—who didn't have the Philadelphia Orchestra to write for worked in an agony of frustration is as incorrect as the analogous notion would be about the painter of that period: the composer's mind operated in the terms of the musical instruments, language, style and forms available to him, and fulfilled its conceptions completely in those terms. That certainly was true of Bach writing for the organ; it was no less true of Bach writing for the unaccompanied violin. He could have written the *Chaconne* for an orchestra; he could have rewritten it for orchestra after writing it for unaccompanied violin (as in fact he made the Prelude of the Sonata No. 6 into a piece for organ and orchestra, the Prelude to the Cantata No. 29); but since he did neither it is clear that he conceived of the piece entirely in the terms provided by the

unaccompanied violin and was entirely satisfied with the ful-
fillment of his conception in those terms.

Nor is it merely that the Bach piece doesn't need completion by Stokowski to fulfill Bach's conception and produce the
effect he intended; it is that the piece as completed by Stokowski does *not* fulfill Bach's conception and does *not* produce
the effect he intended. When Bach himself makes a violin concerto out of his clavier concerto, a cantata prelude out of a
sonata movement for unaccompanied violin, we hear the
same mind, personality and feeling operating in the new work
as in the old; and this undoubtedly would be so if he were
himself to transcribe one of his organ works for the orchestra
of today. What his own orchestral transcription of the work
would demonstrate is that a composer's instrumentation is no
less an integral part of his art than is a painter's color, his
way of scoring no less an expression of his feeling than is his
way of writing melody and harmony. This means that even
a Schönberg, applying orchestral color to the lines of Bach's
texture with precision and subtlety that express his fastidiousness and taste, gives the music the impress of his own mind
and feeling. The others—Stokowski, Ormandy, Elgar, Respighi—call to mind a remark of Ernest Bloch about Richard
Strauss: "Debussy is like a painter who looks at his canvas to
see what more he can take out; Strauss is like a painter who
has covered every inch and then takes the paint he has left
and throws it at the canvas"; and such transcribers give us
Bach with the impress of their own vulgarity. Stokowski's
orchestrations and performances, in particular—with their
lurid phrasing, their tonal heaving and billowing—give us
not the religious feeling and structural power that are Bach's,
but the feverish, orgiastic excitement that is Stokowski's.

In other words, a work of Bach as completed by Stokowski
fulfills not Bach's conception but Stokowski's, and produces
not the effect Bach intended but the effect Stokowski wants.
Now composers have always made music out of other composers' music: Beethoven wrote sets of variations on themes

from Mozart's *Magic Flute;* Brahms wrote sets of variations on themes of Handel and Paganini; Stravinsky in our own century has made one ballet score out of music by Pergolesi, another by using thematic fragments from a number of pieces by Tchaikovsky as the ideas for a work of his own. And what they have done Stokowski certainly may do. But Beethoven, Brahms and Stravinsky haven't offered their products as fulfillments of the unfulfilled conceptions of Mozart, Handel, Pergolesi and Tchaikovsky; they have offered them as works of their own, to be evaluated as such. And that, it seems to me, is how Stokowski may present what he makes of the works of Bach and the other composers, earlier and later, that he fancies up.

I have been discussing in connection with Bach the problem which arises with other music of his period and earlier periods that we shall be considering very shortly. The musical notation reproduced in this book is a series of directions for performance which tell the players what notes to produce, how loud to make them, how long to hold them, and other things of that kind. Ever since Mozart's and Haydn's time the directions have been increasingly numerous and detailed; but the most detailed directions have to leave something to the player—certain subtle differentiations of loudness, certain time-values a little longer or shorter than written, which cannot be specified in notation, and which the player supplies in accordance with the tradition of performance that he has learned, and with his own judgment and taste. On the other hand the further back we go from Mozart and Haydn the less numerous and detailed are the directions for the player; and even the directions concerning the notes to play are summed up in a form of notational shorthand—the melodic ornaments and figured bass which the player was expected to translate into melody, harmony, rhythm and figuration in the language and style of his period. This shorthand is something most people today, including most musicians, know very little about; but it, and the language and style it summarizes, have to be learned by anyone who wants to play the music correctly. For this is music that does have to be completed in performance; but the completion, the filling in of melody and harmony, must be done in the music's own language and style, not in the language and style of our music of the past two hundred years. Which does not mean, however, that a composer of today may not use sixteenth- or seventeenth-century music as the material for a piece of his own.

11

OTHER MUSIC OF THE
EIGHTEENTH CENTURY

We have been concerned thus far with the work of a few major figures among the composers of the music that falls within the normal range of our interest—European music of the past three or four centuries. There remains for us to explore the large amount of great or moving or enjoyable music produced by their contemporaries, their predecessors, their successors.

Thus, in the early part of the eighteenth century there is the music of Bach's contemporaries—Handel, Vivaldi, Domenico Scarlatti, Couperin, Rameau; and later in the century the music of the contemporaries of Haydn and Mozart—Gluck, Bach's son Carl Philipp Emanuel, Boccherini. The music historians would insist that these are not the only eighteenth-century composers worth your attention: they object to the practice, in the concert hall and the appreciation course, of having a period represented by a few outstanding figures and neglecting the other composers who they insist produced equally good music; and they contend that this has resulted in our knowing only a small part of the masterworks of the past.

Well, in the past few years LP recording has provided the opportunities to hear a great amount of music that previously wasn't performed or recorded; and some of it has indeed proved to be music we had been the poorer for not knowing. But most of the newly revealed masterworks have been products of the well-known outstanding figures rather than of their obscure contemporaries: in eighteenth-century music I can recall a couple of charming quartets by Stamitz and Richter, a couple of arresting symphonies by Brunetti; but the works of major stature that come to mind are Couperin's *First Tenebrae Service*, a couple of Carl Philipp Emanuel Bach's symphonies and a few of his sacred songs, Haydn's masses and some of his unfamiliar quartets. It is true, as the historians contend, that many others besides Haydn used the musical language and style of his time; it is not true that these others produced with them music as good as his: the historians' difficulty is their inability to tell when a language and style are being used in a work of great art, and when they are merely being used, period.

As a matter of fact there are works in which even the great masters use the language and style of their time uninterestingly. They are among the things on LP records that could have been left unrecorded. And we can leave them unheard.

But we do want to hear the magnificent and joyous choruses and beautiful solos of Handel's *Messiah;* the dramatic and imaginative writing, mostly for chorus, of his *Israel in Egypt;* the ear-ravishing lyricism of his *Acis and Galatea;* the similar writing in *Alcina, Julius Caesar, Semele, Solomon,* the *Dettingen Te Deum,* the *Ode for St. Cecilia's Day, L'Allegro ed il Penseroso;* the fine instrumental writing of the *Water Music,* the Concerti Grossi Op. 6, the Sonatas Op. 1, some of the harpsichord suites. We want to hear the poignantly lovely writing of Vivaldi's *L'Estro Armonico, The Four Seasons* and some of his miscellaneous concertos. We want to hear Scarlatti's harpsichord sonatas, fascinating and exciting in their endless invention, their harmonic daring, the power of some of the ones in slow tempo, the verve and brilliance of some of the ones in fast tempo, which utilize the sharp, biting, flashing sounds of the instrument for their effect. We want to hear not only the charming harpsichord pieces of Rameau and Couperin, but Rameau's *Concerts en sextuor*, which have some of this composer's loveliest music, and Couperin's *Tenebrae Services*, extended vocal declamations which are made remarkable by their unique style and expressive force. We want to hear not just the familiar aria *Che farò senza Euridice*, but the other beautiful and affecting music of Gluck's *Orfeo ed Euridice*. We want to hear the works of Carl Philipp Emanuel Bach—symphonies, sacred songs, a *Magnificat*—that exhibit the operation of a mind excitingly individual, daring and dynamic. And of Boccherini we want to hear not the Cello Concerto in B flat that Grützmacher put together with materials from Boccherini's works, but Boccherini's own quartets, quintets and trios, which are engagingly and at times excitingly individual in invention and procedures.

12

MUSIC OF EARLIER CENTURIES

It isn't very many years since music, in the concert hall and the appreciation course, began with Bach and Handel, and everything before them was dark and unknown except for the distant gleams of Palestrina and—a few centuries beyond—Gregorian chant. Gradually this situation changed, and the public learned there was a great deal more in those early centuries—though again not as much as the historians claimed.

Today there are LP records which offer, in historical sequence, specimens of the music produced in that period from Gregorian chant to Bach. And while many of the examples of the first types of polyphonic music do no more than satisfy our interest in how the music of the ninth or tenth or eleventh century sounded, there are, as early as the twelfth century, pieces (e.g. Nos. 7 and 8 on Haydn Society 9038) which the ear of today finds esthetically effective. There is no question about the effectiveness of some of the more developed polyphony of Machaut, Dufay, Ockeghem, Obrecht and Josquin des Prés in the fourteenth and fifteenth centuries. Nor is there any such question, later, with the beautiful vocal writing of Lassus and Palestrina, the dark intensity of Victoria. Nor, still later, with the power of Gesualdo, though it is achieved by harmonic progressions that are amazingly bold and strange even to twentieth-century ears. And certainly not with the variety of beauty and expressive power in the works of Monteverdi —among others the famous *Lagrime d'Amante al Sepolcro dell' Amata* and the *Vespers of 1610.*

We find some of the most beautiful and affecting music of the sixteenth and seventeenth centuries in the works of English composers—notably the superb *Mass for Four Voices* and other religious works, the lovely madrigals, the fine instrumental pieces that make Byrd a major figure of this great period of English music. Dowland, Farnaby, Wilbye, Weelkes, Bull, Morley and Gibbons are among those who produced other lovely songs and madrigals, and other fine instrumental pieces.

We come in this way to another great figure, the last in English music—Purcell. His individuality and power are strikingly evident in the famous *Fantasia in Five Parts on One Note,* one of the Fantasias for strings, all superb pieces, in whose slow sections we follow a mind that moves in strange, daring, and at times startling ways—as it does also in the Pavane and Chacony on Bartók 913. The chaconne's reiteration of a ground-bass is a favorite procedure with Purcell (as in fact with his English predecessors)—one that he uses with impressive effect not only in instrumental but in vocal pieces. Thus, the phrases of *When I Am Laid in Earth* in the opera *Dido and Aeneas* succeed each other over the repetitions of a ground-bass. And so with *O Let Me Ever Ever Weep!* and *Next Winter Comes Slowly* in *The Fairy Queen,* a work that is overwhelming not only in the profusion but in the expressive range of its superb writing. And on the other hand *I Love and I Must* and *Tell Me Some Pitying Angel* are two magnificent examples of Purcell's powerfully expressive florid vocal style.

I referred a moment ago to the claims of the music historians—the musicologists, as these scholars are called— about the music of early centuries. Intent on establishing the value of their explorations and excavations, but reasoning in a world of concept thousands of miles from the facts they are digging away in, they have produced one of their pat schematizations: not only, they say, has each period had *its* music, produced by *its* creative energies, and satisfying *its* esthetic needs, but since human creative energies must be presumed to have been equal in all periods, it follows that the music of the tenth or eleventh or twelfth century was the equal of the painting and architecture, and the equal also of the music of the eighteenth or nineteenth century. And so we have had one of these men introducing some recordings of keyboard pieces from 1350 to 1700—most of them insignificant in ideas, structure, and even mere size—with the pronouncement that "the music in this album is not 'ancient music,' stale, dusty, and at best a curio for historically minded snobs. It is no more 'ancient' than Rembrandt's painting or Gothic cathedrals."

Actually, human creative energies have not been equal in all periods, or in all the arts of any one period. We find no important or even interesting poetry in England from the death of Chaucer in 1400 to the publication of Wyatt's poems in 1557; we find only minor poets between Pope and Blake; we find no painting of any consequence in the eighteenth- and nineteenth-century Germany that produced the music of Bach, Haydn, Mozart, Beethoven, Schubert, and other great composers whom we have still to investigate. And the music of an early period that satisfied *its* esthetic needs will not always satisfy ours.

13

BRAHMS

People change for us as we ourselves change in time; the things they said come to make more sense or less; and works of art, which are personal communications of a special kind, also change in significance and value for us. From which it follows that for someone to think less than he once did of certain pieces of music, as I have come to do of certain works of Brahms, is not to be guilty of unnatural behavior, of an enormity beyond comprehension. It probably will happen to you with one composer or another. And the reason it happened to me with Brahms is something to talk about here, because it has to do with the nature of his music.

For many years Brahms's music was for me, every note of it, the greatest of all. Until one day, as I was playing through the slow movement of the Cello Sonata Op. 99 at the piano, I suddenly was aware of hearing not real creative activity but the pretense, the pose of such activity—the pretense of feeling in synthetically contrived themes that were being manipulated by formula to fill out the pattern of the movement. And having heard it here I began to hear it in other works.

I recall a broadcast of a performance of the Piano Concerto No. 2 by Toscanini and the NBC Symphony with Horowitz as soloist. Sounds came through my radio that were evidence of attentive, purposeful activity by Brahms, Toscanini, Horowitz, the orchestra, the audience; but what also came through powerfully was the impression that this was the activity of people under a spell continuing to go through a long-established ritual that was without reality or meaning—performers and listeners going through the motions of esthetic response to a piece of music in which the composer went through the motions of esthetic creation. Anyone not under this spell, anyone able to listen freshly to the agitated statements of the piano that broke in on the quiet opening of the first movement, would, it seemed to me, perceive that they were the noisy motions of saying something portentous that really said absolutely nothing; and listening further he would discover that the entire movement was a succession of such attempts at now one such effect and now another.

Tchaikovsky's comments on Brahms have been quoted as an illustration of one composer's inability to understand and justly appraise the work of another; but actually composers have sometimes written about other composers with the special insight of the practitioner of an art; and when Tchaikovsky criticizes in Brahms's music the conscious aspiration to something for which there is no poetic impulse, the striving for something that must be unstriven for, the conscious attempt at Beethoven's profundity and power that results in caricature of Beethoven, and the operation, for these purposes, of the technical mastery that produces "so many preparations and circumlocutions for something which ought to come and charm us at once"—when Tchaikovsky speaks of all this he is describing what is plain to hear in the works that Brahms wrote, as he himself expressed it, with the consciousness of the tramp of Beethoven behind him.

The superb song *Botschaft* exhibits the genuine emotional impulse and musical gift of a lyricist, a creator of small forms; the *Variations on a Theme of Haydn* is one of the fine works the small-scale artist produces when he employs his technical skill to say the one small thing a number of different ways, and creates a large form by writing a continuous series of small ones. On the other hand the opening movement of Brahms's first published work, the Piano Sonata Op. 1, exhibits the labored and bombastic proclamations, the stretches of arid manipulation, that are the results of the small-scale artist's attempt to write greater than he feels and to produce with technique what doesn't issue from emotional impulse. Similar striving for portentous utterance and similar arid manipulation are exhibited by the opening movement of the Piano Concerto No. 1, which grew out of Brahms's first attempt at a symphony after hearing Beethoven's Ninth; by the opening movement of the Symphony No. 1 that he did produce after twenty years' labor with the tramp of Beethoven behind him; by the other concertos, the equally pretentious chamber music and choral works. Nor are the cloying saccharine sweetness of many of the slow movements, the archness of many of the scherzo movements, easier to endure.

As a matter of fact the cloying sweetness and archness are heard also in small-scale works—some of the songs, most of the Intermezzos and Capriccios and other small pieces for piano that are, to my ears, arid artifice dipped in treacle. And as a matter of fact a few examples of large-scale operation come off for me—the finale of the Symphony No. 2, the second and final movements of the Symphony No. 3, and all but the third movement of the Symphony No. 4, whose concluding passacaglia is one of Brahms's finest essays in variation form.

These few symphony movements, then, the sets of variations on themes of Handel, Haydn and Paganini, and some of the songs are the music of Brahms that I have continued to hear with belief and pleasure. But the rest, which is only the pretense of artistic creation to my ears, may be the real thing to yours; and yours are making the decisions for you.

14

WAGNER

In the preceding chapter I spoke of my impression of the musicians and audience at a performance of Brahms continuing, under a spell, to go through a long-established ritual. And it is interesting to find an English critic, Richard Capell, writing thirty years ago about Wagner's success in imposing on the world his own idea of his work as a prophetic mission, in having the music-dramas presented in a darkened theatre "more austere than many cathedrals" and to an audience—formerly a prominent part of the spectacle—that was now "a dark and huddled anonymous throng assisting almost clandestinely at the enacted mysteries." No European music before Wagner's, said Capell, had worked "this quasi-hypnotic spell"; and although esthetic fashions had changed there still remained great numbers of "these 'perfect Wagnerites' who religiously adore many things in Wagner which in detachment could only be considered as incoherent, tautologous, morally reprehensible, or even dull."

Capell was writing as an admirer and enjoyer of Wagner, but one with the detachment that made him aware of what he termed the "radical falsity" of the libretto of the *Ring* tetralogy—"that the simple barbarians of the old saga are endowed by Wagner with a new consciousness and a manner of expressing themselves which are by no means simple—and all the while they retain their antique savagery of action. Wotan's cunning and Siegfried's brutal prowess were all very well before these persons took to heroising themselves, but then they became unpardonable." Thus, the Siegfried who robs Brünnhilde of the ring is "a symbol and an ideal, a demi-god, a savior. He is Siegfried, Wagner's 'ordained man of the future'—and he is nothing but an ordinary looting *soudard*. Similarly, Wotan, 'the substance of the Intelligence of the Present,' turns out to be the substance of a fraudulent army contractor."

Now I once had occasion to remark myself—concerning a performance of *Das Rheingold* that initiated a matinee *Ring* series for perfect Wagnerites at the Metropolitan—that the famous long-sustained opening E flat from the orchestra pit "cast a spell over the people who crowded the auditorium to capacity, a spell under which the visual and aural presentation of a story about mighty beings symbolized to them mighty significances." But, I added, to "one listener whom the E flat did not place under this spell . . . no mighty significances were conveyed by what he saw and heard." And I will add now that none were conveyed to me by the subsequent music-dramas of the *Ring* tetralogy. For me, then, it isn't only the libretto that doesn't work; it is also the music. I am aware of the prodigious musical powers operating in those scores, and the wonderful moments they achieve here and there (to say nothing of the wonderful pages in the other works we shall come to in a moment). But I find that the endless narrative declamation, the endless bombastic proclamation, the endless literal illustration of words and action (of which the *Ride of the Valkyries* is only the worst example), and the occasional tawdriness and cheapness (notably in the final scenes of *Siegfried* and *Die Götterdämmerung*) are as unendurable as the philosophical posturings and the equally pretentious and laughable verbal jargon of the texts (e.g. *Winterstürme wichen dem Wonnemond*, or *Starke Scheite schichtet mir dort*, or *Schweigt eures Jammers jauchzenden Schwall*). But again you may find them all convincing and impressive; and you will act in accordance with your findings, not mine.

The Prelude to *Tristan und Isolde*, on the other hand, from its very first statement, does cast its spell over me—despite which I manage, at its conclusion, to remember to skip the next half-hour or so of boring declamatory narration, explanation and argument to the point where the music of the Prelude returns as Tristan and Isolde drink the love potion. King Marke's fifteen-minute reproach near the end of the second act is something else I skip; but most of the music in this act is marvelous in its luxuriant tonal beauty and expressiveness, rising to sheer incandescence in the part that begins with *O sink hernieder*. In the Prelude to Act 3 we hear one of Wagner's most wonderful pages—wonderful as a musical evocation of the desolate scene and the wounded Tristan's bodily illness and sickness at heart that will be revealed when the curtain rises. And after Kurwenal's conversation with the shepherd and his first exchanges with the awakening Tristan we come to the powerful music of Tristan's delirium, which rises to the climax of his curse of the potion, and ends with the exquisite passage *Wie sie selig*.

Though Tristan and Isolde are—compared with the characters of the *Ring*—human beings, even they are somewhat dehumanized and monumentalized in Wagner's music-drama (the music, says Capell, "is accompanied on the stage by rather more than life-size gestures of actors who, no matter how gifted, never can avoid bringing to mind the Siegesallee statuary"). But Wagner's only comedy, *Die Meistersinger von Nürnberg*, is, for once, concerned with characters who are, act like, and are involved in the situations of, real human beings—with the exception of Beckmesser, who is a caricature, and as such a major and deplorable defect in the work. It is true that, as Capell puts it, "for the pint pot of this comedy Wagner poured out music in quarts and gallons"; but if Wagner is characteristically long-winded in the work, he is also uncharacteristically genial and sunny—except with Beckmesser, in whom he is revenging himself on the venomous critic Hanslick—which is to say that the exhaustingly garrulous outpouring includes a large amount of extraordinarily lovely music. Formerly the only thing one could do was arrive in the first intermission: one missed the good moments in Act 1, but was fresh for the beautiful passages in Act 2—the gay opening dance, the entrance of Pogner and Eva, Sachs's monologue *Was duftet doch der Flieder*, his conversation with Eva, her *Geliebter, spare den Zorn*, the watchman's song, Sachs's cobbling song, and the quiet closing pages after the riot. And after these one still wasn't too exhausted for the lovely things in Act 3—the affecting Prelude, Sachs's monologue *Wahn! Wahn!*, Walter's description of his dream, Eva's *Meister, 's ist nicht so gefährlich*, the ensuing scene of Sachs, Eva and Walter, the baptism of Walter's song, the quintet, the charming dances and songs of the apprentices, the crowd's *Wach auf* in greeting to Sachs, Walter's song. Now, with the entire opera on LP records, one can listen to an act at a time.

Parsifal was presented by Wagner, and still is accepted by the perfect Wagnerites, as a work of religious character; but I find this sensualist's exaltation of chastity decked out in religious mumbo-jumbo repellent, and would expect a religious person to find it offensive. In addition, the long dull stretches in the music reveal an astonishing enfeeblement of the powers of invention and manipulation that are so prodigious in the earlier works. But in the radiant closing pages of the lovely *Good Friday Spell* we hear his language marvelously enriched and subtilized—e.g. the ascending scale of clarinet, bassoon and horn in the seventh and eighth measures from the end.

In addition to the music-dramas there are the five Wesendonck songs, of which *Im Treibhaus* uses the thematic material of the Prelude to Act 3 of *Tristan und Isolde* in a piece of extended vocal declamation that is in its own way as wonderful as the Prelude.

And there is the *Siegfried-Idyll*, the charming orchestral piece Wagner fashioned out of some of the better themes of the final scene of *Siegfried* to celebrate the birth of his son.

15

VERDI

Verdi, unlike Wagner, did not spin vast ad hoc fantasies about the past and future of art to rationalize his own present practice, but simply addressed himself to the task of setting a libretto to music as well as he knew how; he set to music not philosophically pretentious dramas about gods and heroes of Teutonic mythology, but melodramas about passionate Italians and Spaniards; for his dramatic purpose he did not weave leitmotifs into hour-and-a-half progressions of continuous *melos*, but produced series of clearly outlined melodic structures. All this was enough to make him an object of condescension for some; and they found additional reason for condescension in the vulgarity to which they attributed his popularity.

There are, certainly, crudities and vulgarities in Verdi's early exercises of his powers; but one thing to say about this is Francis Toye's observation that the occasional vulgarity of *Il Trovatore* is "a by-product of the vitality and passion without which there can be no great art." Another is that the powers, operating with vitality and passion, give us in *Il Trovatore* such wonderful melodic structures as Leonora's *Tacea la notte placida* and *D'amor sull' ali rosee*, the Count's *Il balen*, Manrico's *Ah! sì, ben mio;* and their composer is not someone to condescend to.

Moreover, even in the still earlier *Macbeth* we get in the vocal and orchestral writing of the *Sleepwalking Scene* an astounding manifestation of the art which later—developed, enriched, subtilized—fills in moment after moment in *Otello* with sustained invention of marvelously wrought details of melody, harmony, figuration and orchestration—such as the orchestral passage leading from Desdemona's *Splende il cielo*, at the end of the choral episode early in Act 2, to her *D' un uomo che geme;* or the developing violin figure and harmonic progressions of Otello's *Dio! mi potevi scagliar* in Act 3. And the man who wrote the chorus's song around the fire, Iago's drinking song, and the duet of Otello and Desdemona, in Act 1; the duet of Otello and Iago, and especially Iago's *Era la notte*, in Act 2; the duet of Otello and Desdemona, Otello's *Dio! mi potevi scagliar*, the trio of Iago, Cassio and Otello, and the final ensemble, in Act 3; Desdemona's *Willow Song* and *Ave Maria*, in Act 4—this man is an artist to whom nobody may condescend.

The art that is incandescent and robust in *Otello* shows a further refinement and subtilization in *Falstaff*, in writing that is all lightness and fluent grace and transparent texture. The writing is largely point-to-point invention for the words; and some of this invention—for example, the opening uproar—is only the product of an experienced artist's resourcefulness; but much of it—for example Falstaff's interviews with Dame Quickly and Ford in the second scene—is a succession of marvels of subtly contrived expressive point, wit and loveliness, whose very subtlety may require repeated hearing for full appreciation. Moreover, the point-to-point invention includes vocal writing as lovely as Dame Quickly's *un angelo che innamora* in her first scene with Falstaff, or Mistress Ford's *Ogni più bel giojel mi nuoce* in her first scene with him, but for the most part also as brief—the two duets and two arias of Nanetta and Fenton being the only examples of extended lyricism. And one thing in *Falstaff* is new: the poignant autumnal quality of much of the music of the last act—for example, Falstaff's *Ber del vin dolce* after the innkeeper has brought him the wine; and the orchestra's phrases accompanying his arrival at Herne's Oak. This music conveys to us for once the emotion of Verdi himself—the emotion, that is, of a man nearing the end of his life.

As for the other operas, we hear in the early ones conventions and formulas of the period to which Verdi's powers give artistic validity and impressive effect. In *Rigoletto* the outstanding example of this is the famous quartet, in which freshly attentive listening enables us to appreciate the individualized writing for the four characters in the dramatic situation that makes it one of the most remarkable ensembles in opera. In *La Traviata* it is Violetta's *Ah! fors' è lui*, with its concluding efflorescence into florid passages that are not mere vocal exhibitionism of the period but an expression of the intensity of her emotion about her meeting with Alfredo, as the florid passages in the following recitative *Follie! Follie!* and aria *Sempre libera* are expressions of her feverish decision to reject love and pursue pleasure. In both operas, moreover, we hear other manifestations of Verdi's powers: in *Rigoletto* not only the Duke's *Quest' o quella*, his *Parmi veder le lagrime*, Gilda's *Caro nome*, their *E il sol dell' anima*, but the tremendous Prelude and the extraordinary first duet of Rigoletto and Sparafucile; in *La Traviata* not only Violetta's *Addio del passato*, her duet with Germont, her *Parigi, o cara* with Alfredo, but the music of the parties in Violetta's and Flora's homes that continues as a background of feverish gaiety for the poignant dialogue and dramatic incidents in the foreground. And in *Rigoletto* there is the *Zitti, zitti* chorus, with a delicacy that foretells the ensembles in *Falstaff;* in *La Traviata* the Preludes to Acts 1 and 3, whose divided violins are an example of the increasingly elaborate and refined orchestral writing we hear with the beautiful melodic invention in *Un Ballo in Maschera* and *Simon Boccanegra*.

It is this orchestral writing that combines with the superb vocal declamation to make *Ella giammai m'amò* in *Don Carlo* one of Verdi's supreme achievements, and that contributes to the impressive effect of the subsequent scene of Philip and the

Grand Inquisitor. And it is this orchestral writing that, with the exquisite vocal writing, gives us the *Nile Scene* of *Aida*.

The same matured powers, the same enriched and refined art, produce the superb *Requiem*. And their final manifestation, five years after *Falstaff*, is the marvelously beautiful *Te Deum*.

16

TCHAIKOVSKY

Tchaikovsky is another popular composer who has been regarded with condescension for which we hear no justification
in his music. Listening to one of his ballet scores—*Swan Lake*,
The Sleeping Beauty, *The Nutcracker* (the entire score of each,
not just the usual excerpts)—listening, that is, to the canvas,
so to speak, being filled in with detail, we hear in the operation a wonderful precision and taste in the use of the entire
complex of musical line, color, texture and mass. And we hear
also this mastery of the medium serving dramatic and imaginative powers of a high order—the powers revealed for example
in the ominous figure that interrupts the opening melodic
passage of *Swan Lake* and is developed with increasing tension
over plucked bass-notes and sustained brass-notes; or in the
music at the end of Act 1 of *The Nutcracker*, and the Prelude
to Act 2, which convey so marvelously the world of a child's
dream.

Listening now to Toscanini's or Cantelli's performance of
the *Pathétique* Symphony we hear the music, as it proceeds in
strict accordance with Tchaikovsky's directions in the score,
take shape as something contrived with the same feeling for
the complex of musical line, color, texture and mass; and we
hear also the dramatic power it has when given these correct
and beautifully integrated plastic proportions. We are then
able to perceive the effect of the more usual performance that
exaggerates every crescendo and decrescendo, every accelera-

136

tion and retardation (to say nothing of the additional changes of tempo and volume Tchaikovsky doesn't request in his score) and makes every *p* a *ppp*, every *f* a *fff*, in the over-emphasis that is traditional in playing Tchaikovsky. We are able, that is, to perceive the distortion of the shape of the work, the consequent falsification of its meaning. It is the traditional overstatement in performance that converts drama and intensity into the melodrama and hysteria for which Tchaikovsky is looked down upon. And this overstatement has become the criterion by which mere statement is judged inadequate for failing to impart to the music "its essential feverish excitement"—which is as though some actor's ranting in Shakespeare had become the criterion by which the correct delivery of the lines were judged inadequate.

Tchaikovsky's music has been treated in this way because of the knowledge about his neurotically disordered personal life; and he provides part of the answer to the contention that knowledge of a composer's life is necessary for complete understanding of his music—a plausible contention until we think of some of the actual cases. On the one hand not one statement of Schubert has been reported to us that reveals the insights communicated in his greatest works; on the contrary, it is from the music that we infer the probability of these insights in the man. And on the other hand it is Berlioz's extravagances of behavior and utterance that are responsible for the ideas about "monstrous works" in which he carried out "extreme and gigantic aims" that people would not have got from mere listening to the works themselves. So with Tchaikovsky: it is, among other things, the neurotic self-accusations of incompetence and insincerity that are responsible for the ideas about the defects and the insincerity of his music that people would not have got from mere listening to the ballet scores, the operas *The Queen of Spades* and *Eugene Onegin*, the Overture-Fantasia *Romeo and Juliet*, the *Manfred* Symphony, and even the intensely subjective Symphonies Nos. 4, 5 and 6 (*Pathétique*).

It is a composer's works that we are concerned with and evaluate, not the circumstances under which they were produced; and by the evidence of the works I have mentioned Tchaikovsky was a superb artist. Nor was he less so for having produced other works inferior to them.

17

MUSORGSKY

One article of Turner published in 1924 that is of particular interest for us today opens with the statement that "the beginning of any live, intelligent interest in any art is the desire to know an artist's work in its pure, unadulterated state as it finally left the hands of its creator." It may seem obvious that one wants to know a painting as its creator painted it, not as it was repainted by someone else, and that the same is true with any other work of art. But it must be equally obvious that Turner had a reason for making his statement—the reason, in fact, that many works of art are presented to us *not* in their pure, unadulterated state as they left the hands of their creators.

Turner cited examples from poetry: Swinburne had exposed editors' alterations of the texts in various editions of Shelley; Sampson's accurate edition of Blake, Grierson's of Donne, had revealed the similar editorial tampering with their poems in previous editions. And the situation in music, he said, was even worse: not only had editors and performers taken even greater liberties with the originals, but there were few critics with the knowledge required to expose them, and even the objections that were made occasionally were ignored. Turner's explanation of this was "the generally lower intellectual integrity of men of music as compared with men of letters," to which I would add the generally lower intellectual sophistication and understanding where music is concerned: those who understand that one mustn't change someone else's painting or poem don't understand that one mustn't change the harmony or texture of someone else's music.

And so we have the many nineteenth-century "editions" of music of earlier centuries in which the editors, not knowing or caring what the music was intended to sound like, "corrected" it to make it conform to nineteenth-century ideas of what music should sound like. We have Gevaert's "edition" of Haydn's Cello Concerto, which in addition to re-orchestrating the work cuts half the recapitulation out of the first movement. Or Leonard's "edition" of Corelli's *La Folia*, which should be called Leonard's *La Folia* since that is what it really is. Or Grützmacher's "edition" of the Boccherini Cello Concerto in B flat, which is actually a work by Grützmacher himself, made out of thematic materials taken from five genuine Boccherini concertos: the themes of Grützmacher's first and third movements are mostly from an unpublished cello concerto in B flat recently discovered in the Dresden Library, but in part also from Nos. 1, 2 and 4 of four concertos published in Paris in 1770-1771, while the Grützmacher middle movement is a free rewriting of the middle movement of No. 3; of the themes themselves not one is even stated by Grützmacher as Boccherini wrote it; and the forms into which the themes are elaborated, the accompaniments and tuttis, the harmonization and orchestration, are entirely Grützmacher's and exhibit no resemblance to Boccherini's own practice. And even the discoverer of the genuine Dresden Concerto in B flat, when preparing the work for publication, cannot forbear to "improve" Boccherini's orchestration.

Moreover, those "editions" are still the ones used in performances today. Though a correct edition of the Haydn Cello Concerto is available, cellists continue to play and record the Gevaert version. Though the Eulenburg score of the genuine Boccherini Concerto in B flat is available, cellists continue to play and record the Grützmacher fake. And in this we see the "lower intellectual integrity of men of music" that Turner spoke of.

But a contributing cause is the lower intellectual sophistication and understanding I spoke of, which is to be seen in this mixture of sense and nonsense in van der Straeten's *History of the Violoncello:*

> . . . Very meritorious was Grützmacher's activity as an editor of classical works which had been practically lost, especially such rare treasures as the concertos by Haydn, P. E. Bach, Boccherini, sonatas by Duport, Geminiani and others. Unfortunately he treated these masters with little reverence as regards the text of their compositions, and in various cases he pieced together "sonatas" from about half-a-dozen original compositions and edited them as if they appeared in their original form. In the case of the six solo sonatas by Bach, he went so far as to edit a "concert edition," in which he crowds additional chords, passages and embellishments, distorting these great and fine works in the most unpardonable manner. Yet for all that, we must be thankful for the many works which he has rescued and made accessible. . . .

Nonsense, since what Grützmacher made accessible was not the great works but his falsifications of them, which kept—and still keep—the true works from becoming known.*

* There is in addition what is to be seen in the statement on the envelope of a Westminster recording of the fake Boccherini concerto—that "this, [Boccherini's] most representative work, is actually a combination of two scores. As widely performed by Pablo Casals, the two movements in B flat are spaced by an adagio in G minor. That arrangement is followed here, though the recently published Eulenburg score restores, as middle movement, an andantino grazioso in E flat. In other textual respects, this treatment follows closely the Casals model." Here the Grützmacher fake—which Casals and a hundred other cellists played when it was accepted as an edition of a genuine work—becomes the "Casals model"; this "Casals model" and the work in the Eulenburg score become merely different combinations of genuine movements from two Boccherini works—the outer movements in the two combinations being the same, but the "Casals model" substituting a middle movement in G minor for the one in E flat restored by the Eulenburg score; and if "this treatment" refers to the Eulenburg work we are told that except for the middle movement it follows closely the "Casals model." All this in the face of the statement in the preface of the Eulenburg score that accuses Grützmacher of combining "wantonly altered parts of [the genuine concerto] with such from other works of Boccherini and Orchestra Tutti of his own. . . ."

Which brings me to the subject of this chapter. The occasion for Turner's article was the announcement that the piano-and-voice arrangement that Musorgsky himself made of his opera *Boris Godunov* for publication in 1874 was to be published again, after having been out of print for many years. What had been performed since 1896 and available in published form was Rimsky-Korsakov's revision, in which he corrected what he considered to be "the fragmentary character of the musical phrases, the harshness of the harmonies and modulations, the faulty counterpoint, the poverty of the instrumentation, and the general weakness of the work from the technical point of view," which he contended had been responsible for its failure when it had been produced in 1874. It would always be possible, said Rimsky, to publish a "musicologically accurate edition"; he was satisfying the immediate "need of an edition for performances, for practical artistic purposes, for making [Musorgsky's] colossal talent known"— purposes which he claimed were in fact achieved by his revision. For after he became chairman of the Society of Musical Gatherings in St. Petersburg in 1896, he said, "there sprang up in the Society the idea of a stage production of *Boris Godunov* in my revision." The success of this production led to one by Mamontov's company in Moscow with Chaliapin, after which as part of his repertory the Rimsky revision was produced at the imperial Mariinsky Theater in St. Petersburg in 1904 and came to Paris in 1908 in the Diaghilev production that carried the work to Western Europe and America. And Rimsky's claim to have in this way "[made] Musorgsky's colossal talent known" to a world that otherwise would not have known it is accepted to this day.

But what led to the republication of Musorgsky's original work in 1924 was the loudly proclaimed discovery of some French critics that Rimsky, far from making Musorgsky's talent known, had concealed it with his corrections. In the famous words of Jean Marnold, "Rimsky-Korsakov cuts . . . one, two or three measures as serenely as he cuts fifteen or twenty. At will he transposes a tone, or a half-tone, makes sharps or flats natural, alters modulations. He even corrects the harmony. During the tableau in the cell of Pimen the liturgical Dorian mode is adulterated by a banal D minor. The interval of the augmented fifth (a favorite device of Musorgsky) is frequently the object of his equilateral ostracism. . . . From one end of the work to the other he planes, files, polishes, pulls together, retouches, embellishes, makes insipid, or corrupts. . . ." Imagine the analogous things being done to a painting or a poem: you will see what violation of the integrity of another artist's work Rimsky-Korsakov was guilty of; and you will see also that it was one which no painter, no poet would commit or be allowed to commit.

Nor is it true that Rimsky's revision, or any other edition "for performances, for practical artistic purposes," was necessary. It is Rimsky himself who, in *My Musical Life*, tells us of *Boris Godunov*—i.e. Musorgsky's own revised 1872 version— being produced in St. Petersburg in 1874 "with great success," and of its continuing to be performed once or twice each year until 1882, when, "the Lord knows why, productions of the opera ceased altogether, although it had enjoyed uninterrupted success." Concerning the reasons which only the Lord knew, Rimsky writes that "there were rumors afloat that the opera had displeased the imperial family; there was gossip that its subject was unpleasant to the censors"; but he says nothing about any practical difficulties that made necessary "an edition for performances, for practical artistic purposes." Musorgsky's original would have been as practical to produce in 1896 as in 1874; and if it had been produced in 1896 it would presumably have repeated its success of 1874-1882. And if it *had* been produced by the Society in 1896 instead of Rimsky's revision it would have taken the same subsequent steps as the revision in becoming the version the world would know today.

The real reason for what Rimsky did was very different from what he claimed, and much less to his credit. Musorgsky was one of the two great originals of the nineteenth century (Berlioz was the other), with stature and powers that triumphed over his insistence on learning solely by doing; Rimsky, on the other hand, was a minor talent who tells us he needed the help of codified practice in harmony and counterpoint for "new living currents to flow into my creative work." What was original and powerful in Musorgsky's writing was to Rimsky's ears, therefore, error which he tried persistently and unsuccessfully to get Musorgsky to change. And having been unable to get Musorgsky to change it when alive, he proceeded to change it himself when Musorgsky was dead.

Nor is it true that "there sprang up in the Society the idea of a stage production of *Boris Godunov* in my revision." The idea "sprang up" in Rimsky; and in another man there would have "sprung up" the idea of a production of Musorgsky's original work. By using the opportunity to produce his revision instead, Rimsky succeeded not, as he claimed, in making Musorgsky's work known to the world, but in keeping it from being known to most of the world to this very day. For though he argued plausibly that whenever the world disapproved of what he had done it could return to Musorgsky's original score, which he had not destroyed, actually once the revision had taken root everywhere in opera houses, in singers' repertories, in people's minds, then routine and inertia combined with lack of conscience and understanding to keep it from being dislodged for Musorgsky's original. And we come here to what is more extraordinary even than what was done to poor Musorgsky's work—namely, the way people's minds have operated in relation to what was done to it.

Thus, with the republication of Musorgsky's score in 1924 it was possible for anyone, by playing through it, to discover that everything was wonderfully right and nothing called for correction, and at the end to be left overwhelmed by what he had heard achieved with such originality, power, and absolutely assured mastery. And some did. But there were others

of whom one could say what Tovey said of Rimsky himself—
that they were incapable of "telling a blunder from a stroke
of genius or feature of style." And you will find them declar-
ing today that a hearing of Musorgsky's original demonstrates
how much it gained from the editing of a man properly
schooled in his craft—which amounts not just to saying that
something like Rimsky's *Le Coq d'or* is good of its kind, but to
setting it up as the good by which the kind of a *Boris Godunov*
must be judged deficient. Imagine that Van Gogh's work had
been tidied up by some academician, or even by someone like
Sargent; and imagine anyone contending that the restored
Van Gogh originals demonstrated how much they had gained
from the tidying up—contending, in other words, not merely
that Sargent was good for what he was, but that his good
was the good for Van Gogh.

Moreover, if it *had* been discovered that someone had repainted Van Gogh's or any other painter's work, there would
have been no debate over whether the work was more effective with the changes or without them, and whether therefore
they should be retained or removed: it would have been taken
as a matter of course that they had no validity and the original work must be restored. But in the case of *Boris* we find the
celebrated English critic Ernest Newman writing that the
difficulty with *Boris* is one of having to choose not merely
between Musorgsky's own two versions, each complete and
with merits of its own, but from these two and Rimsky's, since
it too is "a good practical proposition" in the theater. We
have had European opera companies producing Musorgsky's
original and going back to Rimsky's revision because it
"sounds better." I have had a man who conducted the
Musorgsky original at Covent Garden a few years ago insist
that the change back to the Rimsky version there had been
a good thing because it had induced the London public to
listen to a great work it had stayed away from before, and
have been unable to get him to understand that this was as
though a museum had induced the public to like an El Greco

painting by having someone touch it up to make its forms and colors more conventional—that what the London public had listened to was no more Musorgsky's great work than the prettied-up painting would be El Greco's. And even the most accurately perceptive and clearest-minded of present-day English critics, Gerald Abraham, in his notes for the HMV and RCA Victor recording of the Rimsky version, recognizes that by applying to *Boris* an art whose "essence . . . is brightly tinted transparency, clear-cut harmonies, and part-writing realized in primary orchestral colors" Rimsky "imprinted his own personality over the entire work," but goes on nevertheless to call this result "a fascinating posthumous collaboration of two very different but very fine musical minds." One would expect Abraham to recognize the obvious disparity and incompatibility of the mind that expresses itself in Rimsky's "brightly tinted transparency, clear-cut harmonies, and part-writing realized in primary orchestral colors," with the mind that produces the somber power of *Boris;* and one would expect him not to want the imprint of a mind like Rimsky's on a work like Musorgsky's.

Thus it is that although Musorgsky's original has been known since 1924, and the full orchestral score has been available since 1928, the Rimsky version continued to be given at the Metropolitan until 1953, when a new manager decided— with a good sense that must be considered something of a miracle—that if one is going to give Musorgsky's *Boris* one should give the *Boris* Musorgsky wrote (and his good sense extended to having its one weakness, Musorgsky's ineffective orchestral realization of his "sonorous image," remedied by improvement of the scoring in accordance with this image, not some other). Thus it is, also, that in the very year that the Metropolitan at last produced Musorgsky's original, HMV in England, making its first complete recording of the work, recorded the Rimsky version; and an English reviewer thought this was justified by the fact that the Rimsky version was the one most people knew—which was like arguing against publishing the accurate texts of Shelley's poems because most people knew the inaccurate ones. Thus it is, also, that Columbia in this country, which had the recording rights for the Metropolitan's productions, decided not to record its production of the original *Boris*. And thus it is, in sum, that if you should wish to hear the original *Boris* you will even at this late date not find any of it on records.

Rimsky-Korsakov's injury to Musorgsky was not just that he made his falsification rather than Musorgsky's own work what most of the world knows as *Boris Godunov* to this very day; it was also that he gave the world the idea of Musorgsky as a clumsy dilettante. This has caused some people, when they have heard Musorgsky's own work, to hear only a dilettante's inept crudities. And it has provided an excuse for others to do with his music what Rimsky did, with the claim that *they* were doing legitimately and well what he had done illegitimately and badly—the legitimacy consisting in their having returned to the original as the basis of changes which they have assured us adhered strictly to Musorgsky's spirit when not strictly to his letter. But that is what Rimsky claimed too; and actually what they have produced has turned out to be based on the original in much the same way as his version.

Thus we had from Stokowski what he called a "symphonic synthesis" of *Boris*, based, he said, on Musorgsky's original score:

    . . . With generous intentions Rimsky-Korsakov tried to re-orchestrate and re-form *Boris*. Instead he made something far from the spirit of Musorgsky. The original orchestration of Musorgsky shows clearly what he was trying to say, but sometimes he failed to express his musical conception, because he was inexperienced in the vast, subtle and highly differentiated world of the modern orchestra. . . . I have tried to help the orchestra more completely say what Musorgsky was aiming to express, keeping the music in the dramatic sequence of Pushkin's poem and Musorgsky's music. The result is something like a free modern symphony. . . .

But to speak of a number of passages torn out of organic context and patched together in what the blurb-writer for once correctly described as "a series of climaxes of almost intolerable brilliance, color and power"—to speak of this as a symphony or even a symphonic synthesis, with its connotation of organic coherence, was to make nonsense of the term. Nor was there more sense in saying an orchestral arrangement was based on the original score if it went back to the original only to depart from it as far as Stokowski's arrangement did. And Stokowski's claim to be merely helping Musorgsky to achieve what he was unable to achieve completely himself was the claim of a man incapable of telling a composer's unfulfilled conception from his mere failure to compose the vast and subtle sonorities Stokowski likes to produce with an orchestra. Musorgsky's sober orchestration does demonstrate clearly what sonorous image he had in mind—or, in Stokowski's way of speaking, "what he was trying to say"; and it demonstrates just as clearly that what he was trying to say was not what is said by the orchestral luxuriance and glitter, the heaving and billowing sonorities, of Stokowski's arrangement.

Musorgsky may have been incapable of using the orchestra in a way that would project his sonorous image of *Boris* effectively in the opera house; but his contemporaries are unanimous about his powers as a pianist, especially in dramatically and pictorially imaginative invention such as we hear in *Pictures at an Exhibition*. For many years I knew this work only in Ravel's orchestral transcription, which I took for granted was more effective than the original for piano— accepting too uncritically the prevailing idea of our time that the orchestra does everything better. And I retain a vivid recollection of my amazement when at last I heard the original played, and discovered how completely achieved an imaginative creation it is. In this work of his maturity—it is dated 1874—Musorgsky writes at every point, in every detail of melody, harmony and figuration, with the unfailing assurance of a man who is absolute master of his style; and in his musical translations of *Goldenberg and Schmuyle, Catacombs,* and *Con mortuis in lingua morta* he writes as a musical artist of the highest rank.

Moreover, listening with knowledge of the piano original I was now able to appreciate fully the imaginative insight and artistic rectitude that made Ravel's version, in its fidelity to the original, almost unique among such orchestral translations. And with knowledge of Musorgsky's and Ravel's achievements I could appreciate fully what other transcribers had done—among them Stokowski, whose version came with the usual statement about the greatness implicit in Musorgsky's mere piano sketch and now completely realized in an orchestration which "aimed to preserve and express the Slavic character" of the work, as against Ravel's "Gallic manner." It was no surprise that a man who heard in Musorgsky's original a mere piano sketch should have fulfilled the conception implicit in this sketch by slashing out whole sections and translating the remainder into the fussy and lush and lurid orchestral sonorities and effects that falsified what Ravel had preserved.

For Stokowski a composer's conceptions are unfulfilled if they aren't realized in Stokowskian orchestral sonorities; for Horowitz they are unfulfilled if they aren't realized in the Horowitz piano fireworks. That means not only Musorgsky but even Beethoven, whose powers as a pianist—one of the most celebrated of his time—also are attested to by his contemporaries, and whose command of the instrument and knowledge of its resources were things his deafness would not affect. But Horowitz thinks otherwise: "It's not that Beethoven's piano writing doesn't sound the way *I* want it to; it's because his writing doesn't sound the way *he* wanted it to"; and the piano writing of Beethoven's last years in particular is for Horowitz a mere groping toward a new style that is not achieved. That, presumably, is what he would say of the passages from the *Diabelli Variations* on pages 49 and 50; but

149

the truth of the matter is that they achieve with precision meanings that are beyond Horowitz's understanding.

But whereas Horowitz is content, fortunately, to leave Beethoven's last piano works unplayed and unrevised, he has made Musorgsky's *Pictures* suitable for performance at his recitals by revising it in terms of the Horowitz way of using the piano—the terms employed in Horowitz's *Carmen* Fantasy and his arrangement of *Stars and Stripes Forever*. And as usual the undertaking is legitimized by a pilgrimage to the original text (which even Rimsky-Korsakov left untouched): we are thus assured that Horowitz has been careful to change only Musorgsky's original work. It was none less than Olin Downes who, as Horowitz's spokesman, assured us that the revision doesn't "introduce any extraneous elements into the music as Musorgsky wrote it," but "is a return to the original text. . . . Following it carefully, Mr. Horowitz has done a little 'piano orchestration' in ways confined to octave doublings, redistribution of passage work between the hands, transpositions of brief passages an octave below or above the original pitch, etc. The effort has been solely to realize the intention of the composer, and to refrain from gratuitous ornamentation or officious 'correction' of any detail of his text as it stands." But my ears, following the recorded performance with the text, note such "officious 'correction' " and "gratuitous ornamentation" and "extraneous elements" as the cut in *The Old Castle;* the omission of the *Promenade* before *Limoges;* the insertion of four measures into a repeat in *Gnomus* from which Musorgsky omitted them; the replacement of bare octaves with rich chords; the completely new figuration in measures 12 to 24 of *Limoges*, realizing the intention not of the composer of *Pictures at an Exhibition* but of the composer of the *Carmen* Fantasy; the changing of a rhythmless octave tremolo in *Con mortuis in lingua morta* to a rhythmed figuration of two upper notes, two lower, two upper, two lower, with a very different effect; the insertion, in the last ten measures of *Con mortuis*, of a reiterated off-beat F sharp in the bass, which introduces rhythmic, pedal, and other effects not intended by Musorgsky.

If, then, you wish to hear a realization of Musorgsky's intention, listen to his own piano version. And if you want an orchestral translation faithful to that intention, listen to Ravel's.

Musorgsky's high-level creative achievements include some of his songs: notably the seldom-heard *Sunless* cycle, with perhaps the finest examples of his fully developed style of subtly inflected vocal declamation; and the better-known *Songs and Dances of Death*, which however until quite recently was sung and recorded only as "corrected" by Rimsky-Korsakov.

18

OTHER MUSIC OF THE
NINETEENTH CENTURY

In contrast to Brahms who produced bad music in the attempt to write greater than he felt, Chopin made a great art of writing small poetic pieces for the piano. I speak, I should say, of the music scraped clean of a hundred years' encrustation of performers' affected, mannered phrasing that has made it seem sentimental and morbid. Even so my use of the term *great* may be questioned—though I don't think there would be any question about the art exhibited in the richly elaborated style of writing and its employment of the resources of the piano, or in the beautiful and subtle invention of pieces like the Impromptu Op. 36, the Nocturne Op. 27 No. 2, the Berceuse, the Barcarolle, some of the Mazurkas—the art exhibited most strikingly perhaps in the Preludes and Etudes, in each of which a piano figuration exercising the hand in a particular segment of piano technique provides the terms with which Chopin creates a piece of music as exquisitely thought and formed as any other. But I think *great* is correctly applied to the Nocturne Op. 48 No. 1, the Polonaises Opp. 44 and 53, the Ballades Opp. 23 and 52, the Sonatas Opp. 35 and 58, the Concerto No. 1—in which there are not only beauty and subtlety but magnificence and power.

We hear another richly elaborated style of writing for the piano used with superb effect by Schumann in his sets of imaginative pieces—*Papillons, Carnaval, Kinderszenen,* the *Fantasiestücke* Op. 12, and parts of *Kreisleriana* and *Davidsbündlertänze;* and in some of his large-scale works—the *Etudes symphoniques,* the Sonatas Opp. 11 and 22, the Fantasia Op. 17, and the Piano Concerto. And this writing for the piano contributes much to the effect of some of the finest songs we have—the great *Dichterliebe* cycle, and among the single songs *Aufträge, Mondnacht, Der Nussbaum, Alte Laute, Du bist wie eine Blume, Loreley, Ständchen, Waldesgespräch, Die Kartenlegerin.* The orchestral works, the chamber music, and almost all the later writing I find less interesting.

What Schumann's songs begin, Hugo Wolf's continue—which is to say that Wolf's writing for the piano again contributes much to the effect of the song, and indeed is often so integrated with the vocal part as to provide the context essential to its continuing sense. Wolf's susceptibility to the stimulation of poetry led him to write almost nothing but songs, and was responsible for what is most remarkable about them—the vocal writing that is like an extension of the words around which the music shapes itself as it points up their meaning. This is true of all the songs; what is true only of some is that the progression which is so remarkably integrated with the poem is in addition a moving or attractive piece of music—like *Anakreon's Grab, In der Frühe, Auf einer Wanderung, Heimweh, Auf ein altes Bild, Die ihr schwebet, Nun wandre Maria, Und steht ihr früh, Herr was trägt der Boden hier?, Auf dem grünen Balkon, In dem Schatten meiner Locken.*

In orchestral music we have in Mendelssohn a minor master who—working on a small scale of emotion and texture—produced the magical overture and the other exquisite pieces for *A Midsummer Night's Dream;* the delightful *Italian* Symphony and scherzo and finale of the *Scotch* Symphony; the fine opening movement of the Violin Concerto; the imaginative *Fingal's Cave* or *Hebrides* Overture.

In opera Bellini exhibits his extraordinary gift for melodic writing in the purely lyrical *La Sonnambula,* and in *I Puritani,* which offers in addition passages of impressive dramatic force. *Norma* I find less interesting; but it has what is perhaps the finest, and certainly the most famous, of his melodic structures, the aria *Casta diva*.

Donizetti too reveals himself as a superb melodist—in the tragic *Lucia di Lammermoor*, and in his masterpiece of operatic comedy, *Don Pasquale*.

Rossini exhibits his powers in operatic comedy not only in the best-known *The Barber of Seville* but in *La Cenerentola*, which has even more impressive writing in his lyric, comic and florid bravura styles—the last in particular often breathtaking in its controlled extravagance. But Rossini had powers for more than operatic comedy, as I discovered only quite recently when Berlioz's comments on *William Tell* led me to listen to a recording of that seldom-performed work, and to be amazed by what had elicited Berlioz's enthusiasm. Concerning Matilda's second-act aria *Selva opaca* he observed correctly that "Rossini has . . . written few pieces as elegant, as fresh, as distinguished in their melody, and as ingenious in their modulations as this one"; and noting in addition the writing for the orchestra Berlioz exclaimed: "This is poetry, this is music, this is art—beautiful, noble, and pure, just as its votaries would have it always." And the passages which follow this one—the duet of Matilda and Arnold, the trio of Tell, Walter and Arnold, the choruses of the three cantons—deserve Berlioz's description of them as the marvel that follows marvel.

In addition to the operas of Bellini and Rossini there are the engaging products of a French minor master—Bizet's *Carmen* and his music for *L'Arlésienne*.

Another French minor master of fascinating originality of mind and style is Chabrier—not in the *España* by which he is known almost exclusively, but in the *Dix Pièces pittoresques* for piano, four of which he made into the *Suite Pastorale* for orchestra; the *Trois Valses romantiques* for two pianos, especially the affecting No. 3; the smaller-scale *Marche joyeuse*.

As for Franck, like Brahms he is most enjoyable when he is

least pretentious—in the *Variations symphoniques* for piano and orchestra, parts of the Sonata for violin and piano, the Prelude and Chorale of the *Prelude, Chorale and Fugue* for piano, the second movement of the Symphony, and *Les Eolides* and *Psyché* for orchestra, though these last two suffer from Franck's repetitious long-windedness. But an observation by Tovey— "The saintliness of Franck shines nowhere more brightly than where his music is most *mondaine*"—describes a combination of qualities that you will hear occasionally and may not like even in these best works.

The Russian nationalists associated with Musorgsky achieved nothing of the stature and power of his work; but the engaging things they did produce are exemplified by the *Polovtsian Dances* from Borodin's *Prince Igor* and the Suite from Rimsky-Korsakov's *Le Coq d'or*.

Even more impressive products of this kind are those of the Czech nationalists. The vein of lovely and richly harmonized melody that we hear in Dvořák's superb *Slavonic Dances* provided much of the substance for his symphonies and chamber music—with the possible exception of the best-known Symphony No. 5 (*From the New World*). And a similar source furnished Smetana with the melodious substance of his beautiful symphonic poem *Die Moldau* and his delightful operatic comedy *The Bartered Bride*.

19

STRAUSS

We come to the end of the nineteenth century and the beginning of the twentieth—to Richard Strauss, Mahler, Debussy.

The powers that operate with youthful vigor and exuberance in Strauss's tone-poems *Don Juan* and *Till Eulenspiegel* exhibit matured refinement and sheer incandescence in *Don Quixote*. This is his masterpiece—inspired in its invention; unflawed by a single Straussian excess or error of taste; every note in the complex texture really counting for something; every detail making its programmatic point brilliantly. So profuse is the programmatic detail, and so subtly achieved at times, that much of it will be caught only by the musically trained listener familiar with the score or capable of reading it as he listens; and other listeners need to have it pointed out to them. This is difficult to do in a book; but here are some of the important things to listen for.

Strauss subtitles the work *Fantastic Variations on a Theme of Knightly Character*, and describes it further as an Introduction, Theme and Variations, and Finale. It makes its points, then, by applying the variation procedure to themes which characterize Don Quixote, Sancho Panza and Dulcinea; and much of the substance of the work is derived from the high-spirited statement of flute and oboe with which the Introduction begins:

This leads to a statement of the violins that will play an important part:

a statement conveying a grace that is a little stiff-jointed and absurd, and whose conclusion:

conveys the fact that things are distorted in the Don's mind. Next a statement of the violas, derived from [1]:

which rambles on until the oboe enters with Dulcinea's theme:

This is interrupted by excited martial calls of muted trumpets over gigantesque mutterings of tubas and string basses that contribute to the absurdity; and now all the thematic substance continues to be heard in an increasingly involved and dense texture representing the Don's increasing confusion of mind, and reaching its conclusion in several loudly proclaimed discordant chords and a final loud and empty note of the trumpets and trombones that tell us his mind has cracked and he has lost his reason.

157

We are now formally introduced to the chief characters of the musical narrative. First, in the words of the score, "Don Quixote, the knight of melancholy countenance," wonderfully delineated by a theme derived from [1] and [4], in minor instead of major, and played by the solo cello, which represents the Don in this work:

He is described further by [2] and [3].

Then Sancho Panza, who is as wonderfully delineated by a new theme from the bass-clarinet and tenor-tuba, which, with the solo viola, represent him in the work:

And the solo viola adds a few marvelously contrived examples of his homely platitudes.

And now the two set out in the first variation of their musical journey—the Don jogging along in the solo cello, Sancho in the bass-clarinet, with the image of Dulcinea (flute, oboe, muted violins) eliciting chivalresque thoughts from the Don ([2] from the solo cello) to an accompaniment of down-to-earth mutterings by Sancho ([S] from bass-clarinet and solo viola). Suddenly they stop: a slowly circling progression by clarinet, bassoon, violins, violas describes the circling of the distant windmills. The Don (solo cello) gallops to a closer point and stops for another look: the windmills continue their circling. Convinced now that they are giants, he gallops up to give battle: there is a crash, a harp glissando; and a sustained note of the solo cello tells us the Don lies prostrate, while the windmills continue their circling. Gradually he revives.

And he is off again in the second variation. A vigorous martial variant of [D] pauses before what the Don thinks is an army, despite Sancho's frantic remonstrances ([S] from the woodwinds) that it is a flock of sheep, whose bleatings are now heard. Again the vigorous martial statement, which tells us of the Don's attack; then piteous cries from the scattering sheep; and once more the vigorous martial statement, now proclaiming the Don's victory.

[S] from the bass-clarinet and tenor-tuba opens Variation 3, which is an argument about the life of chivalry, with Sancho expressing doubts and the Don affirming belief. A series of brief exchanges, with [3] from the first desk of first violins repeatedly expressing the Don's growing impatience with Sancho's persistent objections, lead to an extensive statement by Sancho (solo viola) of all his nuggets of homely wisdom. Eventually the Don interrupts angrily ([3] from the violins), quieting down for an affirmation of his belief which becomes impassioned, reaches a great climax, and ends on a sustained chord of finality—only to have Sancho venture another doubt ([S] from the bass-clarinet), which the furious Don silences ([3] from the violins).

And they set out again in Variation 4, jogging along until they see some pilgrims approaching, in whom the Don sees a band of ruffians. He attacks; there is a crash; and a sustained note of the low strings tells us he lies prostrate while the pilgrims recede into the distance. Sancho utters mournful cries ([S] from the bass-clarinet, tenor-tuba and solo viola); when the Don (solo cello) begins to revive, the exuberant bass-clarinet and tenor-tuba express Sancho's joy.

In Variation 5 the Don, at night, keeps vigil in extended declamation of the solo cello, in the course of which his thoughts of Dulcinea make him giddy (harp glissandos, tremolos of the other instruments).

Resuming their journey in Variation 6 the two meet a

peasant girl mounted on an ass (parody of Dulcinea's theme from the oboes, with punctuating strokes of the tambourine). She is, says Sancho, Dulcinea transformed by an enchanter. The Don is indignant ([2] from the solo cello); Sancho insists (solo viola).

In Variation 7 the soaring aloft of [2] (strings) and [4] (horns), the glissandos of the harp, the rolls of the kettle-drums, the chromatic scales of the flutes, the rushing and whistling of a wind machine all combine to describe the Don—seated on a wooden horse and fanned by a huge bellows—imagining himself riding through the air, while the note D held throughout by the string basses tells us he never leaves the ground.

Next, in Variation 8, a lilting barcarolle ([2] transformed by solo violin and oboe, with the notes of [D] spaced out by English horn, trombone and strings) gives us the episode of the ride in the boat which capsizes. The notes of [D] plucked by the strings suggest the struggling to shore; then [D] *religioso* from flutes, clarinets and horns constitutes a little prayer of thanksgiving.

Galloping off again in Variation 9 the Don meets two monks (two bassoons engaged in a dry-as-dust theological wrangle) whom he takes for magicians and puts to flight—only to encounter, in Variation 10, a fellow-townsman disguised as a knight, who defeats him in a joust and exacts the penalty that he return home.

And now the finale, which depicts the dejected Don plodding homeward, then his last reflections (solo cello's sustained melody derived from [1]) and peaceful death (solo cello's expiring octave-drop to its final note).

Of Strauss's other tone-poems the earlier *Tod und Verklärung* and *Also sprach Zarathustra* are inferior in musical substance; the later *Ein Heldenleben* has pages of superb writing (the love scene, the hero's works of peace, the conclusion) and other pages of Strauss's worst. As for the still later *Sinfonia Domestica*, it is only one example of the deterioration in the later Strauss—a deterioration in the quality of his musical ideas, with no diminution in the prodigious technical virtuosity and garrulous facility, so that although genuine creative activity stopped, the production of endless pages of empty tonal luxuriance went on almost to the day of his death.

This deterioration is heard also in the later operas—in *Elektra*, in *Ariadne auf Naxos*, and in the vastly overrated *Der Rosenkavalier*. Most of this opera is, to my ears, an expertly made hubbub of sounds with no musical significance in themselves and none in relation to the words and action they carry; of the rest the Princess's first-act monologue and the third-act trio seem to me not equal to the demands of the texts; and the one moment of inspired creation and beauty is the second-act *Presentation of the Rose*, with its first exchanges of Octavian and Sophie.

It is the earlier opera *Salome* that offers passages of impressive power achieved by the enormously complex writing—notably the final scene. But it offers others in which the complexity gets to be a luxuriance out of control of artistic purpose or taste. And it offers also the appalling *Dance of the Seven Veils*.

In addition, some of the songs—*Ständchen, Freundliche Vision, Die Nacht, Traum durch die Dämmerung, Ruhe meine Seele, Heimkehr*—are lovely.

20

MAHLER

It is with Strauss that one can begin to speak of gigantic means and aims; and even more with Mahler. The aim was expressed once in Mahler's statement: "For me 'symphony' signifies using all the means of available technique to construct a world for myself"; and the means are the huge orchestras, choruses and vocal soloists, the enormous formal structures in which they are employed. But the employment of the huge orchestras is not the opulent daubing of Strauss; rather it resembles Berlioz's practice in the fastidiousness, precision and originality of its use, frequently, of now only these few instruments and now only those few to produce contrapuntal textures as clear as they are complex. Mahler's use of the orchestra is in fact only one part of an entire operation that resembles Berlioz's in the fact that nothing in the music is perfunctory or mechanical: if an instrument plays or an inner voice moves, the activity is never a routine instrumental doubling or filling in of texture, but always something done with attention, thought and purpose. And this evidence of a mind always working—working, moreover, in unexpected, individual, original and fascinating ways—holds interest even through one of Mahler's long-winded twenty-minute symphony movements.

The best introduction to Mahler, I think, is the Symphony No. 4, whose expansively relaxed and genial earlier movements lead to a gay final movement—a setting for soprano of one of the poems in Arnim and Brentano's collection of German folk-song poetry, *Des Knaben Wunderhorn*. The work thus illustrates one outstanding fact about Mahler—that his musical imagination was rooted in the Bohemian folk song he heard in his youth. Much of his creative energy went, as a result, into the writing of songs—the settings of poems from *Des Knaben Wunderhorn*, the *Lieder eines fahrenden Gesellen*, the settings of poems by Rückert, *Das Lied von der Erde*. And another result was the close relation of his vocal and instrumental writing: the folk-song-like character of much of his instrumental lyricism; the introduction of actual song into movements of several of the symphonies. Thus, the dramatic and brooding first movement of the Symphony No. 2 (*Resurrection*) is followed by an engaging *Ländler;* this by a gigantic Scherzo which is an orchestral reworking of the delightful song, *St. Anthony's Sermon to the Fishes;* this by a song, *Urlicht*, in which the contralto sings that "man lies in greatest need," but that God "will light my way to eternal blissful life"; and this by a setting of Klopstock's Resurrection Ode, sung by the soprano and chorus. And in the Symphony No. 3, two vocal movements lead to another consoling conclusion, this one for the orchestra alone, and Mahler's most sublime utterance.

It is these works that I find accessible and moving, not the ranting later symphonies.

21

DEBUSSY

The fastidiousness and precision and originality that Mahler exhibits in his use of the orchestra we hear in even greater degree in Debussy's music, and not only in the orchestration but in the melody and harmony. Debussy is another of the great originals; and he exhibits his originality not only in a substance quite different from that of the music we have been considering until now, but in equally different procedures, and in the completed entities which these procedures result in—entities without the kind of continuity of melody, development and structure we have been hearing. In one of Debussy's mature works we hear a substance of evocative fragments of melody, figuration, harmony and instrumental color; and a fitting together of such fragments in a progression with coherence and cumulative effect.

The originality of substance and procedure begins to show itself in the varied play with the flute theme in the opening section of Debussy's first major orchestral piece, the *Prélude à L'Après-midi d'un faune*, and in the similar closing section; while the expansive melody of the middle section reminds us of the astonishingly conventional and sugary idiom of the music that preceded this piece—such as the *Arabesques* and *Suite bergamasque* for piano.

But there are no such reminders in *Nuages*, whose thematic fragments and precisely achieved subtleties of orchestral coloring evoke marvelously, from the first measures, the still atmosphere of the scene of clouds moving across the sky. As for those orchestral subtleties, note the opening two measures of clarinets and bassoons alone, then the addition of an oboe, then its withdrawal; note then the entrance of the English horn, the addition of flutes and horns, then of the chord of the muted violins *pp* (with clarinets and bassoons), and with this the kettledrum roll *ppp;* note in that violin chord:

the change from G natural to G sharp, then the change from chord to simple octave.

We have here the beginnings of the method that exhibits its matured development in the rich, complex textures of *La Mer* (particularly its marvelous second movement), *Ibéria* (particularly, again, its second movement), and the smaller-scale *Gigues* and *Rondes de printemps*, in the last of which the idiom is especially rich, lending itself wonderfully to the purposes of an aural "image" of spring (*Gigues, Ibéria* and *Rondes de printemps* constitute the *Images* for orchestra).

The same matured orchestral style is to be heard in the opera *Pelléas et Mélisande;* and it is in fact the superb orchestral writing that I find effective and impressive in the work, not the tenuous vocal declamation. Nor do I find this declamation more interesting in Debussy's songs.

As astonishingly original in the light of its conventional and sugary antecedents is the style of writing for the piano that we hear fully matured in *Soirée dans Grenade* and *Jardins sous la pluie* of *Estampes*, in *L'Île joyeuse*, in *Reflets dans l'eau, Hommage à Rameau* and *Poissons d'or* of the *Images* for piano, and in a few of the Preludes—*La Cathédrale engloutie, La Sérénade interrompue, La Puerta del vino*. The various elements of that piano style are elaborated in the Etudes, some of which I find interesting only in that way (as in fact I do some of the pieces with titles), but a few of which are in addition engaging and impressive as pieces of music. And *Doctor Gradus ad Parnassum*, *The Snow is Dancing* and *Golliwog's Cake-Walk* of *Children's Corner* are charming.

Of the chamber music the early Quartet, though not one of Debussy's best works, has a second and third movement that are exquisitely wrought and lovely; but the late Sonatas for cello and piano, for flute, viola and harp, and for violin and piano offer what to my ears is style carried to a high point of refinement and subtlety, but with little or no content.

22

MUSIC OF

THE TWENTIETH CENTURY

The originality I have referred to in the work of certain composers was something incidental to their achievement of the works of art their minds were concentrated on. With the twentieth century we come to originality—in melody, harmony, rhythm and form—that was consciously striven for, and that was carried to the point where some composers were no longer in communication with the general music public. And so we come to the problem of modern music and the arguments about it.

On the one hand some have contended that the situation is an old one—that the great composers of the past were obscure to *their* contemporaries—and have argued from this that the music which the public has trouble in understanding today is as good as the music it had trouble in understanding in the past. Mozart has been cited as one composer who starved to death for lack of appreciation; but his great contemporary Haydn flourished handsomely, and actually Mozart's difficulty was not the public's failure to recognize his greatness, which it did recognize, but his own lack of skill—whether he was dealing with a French duke who didn't pay him for his daughter's lessons, or an Austrian emperor who paid him only half the salary he had paid Gluck, or a manager who paid him only half the customary fee for an opera, or a publisher who paid him nothing for some quartets—his lack of skill in manipulating the musico-economic machinery of the period to convert the public's appreciation into the money that would have kept him from dying of poverty and overwork at thirty-five. Beethoven also has been cited: the difficulties his contemporaries had with his last quartets have been offered in support of the contention that he too died in want for lack of understanding of his music; but actually he did not die in want, and not only the financial support he received from his noble patrons but the sums he was paid by publishers who competed for his works are evidence of the lifelong contemporary recognition of his greatness even by those who had trouble with his last quartets at first hearing. Schubert is still another who is alleged to have starved to death for lack of recognition; but actually, though he was always poor, it was not privation but an earlier venereal disease that weakened his body's resistance to the typhus of which he died; and he died at the point where his music, which had been appreciated from the start by those who knew it, was beginning to be sufficiently known and recognized for publishers to ask him for works (in the year of his death the Vienna correspondent of the Dresden *Abendzeitung* referred to "the inspired Schubert" whose "name already resounds from all lips"); so that if he had lived he probably would have been able in a few years to command adequate compensation for what was published. The scurrilous attacks on Wagner have been cited as evidence of his contemporaries' inability to understand his music; but he was no less warmly defended, and the Bayreuth Festspielhaus is merely the surviving concrete evidence of the enormous interest, recognition and support that his work commanded in his own lifetime.

On the other hand some have contended, correctly, that the situation is new, but have gone on with further contentions that are incorrect. The American composer Aaron Copland, in his excellent book *Music and Imagination*, quotes from an address at Harvard University some years ago in which E. J. Dent pointed out that "in the days of Handel and Mozart nobody wanted old music; all audiences demanded the newest opera or the newest concerto, as we now naturally demand the newest play and the newest novel," and asked why in music today we demanded the old and were hostile to the new. One reason, said Dent, was the excessive reverence for the classics, which he suspected began in England at the Handel commemoration of 1784 (Germany apparently didn't count). And another reason was the change in public. "In Handel's day there was in all European countries an inner ring of cultivated connoisseurs who were the direct patrons of the composers," whereas "the bourgeois public of the nineteenth century had no tradition of connoisseurship . . . and it had no sense of patronage." This was Dent's formulation of the myth of the golden age of eighteenth-century patronage. The fact was patronage by an aristocracy of birth and rank; the myth converts this into patronage by an aristocracy of mind, spirit and taste; and similarly it converts the change from the eighteenth-century aristocratic to the nineteenth-century bourgeois public into a change from an educated, cultivated and enlightened public to an uneducated, uncultivated and unenlightened one. Actually eighteenth-century patronage of music was part of the ritual of aristocratic existence; and you need only read Mozart's letters to learn that the ritual was practiced by many aristocrats of birth and rank who lacked aristocracy of mind, spirit and taste. Actually too the musico-economic set-up of direct patronage for the creation and performance and hearing of music was replaced largely by the nineteenth-century set-up of the public concert and generally distributed printed editions; and in this set-up the new bourgeois public included people who attended concerts under no other compulsion than their interest in the music—the enlightened interest of the educated, cultivated people many of them were. This public listened to the old music which the new widely distributed editions made it possible to perform; but it listened also to the music that was newly composed; and it continued to listen to both old and new all through the nineteenth century and into the twentieth. If therefore at that point it began to be hostile to the new, the reason cannot have been excessive reverence for the old; it must have been rather the particular nature of those new works of Schönberg, von Webern and the rest—the experiences they offered the ear, mind and spirit, as against the experiences that had been offered by new music until then.

But on this point Copland, in an earlier book called *Our New Music*, advanced another argument. In that book he undertook to describe and explain the changes in expressive content and extensions of vocabulary in modern music, in order to remove from the reader's mind the "fantastic notions" with which he said "newspaper writers and radio commentators who ought to know better" had misrepresented modern music and prejudiced the public against it—to remove, that is, the notions that the music lacked emotion and melody, that it was over-complicated in rhythm and ugly in harmony. In this way he undertook to make it possible for the reader to recognize in the emotion that was merely changed in quality and intensity, in the melody, harmony and rhythm that were merely enriched, the things that made Schönberg and von Webern "*our* music," as natural and acceptable to our ears, as interesting and significant to our minds, as people a hundred and two hundred years ago found *their* music.

And the argument about the extension of vocabulary was stated somewhat differently by Gerald Abraham in his excellent book *This Modern Music*, which provided an admirably clear explanation of the extensions of vocabulary and syntax in the music the public had found incomprehensible. As in the case of a foreign language, Abraham contended, one could not understand modern music merely by listening to it, but had to learn its vocabulary and grammar—though the converse was no less true, that "no amount of knowledge of the why and wherefore of [the] musical speech will make that language your own, as natural to you as Bach's or Wagner's, without a great deal of keen listening practice." But children learn their native language by ear long before they study its grammar; and I know from personal experience that foreign languages are best learned in the same way: after a few months in Vienna, as a boy of ten, I spoke German without having seen a grammar. And this is even more true of music, which, as Abraham himself observed in another connection, "has no sense outside itself": the internal coherence of the progression of sounds is conveyed directly by, and on the other hand apprehended directly from, the sounds themselves as heard. That was how I learned to understand the simplest musical vocabulary and syntax in earliest childhood long before I learned anything about chord progressions; it was how I extended that vocabulary and syntax later to include Debussy, Ravel, early Stravinsky (to *Le Sacre du printemps*), Prokofiev, Bloch. And when that way no longer worked—when in the twenties I began to hear music by Schönberg and others that conveyed no sense to me—I found that no amount of reading of explanations of vocabulary and syntax caused the music to begin to make the sense it had not made. So it has continued to be. When, a few years ago, I began to enjoy some of the later works of Stravinsky I had previously found arid and ugly, it was as a result of listening—listening, it is true, with help, but the help of Balanchine's ballet choreography for the works, not of the incomprehensible explanations by the Stravinskyites or Stravinsky himself. Similarly, when I found Schönberg's *Erwartung* expressively effective, the expressive effect was something imposed on my mind directly by the progression of sounds that I heard for the first time; whereas the principle of organization that Abraham pointed out in a passage of Schönberg's *Five Piano Pieces* still doesn't work for me as a principle of coherent sense in the progression of sounds as heard. And this is true not only of me but of the general public.

Which brings us back to Copland's argument. When the public rejected Schönberg and von Webern it didn't do so under the influence of the critics' misrepresentation of them; it acted on the basis of its own direct experiences of the music; and the critics merely described the experiences they had shared with the non-professional, non-writing listeners. To this day the countless explanations like those by Copland and Abraham haven't induced the public to hear in Schön-berg and von Webern "*our* music," as natural and acceptable to our ears, as interesting and significant to our minds, as people a hundred and two hundred years ago found *their* music. But readers of mine have reported finding in Bartok the meaning I have said I don't find—which is to say that where the public has come to accept a composer, there too it has acted on the basis of its own direct experiences of the music.

And so will you act: with twentieth-century as with earlier music my experiences and judgments are offered subject to confirmation by your own ears and mind. I must report that the writing of Alban Berg has expressive accuracy and power for me in relation to the situations and text of his opera *Wozzeck* but communicates no coherent sense to me in self-contained instrumental structures like his Violin Concerto; but you are free to find it as meaningful in the concerto as in the opera. And so with Hindemith: there was no difficulty in understanding the harmonically sour and emotionally dry works that he kept grinding out for many years with enor-mous technical efficiency, but there was, for me, no pleasure in listening to them such as I have had recently with parts of *The Four Temperaments* and *Symphonic Metamorphoses on Themes of Weber*, whose astonishingly conventional and sensuous idiom raises questions about the earlier sourness and aridity; but you are free to enjoy the earlier works.

Among the century's experimenters and innovators who have proved to be fruitful artists Stravinsky stands out as the towering figure. I mentioned that I have only recently en-joyed some of his later works; I should add that there are some I still don't like, but also that there is one—the ballet score *Le Baiser de la fée* (1928)—that I enjoyed at first hearing. What I liked were things it had in common with his earliest masterpiece, the ballet score *L'Oiseau de feu* (1910); and for some years I failed to perceive what it had in common with the later works I disliked.

One striking thing about *L'Oiseau de feu* is how beautifully it is wrought: we hear, for example, a use of the orchestra as precise and fastidious, to achieve coloring often as delicate and subtle, as Debussy's—the most beautiful example being the transition from the Berceuse to the Finale. And there is the mosaic-like fitting together of substance, instead of its development, that we noted in Debussy. But there is no resemblance to Debussy in the bold, raw dissonance at the end, or in the reiteration of dynamic syncopated figures that builds up tension and excitement in the *Infernal Dance*. And it is the further exploitation of this dissonance and rhythm that we hear in the music for one of the great artistic masterpieces of the century, the ballet *Petrushka* (1911), and that achieves the overwhelming power of the ballet score *Le Sacre du printemps* (1913).

In addition to being beautifully wrought *L'Oiseau de feu* is unusual, for Stravinsky, in its direct expressiveness. And both of these things are true of *Le Baiser de la fée*, but in even greater degree: *Le Baiser*, for me, is Stravinsky's most beautiful score, with an expressiveness that has a wider range than that of *L'Oiseau* and is more touching in the lyrical episodes of the boy and his bride, more powerful in the dramatic episodes of the boy and the fairy. And two other beautifully wrought and directly expressive ballet scores are the genial *Apollon Musagètes* (1928) and the grave and haunting *Orpheus* (1948).

On the other hand we hear in *Le Baiser* the tension-producing syncopations and ostinatos characteristic of Stravinsky's abstract works, like *Danses Concertantes* (1942) and the *Symphony in Three Movements* (1945). And *Le Baiser*, finally, throws light on a practice of Stravinsky that has been misunderstood—his use of themes and styles of composers of the past. At the beginning of the village scene of *Le Baiser* we hear repeatedly a fragment of Tchaikovsky's piano piece *Humoresque*— but only this fragment, and worked into a context of Stravinsky's own. This is the way he uses the other bits of thematic substance of Tchaikovsky in *Le Baiser;* and it is the way he uses the substance and styles of other composers. It is analogous to the old practice of writing variations on another composer's theme: Brahms writing variations on a theme of Paganini wasn't imitating Paganini but writing music of his own that resulted from letting his mind play with Paganini's theme; and Stravinsky has given us music of his own that has resulted from letting his mind play with themes and styles of composers of the past.

I say "play"; and sometimes it sounds as though it *is* for fun; but in *Oedipus Rex* (1927) we hear in the arias a manipulation of the old styles to achieve not the melodic beauty they achieved originally but a harshly austere and monumental utterance suited to this drama of man pursued and destroyed by implacable destiny.

Gerald Abraham points out in *L'Oiseau de feu* elements derived from Rimsky-Korsakov and other Russian predecessors of Stravinsky; but we hear also what the mind of Stravinsky made of them. Similarly one hears in Prokofiev's *Scythian Suite* things which suggest the possibility that the man who wrote this music about pagan Scythia in 1914 knew the music Stravinsky had written about pagan Russia the year before; but we hear also that these things, if they do represent the influence of *Le Sacre du printemps*, are part of the personal and individual way of writing that Prokofiev exhibits in this and other early works. And it is in fact these early works—the Piano Concerto No. 1, the Violin Concerto No. 1, the *Scythian Suite*, the ballet score *Chout*, the Piano Concerto No. 3—that are the most engaging by virtue of the astonishing imaginative and musical powers that operate with youthful freshness and exuberant creative energy. Not that fine works aren't produced later by the more experienced composer—notably the superb score for the ballet *The Prodigal Son* (1928). And even when, much later, what appears to be operating in some works is the developed craftsmanship that could grind out music on demand, there is also the occasional exception like the Symphony No. 5, unusual and impressive in the sustained and involved construction of its first and third movements.

Another personal and individual way of writing, somber and impassioned, is heard in the music of Ernest Bloch. His finest work is the Piano Quintet; and there are impressive pages also in the Violin Sonata, the Viola Suite, the Hebrew Rhapsody *Schelomo* for cello and orchestra, and *Voice in the Wilderness* for cello and orchestra or piano. The more recent String Quartet No. 2 exhibits a refinement and subtilization of the idiom of those earlier works; and its slow portions offer some of the most beautiful writing Bloch has done.

A work by Janáček with extraordinarily powerful writing in a highly individual language and style is his *Slavonic Mass*.

And an arresting new voice in recent years has been that of Benjamin Britten, one of whose outstanding characteristics is a technical resourcefulness and facility which on occasion has turned out a mere pretense at writing music, like the opera *The Rape of Lucrece*, but which on other occasions—in the *Serenade for Tenor, Horn and Strings*, the operas *Peter Grimes* and *Albert Herring*—has served genuine creative imagination and effort.

In addition there is some of the unprofound and enjoyable music that has presented no difficulties to anyone's ears and mind: Delius's exquisitely wrought *Walk to the Paradise Garden* and *Brigg Fair;* the delightful Sitwell-Walton *Façade;* the engaging piano pieces in Albéniz's *Ibéria;* Falla's engaging ballet score *The Three-Cornered Hat;* Sibelius's Symphonies Nos. 5 and 7; Respighi's *The Birds* and *Old Airs and Dances for Lute*, his *Fountains* and *Pines of Rome.*

23

AMERICAN MUSIC

Virgil Thomson once observed in a review of a work by Howard Hanson that Hanson had written lots of music, which made him a real composer, but that the music was as standardized in expression as it was eclectic in style, which made him not a real creator. I would say this of a great many other American composers, past and present—among them Samuel Barber and Gian-Carlo Menotti. And I would go further and say that some Americans haven't really created anything even in music that has *not* been standardized and eclectic. I felt this about Roy Harris, whose music was heard a great deal a few years ago; and I feel it about William Schuman and others whose music is heard a great deal nowadays.

But the stamp of real creative power is, I think, unmistakable in the music of Charles T. Griffes (1884–1920)—in the early *Roman Sketches* for piano that he wrote in a language and style derived from French impressionistic piano music of fifty years ago; in the later Sonata in which he struck out in a new language and style related to the "modern" tendencies of his time, producing a work that is impressive by the authoritative manipulation of the materials rather than effective as musical communication.

That creative power was as unmistakable in Aaron Copland's engaging *Music for the Theater* when it was first heard in 1925. And it remained so even in the unattractive, inaccessible works written in an austere, harshly dissonant "modern" idiom that came after *Music for the Theater*—notably the *Piano Variations* (1930). But one was glad to have it manifest itself again in the lovely and accessible ballet score *Billy the Kid* (1938), the first of a series of such ballet and film scores written in this new, simpler and more attractive idiom, which have continued to be more engaging than the occasional instrumental works. And the most recent dramatic score, the opera *The Tender Land*, seems to me the finest—Copland's largest and most richly filled-out canvas, so to speak. (Earlier I spoke of Copland's attempt, in a book he published in 1941, to persuade us that music like Schönberg's in Europe or his own *Piano Variations* here, when rightly heard and understood, was as natural and acceptable to our ears, as interesting to our minds, as people a hundred years ago found their music. In that connection it is interesting to note that in 1938 Copland had written the first of the ballet and film scores which Arthur Berger, in his excellent book on Copland, tells us represented his decision to stop writing esoteric abstract works for a small special public and write instead music that would interest the large general music public—a decision implying recognition that music like Schönberg's in Europe or Copland's *Piano Variations* here was *not* as natural and acceptable to our ears, as interesting to our minds, as people a hundred years ago found their music.)

In more recent instrumental music Harold Shapero's *Symphony for Classical Orchestra* has impressed me with the creative power I have been talking about. It is evocative of the past but stamped with the impress of Shapero's mind in the way some of Stravinsky's works are; and it is like Stravinsky's also in the assured mastery of the operation and the engaging result.

In opera the distinguished creative achievements other than Copland's *The Tender Land* have been Virgil Thomson's *Four Saints in Three Acts* and *The Mother of Us All*. Thomson, whom I don't find successful with autonomously organized instrumental pieces, is brilliantly successful with music organized around words—specifically the words of Gertrude Stein, which he uses in those two works. His music separates, differentiates, articulates the endless repetitions, gives them point, structure, climax, and achieves something unique, delightful, often very funny, sometimes very moving. Also very fine is Thomson's score for the ballet *Filling Station*.

But what about Menotti's operas? I have already indicated that the music is derivative in a profusion of styles ranging from contemporary down to Puccini and even lower; and I listened to *Amahl and the Night Visitors*, as I have in fact listened to Menotti's other operas, with incredulous amazement—finding it difficult to believe I was really hearing these sugary, trashy tunes, that they could even have occurred to anyone operating as a serious composer today, that he could not have been too embarrassed to let anyone else hear them, and that other people could have considered them worth publishing to the world. But a lot of people like Puccini and worse; and the other reason for Menotti's success—his success even with sophisticated and professional listeners—is his choice of dramatic subjects whose development powerfully engages the audience's interest and emotions—so powerfully, in fact, that the audience is misled into thinking its interest and emotions are being powerfully engaged by the music, whereas actually the most striking fact about *The Consul* was the expressive inadequacy of the mellifluous melodic idiom for the moments of dramatic climax that it expanded in the arias and ensembles.

And what about Gershwin's *Porgy and Bess?* Gershwin's career as a serious composer represented the fallacious idea that since he was an outstanding writer of distinctively American show tunes, he was the man to write the distinctively American symphony and opera, and those show tunes were the material to make it out of—which was like saying the Austrian symphony or opera had to be made by Johann Strauss out of his waltzes. If Johann Strauss had acted on this idea he would have produced works like Gershwin's Piano Concerto and *Porgy and Bess*, which are filled with characteristic Gershwin show music that communicates exactly what it would communicate in a musical show. And *Porgy* represents the additional fallacy, that because the American Negro has contributed to the amalgam of Broadway show music, Broadway show tunes are the right musical medium for any drama about Negroes: we have, then, Negro life in Catfish Row expressed in tunes like *Summertime* and *Bess, You Is My Woman Now* that one might have heard sung by white singers in a Gershwin musical, and that don't acquire any meaning connected with Negroes in Catfish Row when they are sung by colored singers in *Porgy and Bess*. In addition we have these tunes alternating with even more glaringly incongruous material in styles borrowed from grand opera—like the recitative in which Catfish Row Negroes sing such facts as that they will have to get up at five o'clock the next morning.

Only in *An American in Paris* does Gershwin invent delightfully imaginative non-show-music material, in addition to the superb blues in the middle. In this piece he also is able to integrate his material in a coherent form; and it is for me his one success as a serious composer.

The fallacious thinking responsible for *Porgy and Bess* is responsible also for what has been called an "American folk opera"—Kurt Weill's *Down in the Valley*. Here it is folk songs that are the right musical medium for any play about rural folk; so that we have the rural characters of *Down in the Valley* singing their anguish and terror and other powerful emotions in expressively unrelated American folk melodies separated from their own texts. And as if this weren't enough, when the man about to be hanged thinks with desperate longing of his girl, or she thinks similarly of him, each breaks into what in actual style—including Robert Russell Bennett style of orchestration—is a leading tenor's or soprano's number in a Broadway musical.

A word, finally, about Charles Ives (1874-1954). The great to-do in recent years about the originality that showed itself in his use of this or that revolutionary procedure many years before Schönberg seems to me to be about what is unimportant: the important thing is what music Ives produced with whatever technique he used. In the Symphony No. 2, then, one hears occasional lovely writing, especially in the slow portions; but one hears it in a progression that rambles on, shifting from one thing to another in one tempo and another, with no integration and no cumulative effect. The best of Ives's music is fitful and eccentric in that way; but some of it is like the Symphony No. 3, which did not, when I heard it, register on my mind as a coherent and meaningful piece of musical thinking.

24

PERFORMANCE

There is a record of a rehearsal at the 1950 Prades Festival in which Casals stops to explain to the orchestra: "Every note is variety—this is what gives life—otherwise it's something dry. . . ." And it is fascinating to hear him achieve with the orchestra the enlivening inflection of melodic phrase and accompanying figuration that makes the Prades Festival performances of Bach so extraordinary.

The principle that Casals states to the orchestra he also illustrates in his own playing of the cello. The record of the rehearsal is included as a bonus in the volume of 1951 Perpignan Festival performances of chamber music of Beethoven (Columbia SL-169); and in the performance of the great *Archduke* Trio one hears an impressive demonstration of the exciting life that Casals creates in music with the bold inflections and distentions of his powerfully sustained tone in powerfully sustained phrasing.

String tone lends itself to sustained phrasing; not so piano tone, which begins to die out as soon as it is struck. And one remarkable feature of Schnabel's playing of the piano in the service of his playing of music was his ability to create continuity and tension from one note to the next, which made a phrase of melody not a mere succession of notes but something with the continuous life one hears in the phrase of Casals. This, and the ability to carry the tension beyond the phrase through the entire movement, can be heard in the famous performance of the concluding movement of Beethoven's Sonata Op. 111 on Angel COLH-63—the sustained progression from the spaciously meditative opening to the superearthly end.

To speak of continuity and cohesive tension is to speak of what is outstanding in a Toscanini performance: once the progression begins it never sags, but keeps going with the unfailing continuity of impetus, tension and shape in the developing form of sound that is as remarkable in the performance of Ponchielli's *Dance of the Hours* on Victor LM-1834, as in the old performance of Beethoven's *Leonore* No. 1 Overture on Victor LCT-1041. The continuity of shape is achieved by the continuity and coherence in tempo and sonority that also are characteristic of a Toscanini performance—the coherence of the tempos that relate the successive sections in the finale of Beethoven's Ninth on Victor LM-6009 in a single coherent progression from one dazzling sublimity to the next.

Toscanini's delighted exclamation once, "It's like reading the score," as he listened to a recorded performance of his, expressed his basic principle that the shape of a work in living sound should be the one indicated by the composer's directions in the printed score. But another observation of his—that Mozart could be boring if the conductor didn't know what to do between the *p* in the first measure and the *f* eight measures later—made it clear that realizing in sound what was on the printed page was not for him a matter just of producing the *p* here and the *f* eight measures later; and in the performance of Mozart's G minor on Victor LM-1789 one hears a great deal of enlivening inflection between the *p* and the *f*—as one hears also in Casals's and Schnabel's performances. The two statements did however define the type of performance these musicians produced: the performance in which the inflections of tempo and sonority stay within the limits set by the composer's directions—whether the infrequent directions of Mozart or the frequent ones of Debussy—and make precisely detailed the forms in sound which those directions outline roughly.

Nor was Toscanini's exclamation concerned only with shape: it expressed his basic principle that whatever is printed in the score must be heard distinctly in the performance. An enormous amount of effort at rehearsals went into balancing the instrumental sonorities to produce the clarity and transparency of texture, the distinctness of strands in that texture, that one hears in his performance—whether of Beethoven's Ninth or of Debussy's *Ibéria* on Victor LM-1833. Not only effort: to make them heard against the weight of strings and brass he doubled the woodwinds in Beethoven's Ninth; and to achieve similar clarity and distinctness he made many such changes in Debussy's scoring of *La Mer*. But there were instances when he had to accept failure: "I have tried everything," he said once sadly, pointing to the bassoon part in one of the tuttis of Beethoven's *Consecration of the House* Overture, "but I am afraid I will never hear these bassoons."

The good in art becomes the criterion by which one recognizes the bad; and that is true of performance, but with at least one qualification. The good performance is the one that realizes in living sound the form indicated by the composer's directions about tempo and sonority; but the performance that changes this shape with tempos and sonorities different from those the composer asks for is not necessarily bad. We accept it as valid if it is consistent with what we think is the expressive character of the work, and if in addition it has the other characteristics I have mentioned: if it is coherent in tempo and sonority, continuous in impetus, tension and shape. What is bad, then, in the performances in which Stokowski changes the composer's tempos and sonorities is that they distort the works to the point of sheer elephantiasis and give music by Bach or Mozart or Musorgsky the expressive effect of the love duet in Wagner's *Tristan und Isolde* or the Bacchanale in *Tannhäuser*. So with the distortions that Koussevitzky introduced into nineteenth-century music with his over-emphatic changes of tempo and sonority. But bad too, on the other hand, were Koussevitzky's performances of eighteenth-century music with no enlivening inflection at all, which revealed his lack of the knowledge of what to do between the *p* here and the *f* eight measures later—the smooth, silky performances of Mozart, for example, that someone characterized well as "a brilliant façade concealing the absence of thought."

There is, then, a distinction to be made between a performer's playing of his instrument and his playing of music. It is a distinction which doesn't occur to most of the people hearing the beautiful and exciting sounds produced by a Stokowski or a Koussevitzky, a Heifetz or a Horowitz, and which is difficult for them to understand when someone else makes it: to perform music is, after all, to produce the sounds; to produce beautiful sounds would seem to be to perform it well; and performances by great virtuosos would seem to be not good and bad but only different. It isn't easy for these people to understand that the dazzling beauty of Heifetz's tone represents masterly playing of the violin, but that his fussy, wailing inflection of this tone often produces a sentimentalizing and cheapening performance of the music he is playing. Or that Horowitz's infinite gradations of piano tone represent masterly manipulation of the piano, but that the unvarying mannered manipulation of melodic phrase employing these infinite gradations of tone is his one way of operating with every composer—whether Chopin or Schubert or Mozart or Scarlatti—and a way that is good for none.

The difference, then, with Toscanini, Casals, Schnabel, Szigeti, Cantelli, and only a very few others is that in addition to being great performers on their instruments (I say this with full awareness of Schnabel's occasional blurring of difficult passage-work and Szigeti's occasional wiry tone) they are great performers of music. And this is true also of singers like Flagstad, Steber, Bjoerling, and in earlier years Rethberg, Matzenauer, Schipa, Hempel, McCormack. In his recorded performance of *O Paradiso!* Caruso, arriving at a high B flat, holds and expands it from *pp* to an overwhelming *ff*, then breaks off to take breath before completing the phrase; whereas Bjoerling, in his recorded performance, connects the expanded B flat with the next note as part of the continuous and beautifully shaped phrase: in the Caruso performance, then, one hears an exceptionally beautiful voice and a mastery in its manipulation; in the Bjoerling not only these but the art in musical phrasing that Caruso did not have. This vocal art in the service of beautiful musical art is what one hears in Flagstad's singing in *Dido and Aeneas*, Rethberg's singing of *Ave Maria* from *Otello*, Hempel's of *Deh vieni non tardar* from *Figaro*.

25

JAZZ

In addition to what the creative powers of a Griffes, a Copland, a Virgil Thomson have produced operating on one emotional level, there is what such powers have produced operating on another emotional level: the superb show music of Kern, Berlin, Gershwin, Rodgers, Porter, and others; the superb creative performances of jazz musicians like Louis Armstrong and Bix Beiderbecke. As against the well-oiled performances of written-out arrangements by large bands—whether in the smooth "sweet" style of Guy Lombardo or the vigorous "hot" style of Benny Goodman —the ones I call creative are the freely improvisatory "hot" performances by small groups of players. Recording has given permanent life to some of these performances and makes it possible to hear and discuss them as one does a piece by Haydn or Berlioz.

As a matter of fact when we listen to an early Armstrong cornet solo we hear something similar to what is so exciting in Haydn and Berlioz: the moment-to-moment working of a mind which we observe this time in the very process of creation, operating with an inventive exuberance that is controlled by a sense for coherent developing form.

In addition to the Armstrong performances with his Hot Five (1925) and Hot Seven (1927) on Columbia CL-851 and 852, there are the ones with Earl Hines at the piano (1928) on 853, and the ones with large commercial bands

(1928) on 854. They document his playing and singing from the time when these operated in the framework and context of the integrated performances of the Hot Five and Seven that were still close to their New Orleans origins of group improvisation, to the time when a big band merely provided a plushy background for the solo entertainer who began with a sensitively ornamented trumpet statement of a current song hit, continued with an extravagantly free vocal treatment of it, and carried this to its climax in a final spectacular trumpet solo. And listening to the groups of performances together we perceive how much better the Hot Fives and Sevens are, as wholes, than the performances of the Earl Hines combination, brilliant and exciting though these are; and also how much better Armstrong's own work is in those early performances, superb and beautiful though it is in later ones— e.g. the 1928 *Muggles* and *West End Blues*, the 1929 *I Can't Give You Anything but Love*. Within the framework and context of the Hot Five and Seven performances Armstrong's solos, no matter how impassioned, how fantastic, how breathtaking in their virtuosity, remain under control and complete their developing structure; but already in the performances with Hines we hear the spectacular getting to be formless at times, as in those series of ever higher high notes; and we hear this carried to its occasionally incoherent extreme in the concluding exhibitions of trumpet virtuosity of the 1929 performances.

Armstrong did some of his finest creative playing with singers—notably with Bessie Smith. Her performances on the four Columbia records document the change in the material she sang—from the authentic blues with which she began as a Negro folk singer, to the popular songs and novelty numbers of her later years as a vaudeville entertainer. They also document the succession of jazz musicians who recorded with her—from Clarence Williams, the pianist of her first recording of *Down-Hearted Blues* in 1923, and Louis Armstrong, Joe Smith, Charlie Green and others of Fletcher Henderson's band, to the group including Jack Teagarden,

Chu Berry and Buck Washington that played at her last re-cording session ten years later. But they document no change in the magnificent voice and style: the long phrases with their powerful momentums and tensions and wonderful inflections of rhythm and pitch that one hears at the beginning are heard all the way to the end, and exercise their effect in her every performance, no matter of what or with whom. Which doesn't keep us from preferring the performances of the best music with the best players; and for me these are the *Cold in Hand Blues*, *You've Been a Good Ole Wagon*, *Reckless Blues* and *St. Louis Blues* that Bessie recorded with Armstrong in 1925, and the *Baby Doll* and *Lost Your Head Blues* that she recorded with Joe Smith in 1926, which are outstanding among the excellent performances on Columbia CL-855 and 857. Smith does some beautifully sensitive trumpet-playing around her singing; and Armstrong produces on muted cornet a pro-gression of delicate, florid and derisive comment that gets to be hilariously funny.

As for Beiderbecke, the one phrase of the late Otis Ferguson that has remained in my memory is his characterization of a Beiderbecke performance years ago: "as fresh and glistening as creation itself." It was more successful than my own at-tempts to describe what made the playing unique and, for some people, more exciting and moving than any other: "the unfailing continuity in the varied invention; the tensile strength of the continuous line of cornet sound, and at the same time its delicacy; the boldly soaring attack or rise to a high point, the sensitive fall away from this high point or at the end of a phrase." I find these terms inadequate; but I have no better ones now for what, in Beiderbecke's first phrase in *I'm Coming Virginia*, sends chills down my spine and brings tears to my eyes. This and other of his outstanding recorded performances—*Singin' the Blues*, *Clarinet Marmalade*, *Ostrich Walk*, *Riverboat Shuffle*—are on Columbia CL-845; and on 844 are the outstanding *Jazz Me Blues*, *Sorry*, *Since My Best Gal Turned Me Down*, *Thou Swell* and *Ol' Man River*—the last two

188

being examples of his wonderfully sensitive "straight" playing of hit songs.

Recording gives continued life to these improvised performances—but only as long as the records continue in print; and a number of outstanding performances have had their lives ended, for the time being, by the discontinuance of the records. There was the Johnny Dodds *Wild Man Blues* on Brunswick 58004, with an Armstrong cornet solo more controlled and less extravagant than the one in the *Wild Man Blues* on Columbia CL-852. There was Jess Stacy's piano-playing in *The World Is Waiting for the Sunrise* on Decca 5133. There were the performances of the pianist Joe Sullivan, the cornetist Muggsy Spanier and the clarinetist Frank Teschmaker in several famous examples of the exciting Chicago ensemble style: the Chicago Rhythm Kings *There'll Be Some Changes Made* and *I've Found a New Baby* on Brunswick 58017; the Miff Mole *Shim-Me-Sha-Wabble* on Columbia CL-632, which had also the McKenzie and Condon Chicagoans *China Boy* and *Sugar*, and the Condon Footwarmers *Makin' Friends* featuring the superb trombonist Jack Teagarden. There were a number of the best—i.e. the early (1927 to 1931)—Duke Ellington performances on Brunswick 58002, in which the band was still small (ten or twelve men); the arranged ensembles and backgrounds were still quite simple in harmony and style, leaving plenty of room for the soloists to play with freedom and at length; and the playing of the entire band had the relaxed freedom and vitality of jazz performance.

Some of these early Ellington performances may now be on Columbia C3L. And as I write, Jess Stacy's playing in the *Blues of Israel* that was on Decca 5134 can be heard on English Parlophone PMC-1222; Victor LPM-1246 still offers some of the best performances of the pianist Fats Waller; LPM-1443 includes the superb performances with Louis Armstrong and Jack Teagarden at a 1948 concert in Town Hall. Also, Columbia C3L-22, with the performances of Mildred Bailey

—each made a delight by the exquisite inflection of the lovely small voice in phrasing whose subtle displacement of accents is controlled by a feeling for the shape of the phrase (as against the extravagant freedom with rhythm and notes in Billie Holiday's later singing that makes what is sung no longer recognizable as the phrases of the song)—offers with Bailey's singing the exciting playing of small groups that have Teddy Wilson, Mary Lou Williams, Billy Kyle and Ellis Larkin at the piano. And several performances recorded late in 1935—in particular *Some Day*, *Sweetheart* and *Willow Tree*— are made especially notable by the fresh and richly inventive playing Wilson was doing at that time. One cannot hear his marvelous playing in the Red Norvo *I Surrender, Dear* and *Blues in E flat* that were transferred to Epic LN-3128; but his incandescent performance in *What a Little Moonlight Can Do* can still be heard on Columbia CL-637, which has *Miss Brown to You*, *I Wished on the Moon* and others that Wilson recorded at that early time with the young Billie Holiday.

26

CRITICISM

The comments of Berlioz on *Selva opaca* from *William Tell* that I quoted in my discussion of Rossini occur in the long essay on *Tell* that Berlioz wrote for the *Gazette musicale de Paris* in 1834 and that is reprinted in Strunk's *Source Readings in Music History*. I consider this one essay well worth the price of the entire volume; but at the very least it is worth a visit to the library; for it is, as far as I know, the only article available in print here of the formal music criticism Berlioz wrote for French periodicals and newspapers, and I know no better introduction to the writing of the greatest of music critics. And remembering again how indiscriminately the word *great* is tossed about, I will establish what I mean when I apply it to Berlioz's criticism.

What I mean is much the same as what I meant when I applied it to Beethoven's music. Not only does one find in Berlioz's criticism the critical perception that is the absolute essential in such writing; not only does one find this perception formulating itself with literary brilliance and delightful gaiety and wit. In addition one finds—behind all the literary brilliance and gaiety—that perception dealing rigorously with the work of art before it; and with this integrity in relation to the material there is an intensity, a passion, a greatness of spirit in the operation that bring tears to my eyes whenever I read the writing.

These personal qualities appear most vividly of course in the personal writing—the *Memoirs*, the letters. Consider for example the letter in which Berlioz tells his father of his determination to become a composer:

I am willingly swept away toward a magnificent career (one can apply no other term to a career in the arts) and not toward my ruin; for I believe I will succeed, yes, I believe it: the matter is no longer one for considerations of modesty; to prove to you that I am leaving nothing to chance I think, I am convinced that I will distinguish myself in music, every outward sign points to it; and in myself the voice of nature is stronger than the strictest decrees of reason. I have all imaginable odds in my favor if you will back me; I won't need to give lessons like so many others to be sure of a living; I possess some fields of knowledge and elements of others, of a kind that will enable me one day to deepen them; and certainly I have experienced passions strong enough for me not to make mistakes whenever there will be need to represent them or give them voice [make them speak].

If I were condemned mercilessly to die of hunger in the event of failure (this would not lessen my persistence, I assure you) your arguments at least and your anxiety would be more justified; but that is not the case, and on the lowest estimate I am convinced that I will be able one day to have an income of two thousand francs; but let us say only fifteen hundred francs, I will live even on this sum; let us say only twelve hundred, I would be satisfied, [and?] even if music were to bring me nothing. In short I want to make a name for myself, I want to leave on earth some traces of my existence; and such is the strength of this feeling, which has within it nothing but what is noble, that I would rather be Gluck or Mehul dead than what I am in the prime of life.

That is the way I think, that is what I am, and nothing in the world will be able to change me; you could withdraw all help from me or force me to leave Paris, but I don't believe that, you wouldn't want in this way to make me lose the best years of my life, and break the magnetic needle which you cannot prevent from obeying the attraction of the poles.

Farewell, my dear papa, reread my letter, and do not ascribe it to some excited impulse, never perhaps have I been more calm. I embrace you affectionately as well as Mama and my sisters.

Your respectful and affectionate son,

H. Berlioz

I share Turner's doubt that one can read this without being moved, and especially moved if one knows what came of those confident hopes—if one has read Berlioz's own account in his *Memoirs* of the experiences that lead him to write twenty years later:

> . . . I end . . . with profuse thanks to sacred Germany where the worship of art has kept itself pure; to you, generous England; to you, Russia, who saved me; to you, my good friends in France; to you, lofty hearts and minds of all nations whom I have known. I was fortunate in knowing you; I have, and I will faithfully keep, the most precious memory of our relations. As for you, maniacs, stupid mastiffs and bulls, as for you my Guildensterns, my Rosencrantzes, my Iagos, my little Osrics, serpents and insects of every kind, "farewell my . . . friends"; I despise you, and I hope not to die before I have forgotten you.

The *Memoirs*, then, is something to read because it is a remarkable and superbly written personal document. But also, in the absence of English translations of published collections of Berlioz's formal critical writings, the *Memoirs* is valuable for the incidental observations on music one encounters in it.

The only collection of Berlioz's letters available in English, the *New Letters of Berlioz 1830-1868*, offers a poor selection (few of the personal letters that are so moving; many letters concerned with plans, negotiations and arrangements for publication and performance) poorly and inaccurately translated.

In addition to his formal music criticism, some of which he collected in the volume *A travers Chants*, Berlioz wrote feuilletons—imaginative, ironic, witty, and often very funny. Of the two published collections, *Les Soirées de l'orchestre* and *Les Grotesques de la musique*, only the first was published here as *Evenings in the Orchestra* in a translation that was old-fashioned but that may turn out to be preferable to the new one by the translator of the *New Letters*.

For music criticism comparable with Berlioz's—the finest written in English, and some of the finest in any language—read the concert reviews and articles of Bernard Shaw. You may be surprised to hear that he did such writing; but the fact is you will do better to read what he said about a performance at Covent Garden in 1890 than what you will find in a newspaper about a performance at the Metropolitan today—or for that matter what Shaw himself said later about world events. He was not a great spirit; but the music criticism he wrote in his early thirties reveals a genial and attractive human being astonishingly different from the perversely unpleasant and silly world-figure of later years. And it reveals him, at that early period, using vast resources of literary brilliance, fun and wit in the service of a distinguished critical perception and taste in music that is an additional agreeable surprise to someone familiar only with the later Shaw who concerned himself almost exclusively with politics and sociology. In his method of operation as a critic, then, Shaw resembles Berlioz; and what makes him a great critic is an integrity like Berlioz's in relation to his material—the fact that behind all the brilliance and fun and wit the critical perception and taste deals rigorously with what is before it. And the result is a flow of comment on the daily events of those distant musical seasons that is still some of the most discerning, the most instructive, the most enjoyable you can read in any language.

You are not likely to be interested in the performance of Boito's *Mefistofele* that Shaw wrote about on May 29, 1889; but it provided the occasion for his observation that Gounod's *Faust* was "a true musical creation, whereas Boito has only adapted the existing resources of orchestration and harmony very ably to his libretto"—which embodies an instructive distinction you will find useful when you listen to much of the new music written today. And relevant to some opera productions you may see today is Shaw's remark that "the house likes Boito's prologue, in spite of the empty stage and the two ragged holes in a cloth which realize Mr. Harris's modest conception of hell and heaven."

In no newspaper today are you likely to encounter the accurate perception and good sense of Shaw's comment after a performance of Brahms's *Requiem*. The audience's delusion that "Brahms is a great composer, and the performance of this masterpiece of his an infinitely solemn and important function" was, he says, "not confined to those who, having found by experience that good music bores them, have rashly concluded that all music that bores them must be good. It raged also among the learned musicians, who know what a *point d'orgue* is, and are delighted to be able to explain what is happening when Brahms sets a pedal pipe booming and a drum thumping the dominant of the key for ten minutes at a stretch, whilst the other instruments and the voices plough along through every practicable progression in or near the key, up hill from syncopation to syncopation, and down dale from suspension to suspension in an elaborately modernized manner that only makes the whole operation seem more desperately old-fashioned and empty." And adding that Brahms seems to have thought he could produce more remarkable effects than Beethoven by keeping his pedal-points going even longer than Beethoven's, Shaw observes that while the academics like this sort of thing the genuine musician dislikes nothing more than "an attempt to pass off the forms of music for music itself, especially those forms which have received a sort of consecration from their use by great composers in the past"—which neatly exposes Brahms's classicism for what it is.

Nor on the other hand will you find anything more perceptive on Verdi than what Shaw wrote after Verdi's death—his

THE NEW LISTENER'S COMPANION

insistence, for example, that there was no evidence in a single measure of his last three operas that Verdi had heard a note of Wagner, but evidence instead that he had heard Mendelssohn and Beethoven, whose music "is the music of a Germany still under that Franco-Italian influence which made the music of Mozart so amazingly unlike the music of Bach. Of the later music that was consciously and resolutely German and German only . . . of the music of Schumann, Brahms and Wagner, there is not anywhere in Verdi the faintest trace. In German music the Italian loved what Italy gave. What Germany offered of her own music he entirely ignored." This is still the answer to those who even today will have it that the writing in Verdi's last operas represents the influence of Wagner.

Of the four volumes of Shaw's music criticism in the complete edition of his writings published in England only the first, *London Music in 1888-1889 as Heard by Corno di Bassetto*, was published here; but the three of *Music in London 1890-1894* can be found in libraries; and a paper-cover volume has just been published with a selection from all four.

The gaiety of Berlioz and Shaw is not in W. J. Turner: even his irony, however intense, is quiet. He writes with a poet's precision of statement, in the expression of a poet's insights. Those insights give us the illuminating statements about Mozart; they also enable him to make this astonishing observation after Toscanini's concerts in London in 1935— that as he had sat watching Toscanini he "was suddenly reminded of Berlioz's remark: 'Do you think I make music for my pleasure?' I am certain that it is not a pleasure for Toscanini to conduct, but rather that he suffers. It is because of his extreme musical sensibility and intense concentration. Here lies the essence of his superiority." Astounding, because it was written fifteen years before an afternoon on which Toscanini said: "Conducting is for me great suffering. When I am alone with the score I am very happy; when I am on the podium

I am always afraid. I am afraid the horn will be late, the clarinet will not play correct. . . ."

Turner, with the same dislike of Brahms the serious composer as Shaw's, expresses it in different terms. Explaining why he rates the Haydn Variations and the final passacaglia movement of the Fourth Symphony highest in Brahms's work, he says it is because in his variation-writing Brahms is not "being a poet (in the Aristotelian sense) or a great creator; he is merely being a musician"—that is, a craftsman. "I do not like Brahms when he goes forth to battle. . . . Brahms was much too earnest, and to be earnest is always to be ridiculous, since it is given only to the elect, the few supremely great—a Beethoven, for example—to be not earnest but serious. . . . But Brahms when he is being entirely natural and self-forgetful, when he is not at all obsessed by the tramp of Beethoven behind him . . . then he is a truly great and inspired musician."

Of the four collections of Turner's reviews and articles only the first, *Music and Life*, was published here and can be found in a few libraries. Of his other books the *Mozart* is still available; the *Beethoven* is in a few libraries; but the *Berlioz* was not published here.

In this country the writings of Philip Hale and H. T. Parker are worth investigating in the library; but the only newspaper music criticism worth reading in recent years was Virgil Thomson's; and the three collections of his reviews and articles —*The Musical Scene*, *The Art of Judging Music*, and *Music Right and Left*—contain numerous examples of the operation of a critical apparatus of perception and intellect that would make the writing a pleasure to read even without its additional delights of felicitous and witty statement. But I must add that with those pieces of distinguished criticism there are many pieces of irresponsible nonsense.

The difference between sense and nonsense with Thomson is most often the difference between the writing in which his mind is in contact with the real facts that are before him—the facts that one recognizes in the music or performance he is discussing; and on the other hand the writing which deals with things one cannot discover in the music or performance—things which exist only in his head, and to which he applies ideas with no more basis in reality. When, in explanation of his opinion that "Horowitz's playing is monotonous and, more often than not, musically false," Thomson writes that Horowitz "never states a simple melody frankly. He teases it by accenting unimportant notes and diminishing his tonal volume on all the climactic ones. The only contrast to brio that he knows is the affettuoso style"—he describes what anyone can hear in the playing. So when he writes that "Mitropoulos has taken over the Philharmonic-Symphony concerts like an occupying army," refers to Mitropoulos's "Panzer division tactics," and amplifies this with the observations that "all is discipline, machine finish, tension and power" and "he makes every piece . . . sound nervous and violent." But I don't recognize in Yvonne Lefebure's pianoplaying what Thomson describes in his statement that "her differentiations between time and accent also aid orchestral evocation, because melodic passages, as on the *bel canto* instruments, are played without downbeat stresses, the accentual pattern being rendered, as in real orchestral playing, by sharp pings, deep bell strokes, and articulations recalling those of harp, bow-heel, and the orchestra's percussion group." Nor do I recognize Toscanini's performances in Thomson's contention that they have meter but not rhythm, and still less in his mumbo-jumbo about the marriage of historical and literary with musical culture in the Great Tradition of Wagner, von Bülow, Nikisch and Beecham that is lacking in Toscanini's conducting.

Much of Thomson's writing is a spinning out of such fancy schematizing ideas about facts imagined or altered to fit; and much of this schematization is concerned with tradition. An article *Tradition Today*, for example, is about the conductors, dominantly exemplified for Thomson by Reiner and Monteux, who operate as the preservers of "the traditions of interpretation as these have been handed down," as against men like Stokowski and Koussevitzky who operate rather with "a highly personalized ability to hold attention"; about American conductors of the second type who "have the excuse of having passed their youth out of contact with a major musical tradition, of not having known the classics early enough to feel at home with them"; and about one of them, Leonard Bernstein, who "knows what American music is all about, but the western European repertory he is obliged to improvise. . . . That is why, I think, he goes into such chorybantic ecstasies in front of it. He needs to mime, for himself and others, a conviction that he does not have. He does no such act before American works of his own time. He takes them naturally, reads them with authority." And I might add that in conversation Thomson once ascribed a similar ignorance to Toscanini, contending that whereas Toscanini had learned the operatic traditions in the opera house, he had found himself, at fifty, having to deal with the symphonic repertory without knowledge of *its* traditions, and had solved the problem by doing a complete streamlining job on the music.

Actually Bernstein and Toscanini learned the classics as early, and in the same way, as Reiner and Monteux. If Toscanini began his career in the opera house it was because that is where a conductor usually begins in Europe: Muck, Mahler, Walter, Reiner all conducted opera before they conducted the symphonic repertory. And when Toscanini began to conduct this repertory—at thirty, not at fifty—it was with the knowledge of the music and of the traditions of its performance that he had acquired in his youth in the same way as those other conductors: from hearing it performed and studying the scores. The striking differences in Toscanini's performances of symphonic music, like those in his performances of opera, represented not his ignorance of tradition but the modification of it by his personal musical taste: what

Thomson called streamlining was actually a personal performing style which, in opera no less than in symphonic music, tended toward plastic simplicity, economy and subtlety—which, for example, tended to set a single subtly modified tempo for the several sections of a movement. Toscanini would have been open to criticism for this only if the tradition had had the authority Thomson mistakenly endows it with: if, that is, it had gone back in a straight line to an authoritative first performance. But actually the line had begun with first performances that had represented nothing more authoritative than the judgment and taste each conductor had applied to what he had found in the score; it had continued with successive modifications of those performances by later conductors in accordance with *their* judgments and tastes; and there was nothing in all this that forbade further modifications by Toscanini in accordance with *his* judgment and taste.

The successive European performances were transferred to this country by the succession of European conductors who came here; and it was from them that American conductors, including Bernstein, learned in their youth the symphonic repertory and the traditions of its performance. It was, then, not for lack of knowledge of these traditions that Bernstein played Beethoven's *Eroica* badly; nor was it possession of this knowledge that caused him to play a Mozart symphony beautifully. And he went into the same chorybantic ecstasies before a Copland piece as before the Mozart.

But such failures of Thomson and the defects responsible for them are those of a man who also has produced some of the finest music criticism written anywhere. And Tovey's observation about Schubert can be applied to Thomson: his occasional weaknesses and inequalities do not make him a critic of less than the highest rank.

Tovey's observation can also be applied to the occasional weaknesses and inequalities of his own writing. These begin with his limitations of sympathy and understanding, which represent the ideas on the history of music that he absorbed from his teacher Parry. But it was also from Parry that he learned his procedure of point-to-point analysis of music; and this procedure, applied to works of composers for whom he does have sympathy and understanding, gives us those excitingly illuminating descriptions of the courses of events in Haydn's symphonies and Mozart's concertos in *Essays in Musical Analysis*—each of which achieves the primary purpose of criticism as it is defined by E. M. Forster: "It considers the [individual work of art] in itself, as an entity, and tells us what it can about its life." Moreover, this examination and description of the life in particular works underlies Tovey's generalizations of a composer's practice, such as are found in the monumental essays on Schubert and Haydn in *The Main Stream of Music*.

With the extraordinary musical perception there is the understanding and knowledge of a mind that has ranged widely in territory outside of music; and there is also formulation of this perception and understanding in statements that are often epigrammatic in their concentration and clarification of sense and their impact and brilliance. But sometimes the mind ranges so far afield, or the formulation becomes so epigrammatic, that the thought is obscure and difficult to follow. It is mostly in the articles and lectures on general matters—*Normality and Freedom in Music, The Main Stream in Music, Stimulus and the Classics of Music,* and others—that one finds the elliptically allusive or epigrammatic obscurities, the embarrassing professorial humor that are additional weaknesses and inequalities in Tovey's writing. And these don't in the slightest degree lessen the magnitude of the powers and achievements he exhibits elsewhere—the powers and achievements of the great critic who is able to describe in such illuminating fashion the courses of events in particular works of Schubert and Haydn, and to derive from these observations of particular behavior the illuminating general statements about each composer like this one about Schubert: "We are right in thinking that his maturest works in large instrumental forms are diffuse and inconsistent. . . . But when we find (as, for instance, in the first movement of the great C major Symphony) that some of the most obviously wrong digressions contain the profoundest, most beautiful, and most inevitable passages, then it is time to suspect that Schubert, like other great classics, is pressing his way toward new forms." Or this one about Haydn: "He is rightly believed to be on a level with Mozart as a master of form; but his form is described as 'regular and symmetrical.' And when you come to look at it, you find not only that all the rules of form as observed by both Mozart and Beethoven are frequently violated by Haydn, but that they are so seldom observed that it would be quite impossible to infer them from his mature practice at all. More recent writers have tried to show some recognition of this by saying that in Haydn's works we see the sonata forms 'in the making.' This only increases the confusion; for Haydn's most nearly regular works are his earlier ones, when he wrote on the lines of J. C. and C. P. E. Bach; whereas his freedom of form becomes manifest just about the time when he came to know Mozart. The mutual influence of Haydn and Mozart is one of the best-known wonders of musical history; and the paradox of it is that while its effect on Mozart was to concentrate his style and strengthen his symmetry, the effect on Haydn was to set him free, so that his large movements became as capricious in their extended course of events as his minuets had always been in the cast of their phrases."

Of the several other excellent books mentioned in earlier chapters Copland's *Music and Imagination*, containing his Charles Eliot Norton lectures at Harvard in 1951-52, includes a little of the fallacious ad hoc reasoning of the propagandist for contemporary music; but for the most part, in these lectures concerned with "the relation of the imaginative mind to the different aspects of the art of music," Copland is the critic—a critic operating with the special insight of the composer and a gift for felicitous statement. Concerning the enormous wealth of color combinations offered by the modern orchestra, for example, Copland remarks that it has been the undoing of the radio or movie orchestrator: "Where there is no true expressive purpose anything goes; in fact, everything goes, and it all goes into the same piece."

Dent's *Mozart's Operas* is a product of the unusual combination of scholarship which provides interesting information about Mozart's materials, problems and methods with each opera; esthetic perception which illuminates the final work of art; and a clear and graceful style which makes the writing a pleasure to read. And equally good is Dent's little Pelican book, *Opera*.

Sullivan's *Beethoven* and Toye's *Verdi* are two of the best books on individual composers; and others are Kirkpatrick's *Domenico Scarlatti*, Toye's *Rossini*, Walker's *Hugo Wolf*, Berger's *Aaron Copland*. And Wotton's *Hector Berlioz*, the one good book on Berlioz other than Turner's, is worth looking for in the library.

Finally, the three volumes of *Letters of Mozart and His Family*. They are interesting for the comments of Mozart and his father on the music of their contemporaries, and for the information they give us about the musical life of the period, which should correct some mistaken ideas about it that are still current. But their chief interest is in what they tell us about the personality and life of the most extraordinary musical genius we know of; and Mozart's own letters are fascinating and moving personal documents.

I should add that what the letters tell us about Mozart does not—as some would leap to conclude—reveal any additional meaning in the music that we wouldn't perceive without them: on the contrary, it is from the music that we learn of emotional and spiritual resources that we wouldn't know of from anything he said—resources which apparently only the artist was able to draw on, and which achieved explicit formulation only in his works of art. That is, Mozart's vivacity and love of fun are delightfully evident in the rush of absurdly mingled German and Italian in which, at the age of fourteen, he describes a performance of opera in Verona to his sister:

> . . . Oronte, il padre di Bradamanta, è un prencipe (fà il sign. afferi) un bravo cantante, un paritono, mà gezwungen, wen er in Falset hinauf, aber doch nicht so sehr, wie der Tibaldi zu Wien. Bradamante, figlia d' orionte, inamorata di Ruggiero mà (sie soll den Leone heyrathen, sie will ihm aber nicht), fà una povera Baronessa, che ha avuto una gran disgrazia, mà non sò che? Recita (unter einem fremden Nam, ich weiss aber den Namen nicht) ha una voce passabile, e la statura non sarebbe male, ma distona come il diavolo. Ruggiero un ricco principe, innamorato di Bradamanta, un Musico, canta un poco Manzolisch ed à una bellissima voce forte ed è già vecchio la cinquanta cinque anni ed à una leuffige gurgel. Leone, soll die Bradamanta heyrathen, reichissima est; ob er aber ausser dem Theatro reich ist, das weis ich nicht, fà una donna, la moglie di Afferri. à una bellissima voce, ma è tanto sussuro nell theatro, che non si sente niente. Irene fà una sorella di Lolli dell gran Violinisto, che abbiamo sentito a Vienna. à una schnoffelte voce, e canta sempre um ein viertil zu tardi, ò troppo à buon ora. . . .

But the letter tells us nothing that we can't hear—and nothing more than we do hear—when we listen to a musical embodiment of the vivacity and love of fun like the final rush of the Piano Concerto K.453. And from the letters we would know nothing of the sublimities we hear in the *Contessa, perdono* passage at the end of *Figaro*.

PART TWO

27

THE GREAT RECORDED
PERFORMANCES OF THE PAST

Replying to Toscanini's letter of resignation in 1954, David Sarnoff wrote that Toscanini's "incomparable re-creations of the great music of the past and present" had, happily, been "recorded and preserved for us, and for posterity." What he failed to add was that the recordings would be available to us and to posterity only if they continued to be bought in quantities that RCA Victor considered sufficient to justify continuing production. And actually, within a few years Victor had stopped producing some of Toscanini's recordings, so that as I write it is not possible to obtain the records with his truly "incomparable" performances of Mozart's Divertimento K.287, Berlioz's *Harold in Italy* and Strauss's *Don Quixote*. One reason for the drop in sales of Toscanini's recordings was the fact that the public buys the recordings of the currently active performers it reads about, not of the inactive performers it no longer reads about, not even inactive performers as famous as Toscanini. Another reason was the advent of stereo recording, which made Toscanini's recordings uninteresting to those who care more about the latest in sound than about the greatest in performance.

What happened in Toscanini's case has been happening ever since the beginning of commercial recording. Always the companies have talked about the phonograph's preserving performers' art for posterity; but always the recorded performances of yesterday have disappeared from the catalogues, to be replaced by those of today; and with each major change in recording technique—from acoustic to electrical 78-rpm recording, from 78-rpm to long-playing microgroove, and most recently from mono LP to stereo—the recordings made with the old technique have been replaced by recordings made with the new. And this chapter is concerned with some of the great recorded performances that have been lost in this way—performances which are worth hunting for in stores that sell old 78-rpm and LP records, and worth watching for among the occasional reissues.

What acoustic 78-rpm recording reproduced accurately was singing; and the records preserved some of the achievements in what has been called the golden age of singing—the age of Caruso, Melba, Tetrazzini, McCormack and their contemporaries. It must be noted that most of the singers in this period misused the music to show off their voices, instead of employing their voices in an effective presentation of the music; and what was recorded was performances like Caruso's of *Una furtiva lagrima,* in which the outpouring of vocal splendor burst the shape of the musical phrase, more often than performances like McCormack's of this aria, in which the beautiful voice was employed in a plastically coherent shaping of phrase. McCormack wasn't the only exception: the soprano Hempel, too, not only had as lovely a voice and as spectacular a technique as Melba and Tetrazzini but was the great musician they were not: no one in my experience has equalled her sustained phrasing in the closing section of *Dite alla giovine* from *La Traviata* in the performance she recorded with Amato. In addition there were at the Metropolitan the sopranos Gadski, Fremstad, Destinn, the contraltos Homer, Ober, Matzenauer, the tenors Slezak, Urlus, Jörn, all with remarkable voices which they used as superb musicians in an amazing variety of styles; and in Austria the soprano Kurz, in Russia the lyric tenor Sobinov.

Though acoustic recording didn't reproduce the symphony orchestra well, Victor did achieve a remarkable approximation of what I retained in my memory as the sound of the Boston Symphony conducted by Muck in its recordings of the Marche Miniature from Tchaikovsky's Suite No. 1, the finale of his Symphony No. 4, and the Prelude to Act 3 of *Lohengrin.*

The advent of electrical recording in the mid-twenties brought the beginning of realistic reproduction of the orchestra; and in the fifteen or twenty years that followed, Victor recordings preserved the achievements of what might be called a golden age of orchestral performance in this country, in which the Philadelphia Orchestra playing under Stokowski, the Boston Symphony under Koussevitzky, the New York Philharmonic under Toscanini —each a group of exceptionally competent performers sensitized to the direction of a conductor extraordinarily equipped with the ear for orchestral precision and sonority and with the personal force and technical mastery to achieve them—produced their marvels of virtuoso execution and, in accordance with the particular conductor's taste, the Philadelphia Orchestra's tonal sumptuousness and splendor, the Boston Symphony's refinement and subtlety of orchestral color, the New York Philharmonic's radiance, transparency and sharpness of definition. And again it must be noted that the Toscanini performances offered orchestral virtuosity in the service of his unfailing sense for plastic proportion and coherence in the shaping of phrase and larger structure, whereas those of Koussevitzky and Stokowski offered orchestral sonorities that were among the wonders of the age, but with Koussevitzky's italicizing plastic distortions of nineteenth-century music, his playing of eighteenth-century music with no enlivening inflection at all, and Stokowski's playing of almost everything with the fever and luxuriance suitable for the Bacchanale from *Tannhäuser* or the second-act duet from *Tristan und Isolde.*

Two Koussevitzky-Boston Symphony performances that were not only examples of dazzling orchestral virtuosity but admirable statements of the music were those of Mendelssohn's *Italian* Symphony, reproduced more realistically by Victor DM-1259 than by the early M-294, and Prokofiev's *Classical Symphony,* reproduced more realistically by DM-1241 than by 7196/7. And two of the best Stokowski-Philadelphia Orchestra performances were the Dances from *Prince Igor* on M-499, and the Debussy *Fêtes* on 2034 of M-630.

As for Toscanini, the incandescent operation with the New York Philharmonic that he never duplicated with another orchestra was reproduced most realistically by the 1936 recordings they made at the end of his last Philharmonic season—of Beethoven's Seventh, Brahms's *Variations on a Theme of Haydn,* Rossini's Overtures to *Semiramide* and *L'Italiana in Algeri,* and Wagner's Prelude to *Lohengrin, Dawn and Siegfried's Rhine Journey* from *Die Götterdämmerung,* and *Siegfried-Idyll.* But it

could be heard even in.the less realistically reproduced performances they recorded in 1929—of Haydn's Symphony No. 101
(*Clock*), Mozart's Symphony K.385 (*Haffner*), Mendelssohn's Scherzo from the music for *A Midsummer Night's Dream,* Rossini's
overture to *The Barber of Seville,* and Verdi's Preludes to Acts 1
and 3 of *La Traviata.*

In addition to documenting the incandescent operation of conductor and orchestra these recordings documented the Toscanini
performing style of that period—relaxed, expansive, articulating
and organizing and shaping the substance of a piece with much
elasticity of tempo, and molding the phrase with a great deal of
sharp inflection—as against the style of the later NBC Symphony
years that was simpler, tauter, swifter, setting a tempo that was
maintained with only slight modification, and giving the phrase
only subtle inflection. Further examples of the more effective and
impressive earlier style were the performances Toscanini recorded
with the BBC Symphony between 1937 and 1939—of Beethoven's
Symphonies Nos. 1, 4 and 6, his Overture *Leonore* No. 1, Mozart's
Overture to *The Magic Flute,* Rossini's Overture to *La Scala di
Seta,* and the Weber-Berlioz *Invitation to the Dance.* To these
were added the performances he recorded with the newly formed
NBC Symphony in 1938 and 1939—of Haydn's Symphony No.
88, Mozart's Symphony K.550 (the great G-minor), Beethoven's
Symphonies Nos. 3 (*Eroica*), 5 and 8, his Overtures *Leonore* Nos.
2 and 3 and *Egmont* (issued only in England), the Lento and
Vivace from his Quartet Op. 135, Rossini's Overture to *William
Tell*—which documented another characteristic of the early NBC
Symphony performances: their extraordinary energy and fire, the
result of the conductor's being stimulated by the unusual capacities and responsiveness of the many young virtuosos in the orchestra, and their being stimulated by his powers and dedication.

And a towering example of Toscanini's earlier style was the
Schubert Symphony No. 9 that he recorded with the Philadelphia
Orchestra in 1941, which Victor did not issue until 1963. Toscanini's untraditional performance gave this work a sustained tension, momentum and grandeur that it had in no other; and he
achieved with the Philadelphia Orchestra the greatest of his realizations of it—one that was more effective than the great performance he recorded in 1953 with the NBC Symphony. (The other

performances Toscanini recorded with the Philadelphia Orchestra in 1941-42—of Mendelssohn's *Midsummer Night's Dream* music, Berlioz's *Queen Mab*, Tchaikovsky's *Pathétique*, Debussy's *La Mer* and *Ibéria*—also were superior to those he recorded later with the NBC Symphony, and should also be issued by Victor.)

Most of the Toscanini performances available on Victor records in recent years were the ones he recorded with the NBC Symphony from 1944 on, and in his later simpler, subtler, tauter and swifter style. If one listens to both the 1941 and 1953 performances of Schubert's Ninth one hears that the early one is more effective than the later; but if one listens only to the later, one cannot imagine anything better. The available NBC Symphony performances are, then, not Toscanini's greatest; but they are great performances which one cannot imagine being surpassed even by Toscanini himself, and which one cannot hear equalled by any others—except the few recorded by Cantelli, and recently the Debussy *La Mer* and Stravinsky *Le Sacre du printemps* recorded by Boulez. And their greatness is evident even when they are defectively reproduced by the recording, as far too many of them are (of that, more later).

The performances on Victor records included the operas Toscanini broadcast with the NBC Symphony, concerning which the opera specialists among the record-reviewers, and Virgil Thomson among the music critics, created the myth that Toscanini used in these performances only the inexperienced and inferior singers who would submit to the tyranny of his "fast and rigid tempos" that "thwarted" singers' attempts to sing "expressively". Actually the singers he used were not inexperienced and inferior but some of the best available—Milanov, Albanese, Nelli, Merriman, Elmo, Peerce, Vinay, Warren, Valdengo—who sang as expressively with him in these concert performances as Hempel, Destinn, Homer, Matzenauer, Urlus, Rethberg, Lotte Lehmann and other famous singers of the past had done with him in the opera house. And one heard in the performances a coherent and beautiful plastic flow created by a beat that was never anything but flexible in relation to the music, and was unyielding in relation to the singers only in compelling them to operate within that flow. As against the usual performances in which the orchestra played perfunctorily in tempos that deferred to the singers' every ex-

hibitionistic extravagance, and which had no continuity, no coherence, no clarity of outline or texture, Toscanini's performances
offered accurately and beautifully shaped vocal phrases that fitted
precisely into the accurate and beautiful orchestral contexts whose
every detail was in active expressive relation to what was being
sung—all this in a progression that was clear, continuous and
coherent. They constituted striking illustrations of W. J. Turner's
analogy in explanation of the superiority of a Toscanini performance—the analogy of a poem printed clearly and correctly on
good paper, as against the poem printed in smudged ink on blot-
ting paper with the punctuation all wrong. And all of them—
the *La Traviata* with Albanese and Peerce, the *Otello* with Nelli,
Vinay and Valdengo, the *Aida* with Nelli and Valdengo, the
Falstaff with Valdengo, Nelli, Elmo, Merriman and Stich-Randall,
the *Un Ballo in Maschera* with Nelli and Peerce, the Act 4 of
Rigoletto with Milanov, Peerce and Warren, and even the *Fidelio*
with the title role sung inadequately by Bampton—produced the
effect of revelation.

An additional fact to mention is that the performances his
players recalled as having surpassed any others in their experience were not only his Schubert Ninth, his Mozart G-minor, his
Verdi *Otello,* his Debussy *La Mer,* but also the performances of
pieces like the *Skaters Waltz* and Overture to *Zampa.* One heard
in these the same exquisite molding of melodic phrase, the same
plastically coherent shaping, the same clarifying of texture and
structure, which produced the same effect of revelation. It was
not just that Toscanini's feeling for music was a feeling for any
music he performed—for the least as well as the greatest: it was
also that he performed the least as if it *was* the greatest—with the
same total commitment of his powers. He recorded a few of these
light or 'pop' numbers in his first years with the NBC Symphony:
Paganini's *Moto Perpetuo,* Strauss's *Tritsch-Tratsch Polka* and
Blue Danube Waltz, Waldteufel's *Skaters Waltz,* Sousa's *The
Stars and Stripes Forever,* the Overture to Thomas's *Mignon.*
And in 1952 he recorded the Overture to Hérold's *Zampa,* the
Dance of the Hours from *La Gioconda,* the Suite from Bizet's
Carmen, the Prelude to Humperdinck's *Hänsel und Gretel.*

Of Toscanini's contemporaries, Beecham, in the late thirties, recorded with his London Philharmonic dynamically phrased and in other ways excellent performances of Mozart's Symphonies K.297 (*Paris*), 338, 385 (*Haffner*), 425 (*Linz*), 543 and 551 (known as *Jupiter*), and Haydn's Symphonies Nos. 93, 99 and 104; admirably shaped performances of Franck's Symphony and Tchaikovsky's Fifth; and a superb performance of Mozart's *The Magic Flute* with a group of outstanding German singers and the Berlin Philharmonic. But the performance of Mozart's Symphony K.550 in G minor was made unacceptable by an unsuitably jaunty treatment of the opening movement; and on the other hand the animation and grace of the Symphony K.201 were destroyed by Beecham's ponderously slow tempos. And many of the performances he recorded with his Royal Philharmonic in his last years —notably the ones of Haydn's last twelve symphonies—suffered from tempos that made the music ponderous or static, and from over-elaborated inflection of phrase and exaggerated accentuation. But two excellent performances were those of Beethoven's Mass in C and Bizet's *Carmen*.

Bruno Walter recorded in the thirties superb performances of Act 1 of *Die Walküre* with Lehmann, Melchior and the Vienna Philharmonic, of Mahler's *Das Lied von der Erde* with Thorborg, Kullman and the Vienna Philharmonic, and of Haydn's Symphonies No. 86 with the London Symphony, No. 92 (*Oxford*) with the Paris Conservatory Concerts Orchestra, and No. 100 (*Military*) with the Vienna Philharmonic. And after the war he recorded the excellent performances of *Das Lied von der Erde* with Ferrier, Patzak (struggling with an old voice) and the Vienna Philharmonic, and Mahler's Symphony No. 2 with the New York Philharmonic, Cundari, Forrester and the Westminster Choir. But his post-war performances of Mozart, Beethoven and Schubert were increasingly nerveless and flabby, illustrating the observation by Toscanini that someone reported to me in Salzburg in 1937: "When Walter comes to something beautiful he melts."

As for Furtwängler, who clearly had to an impressive degree what the twenty-year-old Bernard Shaw described so well as "that highest faculty of a conductor, which consists in the establishing of a magnetic influence under which an orchestra becomes as amenable to the *bâton* as a pianoforte to the fingers," I found it impossible to accept what Beethoven and Schubert were made to mean by the self-indulgent vagaries and excesses in tempo which distorted shape and destroyed continuity in the works. In the amorphous music of Wagner, however, Furtwängler operated with a feeling for continuity; and the superb *Tristan und Isolde* he recorded with Flagstad and Suthaus is for me the monument to his capacities as conductor and musician. The possibility that he might have exhibited the same feeling for continuity in Mahler's symphonies is suggested by the orchestral context he provided for Fischer-Dieskau's singing in *Lieder eines fahrenden Gesellen*.

One extraordinary performance of an orchestral work was recorded in the thirties by someone who was not primarily a conductor—the pianist Fischer, whose performance of Haydn's Symphony No. 104 with his chamber orchestra not only was admirably paced and shaped but offered the additional delights of incandescent small-group ensemble operation.

Cantelli's death in 1956 deprived us of the one young conductor with technical and musical powers of the magnitude of Toscanini's, a fanatical integrity and dedication like Toscanini's, a similar way of operating in relation to music that produced a similar result: a similar shaping of the work strictly on the lines laid out by the composer's directions about tempo and dynamics; a shaped progression with a similar steadiness, continuity and organic coherence, a similar clarity of outline, texture and structure, achieved with a similar precision of execution and sonority. But there were also important differences: as against the powerful tension in a Toscanini performance, one heard in Cantelli's performances serenity and youthful lyricism and grace; and in addition to this difference in general character and style there were differences in tempo, inflection of phrase, shaping of larger structure, which revealed Cantelli as someone with a mind and taste of his own. And though they were the performances of a young man, they didn't exhibit a trace of the immaturity which, inevitably, some critics claimed was detected by their discerning ears: the performances undoubtedly would have changed in time, but each as it was produced then emerged as something completely achieved and completely satisfying.

His early death resulted in his leaving only a small number of recordings—of Tchaikovsky's Fifth with the orchestra of La Scala; Haydn's Symphony No. 93 and Musorgsky's *Pictures at an Exhibition* with the NBC Symphony; Mozart's Symphony K. 201 and *Ein musikalischer Spass*, Beethoven's Seventh, Schubert's *Unfinished*, Mendelssohn's *Italian*, Tchaikovsky's *Pathétique* and *Romeo and Juliet*, Wagner's *Siegfried-Idyll*, and Debussy's *Prélude à l'Après-midi d'un faune*, *Nuages* and *Fêtes*, and *La Mer*, all with the Philharmonia.*

And the premature death of another remarkably gifted conductor, Argenta, resulted in his leaving even fewer recordings— of Berlioz's *Symphonie Fantastique* with the Paris Conservatory Concerts Orchestra, Rimsky-Korsakov's *Capriccio espagnol* with the London Symphony, Tchaikovsky's Fourth and Debussy's *Images* with L'Orchestre de la Suisse Romande.

The pianist in whose performance of a Beethoven sonata one heard—as in Toscanini's performance of a Beethoven symphony —a clarifying articulation which seemed to reveal the structure and expressive content of the work for the first time, was Schnabel. And the force and authority of this new image of the work were such as to establish Schnabel's performances of the sonatas and concertos, like Toscanini's of the symphonies, as definitive— the ones by which others were judged and, to this day, found less satisfying. There were listeners for whom Schnabel's playing was an operation of intellect without emotion; but actually, though the operation of a powerful mind was evident, it was excess of emotion, not of intellect, that produced the flaws in the performances—the occasional distention of phrase to the point of distortion, the occasional tempo too fast for clarity or accuracy, the

* A large number of Cantelli's performances are on the tapes of his broadcasts with the NBC Symphony and the New York Philharmonic that were handed over to Walter Toscanini and placed by him in the archives of Yale University Library to be kept forever from the hearing of the public. But some, recorded off the air, have been issued on underground records; and one hopes others will be.

occasional fortissimo beyond the limit of agreeable sound—these in addition to the occasional inaccurate execution of some of Beethoven's awkward passage-work that Schnabel's fingers couldn't manage, though he was a superb pianist with a technique equal to the demands of most of the music he played.

Inevitably one thinks first of his performances of the last and greatest of Beethoven's piano music, in which the concluding variation movements of the Sonatas Opp. 109 and 111, the concluding Arioso dolente and fugue of Op. 110, the slow movement of Op. 106 (*Hammerklavier*) and No. 20 of the *Diabelli Variations* communicated their special expressive content as they did in no one else's performances. But what operated in these operated with similar effect in the earlier music: what made the slow movement of Op. 106 overwhelming was the Schnabel way of prolonging time values which, enlarging the physical shape of the music, enlarged its expressive dimensions; and the same prolonging of time values made the Adagio of the Sonata Op. 53 (*Waldstein*) the spaciously, profoundly meditative and powerfully dramatic utterance that it was in no other performance. Similarly, what caused the uninteresting Variations Op. 34 to hold one's attention was the same lyrical grace that he imparted to the opening movement of the Sonata Op. 101. And these achievments were not lessened by the first movement of Op. 106 that Schnabel—in an obedience to Beethoven's metronome marking which Tovey rightly called a "mistaken form of piety"—made into a frenetic rush which he couldn't even execute clearly; or by the similar frenetic rush he made of the finale of the Sonata Op. 57 (*Appassionata*); or by the first movement of the Sonata Op. 26 which should flow gracefully, but which—in his attempt to give it greater expressive weight with slow tempo and intensifying inflection—he made unattractively pretentious.

As with late Beethoven so with late Schubert: with his enlarging of its physical shape and expressive dimensions Schnabel made the exalted slow movement of the posthumous Sonata in B flat an overwhelming utterance that no other performance in my experience achieved. Nor did any other performance give the Scherzo the enchanting grace that Schnabel gave it. This grace also produced incomparable performances of Schubert's smaller pieces, the *Moments musicaux* and Impromptus. And again the great achievements were not lessened by the Impromptu Op. 90 No. 1 performed with unsuitable turbulence, or the lyrical opening section of the second movement of the Sonata Op. 53 distorted in shape by the pauses at the ends of the phrases.

The grace was prominent also in Schnabel's playing of Mozart, unique in its subtle articulation of clearly outlined melodic phrase, its delicacy and suppleness and at the same time its cohesive tension and strength. There has been on records nothing comparable with his delivery of the long progression of melody in the extraordinary Andante of the Concerto K.467, and with the effect it imparted to the music. And again an achievement like that, or like the powerfully phrased performance of Mozart's extraordinary Rondo K.511, was not lessened by things like the excessively turbulent and rhythmically unsteady first movement of the Sonata K.310.

Outstanding performances recorded by contemporaries of Schnabel included, in the twenties, two by Backhaus, an uninteresting musician but the possessor at that time of a phenomenal technique, which produced the figurations of Chopin's Etudes Opp. 10 and 25 with transcendant ease and grace in completely straightforward, unmannered performances that I remember as the best in my experience, and an equally straightforward and effective performance of Brahms's *Variations on a Theme of Paganini.*

Rachmaninov recorded his superb performance of Schumann's *Carnaval,* and in addition contributed excitingly enlivened playing to performances with Kreisler of Beethoven's Violin Sonata Op. 30 No. 3 and Schubert's Op. 162.

Gieseking, in the thirties, recorded sparkling performances of Mozart's Concerto K.271 and Beethoven's No. 1 and an excellent one of Beethoven's Sonata Op. 31 No. 2—all quite different from his usual finely chiseled small-scale playing, which was effective in Debussy's music and some of Mozart's, but not in Beethoven's Concertos Nos. 4 and 5 and *Waldstein* and *Appassionata* Sonatas.

And in the few years before his death in 1950 the young pianist Lipatti recorded a few performances—of Bach's Partita No. 1, a couple of Scarlatti sonatas, Mozart's Sonata K.310, Schumann's Concerto, Chopin's Sonata Op. 58, Waltzes, Barcarolle, Nocturne Op. 27 No. 2 and Mazurka Op. 50 No. 3—in which one heard the lyricism, grace, elegance and verve, the unfailing taste and feeling for continuity in phrase and large structure, in addition to the precision of execution and the tonal beauty, that made the playing outstandingly distinguished and his death an irreparable loss.

As for the celebrated harpsichordist Landowska, it was some of the performances she recorded in Europe in the thirties—of Bach's *Chromatic Fantasy and Fugue* and Toccata in D, Scarlatti sonatas, Handel suites and music of Rameau—that deserved the adulation she demanded and received. Her post-war gigantesque pounding and distortion on Victor records—offered by her, and accepted by awed listeners, as divine revelation—I heard as unmitigated murder.

What I remember as the greatest playing of music on the violin was Szigeti's in the thirties and forties—its excitingly enlivening inflection of phrase with continuity of tension and outline from note to note, its further continuity of tension and shape from phrase to phrase in the larger structure. I have heard nothing like the tremendous performance this produced of Bach's *Chaconne;* nothing like the incandescent performance of Bach's Concerto in D minor that Szigeti recorded with the New Friends of Music Orchestra under Stiedry (in his post-war performance with the Prades Festival Orchestra under Casals his tone was wiry and granular, his phrasing unimpressive). No other violinist has made of the violin's first entrance in Beethoven's Violin Concerto what Szigeti made of it, in the first (1932) performance he recorded with an unnamed orchestra under Bruno Walter, with his dynamic inflection of the very first phrases, his breathtaking crescendo of energy in the ascending rush of two-note figures to the conclusion of the passage; and no one has achieved anything like his similarly dynamic playing in the rest of the work. (Szigeti himself didn't achieve its equal in the excellent performance he recorded some years later with the New York Philharmonic under Walter.) Nor has anyone else achieved the impassioned elegance of Szigeti's performance of the first movement of Mendelssohn's Concerto with the London Philharmonic under Beecham, with whom he recorded also superb performances of Prokofiev's Concerto No. 1

and Mozart's K.218. And to these he added similar performances of Handel's Sonata Op. 1 No. 13 and Mozart's Sonata K.304.

Other great violinists of the twenties and thirties were Thibaud, who contributed his elegance of style to the famous performances of trios with Casals and Cortot; Flesch, with whom Szigeti recorded Bach's Concerto in D minor for 2 violins; and Hubermann, who recorded highly individual performances of the Beethoven and Tchaikovsky Concertos and Mozart's Concerto K.216. And the considerably younger Goldberg, in the thirties, recorded incandescent performances of Mozart sonatas with the pianist Lili Kraus and Haydn trios with Kraus and the cellist Pini, and fine performances with Kraus of Beethoven sonatas. Goldberg also recorded several distinguished performances after the war—of Bach's Concerto No. 2, Mozart's Concertos K.216 and 218, Handel's Sonata Op. 1 No. 13, and Mozart's Trios K.502 and 548 with Joanna and Nikolai Graudan (except for an excellent pre-war performance of Mozart's Concerto K.456 Kraus's playing without Goldberg was, and still is, poor).

As a solo performer the violinist Adolf Busch produced an unattractive tone and was musically uninteresting; but he operated more effectively in the Busch-Serkin Trio, whose performance of Schubert's Trio Op. 100 had the sensitive and beautiful-sounding playing that Rudolph Serkin did in ensemble performances with Busch in those early pre-American years. And Busch also led his Chamber Players in performances of Bach's *Brandenburg Concertos* and Suites that set new standards for these works.

As for cellists, one of the high points of the performer's art in my experience occurred in Casals's pre-war performance of Beethoven's Sonata Op. 102 No. 2 with Horszowski, at the return of the opening section after the middle section of the slow movement: Casals's inflection and timing of the cello's comments on the piano's statements, and at the end of the section his sustained delivery of the raptly meditative passage leading to the concluding fugue. And the unique powerfully sustained tone and phrasing produced comparable performances of the Sonatas Op. 102 No. 1 with Horszowski and Op. 69 with Schulhof.

In addition there were the famous performances of Beethoven's Trio Op. 97 (*Archduke*), Schubert's Op. 99 and Haydn's Op. 73 No. 2 that Casals recorded in the twenties with the violinist Thibaud and pianist Cortot, after the three had been playing together for their own pleasure almost twenty years. They were fascinating as the incandescent working together of three strikingly dissimilar players—Casals with his power of tone and phrasing, Thibaud with his grace and elegance, Cortot with his warmth and intimacy.

In the post-war Perpignan Festival performance of Beethoven's Trio Op. 97 and Prades Festival performance of Schubert's Op. 99 one heard the pianist Istomin and violinist Alexander Schneider playing with less grace and more force than Cortot and Thibaud, but Casals dominating again with the power of his tone and phrasing. And this was true also of the Prades Festival performance of Schubert's Op. 100 by Horszowski, Schneider and Casals. Casals's playing in Beethoven's Sonatas Op. 69 and Op. 102 No. 2 didn't equal his pre-war playing in those works; but it was powerful and moving for someone who didn't know that pre-war playing. (Rudolph Serkin, striving for comparable power in his playing of the piano parts, achieved mere loudness and crudeness.)

The one cellist of the same towering stature as Casals was Feuermann, whose early death resulted in his leaving a comparatively small number of recorded performances—of Beethoven's Trio Op. 8 for strings with Goldberg and Hindemith, his Sonata Op. 69 with Hess, his Variations on *Ein Mädchen oder Weibchen* from *The Magic Flute* with the incomparable ensemble pianist Rupp, Mozart's Divertimento K.563 for string trio with Heifetz and Primrose, Beethoven's Trio Op. 97 (*Archduke*) and Schubert's Op. 99 with Heifetz and Rubinstein, Schubert's *Arpeggione* Sonata with Moore, Strauss's *Don Quixote* with the Philadelphia Orchestra under Ormandy.*

In the thirties the Budapest Quartet's first European recordings,

---

* He was the solo cellist in Toscanini's marvelous 1938 NBC Symphony performance of *Don Quixote*—far superior to the 1953 performance issued by Victor—which has been issued on a defective underground record.

issued here by Victor—of Mozart's Quartets K.465, 499 and 590, Beethoven's Op. 18 Nos. 2 and 3, Op. 59 No. 2, Op. 74 (*Harp*) and Op. 130, Schubert's Op. 29, and Wolf's *Italian Serenade*—acquainted American listeners with a tonal, musical and ensemble excellence beyond any previously experienced here in quartet performance. After recording for Victor Haydn's Op. 54 No. 1 and Mozart's K.458 (*Hunt*), the group began its association with Columbia, for which it recorded in the forties Mozart's K.387 and 421, his Quintets K.406, 515, 516, 593 and 614 (all with the violist Katims), Haydn's Op. 64 No. 5, Op. 74 No. 3 and Op. 76 No. 4 (*Sunrise*), Beethovens Op. 18 Nos. 1, 4' and 6, Op. 59 No. 3, Opp. 95, 127, 131, 132 and 135, his Quintet Op. 29 (with Katims), and Schubert's Quintets Op. 114 (*Trout*) (with Horszowski) and Op. 163 (with the cellist Benar Heifetz).

In the fifties it recorded for the new LP mono records all of Beethoven's quartets, all of Mozart's quartets and quintets (with the violist Trampler this time), all three of Schubert's major quartets and all six of Haydn's Quartets Op. 76. If one listened to these performances by themselves one found them completely satisfying; only if one listened to them after the early ones—to the LP Mozart K.499, for example, after the European 78-rpm K.499, or to the LP Mozart quintets after the 78-rpm ones of the forties—did one discover the loss in the later ones of some of the earlier sensitiveness, grace and life.

But it was in the performances recorded in the sixties for stereo —of all the Beethoven quartets, Mozart's Quintet K.581 for clarinet (Oppenheim) and strings, his Quartets K.478 and 493 for piano (Horszowski) and strings, and Schubert's Quintets Opp. 114 and 163—that the deterioration in tone and intonation and even in the treatment of the music reached the point where the playing was not only musically unsatisfying but unpleasant to listen to.

Already in the mid-forties the short-lived New Music Quartet was exhibiting an unprecedented technical, musical and ensemble incandescence in its performances. After recording pieces by Gibbons, Locke, Purcell, Tartini, Scarlatti and Boccherini and Beethoven's Quartet Op. 59 No. 3 for Bartók Records, it recorded for Columbia four delightful Boccherini quartets and three early Mozart quartets before it disbanded.

In the thirties the recordings of the Glyndebourne Festival performances of Mozart's *The Marriage of Figaro, Don Giovanni* and *Così fan Tutte* offered not only the first performances of the entire works on records, but performances conducted by Fritz Busch with elegance, style, wit and, in the case of *Don Giovanni*, power that made them definitive—the ones by which others later were judged and usually found inferior.

Busch returned to Glyndebourne after the war; and recordings were issued of excerpts of the *Idomeneo* and *Così fan Tutte* he conducted—the first with Jurinac, Richard Lewis and Alexander Young, the second with Jurinac, Thebom, Lewis and Kunz. A later recording of *Idomeneo* in its entirety (with some cuts) offered a bland performance conducted by Pritchard, but superb singing by Jurinac, Lewis and Simoneau. And when Glyndebourne added works of other composers to those of Mozart, the Rossini *La Cenerentola* conducted by Gui was one of the most extraordinary examples of the combined operation of operatic performance ever put on records, and was followed by Gui's impressive performances of Rossini's *Le Comte Ory* and *The Barber of Seville.*

Caruso's death at the beginning of the twenties may have marked the end of the particular period referred to as the golden age (though a few of the greats of that period—McCormack, Homer, Matzenauer and De Luca—continued to sing); but it didn't mark the end of extraordinary voices and great singing. One of these voices, Ponselle's, was in fact first heard at the Metropolitan with Caruso's in the company's first production of *La Forza del Destino* in 1918. Her recorded performances reveal insufficient feeling for the shape of the musical phrase; but *Tu che invoco* from *La Vestale* and *Vedi? . . . di morte l'angelo* in the final duet of *Aida* show her to have been capable in some instances of being taught to sing with better taste than her own—something the tenor Gigli was *in*capable of.

Rethberg, on the other hand, had not only an extraordinarily lovely voice but flawless musical taste; and her performance of *Ave Maria* from *Otello*—the seemingly effortless emission of ear-ravishing vocal sound in a sustained flow which articulates and shapes the phrases with plastic perfection—is one of the examples of great vocal art on records.

The same may be said of Schipa's electrically recorded singing at the beginning of *Parigi, o cara* from *La Traviata* (with the unbearable singing of Galli-Curci) or in *Parmi veder le lagrime* from *Rigoletto*—the use of his distinctive light tenor voice with a style of phrasing enchanting in its grace and elegance—which leaves one unprepared for the tasteless accelerations and retardations and distortions of phrase in earlier performances.

And a soprano of that time who exhibits similar enchanting style in the use of her exquisite voice is Ivogün.

Gigli was one of the tenors whom it was considered possible to discuss as Caruso's successor, but whose voices actually didn't resemble Caruso's at all. However the tenor Piccaver, whom I don't recall being discussed in that way—possibly because he sang only in Vienna and Berlin—did, by the evidence of his recorded performances of the early twenties, have a voice with something like the unique timbre of Caruso's, its power and its freedom, which he used with musical taste that Caruso didn't have. (Singing at the same time as Piccaver in Vienna was the superb soprano Wildbrunn, who never sang here; and in Berlin the contralto Onegin, whom I heard, in the early twenties, flood the Metropolitan with her opulent singing of *Brangaene's Warning* in *Tristan und Isolde;* the fine bass Kipnis, whom I heard later in Salzburg in the *Fidelio* and *Magic Flute* conducted by Toscanini.)

It was in the thirties, in the singing of Bjoerling, that one heard the tenor whose voice stood out among all others as Caruso's had done, in its unique timbre—a silvery luster as against Carusos's darker splendor—combined with extraordinary range, power and freedom; and who exhibited in his use of that voice an unfailing sense for continuity and shape in the musical phrase that Caruso distorted. The performance of Lensky's aria from *Eugene Onegin* recorded at the last concert before Bjoerling's sudden death is the only one comparable with Sobinov's in vocal beauty and expressive effect.

As unique a phenomenon among soprano voices as Caruso's among tenors was Flagstad's; and as phenomenal as the voice itself, with its voluminous splendor all the way to the top when it was first heard here, was the manner of its production and deployment—the production that made the singing seem as natural and casual as speech, the deployment that had the voice go effortlessly wherever the music required it to go, rising to a squarely attacked and securely held high note, and from this one to another and still another, before descending to complete the phrase—all as though this presented no difficulty and breath were not even involved. And in addition there was the musical rightness of the singing—the unfailing perfection of the simply shaped phrases of the early years, as in the first recorded finale of *Tristan,* and the subtly inflected ones of the post-war years, as in the complete *Tristan* recorded with Furtwängler.

Someone reported to me the opinion Stokowski had expressed to him that the three greatest musical performers of this century had been Toscanini, Caruso and Chaliapin. And Chaliapin is one of the two singers—Gerhardt is the other—who stand out in my recollection of the twenties. What I recall chiefly, of course, is his Boris Godunov, one of the greatest operatic impersonations of all time, which I imagine Stokowski had in mind. But what I was shocked to discover from a recent chance hearing of Chaliapin's performances of the *Catalogue Aria* from *Don Giovanni* and the *Serenade* from *Faust* was his use of his extraordinary powers in a hamming up of some of his other roles to the point of ludicrous travesty.

As for Gerhardt, her mezzo-soprano voice, though still lovely, was past its prime and a little tremulous; but her use of it—her subtle inflection of it as she deployed it with sensitiveness to the shape as well as the expressive content of the musical phrase—made her performances of the songs of Schubert, Schumann, Brahms, Wolf and Strauss some of my most exciting and memorable experiences of those years.

It was not until the thirties that I began to hear on records the equally exciting performances of these songs by Elisabeth Schumann—the distinguished art in her use of her unique silvery voice, which had a tensile strength in its delicacy that made her spinning out of the sustained phrases of Schubert's *Nacht und Träume, Litanei* and *Nähe des Geliebten* especially effective— the performance of *Nacht und Träume* being, in fact, the definitive one in my experience, which I have heard no other singer equal. Enchanting too were her performances of the arias from the Mozart operas in which she appeared in Europe, her Sophie in the historic recorded performance of *Der Rosenkavalier* with Lotte Lehmann's Marschallin, Olszewska's Octavian and Mayr's Baron Ochs.

Chaliapin is the pre-eminent figure among a number of singers who used extraordinary voices in the service of extraordinary dramatic powers. One who is accepted as having been such a singer, Mary Garden, I found—when she appeared in New York with the Chicago Opera Company from 1917 to 1922—to be the possessor of an unattractive voice and a few dramatic mannerisms. But the tenor Muratore who appeared with her did have the superb voice and compelling stage presence of the great singing actor she was not.

Such compelling stage presence and a voice of remarkable dramatic expressiveness made Leider the outstanding Isolde and Brünnhilde of the twenties and thirties (these roles were all she did outside of Germany; but her recorded performances indicate that she was an equally impressive Fidelio and Donna Anna); and Thorborg her mezzo-soprano counterpart of the thirties and forties—among other things the Fricka of comparable magnitude with Leider's Brünnhilde.

As against the grandeur achieved by these two, Lotte Lehmann offered warm humanity. The short-breathed singing she did with her distinctively luscious voice even in her prime, in the twenties and thirties, broke the musical phrase too often, but was suffused with the personal warmth and magnetism that achieved the miracle one witnessed in the opera house—of dull Elisabeth and pallid Elsa being transformed into living beings who touched one's heart—and that made her Fidelio and Marschallin historic achievements in operatic impersonation. In her *Lieder*-singing of these years Lehmann loaded onto a dramatic song like Schubert's *Der Doppelgänger* the expressive intensity and projection suited to the operatic aria, which burst through the musical shape within which the song's expressive content was contained; but she did well with a quiet song like *An die Musik* or a vivacious one like Schumann's *An den Sonnenschein,* and was incomparable in his humorous *Die Kartenlegerin.* By the forties the need of care and skill in the use of an aging voice resulted not only in an improved quality of the high notes that had been constricted and shrill, but in a refinement and subtilization of style: expressive effect was no longer achieved directly by bursts of vehemence without regard for the damage to the musical phrase, but was achieved instead by inflection of the voice within the phrase that retained continuity and shape.

Another distinguished singing actor of that period was Schorr, whose fine baritone voice served his outstanding impersonation of Hans Sachs.

And finally Pinza, with a magnetic stage presence in *Don Giovanni* and *Figaro,* and a bass voice which in the recorded performances of the late twenties had an amplitude and richness all the way down to its lowest notes that it gradually lost as his use of it gained the refinement of musical phrasing and style of the performances of the forties, but which retained a dusky magnificence even in those later performances. The change is demonstrated most clearly in the early and late performances of Philip's monologue from *Don Carlo.*

The German singers whom Beecham chose for his *Magic Flute* in the late thirties included the brilliant coloratura soprano Berger, who sang at the Metropolitan after the war, and three who did not sing here: the soprano Lemnitz, who deployed her extraordinarily lovely delicate voice in exquisitely nuanced phrasing; the tenor Roswaenge, the possessor of a tenor voice of unusual splendor; and the baritone Hüsch.

A contemporary of theirs who also did not sing here was the lyric tenor Patzak, whom one heard of as an outstanding singer of Mozart, but who sang other music as effectively.

And another was the mezzo-soprano Supervia, who exhibited an excitingly individual voice and style in recorded excerpts from Rossini operas and *Carmen.*

With Flagstad in her first Metropolitan *Tristan und Isolde* were Melchior, past his prime but enduring, and the excellent contralto Branzell.

The years that followed brought to the Metropolitan Sayão, who had a lovely lyric soprano voice; Milanov, whose dramatic soprano at that time was extraordinarily beautiful when it was under control, as it frequently was not—though it was invariably under control when she sang under the hypnotic direction of Toscanini; the soprano Albanese, whom he chose for his NBC Symphony performances of *La Bohème* and *La Traviata;* the soprano Traubel, whose voice was at its peak, and deserved his delighted exclamation *"Che bella voce!"*, in the finale of *Die Götterdämmerung* she recorded with him in 1941; the mezzo-soprano Tourel, whom he chose for his first performance of Berlioz's *Romeo and Juliet* in its entirety with the New York Philharmonic in 1942; the tenor Peerce, whom he chose for his first NBC Symphony performance of Beethoven's Ninth and continued to use thereafter.

But it was Steber's performances—above all her Countess in *Figaro,* one of the outstanding operatic characterizations in my experience, her Donna Anna in *Don Giovanni,* her Fiordiligi in *Così fan Tutte*—that offered in voice, phrasing and style what added up to the grandest and greatest singing after Flagstad's at the Metropolitan.

And in the post-war years one made the acquaintance of the beautiful singing of the sopranos Baillie, Ritchie and Stader; the contraltos Stignani, Klose, Nikolaidi and Ferrier; the tenor Valletti, who had something like the voice and style of Schipa; the baritone Hotter.

In the fifties a large number of performances of the past on 78-rpm records were transferred to LP records—among them the records of Victor's LCT series and its later low-priced Camden series, and those of Angel's COLH series. The Victor LCTs and Camdens were discontinued after a few years; the Angel COLHs in 1969. But some of the discontinued performances have reappeared, and previously unissued ones continue to appear—in Victor's low-priced Victrola series, Columbia's Odyssey series, Angel's Seraphim series. Angel, in the fall of 1969, reissued a number of the COLH performances in Seraphim collections; and as I write it is about to reissue on Seraphim all the Schnabel COLH performances of Beethoven's music for solo piano—which encourages the hope that his other performances on COLH

records, and those of other great performers, will also be so reissued. And meanwhile a number of the COLH records discontinued by Angel here are still available in Europe. Nor is this
true only of performances originally on 78-rpm records: some of
the performances recorded on mono LP in the fifties that were
discontinued with the advent of stereo are also being reissued,
and others are available in Europe.

The discography that follows is a selection from the records
listed in the catalogues as being available here and in Europe—
to which are added discontinued records to look for in shops
which deal in them, and performances to watch for on newly
issued records. Several shops stock, or can obtain, European
records—among them Discophile and Darton in New York; and
what they may not be able to obtain may be obtainable from
Discurio, 9 Shepherd's Market, London W.1. Rococo and Cantilena records, made in Canada, can be obtained from Charles
Consumer Service, 30 West 21 Street, New York.

In addition I take note this time of the so-called underground
records and tapes—with performances recorded originally from
broadcasts or reproduced from discontinued commercial records,
and issued without authorization by the performers or the record
companies with contractual rights to make and issue the performers' recordings—that have appeared in increasing numbers
in the past few years.

RECORDED PERFORMANCES LISTED
UNDER NAMES OF PERFORMERS

Albanese. Watch for a reissue of the 78-rpm performances that were on Victor LM-2286—of the *Letter Scene* from Tchaikovsky's *Eugene Onegin* and arias from *Figaro, Don Giovanni, Carmen* and *Don Pasquale*. The voice is sometimes dry and afflicted with strong vibrato; but the singing is made exciting by its style and intensity. Meanwhile one can hear her sing Violetta in Toscanini's *La Traviata.*

Argenta. London STS-15006 has the performance of Berlioz's *Symphonie Fantastique;* London 6006 the performance of Rimsky-Korsakov's *Capriccio espagnol* (with Chabrier's *España*).

Backhaus. Parnassus 3 (Parnassus Records, 130 Arnold Street, Staten Island, N.Y. 10301) has the marvelous 1927 performance of Brahms's *Variations on a Theme of Paganini*, regrettably not with the one of Chopin's Etudes but with a shapeless 1938 performance of Schumann's Fantasia.

Baillie. Imported Odeon HQM-1015 (E)* has her performances of Purcell's *Tell Me Some Pitying Angel, With Verdure Clad* from Haydn's *The Creation, I Know that My Redeemer Liveth* from Handel's *Messiah,* and pieces from his *Samson* and *Judas Maccabaeus.*

Beecham. His performance of Beethoven's Mass in C is on Capitol SG-7168; the one of Bizet's *Carmen,* with de los Angeles and Gedda, on Angel S-3613; the one of Delius's *Brigg Fair* on Capitol SG-7116; the pre-war *Magic Flute,* with sound that lacks amplitude and solidity of bass, on Turnabout 4111/3.

Berger. She sings in Beecham's *The Magic Flute* and in the *Rigo-*

---

* (E) after the number of an imported record means England, (F) means France, (G) means Germany, (I) means Italy.

letto on Victor LM-6021; and imported Odeon 73384 (G) has performances of *Martern aller Arten* from Mozart's *Seraglio,* only the first half of *Et incarnatus est* from his *Mass in C Minor* (a butchery without precedent), and arias by Rossini, Donizetti and Verdi.

Bjoerling. In addition to Victor LM-6008, which has the *Il Trovatore* with Milanov and Warren, there are imported Odeon HQM-1190 (E), with early performances of arias from *Il Trovatore, Rigoletto* and *Un Ballo in Maschera* sung in Swedish and Italian, and *Ingemisco* from Verdi's *Requiem;* HMV (imported as Odeon) ALP-1620 (E), with the arias from *L'Elisir d'Amore, L'Africaine, Carmen* and *Rigoletto,* among others, recorded between 1936 and 1948, that were on Angel COLH-148; ALP-1841 (E), with the arias from *Faust, Il Trovatore, Rigoletto* and *Aida,* among others, recorded in the same period, that were on Angel COLH-150; Victor LM-2003, with a 1955 Carnegie Hall recital in which Bjoerling is a little breathless in the arias from *Don Giovanni* and *Carmen* but produces a brilliant performance of Strauss's *Cäcilie* and ear-ravishing *mezza voce* singing in his *Traum durch die Dämmerung* and Foster's *I Dream of Jeannie with the Light Brown Hair;* Victor LM-2269, with 1958 performances of arias from *L'Elisir d'Amore, Prince Igor* and *Eugene Onegin* (the last two in Swedish) and excerpts from the complete recordings of *Aida, Rigoletto* and less consequential operas; Victor LM-2784, with the amazingly beautiful singing he did in the aria from *Eugene Onegin* and *Lohengrin's Narrative* (both in Swedish) at the last concert in Göteborg, and in songs by Schubert, Strauss and others at a Carnegie Hall recital two years earlier. In addition he contributes marvelous singing to Toscanini's 1940 *Missa Solemnis* and *Requiem* on underground tapes.

Bohnen. He sings with Lehmann in the second-act duet from *Die Meistersinger* on Rococo 5257.

Branzell. Rococo 5214 has her performances of arias from *Dido and Aeneas, Orfeo ed Euridice* (in German), *La Favorita* and *Il Trovatore* and *Erda's Warning* from *Das Rheingold,* among other things.

Budapest Quartet. Of the Beethoven quartets recorded in the fifties, the six of Op. 18 on Columbia SL-172 have been reissued on Odyssey 32-36-0023 (reduce treble, increase bass); and it is to be hoped that the others originally on SL-173 and 174 will also be reissued. In addition there are the Mozart quintets recorded with Trampler in the fifties, listed as available on Columbia D3L-347 (mono), which I would acquire in preference to D3S-747 (stereo); and good performances with Trampler of Beethoven's Quintet for strings Op. 29 and Dvořák's Op. 97 on Columbia MS-6952.

Busch Chamber Players. Of the *Brandenburg Concertos* formerly on Angel COLC-13 and 14 only No. 5 is at present in the Seraphim collection, *Six Concertos,* 6043.

Busch-Serkin Trio. The performance of Schubert's Trio Op. 100 formerly on Angel COLH-43 is available on Electrola (imported as Odeon) E-80792 (G).

Cantelli. His performance of Beethoven's Seventh is on Seraphim S-60038; the ones of Schubert's *Unfinished* and Mendelssohn's *Italian* on Seraphim 60002; the ones of Debussy's *Prélude à l'Après-midi d'un faune, Nuages* and *Fêtes,* and *La Mer* on Seraphim 60077. And imported Odeon QIM-6381 (I) has Mozart's Symphony K. 201 and *Ein musikalischer Spass.* Watch for possible reissues of the others, and possible underground releases of performances from his broadcasts.

Caruso. Victrola VIC-1430 has most of the performances he recorded at his first American sessions (1904-6)—of arias from *L'Elisir d'Amore, Don Pasquale, La Favorita, Les Huguenots, Rigoletto, Il Trovatore* and *Aida,* among others—which exhibit the ear-ravishing beauty of his voice at that early time and the flawed musical taste in its deployment that he retained to the end.

Casals. Of his pre-war performances, the Beethoven Trio Op. 97 with Thibaud and Cortot formerly on Angel COLH-29 is on imported Voce del Padrone COLH-29 (I); the Schubert Op. 99 and Haydn Op. 73 No. 2 formerly on Angel COLH-12 are on Voce del Padrone COLH-12 (I) and Electrola E-80487 (G); and one must hope for an underground reissue of the Beethoven sonatas. Of the Prades and Perpignan Festival performances only the Beethoven sonatas have been reissued on Odyssey 32-36-0016 (electronic pseudo-stereo); and one hopes for reissues of the Beethoven and Schubert trios. World Series PHC-9099 (stereo) has his performances of Beethoven's Sonata Op. 102 No. 2—a little dry in tone, but still supreme in understanding—and the Sonata Op. 5 No. 2, both with excellent playing by Horszowski, at a later Bonn Festival.

Cebotari. She is the Sophie with Lemnitz's Octavian in the *Presentation of the Rose* from *Der Rosenkavalier* on Rococo 5300.

Chaliapin. The excerpts from *Boris Godunov* formerly on Angel COLH-100, including the final scene recorded at a Covent Garden performance in 1928, are on imported Pathé Voix Illustres VOI-50.020(F), Electrola E-80981 (G) and Voce del Padrone COLH-100 (I). (The first LP transfer years ago, Victor LCT-3, had also the Covent Garden second-act *Monologue* and *Hallucination Scene,* made excit'ng by the sound of Chaliapin's hurling the stool at the ghost of Dimitri, in place of the studio performances on COLH-100.) And the *Monologue* is in *Great Voices of the Century,* Seraphim 60113.

Dal Monte. She sings with Schipa in duets from *Don Pasquale* and *La Sonnambula* on imported Voce del Padrone COLH-117 (I).

De Gogorza. In Handel's *Where'er You Walk,* on Cantilena 6203, the voice is the hoarse one I heard in 1914; but in earlier performances he uses an agreeable baritone with musical taste and achieves delightful subtleties of phrasing in the *Serenade* from *Don Giovanni* that I don't remember hearing from anyone else. In the duet from *Il Trovatore* the famous soprano Eames achieves nothing like the power of Gadski's phrasing and style; but Sembrich's singing in a duet from Thomas's *Hamlet* enables one to understand the superlatives that were written about her.

De Luca. The early performances on Rococo 24 I haven't heard. The later ones originally on Camden CAL-320 here, until recently on Camden CDN-1012 in England, and now on Camden LCC-17 in Italy, include *Povero Rigoletto* and *Cortigiani, vil razza dannata* from *Rigoletto,* which—for listeners accustomed to the usual bellowing in this scene—is made notable and exciting by the fact that every note is *sung* with a style and art that achieve the most intense expressiveness and dramatic force. The beautiful voice isn't damaged by the artificial echo added in some of the performances. See also under Collections: *Unforgettable Voices from Italian Opera,* Victrola VIC-1395.

Destinn. Cantilena 6202 provides a glimpse of Toscanini's 1915

232

revival of *Il Trovatore* at the Metropolitan with the accurately and beautifully sung *Miserere* that Destinn and Martinelli recorded at the time. It also documents her Pamina of that period with a beautiful performance of *Ach, ich fühl's,* and her pre-Metropolitan singing with a duet from *Les Huguenots* with the tenor Jörn, among other things. See also under Collections: *Unforgettable Voices from Italian Opera,* Victrola VIC-1395.

Farrar. One hears on Rococo 5216—in the *Alleluja* from Mozart's *Exsultate, jubilate,* a piece by Gluck, the *Jewel Song* from *Faust,* and *L'altra notte* from *Mefistofele,* among less consequential things—what an extraordinarily beautiful voice she had.

Ferrier. She sings on London 4212 in Mahler's *Das Lied von der Erde* and three songs to texts of Rückert with the Vienna Philharmonic under Walter. Still listed, but reported difficult to obtain, are London 5103, with excerpts from the Glyndebourne Festival performance of Gluck's *Orfeo ed Euridice* conducted by Stiedry (reproduced poorly at times by the LP transfer); London 5258, with songs of Schubert and Schumann and arias from Handel's *Xerxes* and Gluck's *Orfeo* (the transferred sound isn't always bright and clean); and London 5291, with arias from Purcell's *The Fairy Queen* and Handel's *Atalanta* and songs of Wolf and Jensen (the sound is at times defective).

Imported Decca ACL-293 (E) has the excerpts from *Orfeo;* ACL-307 has the songs of Schubert, Schumann and Wolf; ACL-308 has the Handel and Gluck arias from London 5258, with excerpts from Bach's *St. Matthew Passion;* ACL-310 has the Handel and Purcell arias from London 5291. And SXL-2234 has arias from Bach's *St. Matthew* and *St. John Passions* and *Mass in B Minor* and Handel's *Messiah, Samson* and *Judas Maccabaeus.*

Feuermann. His performances of Beethoven's Sonata Op. 69 with Hess and Schubert's *Arpeggione* Sonata with Moore are on Seraphim 60117; his performances of Beethoven's Variations on *Ein Mädchen oder Weibchen,* two fine transcribed movements of a Handel organ concerto, and a dull Mendelssohn sonata with Rupp on Victrola VIC-1476; his performances of Beethoven's Trio Op. 97 and Schubert's Op. 99 with Rubinstein and Heifetz on Victor LM-7025. The earlier LP transfers of Strauss's *Don Quixote* on Camden 202 and Mozart's Divertimento K.563 on Victor LCT-1021 being no longer available, one hopes not only for new ones of these, but for an underground recording of Toscanini's NBC broadcast of *Don Quixote* with Feuermann that will be free of the technical defects of the one on MJA 5001.

Flagstad. Of her early Victor recordings, the very first, the 1935 finale of *Tristan und Isolde,* is now on Victrola VIC-1455, *Unforgettable Voices from German Opera,* which produces the performance with less amplitude and splendor than did the original 78-rpm record, but with enough to give an idea of what overwhelmed listeners that first year. (There is also an underground recording of the *Tristan* broadcast in March 1935.) The collection that was on Camden CAL-462 here and Victrola 1208 in England—with Beethoven's *Ah! perfido, Abscheulicher!* from *Fidelio,* and excerpts from *Oberon, Lohengrin, Tannhäuser* and *Die Walküre*—is now on imported RCA LM-20063 (I). The newly issued Victrola VIC-1517 omits from the preceding group the *Fidelio* and *Tannhäuser* arias and adds the finale of *Die Götterdämmerung.* And the duets from *Lohengrin* and *Tristan* with Melchior (and *Brangaene's Warning* sung by Flagstad) are on Victor LM-2618.

Of her post-war performances, Angel 3588 has the *Tristan und Isolde* with Suthaus conducted by Furtwängler; London 25101 has Wagner's wesendonck songs with the Vienna Philharmonic under Knappertsbusch; imported World Record Club SH-117 (E) has the Purcell *Dido and Aeneas* conducted by Geraint Jones; London 25141 has arias of Bach and Handel, with crude orchestral contexts provided by Boult with the London Philharmonic; London 5262 (reported difficult to obtain) has songs of Schubert and Schumann, which are available on imported Decca LXT-5263 (I); and imported Odeon HQM-1057 (E) has an earlier performance of *When I Am Laid in Earth* from *Dido and Aeneas, Erbarme dich* from the *St. Matthew Passion,* and the finale of *Die Götterdämmerung,* among other things.

Furtwängler. His performance of *Tristan und Isolde* with Flagstad and Suthaus is on Angel 3588; the one of Mahler's *Lieder eines fahrenden Gesellen* with Fischer-Dieskau and the Phil-harmonia on Angel 35522.

Gadski. In her last years at the Metropolitan she sang Wagner; but her superb earlier singing of Verdi is documented in the duets from *Il Trovatore* and *Aida* with Amato on Cantilena 6201. (The *Trovatore* duet is also on Victrola VIC-1395, *Unforgettable Voices from Italian Opera*.) It is these duets and one from *Rigoletto* with Hempel that make the record valuable, not Amato's solo performances.

Gerhardt. Rococo 5245 offers songs of Schubert, including eight from *Die Winterreise,* most of them with the marvelous piano accompaniments of Bos. Rococo 5202 offers the songs of Wolf she recorded with Bos for Volume 1 of the Hugo Wolf Society in 1932, with an additional song recorded in the mid-twenties, and three recorded in 1907 with Nikisch at the piano. The 1932 voice is a tremulous shadow of the beautiful voice of 1907, but still lovely much of the time. And Rococo 5207 has a number of other songs of Schubert, Schumann, Wagner, Wolf and Strauss recorded with Nikisch in 1907 and 1911, in which one hears not only the loveliness of the young voice but, astonishingly, the same wonderful inflection of voice and phrase as in the performances recorded at fifty.

Gieseking. Angel 35065 has his performances of Debussy's *Estampes* and *Images;* 35250 his performances of Debussy's Etudes; Odyssey 32-16-0371 his performance of Mozart's Concerto K.488 with the Philharmonia under von Karajan; and the three volumes of Seraphim 6047/9 have the performances of all of Mozart's piano music formerly on Angel 35068/78, which includes a number of pieces most of us have never heard—the earliest interesting chiefly for what they reveal about Mozart's initial talent and its development, some later ones interesting only as exercises of his exquisite craftsmanship, but others achieving impressive effect as works of art. Gieseking's sensitive playing often lacks sufficient force and—in slow tempo—sustained tension; but some of the unfamiliar pieces he plays with the force and tension that are lacking in the familiar ones.

An underground recording has the most extraordinary Gieseking performance in my experience—the one of Mozart's Concerto K.467 with the New York Philharmonic under Cantelli.

The listener familiar with Gieseking's customary finely chiseled playing of Mozart is amazed to hear him this time, presumably under the magnetic compulsion of Cantelli, play with an unprecedented power of tone and style that must have surprised him as much as it did the audience. That power in the enunciation of the long flow of melody in the great Andante produces the only performance of it that equals Schnabel's in musical and expressive effect; and unlike Schnabel's it is supported by a superb orchestral context provided by Cantelli.

Glyndebourne Festival. Of the pre-war performances conducted by Busch, *The Marriage of Figaro,* its transferred sound agreeable and clear but occasionally dim, is on Turnabout 4114/6; the *Don Giovanni,* with brighter and otherwise better sound, on Turnabout 4117/9; the *Così fan Tutte,* with heavy bass and peaked treble, on Turnabout 4120/22. The excerpts on Victor LM-1186 and LHMV-1021 from the post-war *Così* and *Idomeneo* conducted by Busch are unavailable. The *Idomeneo* conducted by Pritchard that was on Angel 3574 is now on imported World Record Club OH-210/3 (E). As for the performances conducted by Gui, *La Cenerentola* is on imported Odeon HQM-1011/3 (E), *Le Comte Ory* on imported Odeon HQM-1073/4 (E), and *The Barber of Seville* on Angel S-3638.

Goldberg. The pre-war performances of Mozart sonatas and Haydn trios transferred to Decca DX-103 and 104 are no longer available. And of the post-war performances only Mozart's Concertos K.216 and 218 are listed on Decca 9609, and his Trios K.502 and 548 on Decca 9722.

Goossens, Leon. Imported Odeon HQM-1087 (E) has this oboist's fine performances of a concerto put together by Benjamin with some lovely pieces by Cimarosa, and a quite lovely Concerto in C minor by Marcello, among other things.

Hempel. Her performance of *Dite alla giovine* from *La Traviata* with Amato and superb performance of *Qui la voce* from *I Puritani* were on imported HMV CSLP-501 (E); and imported Odeon COLH-135 (E) had her performances of arias from *The Magic Flute, The Seraglio, Ernani* and *La Traviata.* Imported Odeon 73397 (G) has her marvelous performance of *O beau pays* from *Les Huguenots,* with lovely performances of arias from *Lakmé* and *La Perle de Brésil* and Mendelssohn's *Auf Flügeln des Gesanges*. And the earlier performances on Rococo 8 include *Martern aller Arten* from *The Seraglio* and a duet from *Lucia di Lammermoor* with the tenor Jadlowker.

Homer. Her rich contralto is heard on Victrola VIC-1519 in arias from Handel's *Messiah*, Gluck's *Orfeo* and *Alceste* and Meyerbeer's *Les Huguenots* and *Le Prophète,* duets from Verdi's *Il Trovatore* with Caruso, and an atrociously cut duet from *Aida* with Gadski.

Hotter. Seraphim 6051 has his beautiful-sounding and understated performances of Schubert's *Die Winterreise* and *Schwanengesang;* Seraphim 60065 his beautiful performances of songs of Wolf, including *Anakreon's Grab* and *Verborgenheit,* and Brahms, including *Botschaft* and *Sapphische Ode*.

Hubermann. His performance of Tchaikovsky's Concerto is on Rococo 2002.

Hüsch. He is the Papageno in Beecham's pre-war *Magic Flute*.

Ivogün. Imported Odeon 73395 (G) has her performances of *Martern aller Arten* from *The Seraglio* and *Der Hölle Rache* from *The Magic Flute,* and arias from *The Barber of Seville* and *Don Pasquale*.

Jadlowker. He sings with Hempel in a duet from *Lucia* on Rococo 8.

Jörn. His amazing tenor voice is heard in a duet from *Les Huguenots* with Destinn on Cantilena 6202.

Jurinac. Her lovely voice and affecting singing are heard, on imported Odeon HQM-1024 (E), in Ilia's two arias from the 1951 Glyndebourne *Idomeneo* conducted by Busch, Cherubino's two arias from the 1950 *Figaro* conducted by von Karajan, the Countess's two arias from the 1955 Glyndebourne *Figaro* conducted by Gui, Marzelline's aria from the lethargic 1953 *Fidelio* conducted by Furtwängler, and excerpts from Smetana's *The Bartered Bride* and Tchaikovsky's *Joan of Arc*.

Kipnis. Seraphim 60076 has his eloquent *Il lacerato spirito* from *Simon Boccanegra* (in Italian), richly sonorous arias from *The Magic Flute* and *Die Meistersinger,* arias from *Figaro* and *The Barber of Seville* to which he gives a humorous bite in spite of the awkward German words, and excellent performances of

Schubert's *Der Erlkönig* and Wolf's *Alles endet, was entstehet.* (A German will be aware that the German words are sung by someone born in Russia.)

Klose. Her opulent contralto is heard in duets from *Orfeo* with Lemnitz on Rococo 5203, and in the quartet from *Don Carlo* on Rococo 5300 (all in German).

Kreisler. Some of his finest playing is heard in the performances of Beethoven's Sonata Op. 30 No. 3 and Schubert's Op. 162 with Rachmaninov on Victor LM-6099. A highly desirable underground release would be his early recording of the Beethoven Concerto with the Berlin State Opera Orchestra under Blech.

Kurz. Her lovely voice and singing—and her occasional liberties with tempo and exhibitionistic interpolations—are heard, on Rococo 37, in arias from *The Magic Flute, Les Huguenots* and *Un Ballo in Maschera* in German, and *I Puritani, La Sonnambula, Rigoletto* and *Il Trovatore.*

Landowska. Her performances of Bach's *Chromatic Fantasy and Fugue* and other pieces are on imported Pathé Gravures Illustres COLH-71 (F); of Scarlatti sonatas on COLH-73; of Handel suites on COLH-310. The Scarlatti sonatas are also on imported Voce del Padrone COLH-73 (I).

Lehmann, Lilli. Though her voice, on Scala 826, no longer has luster or warmth, it is steady and powerful; and her florid singing in an aria from Handel's *Joshua,* her phrasing and style in arias from *The Seraglio* and *Don Giovanni,* are breathtaking.

Lehmann, Lotte. Her Fidelio, Elisabeth, Elsa and Sieglinde (another character she brought to exciting life) are documented by some of the performances on imported Odeon 73396 (G); her Sieglinde further on imported Pathé Voix Illustres VOI 50.013 (F), by the excellent performance of Act 1 of *Die Walküre* with Melchior, conducted by Walter, that was on Angel COLH-133; her Marschallin by the historic performance of parts of *Der Rosenkavalier,* with Olszewska, Schumann and Mayr, on Seraphim 6041. And Rococo 5257—with her acoustically recorded performances of arias and duets from *Figaro* and *Don Giovanni* (with Schlusnus), *Die Meistersinger* (with Bohnen), *Tannhäuser, Lohengrin, Der Freischütz* and *Carmen,* among others—reveals her lovely light soprano voice of that early period, used with ease, simplicity, feeling for the musical phrase, moving expressive effect, and, already then, dramatic point that is most striking in the *Meistersinger* duet.

Victrola VIC-1320 has all the songs of Brahms and Wolf that Lehmann recorded for Victor between 1935 and 1947, except Wolf's *In dem Schatten meiner Locken,* but including four of Wolf previously unissued. Several of her best early Victor performances—of Beethoven's *Ich liebe dich,* Schubert's *An die Musik* and *Erlkönig,* Brahms's *Botschaft,* Wolf's *In dem Schatten meiner Locken, Anakreon's Grab* and *Auf ein altes Bild*—were on Camden CAL-378, and later on CDN-1015 in England; now most of them are on RCA 430.661, listed as available in France. Victor LCT-1108, and later RCA 430.529 in France, had other early Victor performances of Schubert's *Im Abendroth* and four songs from *Die Winterreise* and Schumann's *Die Kartenlegerin* and *Alte Laute,* among others. The remaining Victor performances of songs from *Die Winterreise* and all the Columbia performances of the rest of that cycle were never reissued on LP; and an underground reissue would seem to offer the only possibility of the entire cycle. But Schubert's *Die schöne Müllerin* was on Columbia ML-5996, later available in Germany as CBS 72209; and one hopes for its reissue on Odyssey. Odyssey 32-16-0315 has Schumann's *Dichterliebe,* with Bruno Walter's tinkly playing of the piano part. And CBS 72703, listed as available in France, has Schubert's *Die junge Nonne* and *Der Doppelgänger* (its shape still destroyed by excessive vehemence), Schumann's *Aufträge* and *Der Nussbaum,* and songs of Beethoven, Brahms, Wolf and Strauss, all formerly on Columbia ML-5778. See also under Collections: *Great Voices of the Century,* Seraphim 60113.

Leider. Imported Pathé Voix Illustres VOI-50.025 (F) has what was on Angel COLH-132: the first-act narrative from *Tristan und Isolde,* parts of the second-act duet with Melchior, and the final *Mild und leise,* to which Melchior adds *Wohin nun Tristan scheidet* from Act 2 and the marvelous *Wie sie selig* from Act 3. In addition the record has Leider's superb performances of *Or sai chi l'onore* from *Don Giovanni* and *Abscheulicher!* from *Fidelio.* (The second-act duet from *Tristan* is also on Seraphim 60113, *Great Voices of the Century.*) And Rococo 5303 has early accoustically recorded and impressive performances of the Countess's arias from *Figaro* and *Or sai chi l'onore* from *Don Giovanni* (in German), Beethoven's *Ah! perfido* (in Italian), *Ozean, du Ungeheuer* from *Oberon,* a song of Wolf, and less consequential pieces.

Lemnitz. She sings in Beecham's pre-war *Magic Flute;* and Rococo 5203 has performances (in German) of arias from *Il Trovatore* and *Aida* and duets from *Orfeo ed Euridice* (with Klose) and Tchaikovsky's *The Sorceress* (with Roswaenge), in addition to arias from *Der Freischütz, Tannhäuser* and *Lohengrin;* 5273 has performances of *Dove sono* from *Figaro* (in Italian), the *Willow Song* and *Ave Maria* from *Otello* (in German), and songs of Brahms and Wolf, among other things; 5300 has several 1942-3 performances which surpass all these—above all the Countess's arias from *Figaro* (in German), but also the fourth-act duet with di Luna from *Il Trovatore* (in German, with Schmitt-Walter), the duet and quartet in Philip's study from *Don Carlo* (in German, with Klose, Hahn and Ahlersmeyer), and the *Presentation of the Rose* from *Der Rosenkavalier* (with Cebotari).

Lipatti. Odyssey 32-16-0315 has his performances of Bach's Partita No. 1 and two chorale-preludes and Mozart's Sonata K.310; 32-16-0369 his performances of Chopin's Sonata Op. 58, Barcarolle, Nocturne Op. 27 No. 2; 32-16-0058 ("electronic stereo") the performances of Chopin's Waltzes that no one has equalled in rhythmic subtlety and grace; 32-16-0141 the greatest of all performances of Schumann's Concerto (reduce treble on all these, and if necessary increase bass). In addition Seraphim 60007 has a performance of Chopin's Concerto No. 1; Angel 35931 the performance of Mozart's K.467 with the Lucerne Festival Orchestra and von Karajan; and Angel 3556 the performances of the same Bach partita, Mozart sonata and Chopin waltzes and of two Schubert Impromptus at his last public recital at the 1950 Besançon Festival, where he was so ill and weak that he could barely climb the stairs to the auditorium, but where, by an almost unimaginable effort of will, he not only managed to play the works with his precision, lyricism, elegance and verve, but—under the stimulation of the occasion—raised the performances to sheer incandescence.

Matzenauer. Her 1912 performance of *In grembe a me* from *L'Africaine* is on Victrola VIC-1395, *Unforgettable Voices from Italian Opera*. And Collectors Guild 611 had additional impressive performances.

Mayr. His historic Baron Ochs is documented by the recorded performance of parts of *Der Rosenkavalier* with Lehmann, Olszewska and Schumann on Seraphim 6041.

McCormack. His famous performance of *Il mio tesoro* from *Don Giovanni* is on Victrola VIC-1472, with arias from Méhul's *Joseph, Carmen, Lakmé, Faust* and *The Pearl Fishers,* among others. And *Una furtiva lagrima* from *L'Elisir d'Amore* is on VIC-1393, with other arias, including *De' miei bollenti spiriti* from *La Traviata,* in which one is surprised by a few distortions of phrase. Both *Il mio tesoro* and *Una furtiva lagrima* are on Rococo 5274, with the same aria from *La Traviata* and others from *Lucia, The Daughter of the Regiment* and *Rigoletto,* duets from *The Pearl Fishers* (with Sammarco) and *Aida* (with Lucy Marsh), and the quartet from *Rigoletto* (with Bori, Jacoby and Werrenrath). See also under Collections: *Great Voices of the Century,* Seraphim 60113.

Melba. Rococo 17 has her impressive coloratura singing in the *Mad Scene* from Thomas's *Hamlet* and her performance of the *Ave Maria* from *Otello,* among other things.

Melchior. His performances of the second-act duet from *Tristan und Isolde* and third-act duet from *Lohengrin* with Flagstad are on Victor LM-2618; his earlier performance of the duet from *Tristan* with Leider is on Seraphim 60113, *Great Voices of the Century;* his performances of *Wohin nun Tristan scheidet* from Act 2 and the marvelous *Wie sie selig* from Act 3, in addition to the duet with Leider, formerly on Angel COLH-132, are now on imported Pathé Voix Illustres VOI-50.025 (F); his performance in the Act 1 of *Die Walküre* with Lehmann conducted by Walter, formerly on Angel COLH-133, is now on imported Pathé Voix Illustres VOI-50.013 (F). And a no longer available set, ASCO 121, had his more impressive earlier singing of the mid-twenties, notably in *Dio! mi potevi scagliar* and *Niun mi tema* from *Otello* and the fourth-act duet from *Aida* with the superb contralto Ober (in German).

Milanov. Her beautiful voice in its prime is heard in Toscanini's performance of Act 4 of *Rigoletto* on Victrola VIC-1314, and in his 1940 broadcasts of Beethoven's *Missa Solemnis* and Verdi's *Requiem* on underground tapes; and it is still beautiful in the later *Il Trovatore* with Bjoerling and Warren on Victor LM-6008; but its thin, unattractive, tremulous sound in the still later *Aida* on Victrola VIC-6119 makes this performance, even with Bjoerling's singing, one to avoid. But just before this *Aida,* at a time in the early fifties when her unpleasant-sounding and wobbly singing at the Metropolitan was painful to listen to, she was able to produce in the recording studio the excellent performances of arias from *Aida, La Forza del Destino* and *Un Ballo in Maschera* on Victrola VIC-1336, and the agreeable-sounding and well-phrased *Casta diva* from *Norma* on Victrola VIC-1395, *Unforgettable Voices from Italian Opera.*

Muratore. One hears a fine voice in the arias from *Carmen, Werther* and *Manon* on Scala 824 (and a few details in its deployment that aren't in good musical taste by today's standards); but in the aria from *Mona Vanna* it has an additional luster which makes it the superb voice I remember hearing in that opera.

New Music Quartet. Bartók 909, with Beethoven's Quartet Op. 59 No. 3; 911, with a Boccherini quartet in A and sonatas *a quatro* by Tartini and Alessandro Scarlatti; and 913, with Gibbons's Fantasies Nos. 1 and 2, Locke's Consort No. 6 for viols, and Purcell's Pavane and Chacony in G minor, can be obtained from Bartók Records, 200 West 57 Street, New York.

Olszewska. She is the Octavian in the historic recorded performance of parts of *Der Rosenkavalier* with Lehmann, Schumann and Mayr on Seraphim 6041.

Onegin. *Brangaene's Warning* from *Tristan und Isolde* is poorly reproduced on Scala 821; but the lustrous beauty of the voice, its extraordinary range, power and suppleness, and its amazing agility are heard in the arias from *Samson et Dalila, Orfeo ed Euridice* and Handel's *Rinaldo* and the *Alleluja* from Mozart's *Exsultate, Jubilate.*

Patzak. Those who know only his quavering old voice in Walter's performance of Mahler's *Das Lied von der Erde* can hear on Rococo 5312 the fine lyric tenor of his youth in arias from *Don Giovanni, The Magic Flute, Così Fan Tutte, The Seraglio, Il*

Trovatore, Un Ballo in Maschera, Eugene Onegin, The Bartered Bride, Mignon and *The Tales of Hoffmann* (all in German). (Where surface noise is strong reduce treble drastically; where there is no surface noise and the sound is muffled increase treble.)

Piccaver. Rococo 5316 has acoustically recorded performances of arias from *Lucia, L'Africaine, Faust* and *Rigoletto,* among other things. (Reduce treble drastically.)

Pinza. Except for a 1940 *Se vuol ballare* from *Figaro* and 1951 *La calunnia* from *The Barber of Seville,* Victrola VIC-1418 has performances recorded in the late twenties—of *O Isis* from *The Magic Flute* (in German), *Ite sul colle* from *Norma,* and arias from *La Favorita* and *I Vespri Siciliani.* And except for a 1939 *Non più andrai* from *Figaro,* VIC-1470 also has performances recorded in the late twenties—of the *Champagne Aria* (rhythmically inexact) and *Serenade* from *Don Giovanni, O Isis* from *The Magic Flute* (in Italian), *Ah! del Tebro* from *Norma,* arias from *La Juive, Faust, Il Trovatore* and *Don Carlo,* and *Confutatis maledictis* from Verdi's *Requiem.* The 1927 *Monologue* from *Don Carlo* is interesting to compare with the one Pinza recorded twenty years or more later on Victor LM-1751, with arias from *Nabucco, I Vespri Siciliani, Ernani* and *Simon Boccanegra,* the two first-act arias from *Figaro,* the two from *The Magic Flute* (in Italian), and a hammed-up *Catalogue Aria,* rhythmically inexact *Champagne Aria* and fine *Serenade* from *Don Giovanni.* And Odyssey 32-16-0335 has the Mozart arias recorded in the mid-forties with the Metropolitan Opera Orchestra under Walter—*Se vuol ballare* and *Aprite un po' quegl' occhi* from *Figaro,* Osmin's aria from *The Seraglio* and *In diesen heiligen Hallen* from *The Magic Flute* (both in Italian), another hammed-up *Catalogue Aria* and rhythmically inexact *Champagne Aria* from *Don Giovanni,* and the concert aria *Mentre ti lascio.* (Reduce treble for the Victrola and Odyssey records.) In addition, his performance of Figaro can be heard in the underground tapes of broadcasts of the 1943 and 44 Metropolitan *Figaro* superbly conducted by Walter, with Steber, Sayão, Novotna and Brownlee.

Ponselle. She is heard on Victrola VIC-1507 in arias from *Norma, Ernani, Il Trovatore, La Forza del Destino, Aida* and *Otello*

243

(with her voice made unrecognizable by incorrect speed in *Ave Maria*) and the final duet of *Aida* with Martinelli. See also under Collections: *Unforgettable Voices from Italian Opera*, Victrola VIC-1395.

Rachmaninov. The performance of Schumann's *Carnaval* that was on Victor LCT-12 and later on Camden CAL-396 is now available on imported Camden LCC-7 (I). And the performances of Beethoven's Sonata Op. 30 No. 3 and Schubert's Op. 162 with Kreisler are on Victor LM-6099.

Rethberg. Camden CAL-335 had her performances of arias from Mozart's *Il Re Pastore* and *Don Giovanni, Faust, Un Ballo in Maschera* and *Otello,* but with fake electronic gloss and resonance. ASCO 115 had her early Brunswick recordings of arias from Handel's *Sosarme, The Magic Flute, Figaro* (the Countess's two, the first in German), *Der Freischütz* and *Aida.* She can be heard in a duet from *Carmen* with Tauber (in German) on Seraphim 60086; and see also under Collections: *Unforgettable Voices from German Opera*, Victrola VIC-1455.

Ritchie. She sings in Handel's *Sosarme* on Oiseau-Lyre 50091/3 and in Mahler's Symphony No. 4 with the Concertgebouw Orchestra under van Beinum on imported Decca ACL-212. Her unequalled performance of Schubert's *Der Hirt auf dem Felsen* with de Peyer is something to hunt for.

Roswaenge. He sings in Beecham's pre-war *Magic Flute;* and imported Odeon 73382 (G) has performances (in German) of arias from *Oberon, Carmen, Rigoletto, Il Trovatore, Un Ballo in Maschera, Aida* and (in Italian) *Der Rosenkavalier.*

Sayão. Her performances of arias from *Figaro, Don Giovanni, La Sonnambula* and *La Traviata,* are on Odyssey 32-16-0377. And she is the Susanna in the superb 1943 and 44 Metropolitan *Figaro* conducted by Walter, on underground tapes.

Schipa. He sings in the *Don Pasquale* on imported Voce del Padrone QSO-53/5 (I); imported Pathé Voix Illustres VOI-50.011 (F) and Voce del Padrone COHL-117 have his performances—regrettably with added artificial resonance—of arias from *Don Pasquale* and *L'Elisir d'Amore,* duets from *Don Pasquale* and *La Sonnambula* with dal Monte, and pieces by Gluck and Alessandro Scarlatti; and imported RCA Italiana LM-20113 (I), which I haven't heard, has arias from *Don*

Giovanni, La Favorita and *Rigoletto.* One hopes for reissues here, commercial or underground, of the arias from *The Barber of Seville, Parmi veder le lagrime* from *Rigoletto* and *Quando le sere* from *Luisa Miller.* See also under Collections: *Great Voices of the Century,* Seraphim 60113; *Unforgettable Voices from Italian Opera,* Victrola VIC-1395.

Schlusnus. He sings with Lehmann in a duet from *Don Giovanni* on Rococo 5257.

Schnabel. Of the performances on the discontinued Angel and imported Pathé (F) COLH records, the first reissued on Seraphim 60115, *The Art of Artur Schnabel,* were the post-war performances of Mozart's Sonata K.570 and Rondo K.511, the least interesting two of Schubert's Impromptus, Weber's *Invitation to the Dance,* and a few pieces by Brahms; included in *Six Legendary Pianists,* Seraphim 6045, was the post-war Schubert *Moments musicaux;* in *Six Concertos,* Seraphim 6043, the post-war Beethoven Concerto No. 2 with the Philharmonia under Dobrowen; in *Six Chamber Music Masterpieces,* Seraphim 6044, the pre-war Mozart Quartet K.478 with members of the Pro Arte Quartet.

As I write, Seraphim is about to reissue all the Beethoven sonatas on 6063/4/5/6, and the Beethoven Bagatelles and variations on 6067.

As for the Beethoven concertos, Angel GR-4006 and COLH-1/5 had not the performances of the thirties with English orchestras under Sargent, which were Schnabel's best, but— with the pre-war No. 1—the post-war Nos. 2, 3, 4 and 5 with the Philharmonia under Dobrowen and Galliera; and of these Nos. 3 and 4 were excellent and satisfying when heard by themselves, but revealed losses in suppleness, grace, and continuity of tension and outline when compared with the early performances. Moreover the Angel records reproduced them with electronically reprocessed sound that was so poor that I recommended acquiring them with the natural and more solid sound they had on imported Electrola 60620/3 and 80845 (G). One hopes, therefore, for an underground reissue of the early performances that were on Victor LCT-6700 years ago. Meanwhile Victrola VIC-1505 offers the performance of No. 4 that Schnabel recorded with the Chicago Symphony under Stock in 1942, which is very close to the early performance and reproduced with more spacious and lustrous sound (reduce bass and increase treble for correct orchestral balance), but with loss of clear definition when Schnabel plays in fast tempo. And VIC-1511 has the excellent performance of No. 5 that he recorded with the same orchestra and conductor at that time (bass must be increased, which increases the low-pitched hum in the sound).

A desirable underground release would be Schnabel's performances of Beethoven's cello sonatas with Fournier, which were on Victor LCT-1124 years ago.

One hopes for Seraphim reissues of Schnabel's performances of Schubert; meanwhile the posthumous Sonata in B flat formerly on Angel COLH-33 is on imported Pathé Gravures Illustres COLH-33 (F), the Sonata Op. 53 formerly on Angel COLH-83 now on imported Gravures Illustres COLH-83, the posthumous Sonata in A on imported Gravures Illustres COLH-84. The *Trout* Quintet formerly on Angel COLH-40 is on imported Gravures Illustres COLH-40, the *Moments musicaux,* as I mentioned earlier, in *Six Legendary Pianists,* Seraphim 6045; but the Impromptus are unavailable.

Of Mozart, the Sonatas K.310, 332 and 570 and Rondo K.511 were listed as available on imported Pathé COLH-305 (F) in the fall of 1969; and the Sonata K.570 and Rondo K.511, as I mentioned earlier, are among the pieces on Seraphim 60115, *The Art of Artur Schnabel.* Of the pre-war performances of the Concertos K.467 and 595 formerly on Angel COLH-67 and the one of K.459 formerly on imported Odeon 80829 (G), only the first and third are announced for reissue in March or April 1971 on imported World Record Club SH-142 (E). The second, and the post-war performances of K.466 and 491 that were briefly on Victor LHMV-1012, are unavailable. But underground records have the broadcast performances of the Concerto K.482 with the New York Philharmonic under Walter, and K.488 with the Philharmonic under Rodzinski; and one hopes for underground releases of the other Mozart concertos I have mentioned if they aren't reissued on Seraphim records.

The underground record with the Concerto K.488 has also the Sonata K.333; the two-record set with the Concerto K.482 has the incomparable performances with Szigeti of Mozart's Sonata K.481 and Beethoven's Opp. 24 and 96 at the Frick Collection in the late forties.

Schorr. His impersonation of Hans Sachs in *Die Meistersinger* is documented by most of the excerpts he recorded between 1927 and 1931, formerly on Angel COLH-137, now on imported Voix Illustres VOI-50.023 (F). They include the quintet recorded with Schumann and Melchior, but not, regrettably, the duet *Sieh' Evchen, dächt' ich doch* that Schorr recorded with Rethberg for Victor.

Schumann. Her performances of Schubert songs that were on Angel COLH-130 and 131 are available on imported Pathé Voix Illustres VOI-50.006 and 50.031 (F); and the one of *Nacht und Träume* is on Seraphim 60113, *Great Voices of the Century*. In addition her Sophie in *Der Rosenkavalier* can be heard in the historic performance with Lehmann, Olszewska and Mayr on Seraphim 6041, which has also her performances of eight Strauss songs. In the early performances on Rococo 6—of Zerlina's arias from *Don Giovanni* and the *Jewel Song* from *Faust* (in German, and with raucous orchestral accompaniments)—one hears her voice with the amplitude and bloom it had at the beginning, used with the flawless musical art that was hers already then. Perennial 1001 (Perennial Records, 130 Arnold Street, Staten Island, N.Y. 10301) has better reproduction of her 1921 performances of Blonde's arias from *The Seraglio* (in reverse order from that of the label), her 1925 *Ach, ich fühl's* from *The Magic Flute* and *Deh vieni* from *Figaro* (in German, but marvelously sung and phrased), a 1928 performance—the voice in its prime, the style superb—of a piece from Zeller's *Der Vogelhändler,* a beautiful 1938 performance of Brahms's song *Bitteres zu sagen,* an enchanting one of his *Blinde Kuh,* a fine 1945 performance of an aria from Bach's *St. Matthew Passion.* Watch for the songs of Strauss and Wolf that were on Angel COLH-102, and the Strauss songs and Mozart arias that were on Angel COLH-154.

Schumann-Heink. When she recorded the performances on Rococo 11 her voice had lost its beauty but retained its steadiness and power, and she deployed it with extraordinary stylistic and expressive force in an amazing variety of styles in pieces ranging from the florid *Brindisi* from *Lucrezia Borgia* (in which she takes the liberties with tempo customary in her period) to *Erda's Warning* in *Das Rheingold*. Rococo 5271 offers, with additional operatic excerpts, impressive performances of songs —Schubert's *Die Forelle,* Schumann's *Mondnacht,* Brahms's *Sapphische Ode,* and above all Schubert's *Erlkönig,* in which she astounds one with the four voices she produces and overwhelms one with her expressive use of them. Her performances are reproduced less well on Victrola VIC-1409. See also under Collections: *Unforgettable Voices from German Opera,* Victrola VIC-1455.

Sembrich. The voice and style that are so impressive in the duet with de Gogorza on Cantilena 6203 are not heard in even the best of her performances on Cantilena 6212—of the arias from *Faust* and *La Traviata;* and some of the performances are shockingly poor.

Slezak. In the performances of arias from *Lakmé, Le Prophète, Stradella, Euryanthe* and *Otello* on Scala 823, and arias from *The Magic Flute, L'Africaine, William Tell, Carmen, Il Trovatore* and *Aida* on 844, one hears a tenor voice of remarkable beauty and power that is capable also of delicate lyricism, and of the sensitive phrasing in the songs of Mozart, Schubert, Wolf and Strauss on the records.

Sobinov. Rococo 19 has his beautiful and affecting performances of Lensky's arias from *Eugene Onegin* and similar performances of arias from other Russian operas and from *Don Pasquale, Mignon, The Pearl Fishers* and *Lohengrin* (all in Russian).

Stabile. The Falstaff of Toscanini's La Scala and Salzburg performances of *Falstaff* is heard on Rococo 5277 in a long excerpt from Act 1 ending with *L'onore!* and in the wooing of Mistress Ford in Act 2 as far as *Quand' ero paggio,* in which his voice is good and used with superb expressive effect. (Regrettably the additional excerpts on Telefunken 78s—the interview with Mistress Quickly in Act 2 and *Ehi! Taverniere!* from Act 3— are not included.) The record has also arias from *Figaro, Don Giovanni, Lucia* and *Otello* (this one inadequately accompanied).

Steber. Odyssey 32-16-0363 has the 1953 performances of Constanza's *Traurigkeit ward mir zum Lose,* Donna Elvira's *Mi tradi,* Donna Anna's *Non mi dir,* Fiordiligi's *Per pietà,* Pamina's *Ach, ich fühl's* and an aria from *The Impresario* with orchestra under Walter. But of the early Victor performances of Constanza's *Martern aller Arten* (in English), the Countess's and Cherubino's arias and Susanna's *Deh vieni,* Zerlina's *Batti, batti,* Pamina's *Ach, ich fühl's* and arias from *Faust* and *Carmen,* only the first has been reissued on Victrola VIC-1455, *Unforgettable Voices from German Opera.* Columbia hasn't yet reissued her performances of arias and duets from Verdi's *Ernani, La Traviata, La Forza del Destino, Don Carlo* and *Otello;* and though her overwhelming performance of Berlioz's *Les Nuits d'été* with an orchestra under Mitropoulos is in the catalogue it 'is unobtainable. But her unforgettable performance of the Countess in the 1943 and 44 Metropolitan *Figaro* superbly conducted by Walter can be heard in underground tapes of the broadcasts; and perhaps there will be underground reissues of the Columbia Verdi and Berlioz performances.

Stignani. She sings in the *Norma* with Callas on Seraphim 6037.

Supervia. HMV (Odeon when imported) HQM-1220 has her performances of arias from *La Cenerentola* and *Carmen.*

Szigeti. The great first (1932) performance of the Beethoven Concerto has just been made available on HMV (Odeon when imported) HQM-1224 (E); and until they are similarly reissued, or released on underground records, the Columbia LPs with the other concertos—ML-4286 with the Bach, ML-2217 with the Mendelssohn, ML-4533 with the Mozart and Prokofiev—are worth hunting for. At present imported Odeon HQM-1127 (E) has a few other performances Szigeti recorded in his prime—of Bach's Concerto in D minor for two violins, with Flesch as the impressive second soloist; Tartini's Concerto in D minor; and two pieces that I find uninteresting: an arrangement of the slow movement of Bach's Concerto in F minor for clavier, and Brahms's Sonata Op. 108, with the pianist Petri. In addition his performance of Bach's *Chaconne* is preserved by the recording of the six Sonatas and Partitas for unaccompanied violin on Bach Guild 627/9; Vanguard VRS-1109/12 has the Beethoven sonata series at the Library of Congress in the early forties, in which Arrau's wooden playing has a dampening effect on Szigeti much of the time, but not in the Sonata Op. 47 (*Kreut-*

zer), where Szigeti's own feeling is strong enough to produce incandescent playing; and in another Library of Congress concert on Vanguard 1130/1 he is stimulated by the piano-playing of Bartók in superb performances of Beethoven's *Kreutzer* Sonata, Debussy's Sonata and two Bartók works; but the Mozart sonatas on Vanguard S-265/7 were recorded when Szigeti could no longer produce bearable sounds with his instrument. Underground records have the imcomparable performances of Mozart's Sonata K.481 and Beethoven's Opp. 24 and 96 with Schnabel at the Frick Collection in the late forties.

Tauber. Seraphim 60086 has fine early performances of the Italian aria from *Der Rosenkavalier* and (in German) arias from *Rigoletto, La Traviata* and *Il Trovatore* and a duet from *Carmen* with Rethberg; but also poor ones, including a badly distorted duet from *Aida*.

Tetrazzini. The extraordinary beauty and spectacular agility of her voice are exhibited on Rococo 13 in several performances in which her deployment of it is enjoyably straightforward, and in several others in which the total absence of musical phrasing and style and mere exactness of time is painful.

Teyte. Her exquisitely pure and bright soprano voice was heard on Angel COLH-138 in *Le Spectre de la rose* and *L'Absence* from Berlioz's *Les Nuits d'été* and songs of Chausson and Duparc, among others. It can be heard in Debussy's *Beau soir* on Seraphim 60113, *Great Voices of the Century*.

Thorborg. Her Fricka in *Die Walküre* is documented by two excerpts on Victrola VIC-1455, *Unforgettable Voices from German Opera*. And she sings in Toscanini's 1940 *Missa Solemnis* on an underground tape.

Toscanini. Music-lovers should not be deterred from acquiring his great performances by the fact that they are reproduced in mono, not stereo, sound, and often in defective mono sound at that—defective not, as is generally believed, because of the acoustic peculiarities of Studio 8H (many of the defective NBC Symphony recordings were made in acoustically excellent Carnegie Hall) but because of the incompetence, equalled by the conceit and presumption, of the Victor men who supervised the recording sessions—not the engineers but the producers who were empowered to tell the engineers where to place the

Toscanini (*continued*)

microphone, and to make other decisions which affected the sound that was imprinted on wax or acetate or tape. The superb Debussy *Ibéria* is evidence of the fact that excellent recordings could be made in 8H when the producer—in this case Richard Mohr—had the single microphone placed at what an NBC engineer named Johnston had established as the optimum location, and also—as Johnston had further discovered to be necessary—had the seats in the hall pushed all the way back toward the wall. But for Debussy's *La Mer* Mohr chose to place the microphone a few feet back from the Johnston location and to push the seats only part of the way back toward the wall; and the result was sound with less than the presence and distinctness of *Ibéria's*. Worse still, at a 1945 session a producer named Richard Gilbert, after following Johnston's directions and achieving a beautiful-sounding Gershwin *An American in Paris*, decided, for the next piece, to place several microphones in a way he had thought up, and achieved the shallow, coarse sound of the Sousa *Stars and Stripes Forever*. As for Carnegie Hall, the microphone-placement with which NBC engineers had obtained the excellent sound of the broadcasts of Toscanini's occasional concerts there was known; but in 1947 Gilbert took it into his head not only to place the microphone further back but to cover the side boxes and parquet with draperies, and in this way produced the lusterless, airless sound of the Tchaikovsky *Pathétique;* and the weaker, dimmer sound of the Mendelssohn *Midsummer Night's Dream* music resulted from his placing the microphone—for this lightly scored music!—even further back. Mohr, told in 1953 the microphone-placement that had achieved the beautiful and balanced sound of the 1940 broadcast *Missa Solemnis,* rejected it; and what he did instead achieved the sound on LM-6013 in which the chorus predominates over the soloists and orchestra.

Thus, whereas it would have been unthinkable that anyone should change what Toscanini produced at a concert, a Victor producer could, and did, change it when Toscanini produced the performance for a recording; and the producers' decisions, in many cases, imprinted on the wax or acetate or tape a faulty transformation of the original spacious, lustrous, balanced

Toscanini (*continued*)

sound instead of the facsimile that correct microphone-placement would have achieved. And the advent of tape gave the producers and editors an additional means of changing what Toscanini had achieved: the sound on the original tape, after being heard and approved by Toscanini, could be, and was, changed when it was transferred to the working tape used in the processing of the metal parts for the final disc records. I happened to hear, on one occasion, the overwhelmingly beautiful, spacious, solid sound imprinted on the original tape of Toscanini's performance of Beethoven's Eighth, and the unrecognizably transformed sound—compressed, thin, shallow, lusterless—on the working tape that an editor named Slick had made for the processing of the records; and on another occasion I heard the similarly beautiful sound on the original tape, from which the working tape had been made with an extreme boosting of treble that produced the ear-piercing trumpet sound at the beginning of Musorgsky's *Pictures at an Exhibition,* the snarling sound of the brass in *Catacombs,* the harsh sound of the violins, the raucous sound of the full orchestra, on LM-1838. Nor was this all that tape made possible: an editor named Gerhardt persuaded Walter Toscanini to authorize his inflicting on the clear, bright, solid sound of the Debussy *La Mer* already issued on LM-1221 increasing amounts of what Victor advertised as "enhancement" by artificial echo-chamber resonance that produced the glossy, blurred and blowzy *La Mer* on LM-1833.* And the transfer of 78-rpm recordings to LP provided Gerhardt and others with the opportunity for various types of electronic "enhancement" that spoiled good recordings and made poor ones worse—an atrocious example being the 1964 version of the 1946 Tchaikovsky *Romeo and Juliet* on LM-7032,

* One reason why this falsification continued and was carried to extremes was the record-reviewers' enthusiastic approval of it, exemplified by Roland Gelatt's review in *High Fidelity* which found that the "enhancement" gave the *La Mer* on LM-1833 "the atmosphere of a concert hall", which was "a real improvement", adding only that electronic trickery couldn't give the recording the "clarity, brilliance and presence" of the recording of Musorgsky's *Pictures*—"clarity, brilliance and presence" being what Gelatt heard in the sound distorted and falsified by the extreme boosting of treble.

Toscanini (*continued*)

in which the solid, bright, clear sound of the original 78-rpm recording was deprived of its solidity by a bass-cut, of its brightness by a treble-cut to eliminate surface noise, and of its clarity by the addition of echo-chamber resonance.

In 1966, after it had discontinued several important Toscanini recordings—including the Act 2 of Gluck's *Orfeo,* Berlioz *Harold in Italy* and Strauss *Don Quixote*—Victor withdrew most of the rest for the announced purpose of commemorating the hundredth anniversary of Toscanini's birth in 1967 by reissuing the recordings on a new series of lower-priced Victrola records with their true sound, which would be obtained by having the editor assigned to the project, Robert Zarbock, make new transfers of the sound from the original metal parts of the 78-rpm recordings or the original tapes of LP recordings, without change, to the working tapes for the new records. But when, in 1967, the first group of the new Victrolas appeared, one discovered that Zarbock had obeyed instructions to the extent of transferring the original clear, bright, solid sound of the Debussy *La Mer* to VIC-1246, but had disobeyed them by giving the transferred sound a treble-boost which made the violins glistening and silky, the brass brighter and sharper—all attractive to the ear, but false. To obtain the true sound of violins and brass one had to be able to cancel the treble-boost—which one could do only with a first-class treble-control that would cut the upper end of the treble without cutting back into the middle (an inferior treble-control which cut back into the middle would remove not only the treble-boost but some of the brightness of the original sound). And comparison of the Dvořák *New World* Symphony on VIC-1249 with the excellent one on the first-issued LM-1778 revealed not only Zarbock's treble-boost in the glistening, silky violins and brighter brass, but a lessened solidity down below, which had to be remedied by increasing bass with the bass-control. As the recordings continued to appear on the new Victrola records most of them had the treble-boost that required reduction of treble and the insufficient solidity that required increase of bass.

In a few instances Zarbock disobeyed instructions further by not making the new transfer from the original recording. Thus,

Toscanini (*continued*)

he chose to transfer to the Victrola Beethoven Eighth not the marvelous sound on the original tape but the transformation of that sound on Slick's working tape, which he was able to make more agreeable to the ear, but to which he couldn't restore the spaciousness, luster and solidity that Slick had removed. Similarly Zarbock transferred to the Victrola Musorgsky *Pictures* the sound not of the original tape but of the working tape with the extreme treble-boost that produced again the ear-piercing trumpet at the beginning, the snarling brass in *Catacombs,* the harsh violins, the raucous sound of the full orchestra. And Zarbock transferred to the Victrola finale of *Die Götterdämmerung* not the sound of the original 78-rpm recording but that of the first LP transfer on LCT-1116, which had not only cuts in treble and bass that reduced the brilliance and solidity of the superb original sound, but a slight bass hum not in the original; and the bass-boost Zarbock gave this LCT transfer in his new Victrola transfer increased that hum to what sounded like a strong sustained organ pedal note throughout the performance. The head of Quality Control at Victor who explained all this to me in reply to my inquiry told me also that Zarbock did not intend to correct the defect; and in this he was not reversed by the Manager of Red Seal, Roger G. Hall (who earlier had expressed his approval of Zarbock's dealing with the Beethoven Eighth and all the Victrola reissues). And so— not for the first time—the intentions of a corporate entity, RCA Victor, were defeated by the actions, behind the corporate façade, of individuals, and this corporate entity was made to bear publicly the responsibility for a scandalously defective recording produced by an individual deficient not only in judgment but in conscience.

Nor was this all. Though the announced intention had been to put the true sound of the original recordings on the Victrola records for the music-lovers interested in Toscanini's performances, the sales division of Victor was able to get the company to begin, early in 1968, to issue the recordings both in their original mono sound on VIC records and in "electronically reprocessed stereo" versions on VICS records for stereo-lovers, who, I would guess, were not interested in Toscanini even in

Toscanini (*continued*)

pseudo-stereo sound. Most retail dealers decided immediately to stock only the VICS records, so that the VIC records were difficult to obtain; and by now, though Victor insists both are available, the Schwann catalogue lists only the VICS', which are in fact the only ones obtainable. But the earlier Victrolas issued only in mono are still available on VIC records. (I was told that the original mono sound could be obtained from a VICS version by reducing bass 4 db in the left channel, increasing bass 4 db in the right channel, and raising the level 3 db in the left channel; but a former Victor technician was reported to have said one could recover the original mono sound by playing the pseudo-stereo in the mono [A+B] mode and adding a step of bass.)

Of the early recordings with the New York Philharmonic (designated by P), the BBC Symphony (B) and the NBC Symphony (N), Victor's first LP transfers were LCT-1013, with Beethoven's Seventh (P); 1023, with the Brahms *Haydn Variations* (P) and Beethoven First (B); 1042, with Beethoven's *Pastoral* (B); 1041, with Beethoven's *Leonore* Overture No. 1 (B), two movements from his Quartet Op. 135 (N) and his Fifth Symphony (N); and 7, with Haydn's Symphony No. 88 (N). And Victor's later Camden transfers of the Philharmonic recordings, with sound of varying quality, were CAL-352, with Beethoven's Seventh; 326, with Mozart's *Haffner* Symphony, Mendelssohn's Scherzo, the Overture to Rossini's *The Barber of Seville*, and the Brahms *Haydn Variations;* 309, with the Overture to Rossini's *Semiramide,* the two *La Traviata* Preludes of Verdi, and Wagner's *Siegfried-Idyll;* and 375, with Haydn's *Clock* Symphony, the Prelude to Wagner's *Lohengrin,* and *Dawn and Siegfried's Rhine Journey* from his *Die Götterdämmerung.*

It is not a new transfer from the original Philharmonic 78-rpm recording of Beethoven's Seventh that is on Victrola VIC-1502, with sound that has less solidity than it had on LCT-1013 and fluctuates in volume and brightness, but a reissue of the transfer that was on Camden CAL-352, which has been released on a Camden record in England. CAL-326 has also been released in England as CDN-1055, CAL-309 as CDN-1045, and

Toscanini (*continued*)

CAL-375 as CDN-1054; and they will presumably be released here as Victrolas.

In commemoration of the hundredth anniversary of Toscanini's birth the BBC Symphony performances of Beethoven's First, Fourth and *Pastoral* Symphonies, his *Leonore* Overture No. 1, and the Overture to Mozart's *The Magic Flute* were reissued on Saraphim 6015, regrettably with sound made unnatural and poor by filtering, boosting of treble and addition of echo-chamber resonance. Reported to be more faithful to the originals are the transfers of Beethoven's First and Fourth on imported World Record Club SH-134 (E) and of his *Pastoral* on SH-112; and imported Odeon QIM-6398 (I) has the *Leonore* No. 1, the Overtures to *The Magic Flute* and Rossini's *La Scala di Seta,* and the Weber-Berlioz *Invitation to the Dance.*

The performance of Schubert's Ninth with the Philadelphia Orchestra is still available on Victor LD-2663.

As for the NBC Symphony performances, several of major importance—Act 2 of Gluck's *Orfeo,* Berlioz's *Harold in Italy,* Schubert's Ninth, Strauss's *Don Quixote*—have not as yet been reissued on Victrola; and a number of those issued on Victrola in England haven't yet been issued here; but a few of these— Mozart's Symphony K.551, Beethoven's *Fidelio* and *Missa Solemnis* and Verdi's *Requiem*—are still available here on the first-issued LM records. In the following listing of the performances —under alphabetically ordered names of composers—the recommendation to reduce treble in the Victrola transfers is expressed by (—t), the recommendation to increase bass by (+b).

Of Beethoven, the 1944 broadcast of the Piano Concerto No. 4 with Serkin is on Victor LM-2797; the 1944 broadcast of *Fidelio,* including the *Leonore* Overture No. 3, with Bampton, Steber and Peerce, is on LM-6025; the 1953 *Missa Solemnis* with Marshall, Merriman, Conley, Hines and the Shaw Chorale, is on LM-6013. And VIC-8000 has the new Victrola transfers of the nine symphonies, the Septet, the two movements of the Quartet Op. 135 (—t, +b), and these overtures: *Prometheus, Egmont* (—t), *Coriolan* (—t, +b), *For the Consecration of the House* (—t, +b). I have described what Zarbock did with the sound of the Symphony No. 8; as for the others, it wasn't pos-

Toscanini (*continued*)

sible for him to give the clear, well-balanced sound of No. 9 the spaciousness of Nos. 3, 6 and 7 that it lacked, or to put the airless sound of the rest of No. 2 into the greater space around the second movement; but he did manage to brighten the dull sound of most of No. 4 and give much of No. 5 the solidity it lacked; and his are the best-sounding versions of the symphonies issued thus far, which can be made even better by increasing bass in all, except for the later three movements of No. 5, and reducing treble in Nos. 1, 3, 6, 7, the second movements of Nos. 2, 4 and 5, the third movement of No. 9. The sound of the other works is good.

VIC-1521 has the 1945 Piano Concerto No. 1 with Dorfmann, with the atrociously reproduced broadcast of the tremendous *Leonore* Overture No. 3 of the 1939 Beethoven cycle.

The greater 1940 broadcast of the *Missa*—more relaxed and expansive, and with the superior singing of Milanov, Thorborg, Bjoerling and Kipnis—is available on an underground tape, and possibly on underground discs. One hopes for such underground releases of the greatest of his Beethoven Ninths—the one he broadcast with the New York Philharmonic in 1936— and the NBC broadcasts of the other symphonies and the overtures in his 1939 Beethoven cycle.

Of Berlioz, the 1947 broadcast of *Romeo and Juliet* is on LM-7034. In the new transfer, on VIC-1398, of the two movements —*Romeo Alone; Festivities at the Capulets'* and *Love Scene*— that Toscanini recorded after the broadcast the beginning of the *Love Scene* wavers in volume and pitch as it does not in the original 78-rpm recording; and the *Queen Mab* Scherzo on VIC-1267 retains the extreme treble-boost in an earlier transfer that makes the delicate antique cymbals near the end sound like big bells. The *Roman Carnival* Overture is on VIC-1244 (—t, +b), with Respighi's *Fountains* and *Pines of Rome* (—t, +b); the *Rákóczy March* is in the collection *Invitation to the Dance,* VIC-1321. Until *Harold in Italy* is reissued, or is released on an underground record, it can be obtained on VRA-2028 from Yamano Music Co., 6-5, 4 Chome, Ginza, Cho-ku, Tokyo, Japan.

The suite from Bizet's *Carmen* is on VIC-1263 (—t, +b),

Toscanini (*continued*)

with Tchaikovsky's *Nutcracker Suite* and Ponchielli's *Dance of the Hours* (both —t, +b).

Brahms's Symphonies and *Variations on a Theme of Haydn* (—t) are on VIC-6400.

The new Victrola transfer of Cherubini's *Requiem,* not yet issued here, is available in England in VCM-10, with Verdi's *Requiem, Te Deum, Hymn of the Nations* and *Va, pensiero* from *Nabucco.*

Debussy's *La Mer* (—t) and *Ibéria* are on VIC-1246, with Franck's *Psyche and Eros* (—t, +b).

The Overture to Donizetti's *Don Pasquale* that was on LM-6026 hasn't been reissued.

Dvořák's No. 9 (old No. 5) (*From the New World*) is on VIC-1249 (—t, +b), with Schumann's *Manfred* Overture (—t, +b, but increase treble in the later half).

Franck's *Psyche and Eros:* see Debussy.

Until the 1952 broadcast of Act 2 of Gluck's *Orfeo ed Euridice* with Merriman, Gibson and the Shaw Chorale that was on LM-1850 and LVT-1041 is reissued, or is released on an underground record, it can be obtained on VRA-2045 from Yamano in Tokyo. An even more desirable underground release would be the superior 1945 broadcast.

Of the Haydn Symphony No. 94 (*Surprise*) (—t, +b) on VIC-1262 the Andante and Minuet are too fast for the proper flow, articulation and effect of the music—sacrificed for the demonstration of a real *andante* and *allegro molto* as against the usual ones Toscanini considered to be "too slow". As for the superb No. 101 (*Clock*) on the reverse side, atrociously recorded in Studio 3A, the new Victrola transfer produces the first two movements with the original ample, solid 78-rpm sound (and surface noise) in the extreme acoustic deadness of the studio, but the last two with thin, pallid sound like that of a poor LP transfer. The 1949 Symphony No. 99 included in *A Toscanini Treasury,* LM-6711, is a fine realization of the incandescent work, but not Toscanini's best: the introductory Adagio hasn't the relaxed, unhurried spaciousness, and the Vivace assai that follows and concluding Vivace haven't the animation and energy of the performance broadcast in 1941, which would be

Toscanini (*continued*)

a desirable underground release. So would the broadcasts of the 1938 Symphony No. 98, more relaxed and spacious than the 1945 performance issued on M-1025 and never transferred to LP; the 1938 No. 88, 1944 No. 92 (*Oxford*), 1943 No. 94, 1942 No. 101 and 1943 No. 104. Meanwhile Yamano VRA-2039 has Nos. 88 and 99 (presumably the 1949 performance).

Mendelssohn's music for *A Midsummer Night's Dream* (+t in the Overture and Scherzo, +b in the Intermezzo, Nocturne and Scherzo) is allegedly on VIC-1337 but actually on VICS-1337, with Schumann's uninteresting Symphony No. 3. And the *Italian* Symphony (—t in the second and third movements, +b in the first, third and fourth) is allegedly on VIC-1341 but actually on VICS-1341, with Weber's Overtures to *Euryanthe, Oberon* and *Der Freischütz* (+b in the last two). Neither the 1947 broadcast of the entire Octet that was on LM-1869 nor the incandescent scherzo movement recorded in 1945 has been reissued; and both would be desirable underground releases. So would the 1947 broadcast of the better—and better reproduced —performance of *A Midsummer Night's Dream* that preceded the recording session.

Of Mozart, the Symphony K.551 (known as *Jupiter*) and Bassoon Concerto K.191 are on LM-1030; the Victrola transfers of the Symphonies K.543 and K.550 (*the* G-minor) (—t, +b) on VIC-1330. The second and third movements of K.543 are played too fast for the proper flow, articulation and effect of the music —sacrificed, again, for the demonstration of a real *andante* and *allegretto* instead of the usual ones that Toscanini contended were "too slow". Victoria transfers included in VCM-7 in England but not yet issued here are the Divertimento K.287 formerly on LM-13 and (with "enhanced" sound) LM-2001; the Symphony K.385 (*Haffner*), also atrociously recorded in Studio 3A and formerly "enhanced" on LM-1038; the Symphony K.551; and the Overtures to *Figaro, Don Giovanni* and *The Magic Flute* formerly on LM-7026. Desirable underground releases would be the 1939 recording of the G-minor Symphony and broadcast of the Symphony K.504 (*Prague*) and 1941 broadcast of the Sinfonie Concertante K.364 for violin and viola.

Musorgsky's *Pictures at an Exhibition* (reduce treble dras-

Toscanini (*continued*)

tically) is on VIC-1273, with Ravel's *Daphnis and Chloë* Suite.

The Prokofiev *Classical Symphony* formerly on LM-9020—with a second movement in strict obedience to the *Larghetto* marked in the score but too slow for the proper flow and effect of the music—hasn't been reissued. A desirable underground release would be an earlier broadcast with a more animated Larghetto.

Respighi's *Fountains* and *Pines of Rome* are on VIC-1244 (—t, +b).

Rossini's Overtures to *L'Italiana in Algeri*, *La Cenerentola* and *The Siege of Corinth* are on VIC-1248, with Verdi's Preludes to Acts 1 and 3 of *La Traviata* (—t, +b) and Overtures to *La Forza del Destino* and *I Vespri Siciliani*. VIC-1274 has Rossini's Overtures to *Semiramide* (—t, +b), *William Tell* (—t) *Il Signor Bruschino* (+t), *La Gazza Ladra* (+t, +b) and *The Barber of Seville* (+b, +t in the second half), and the *Passo a sei* from *William Tell* (+t).

Schubert's Symphony No. 5 (—t, +b) and *Unfinished Symphony* (—t in both movements, +b in second) are allegedly on VIC-1315 but actually on VICS-1315. The 1953 Symphony No. 9 formerly on LM-1835 is unavailable; and if there is no Victrola reissue an underground one would be desirable.

Schumann's *Manfred* Overture: see Dvořák.

Smetana's *Die Moldau* (—t, +b) is on VIC-1245, with Tchaikovsky's *Romeo and Juliet* (—t, +b), which exhibits a loss of brightness and solidity beginning near the end of the introduction and continuing until the suddenly quiet passage for muted violins in the exposition. The record has also Glinka's *Kamarinskaya* and Liadov's *Kikimora*.

Strauss's *Don Juan* and *Till Eulenspiegel* are on VIC-1267 (—t), with Dukas's *The Sorcerer's Apprentice*. Until the 1953 *Don Quixote* formerly on LM-2026 is reissued it can be obtained from Yamano on VRA-2023; but a desirable underground release would be the more animated and energetic performance broadcast in 1938 with Feuermann as cello soloist (the one now available, MJA-5001, is defective).

Tchaikovsky's *Manfred* (—t in the third movement and the later half of the finale) is allegedly on VIC-1315 and actually on

Toscanini *(continued)*

VICS-1315; his Symphony No. 6 *(Pathétique)* is on VIC-1268, which produces the first three movements with the original clear but lusterless and airless sound that can be brightened with additional treble, the first half of the finale with murky, unclean sound, and the second half with clear, clean sound that needs additional bass (and throughout there are 78-rpm swishes and other noises). For the *Romeo and Juliet* on VIC-1245 see the paragraph on Smetana's *Die Moldau;* and the *Nutcracker Suite* (—t, +b) is on VIC-1263, with the suite from *Carmen* and the *Dance of the Hours,* from *La Gioconda* (both —t, +b). Desirable underground releases would be the extraordinary *Nutcracker Suite* broadcast in 1940 and the superior 1940 broadcasts of the *Pathétique* and *Romeo and Juliet.*

Verdi's *Aida* (—t, +b) is allegedly on Victrola VIC-6113 but actually on VICS-6113; his *Un Ballo in Maschera* is still on LM-6112; his *Falstaff* is still on LM-6111; his *Otello* is still on LM-6107 (but on Victrola VICS-6120 in England); his *La Traviata* is still on LM-6003; Act 4 of his *Rigoletto* is allegedly on Victrola VIC-1314 but actually on VICS-1314, with the trio from *I Lombardi* and the Overture and aria *Quando le sere al placido* from *Luisa Miller* (—t in all, +b in the first); his *Requiem* is still on LM-6018; his *Te Deum* (—t, +b) is allegedly on Victrola VIC-1331 but actually on VICS-1331, with the *Hymn of the Nations* (—t) and the choral piece *Va pensiero* from *Nabucco* (+b). Toscanini's even greater 1940 NBC broadcast of the *Requiem*—more relaxed and expansive, and with the superior singing of Milanov, Castagna, Bjoerling and Moscona—is available on an underground tape, and possibly on underground discs.

Wagner's Prelude and Finale from *Tristan und Isolde* and Prelude and *Good Friday Spell* from *Parsifal* are on Victrola VIC-1278 (—t, +b in both); VIC-1247 has his Preludes to Act 1 and Act 3 of *Die Meistersinger* (—t, +b in the second), Preludes to Acts 1 and 3 of *Lohengrin* (—t, +b), *Siegfried-Idyll* (—t) and *A Faust Overture* (—t, but +t in the later half). The overwhelming performance of *Siegfried's Death and Funeral Music* (—t, +b) is allegedly on Victorola VIC-1316 but actually on VICS-1316, with the 1941 broadcast of the last scene of Act 1

Toscanini (*continued*)

of *Die Walküre* (—t), in which the clarity of orchestral texture, the sensitive, enlivening phrasing, the unfailing continuity and coherence, the unfailing immediate relation to the singing are an unending marvel, but the singing of Traubel and Melchior is undistinguished and reproduced, on the mono record I heard, with high-frequency distortion. Traubel is at her best in the finale of *Die Götterdämmerung* allegedly on Victrola VIC-1369 but actually on VICS-1369, which is disfigured by the enormous low-frequency hum I mentioned earlier; and the reverse side has the 1941 broadcast of *Dawn and Siegfried's Rhine Journey* from *Die Götterdämmerung* with, in addition this time, the duet of Brünnhilde and Siegfried sung by Traubel and Melchior.

The Overtures to Weber's *Euyranthe, Oberon* and *Der Freischütz* (+b in the last two) are allegedly on Victrola VIC-1341 but actually on VICS-1341, with Mendelssohn's *Italian* Symphony (—t in the second and third movements, +b in the first, third and fourth).

The five-record *Toscanini Treasury of Historic Broadcasts,* LM-6711, offers a group of previously unissued performances which includes only one of a work of major stature, Haydn's Symphony No. 99, and this one not Toscanini's best performance of the work, which is the one he broadcast in 1941. On the remaining nine sides the Toscanini powers are applied to lesser works that he performed only once or twice: Haydn's Sinfonie Concertante in E-flat, Leopold Mozart's *Toy Symphony,* Sibelius's Symphony No. 2 and his inferior *Pohjola's Daughter,* Brahms's saccharine *Liebeslieder Walzer* (enchantingly performed), his boring Serenade in A and *Gesang der Parzen,* Shostakovich's trashy Symphony No. 1, and—on three sides!—that inflated monstrosity of portentous banality, his Symphony No. 7 (*Leningrad*).

The collection of Toscanini's performances of 'pop' and light music, *Invitation to the Dance,* Victrola VIC-1321, doesn't include the superb Overtures to Hérold's *Zampa* and Suppé's *Poet and Peasant* and Sousa *The Stars and Stripes Forever,* but offers the Waldteufel *Skaters Waltz,* the Strauss *Blue Danube Waltz* and *Tritsch-Tratsch Polka,* the Paganini *Moto Perpetuo*

Toscanini (*continued*)

(the last two enable one to hear the hair-raising energy and fire of the early NBC Symphony performances), to which it adds the Berlioz *Rákóczy March,* the Weber-Berlioz *Invitation to the Dance* and the *Ballabili* from Verdi's *Otello* (+t, +b in the first four, +b in the *Rákóczy March,* —t, +b in the last two).

Of the pieces in the discontinued collection *Toscanini Conducts Overtures,* LM-7026, the Rossini Overtures to *The Siege of Corinth* and *L'Italiana in Algeri* are on Victrola VIC-1248, and the Victrola transfers of the Mozart Overtures to *Figaro, Don Giovanni* and *The Magic Flute* are included in VCM-7 in England; but the Overtures to Gluck's *Iphigénie en Aulide,* Cherubini's *Anacreon* and *Medea,* and Cimarosa's *The Secret Marriage* have not been reissued. (The discontinued collection is obtainable from Yamano on RA-2198/9.)

Traubel. The singing that delighted Toscanini in the finale of *Die Götterdämmerung* she recorded with him and the NBC Symphony in 1941 can be heard on Victrola VIC-1369 (which reproduces the performance with an enormous low-frequency hum). On the reverse side she sings the first-act duet with Melchior; and VIC-1316 has the final duet of Act 1 of *Die Walküre,* in which their singing is undistinguished. See also under Collections: *Unforgettable Voices from German Opera,* Victrola VIC-1455.

Urlus. His amazing singing in the various styles of the arias from *The Magic Flute, William Tell, Carmen, Otello, Die Meistersinger* and other works of Wagner is heard on Rococo 5238.

Valletti. He sings in the *Don Pasquale* on imported Cetra (Eurodisc) (G) and Cetra (I) LPC-1242; and imported Cetra LPC-55002 (I) has his beautiful singing in arias from *Don Giovanni, The Barber of Seville, L'Italiana in Algeri* and *La Sonnambula,* among others. (The electronically altered sound produced by Everest's versions of Cetra recordings is something to avoid.)

Walter. The pre-war performance of Act 1 of *Die Walküre* with Lehmann and Melchior that was on Angel COLH-133 is on imported Pathé Voix Illustres VOI-50.013 (F); the post-war performance of Mahler's *Das Lied von der Erde* with Ferrier and Patzak is on London 4212; the one of Mahler's Symphony No. 2 with the New York Philharmonic is on Columbia M2S-601,

And his superb 1943 and 44 Metropolitan *Figaro* with Pinza, Steber, Sayão, Novotna and Brownlee is on underground tapes. Wildbrunn. Rococo 5220 has her acoustically recorded performances (in German) of arias from *Don Giovanni, Un Ballo in Maschera* and *Fidelio* and excerpts from the Wagner music dramas.

RECORDED PERFORMANCES LISTED
UNDER NAMES OF COLLECTIONS

The Fabulous Forties at the Met, Odyssey 32-16-0304 (electronic pseudo-stereo), has, among others, Risë Stevens in *Che farò* from *Orfeo,* Baccaloni in *A un dottor* from *The Barber of Seville,* Tourel in *Una voce* from *The Barber,* Pinza in *Se vuol ballare* from *Figaro,* Singher in the *Queen Mab* Ballad from Gounod's *Romeo and Juliet,* Ralf in the *Prize Song* from *Die Meistersinger,* Sayão in an aria from *Manon,* and Traubel in *Elsa's Dream* from *Lohengrin,* in which her voice has lost some of its beauty in the earlier performance in the Victrola *Unforgettable Voices* below.

Great Voices of the Century, Seraphim 60113, has Schumann in Schubert's *Nacht und Träume,* Chaliapin in the *Hallucination Scene* from *Boris Godunov,* McCormack in *Where'er you Walk* from *Semele,* Leider and Melchior in the second-act duet from *Tristan und Isolde,* Maggie Teyte in Debussy's *Beau Soir,* Lehmann in *Mein Herr, was dächten Sie* from *Die Fledermaus,* Caruso in the 1902 *Questa o quella* from *Rigoletto,* Schipa in *Ah! dispar, vision* from *Manon.*

Unforgettable Voices in Unforgotten Performances from the German Operatic Repertoire, Victrola VIC-1455, has Flagstad's very first recorded performance (1935) of the finale of *Tristan,* Rethberg in *Senta's Ballad* from *Der fliegende Holländer,* Traubel in *Elsa's Dream* from *Lohengrin,* Thorborg in two passages from Fricka's berating of Wotan in *Die Walküre,* and Schumann-Heink in *Waltraute's Narrative* from *Die Götterdämmerung.*

Unforgettable Voices . . . from the Italian Operatic Repertoire, Victrola VIC-1395, has Caruso taking breath between words that should be connected in the 1904 *Celeste Aida,* Destinn distorting a few phrases in *D'amor sull' ali rosee* from *Il Trovatore* as I am sure she did not with Toscanini, Matzenauer in an aria from *L'Africaine*, Gadski in the fourth-act duet from *Il Trovatore* with Amato, Ponselle exhibiting no sense for coherent musical shape in *Ritorna vincitor* from *Aida*, Schipa spoiling some of *Una furtiva lagrima* from *L'Elisir d'Amore* with tasteless accelerations and retardations, Onegin in a hammed-up *Brindisi* from *Lucrezia Borgia*, De Luca's distinguished singing with Pons's pipings in *Il nome vostro* from *Rigoletto*, Milanov, past her prime, in an agreeable-sounding and well-phrased *Casta diva* from *Norma*.

Unforgettable Voices . . . from the French Operatic Repertoire, Victrola VIC-1394, has the sopranos Alma Gluck in an aria from Rameau's *Hippolyte et Aricie* and Mabel Garrison in *Je suis Titania* from *Mignon*, the contraltos Homer in *O prêtres de Baal* from *Le Prophète* and Gerville-Réache in an aria from Massé's *Paul et Virginie*, the tenors Lauri-Volpi in an excerpt from *The Tales of Hoffmann* and Peerce in an excerpt from *La Juive*, and the baritone Ruffo in the *Brindisi* from *Hamlet*.

28

THE BEST RECORDED
PERFORMANCES OF TODAY

(November 1970)

This section is concerned with the recorded performances in the current catalogue by musicians who are active today.

The first thing to mention about it is that it is selective: it doesn't evaluate all the performances of all the works of all the composers, which one person couldn't even hear; but instead limits itself to the works discussed earlier in the book, and limits itself further to recommending the performance or performances of a work that I consider to be the best of the ones I have heard.

It is the best performance that I recommend, not the best or latest sound: I prefer the better performance, reproduced adequately, to the poorer one that is reproduced with more beautiful sound; the great Toscanini performance with the mono sound of his time, to an undistinguished one with the stereo sound of today. In most instances I say nothing about the recorded sound, and one may assume that I consider it satisfactory. But a defect in the sound is something the reader should be informed of, and I therefore mention it.

When I prepared this section for the first edition of 1967 both mono and stereo versions of recordings were available, and in most instances I listed the mono in preference to the stereo because my ear found the mono to be more accurate in its greater solidity, its more clearly and strongly defined bass. Since then the mono versions have been discontinued; and an asterisk next to a number indicates a stereo version of a recording of which I originally preferred the mono. If it lacks solidity and well-defined bass, one may be able to remedy this by adding bass with the bass-control.

My recommendations of what I think are the best performances will reveal that in performance as in music I have done my own listening and evaluating and reached conclusions which frequently differ from those of other critics and from generally held opinion. Generally held opinion—whose effect was bad enough fifty years ago but has been enormously increased by present-day publicity media like record magazines and radio programs—regards all performances by well-known performers as valid, so that one can say Ashkenazy's performance of Chopin's G-minor Ballade is different from Horowitz's, but not that one is an effective realization of the piece of music and the other a monstrous distortion of it. But my ears tell me that Horowitz's excessively mannered enunciation of melody in alternation with his explosions of supercharged virtuosity, though they alternately titillate and excite his audience, monstrously distort the shape of the piece; so I advise against them and recommend Ashkenazy's beautifully shaped performance. Similarly I hear and advise against Rudolph Serkin's violent belaboring of instrument and music that generally held opinion regards as impressive performance of Beethoven; his nerveless playing—with its tone that changes from a pallid *piano* only to an unpleasantly percussive *forte,* its melodic legato that is without continuity of dynamics, cohesive tension and outline— that generally held opinion regards as a model of Mozart style. And what Irving Kolodin, expressing generally held opinion of Cliburn as a musician, once wrote of Cliburn's performances of several Chopin pieces on a record—that they exhibited no more than the talent exhibited by any number of students in the Eastman and Juilliard Schools—I consider not to be true of those Cliburn performances, which I think show him to be one of the outstanding musicians of our time; but I consider it to be true of the performances that Barenboim has managed to get generally held opinion to take at his own excessive evaluation. ("Egoism, not artistry," the critic Harris Green observed, "is the little motor that drives Barenboim, and gall is its fuel.")

And as in music so in performance: I give my opinion on the assumption that it is asked for; but the reader is free to decide that he prefers Horowitz's playing of Chopin to Ashkenazy's, Serkin's or Barenboim's playing of Beethoven and Mozart to Cliburn's, Nilsson's singing in *Tristan und Isolde* to Flagstad's, Klemperer's performance of *Fidelio,* or Bernstein's of *Falstaff,* to Toscanini's.

Recorded Performances of Works Listed Under Names of Composers

Albéniz

Ibéria. Watch for a possible reissue of Epic SC-6058, with de Larrocha's performances of the twelve piano pieces, which are made fascinating by the harmonically sophisticated treatment of their Spanish folk-style material.

Bach, Carl Philipp Emanuel

Magnificat. Victrola VICS-1368 has Kurt Thomas conducting the Collegium Aureum and soloists including Ameling.

Bach, Johann Sebastian

(The) Art of Fugue. Nonesuch 73013 has Ristenpart conducting the Saar Chamber Orchestra.

Cantata No. 4, *Christ lag in Todesbanden.* Bach Guild 5026* has Prohaska conducting the Vienna Chamber Choir and soloists.

Chaconne (from Partita No. 2 for Unaccompanied Violin). See in Chapter 27: Szigeti.

Chorale-Preludes for Organ. Vanguard C-10027/8 has Heiller's performance of the *Orgelbüchlein,* with the great *O Mensch, bewein' dein' Sünde gross* and *Ich ruf' zu dir, Herr Jesu Christ* and other good pieces, in addition to uninteresting ones.

Vanguard C-10039/40 has Heiller's performance of the *Eighteen Chorale-Preludes,* which similarly include uninteresting pieces in addition to the great *Nun komm', der Heiden Heiland* and *Schmücke dich, o liebe Seele* and other good ones.

See also under *Clavierübung: German Organ Mass.*

Chromatic Fantasy and Fugue for Clavier. Lyrichord 47 has

Valenti's superb performance, with the Toccatas in C minor and D.

Clavierübung. Glenn Gould's remarkable performance of the *Goldberg Variations,* originally on Columbia ML-5060, is now on MS-7096 (electronic pseudo-stereo); his performances of the *Italian Concerto* and Partita No. 1, originally on Columbia ML-5472, are now on MS-6141 (pseudo-stereo). For the Partita No. 1 see also in Chapter 27: Lipatti.

Of the *German Organ Mass* only the opening Prelude and concluding Fugue in E-flat (BWV. 552) are on Deutsche Grammophon ARC-198-307, performed by Walcha, with the Prelude and Fugue in A minor (543). Watch for a possible reissue of Walcha's performance of the entire work on ARC-3022/4, with several of the longer and more elaborate chorale-preludes that are outstanding: *Gott Vater in Ewigkeit* (BWV. 669), *Wir glauben all' in einen Gott* (680), *Aus tiefer Not schrei ich zu dir* (686) and *Gott heiliger Geist* (674).

Concertos. Benjamin Britten's enlivening performance of the *Brandenburg Concertos* with the English Chamber Orchestra on London 2225 is the one to acquire.

The Concerto in D minor for clavier or violin is performed superbly by Gould on the piano with an orchestra under Bernstein on Columbia ML-5211 (with Beethoven's Concerto No. 2), and effectively on the harpsichord by Malcolm with the Stuttgart Chamber Orchestra under Münchinger on London 6392.* See also in Chapter 27: Szigeti.

The Concertos in A minor and E for violin are performed with effective simplicity by Milstein with a group of strings on Angel S-36010;* and more robustly by Stern on Columbia MS-6949*—the A-minor with members of the London Symphony, the E-major with the New York Philharmonic under Bernstein. Columbia ML-6401 had keyboard versions of these works performed on the piano by Gould with dynamic phrasing and passage-work that made them more exciting than any of the performances of the violin versions.

The Concerto in D minor for two violins is performed by David and Igor Oistrakh with the Royal Philharmonic under Goossens on Deutsche Grammophon 138-820;* but even better is the Szigeti-Flesch performance (see in Chapter 27: Szigeti).

Fugues for Organ. Walcha's performances of the Toccata and Fugue in D minor (BWV. 565) and Toccata, Adagio and Fugue in C (564) are on Deutsche Grammophon ARC-198-304* (with the *Dorian* Toccata and Fugue in D minor).

His performances of the Fantasia and Fuge in G minor (542) and *Passacaglia* (with Fugue) in C minor (582) are on ARC-198-305.*

His performance of the Prelude and Fugue in B minor (544) is on ARC-198-306* (with the Preludes and Fugues in E minor (548) and C (547), impressive as pieces of fugal construction).

His performance of the Prelude and Fugue in A minor (543) is on ARC-198-307, with the opening Prelude and closing Fugue in E-flat of the *Clavierübung*.

Richter's performances of the Toccata and Fugue in D minor and Fantasia and Fugue in G minor are on Deutsche Grammophon 138-907.

German Organ Mass. See under *Clavierübung*.

Goldberg Variations for Clavier. See under *Clavierübung*.

Italian Concerto for Clavier. See under *Clavierübung*.

(Die) Kunst der Fuge. See *(The) Art of Fugue*.

Mass in B Minor. Having heard Richter's performance at a concert, I feel able to recommend it on Deutsche Grammophon ARC-198-190/2; and Shaw's on Victor LSC-6157* also is good.

Orgelbüchlein. See under Chorale-Preludes.

Partita No. 1 for Clavier. See under *Clavierübung*.

Passacaglia (with Fugue) for Organ. Deutsche Grammophon ARC-198-305 has Walcha's performance, with the Fantasia and Fugue in G minor (542) and other pieces.

St. Matthew Passion. Having heard Richter's performance at a concert, I can recommend it on Deutsche Grammophon ARC-198-009/12; and Gönnenwein's on Angel S-3735 also is good.

Sonata No. 3 for Violin and Harpsichord. I prefer Schneeberger's more quietly lyrical performance with Müller on Nonesuch 73017 to Grumiaux's more powerfully projected performance with Sartori on Philips PHS-2-997.

Suites Nos. 2 and 3 for Orchestra. Philips 839-793 has Leppard conducting excellent performances with the English Chamber Orchestra.

Toccatas for Clavier. Lyrichord 47 has Valenti's performances of the ones in C minor and D, with the *Chromatic Fantasy and Fugue.*

Toccatas for Organ. See under Fugues for Organ.

(The) Well-Tempered Clavier. Book 1 is on Columbia D3S-733,* Nos. 1 to 8 of Book 2 are on MS-7099, Nos. 9 to 16 on MS-7409, performed by Gould on the piano with impressive effectiveness at times, but much of the time with damaging eccentricities and perversities of tempo and touch.

Collections. London 26067 has Horne's superb performance of *Erbarme dich* from the *St. Matthew Passion,* among others (with arias of Handel). See also in Chapter 27: Flagstad.

BEETHOVEN

An die ferne Geliebte. See under Songs.

Bagatelles for Piano. See in Chapter 27: Schnabel. And a performance of Op. 126 by Jacob Lateiner, similar to Schnabel's in conception and comparable in effect, is on Victor LSC-3016, with the Sonata Op. 111.

Concertos for Piano. See in Chapter 27: Schnabel.

Watch for possible reissues of Gould's excitingly enlivening performance of No. 1 on Columbia ML-5298 and MS-6017, regrettably in a crude and blaring orchestral context; and his performance of No. 3 with an orchestra under Bernstein on ML-5418 and MS-6096, whose slower than usual tempos produced a powerfully sculptured first movement, an excitingly energetic finale; but not his performance of No. 4 on ML-5662 and MS-6262, with its unusual and frequently unconvincing manipulation of phrase, its eccentricities and sheer perversities. ML-5211 still has his superb performance of No. 2 with an orchestra under Bernstein (with Bach's Concerto in D minor); MS-6888* his performance of No. 5 *(Emperor)* with the American Symphony under Stokowski, in which an unprecedentedly slow tempo in the first movement and other unusual features produce results that are at times impressively effective, at other times eccentric, perverse and impossible to hear as valid statement of the music.

In contrast with Gould, Cliburn—in Nos. 4 and 5, on Victor LSC-2680* and 2562*—exhibits complete naturalness and rightness in the shaping of the music with his unfailing sense for note-to-note continuity of tone, tension and outline, in performances characteristic in their simply, subtly achieved grandeur. (Unfortunately Reiner, who conducts the Chicago Symphony, indulges in overemphatic and ponderous distention in No. 4, which is made worse by the inflated recorded sound in excessively resonant space that requires drastic reduction of bass.)

Rubinstein's performance of No. 5 with the Boston Symphony under Leinsdorf on Victor LSC-2733* was the first to exhibit—in addition to the new repose and continence of recent years—a correctness of style that his earlier playing of Beethoven didn't have; and similar playing is heard in No. 3 on LSC-2947.* The performance of No. 1 on LSC-3013* is relaxed and sensitive where Gould's was excitingly enlivening, but is effective in its own way.

The performance of No. 5 on Philips 839-794 is made notable by the musically sensitive orchestral context that Davis creates with the London Symphony for Bishop's excellent playing, and by the fact that it is a real ensemble performance in which for once the piano's passage-work doesn't obscure the orchestra's melodic writing.

Gilels's performances on Angel S-3731 are much of the time a mere blandly fluent playing of the notes in music which, even in the two early concertos, calls for an energy that he exhibits only in some of the powerful moments of the later three.

Sampling the performances on Angel S-3752 with No. 4, I found it to be a combination of Klemperer's ponderously slow tempos (even in the *Vivace* finale) and—totally unrelated to these—Barenboim's pretty sounds and finicky phrasing; and decided to let the others go unheard.

Watch for a possible reissue of Fleisher's superbly conceived and achieved performance of No. 4 with the Cleveland Orchestra under Szell on Epic LC-3574 and BC-1025 (with Mozart's K.503).

Concerto for Violin. Except for the beautiful writing in the development section of the first movement, at the solo violin's second entrance, this work would be regarded with less awe if

Beethoven's name were not attached to it. Until one of Szigeti's performances with orchestras under Walter is available again there is Oistrakh's performance with the French National Radio Orchestra under Cluytens on Angel S-35780.*

Fidelio. Fricsay's pacing of the work, on Deutsche Grammophon 138-390/1, is not as right and effective throughout as Toscanini's, but may be preferred by some for its superior singers— Rysanek, Seefried, Häfliger, Fischer-Dieskau and Frick—and recorded sound. The ineffectively paced performances of Furtwängler, Klemperer and the rest are things to avoid. See also in Chapter 27: Flagstad, Jurinac, Leider, Lotte Lehmann, and under MISCELLANEOUS COLLECTIONS: Evans, Farrell, Horne, Rothenberger, Schwarzkopf.

Mass in C. In addition to the Beecham perforamnce on Capitol SG-7168 there is the excellent one in which Richter conducts his Munich Bach Choir and Orchestra and soloists on Deutsche Grammophon 139-446.

Missa Solemnis. Toscanini's remains the performance to acquire —only one of many reasons being the raptly mystical character that he, and no other conductor, imparts to the hushed orchestral Prelude to the *Benedictus.*

Overtures. Not only the *Coriolan* but the *Leonore* Overtures, on Deutsche Grammophon 2707-046, suffer from von Karajan's ponderously slow tempos—the impression they give being that he is lost in a trance of admiration for the Berlin Philharmonic's beautiful playing.

Quartets. First in the performances of Opp. 59, 74 and 95 in Victor VCS-6415, then in the performances of the last quartets in VCS-6195, and finally in the performances of the first six in VCS-6195, the Guarneri Quartet has demonstrated an operation on the highest level of instrumental virtuosity, tonal beauty, ensemble precision and musical understanding, but has revealed something less than the flawless judgment and taste of its only peers, the Yale Quartet and the Quartetto Italiano. It has revealed this in some of its tempos—e.g., those of the third movement of Op. 130, too sluggish not merely for Beethoven's direction *Andante con moto,* but for the *scherzando* character he also specifies, the lilting grace the music should have; and of the following movement, too sluggish not merely for the direction *Allegro assai* but for the *danza tedesca* the music is intended to be. It has revealed it also in the monkeying with tempos—the excessive slowing down of second subjects or lyrical episodes that has destroyed continuity and momentum; the enormous slowing down of the series of half-notes following the series of quarter-notes in each of the statements of the opening section of the variation movement of Op. 132; the even more damaging slowing down of the development in the first movement of Op. 130, destroying the effect it has in the correct tempo—the urgency of the reiterated rhythmic figure over which the plaintive melodic exclamations are heard.

The Guarneri performances of the so-called middle quartets in VCS-6415 exhibit the fewest such defects—in Op. 59 No. 2 the slowing down of the second subject in the first movement; in Op. 59 No. 3 the first violin's arch anticipatory retardations before bars 42 and 49 in the second movement—and are the best available. But of the last quartets the performances to acquire are either those of the Quartetto Italiano, which has astonished music-lovers recently with an ability it didn't have twenty years ago to play this music as superbly as it plays its instruments, and which has recorded all the last quartets and *Grosse Fuge* for Philips (Opp. 127 and 135 on 839-745, Op. 130 and the *Grosse Fuge* Op. 133 on 839-795, Op. 131 on 802-915, Op. 132 on 900-182); or those of the Yale Quartet, which are better recorded (thus far Op. 127 on Vanguard C-10054, Op. 131 on C-10062, and Op. 132 on C-10005). And of the six of Op. 18 the performances to acquire are the Budapest Quartet's of 1951 reissued on Odyssey 32-36-0023 (mono) (reduce treble and increase bass).

Quintet Op. 29. A good performance by the Budapest Quartet and Trampler is on Columbia MS-6952 (with Dvořák's Quintet Op. 97).

Septet for Winds and Strings. This is a piece I used to find uninteresting, until I heard it with the life imparted to it by the animation and phrasing of Toscanini's performance (see in Chapter 27) with an increased number of strings for proper balance with the winds.

Serenade Op. 8 for String Trio. Philips 900-227 has the performance of Grumiaux, Janzer and Czako.

Sonatas for Piano. See in Chapter 27: Schnabel.

In the first movement of Op. 106 (*Hammerklavier*) on London 6563 Ashkenazy succeeds where Schnabel fails, by not obeying the Beethoven metronome marking that Schnabel obeys, and instead finding the tempo in which he can articulate and shape the movement in what becomes the most effective statement of it in my experience. He doesn't give the slow movement the enlargement of shape, and through this of expressive dimensions, that Schnabel does; but he performs it with moving expressive eloquence. And he achieves in the formidable concluding fugue an extraordinary clarification of texture and structure.

In Gould's performances of Opp. 109, 110 and 111 on Columbia ML-5130 one hears his remarkable musical intelligence operating independently with results that are impressively effective in Op. 110 and the finale of Op. 111, but also his eccentricity and perversity operating at times in the finale of Op. 109 and the first movement of Op. 111 with results that I find impossible to hear as valid statements of the music. I feel the same impossibility with the first movement of Op. 57 (*Appassionata*), on MS-7413, that proceeds *Andante sostenuto* instead of the *Allegro assai* Beethoven prescribes, and the second movement that proceeds *Adagio molto* instead of Beethoven's *Andante con moto;* I feel it also with the finale of Op. 27 No. 2 (known as *Moonlight*) as it is speeded up by Gould, but *can* go along with the first movement played *Andante con moto* even though I am sure it is not what Beethoven˙intended with his direction *Adagio molto*. And I feel the impossibility with the speeded-up Allegros of the Sonatas Op. 10 on MS-6686.

In Cliburn's performance of Op. 81a (*Les Adieux*) on Victor LSC-2931* (with Mozart's Sonata K.330) each note goes on to the next with unfailing continuity and cohesive tension and rightness of relation in what emerges as a completely imagined and completely realized integrated progression; whereas Barenboim's performance on Angel S-36424 is a progression without continuity, cohesive tension and integration. Which is to say that Cliburn has—and Barenboim does not have—the ultimate gift of the finished artist: the discipline that has other pianistic and musical gifts under the control which produces an ordered, coherent conception of the musical work in his mind and an accurate realization of this conception from his instrument. And what is true of this Barenboim performance I have found true of the others—which makes them things to avoid.

Jacob Lateiner's performance of Op. 111 on Victor LSC-3016* (with the Bagatelles Op. 126) is similar to Schnabel's in structural and expressive conception, but the detailed playing is Lateiner's own and very fine. His performances of Opp. 53 and 109 on LSC-3173, however, are not good.

Kuerti offers excellent performances of Op. 81a (*Les Adieux*), the rarely played but fine smaller-scale Opp. 78 and 79, and the early Op. 10 No. 2 on Monitor S-2075.

Haskil's performances of Op. 31 Nos. 2 and 3, on Philips World Series 9001, are very good.

Sonatas for Piano and Violin. See in Chapter 27: Szigeti, Rachmaninov, Goldberg.

The performances by Haskil and Grumiaux that were on Epic LC-3381, 3458, 3400 and 3488 are available on Philips 6733-001 (6588-001/4).*

Sonatas for Piano and Cello. In addition to Casals's performances (see in Chapter 27) there are the superb performances of Op. 69 and Op. 102 No. 2 by Bishop and Du Pré on Angel S-36384.*

Symphonies. Toscanini's performances of the nine (see in Chapter 27) not only are definitive but are free of the occasional errors in tempo or change of tempo that damage shape and effect in von Karajan's performances with the Berlin Philharmonic on Deutsche Grammophon 2721-001, and in Jochum's with the Amsterdam Concertgebouw on Philips S-C71AX900. Klemperer's excessively slow tempos make his performances with the Philharmonia on Angel S-3619 something to avoid. And this must be said also of the slow tempos of the first and third movements in Boulez's performance of the Symphony No. 5 on Columbia M-30085.

See also in Chapter 27: Cantelli.

Trios. The Istomin-Stern-Rose performances on Columbia M5-30065 are excellent; but avoid the performance of Op. 97 (*Archduke*) on the earlier MS-6819, in which the piano is obtrusively loud in the first two movements.

Barenboim's deficiencies as pianist and musician outweigh

the merits of Zukerman and Du Pré in the performances on Angel S-3771.

For the Cortot-Thibaud-Casals performance of Op. 97 see in Chapter 27: Casals. And watch for reissues of the Istomin-Schneider-Casals Perpignan Festival performance of Op. 97 that was on Columbia ML-4574, and of the performances of Op. 1 No. 2 and Op. 70 No. 2 on 4573 and 4571.

A performance of Op. 97 by the superb Trio di Trieste is on imported Deutsche Grammophon SLPEM-196-220 (G + I).

Variations. See in Chapter 27: Schnabel.

Bishop has a fine performance of the *Diabelli Variations* on Philips 900-220.

Gould's performances of the 32 Variations in C minor and the Variations Opp. 34 and 35 (*Eroica*) on Columbia M-30080 suffer from his various eccentricities and perversities.

For Variations on *Ein Mädchen oder Weibchen* from *The Magic Flute* for cello and piano see in Chapter 27: Feuermann.

BELLINI

Beatrice di Tenda. A lesser work, in which Sutherland's singing of recitative and melody, on London 1384, is irritatingly mannered.

Norma. Callas's early performance on Seraphim 6037 is the one to acquire, not her later one on Angel S-3615, and not Sutherland's on London 1384* or Suliotis's on London 1272.

(*I*) *Puritani*. Sutherland's singing on London 1373* is some of her best on records; but Callas's in her early performance on Angel 3502 (or imported Columbia 33CX-1058/60) is lovelier and more moving.

(*La*) *Sonnambula*. The Callas performance that was on Angel 3568 and is now on imported QCX-10278/80 (I) is the one to acquire in preference to Sutherland's mannered moaning on London 1365.

Collections. Victor LSC-2862* has Caballé's performances of *Casta diva* from *Norma* and *Col sorriso d'innocenza* from *Il Pirata* (with arias of Donizetti), in which she deploys her agreeable voice with a sense for emerging shape of phrase, for style, for dramatic expressiveness, that makes the result impressive and even exciting.

Westminster 17143 has Sills's performances of arias from *La Sonnambula* and the unfamiliar *I Capuleti ed i Montecchi* (with arias of Donizetti), in which her voice—except for an occasional edge and tremulousness—is agreeable to the ear, and an instrument for her impressive security and musical style in the ornamented melody and spectacular florid passages. Some of the specially composed variants in repeats seem to me excessive; and I am not convinced that because Bellini and Donizetti and Rossini had to let singers indulge in this practice it should be indulged in today.

See also in Chapter 27: Schipa, Valletti; under MISCELLANEOUS COLLECTIONS: *The Age of Bel Canto,* Callas, Horne, Simionato, Sutherland.

BERG

Wozzeck. I prefer the Berlin Opera performance conducted by Böhm on Deutsche Grammophon 138-991/2,* with the accurate singing of Fischer-Dieskau and Lear, to the one on CBS 32-21-0001 in which Boulez produces with the Paris Opera Orchestra a marvelously clear-textured and powerful context for singing by Berry and Isabel Strauss, among others, that departs from the printed score to a surprising degree.

BERLIOZ

Beatrice and Benedict. From the excellent performance on Oiseau-Lyre S-256/7*—with Cantelo, Veasey, Watts, the St. Anthony Singers and the London Symphony conducted by Davis—one learns that the familiar overture includes the only outstanding pages of vocal writing in this late work—Beatrice's aria *Il me souvient le jour du départ* and the finale.

(The) Damnation of Faust. Baker's Marguérite, Gedda's Faust, Becquier's Mephistopheles and L'Orchestre de Paris make the performance conducted by Prêtre on Angel S-3758 the one to acquire.

(L') Enfance du Christ. Oiseau-Lyre 60032/3* has the excellent performance with Pears, Morison, the St. Anthony Singers and the Goldsborough Orchestra conducted by Davis; Nonesuch 73022 the one conducted effectively by Martinon, with the

Chorus and Orchestra of the French National Radio and good soloists.

Harold in Italy. I can recommend no performance other than Toscanini's (see in Chapter 27).

(La) Mort de Cléopâtre. Berlioz submitted this lyrical scene in his third unsuccessful attempt to win the *Prix de Rome* while a student at the Paris Conservatoire; but the orchestra's very first bars proclaim what is evident throughout, though most impressively in Cleopatra's invocation *Grands Pharaons* over the orchestra's powerful bass ostinato—that this is not a fumbling of unmatured gifts but an operation with absolute assurance in a style completely individual and completely formed. Baker uses her beautiful voice with superb musical and expressive effect in the performance with the London Symphony under Gibson on Angel S-36695, which has also her performance of the final scenes of *The Trojans.* And Davis conducts an excellent performance with Pashley and the English Chamber Orchestra on Oiseau-Lyre SOL-304, which has also three lovely pieces for chorus and orchestra—*Sara la baigneuse, Méditation religieuse* and *La Mort d'Ophélie.*

(Les) Nuits d'été. In addition to Steber's great performance (see in Chapter 27), the fine one of De los Angeles with the Boston Symphony under Munch that was on Victor LM-1907, the great one of Price with the Chicago Symphony under Reiner on Victor LSC-2695* (flawed only by a couple of Reiner's tempos), there are now Baker's beautiful performance with the New Philharmonia under Barbirolli on Angel S-36505, and the one on Philips SAL-3789 in which Davis and the London Symphony provide a superb orchestral context for the excellent singing of Armstrong, Veasey, Patterson and Shirley-Quirk.

Overtures. Victor LSC-2695* has Munch's performances with the Boston Symphony of *The Roman Carnival, The Corsair, Benvenuto Cellini* and *Beatrice and Benedict,* with *Royal Hunt and Storm* from *The Trojans.*

Philips 900-138 has Davis's performances with the London Symphony of *The Roman Carnival, The Corsair, Waverly, Les Francs-Juges* and *King Lear.* See also in Chapter 27: Toscanini.

Requiem. Munch's earlier performance with the Boston Symphony on Victor LDS-6077* is good, but has a poorer chorus than the later one with the Bavarian Radio Orchestra and Chorus on Deutsche Grammophon 139-264/5; but Simoneau in the earlier performance sings more beautifully in the *Sanctus* than Schreier in the later one; and without the addition of a large amount of bass the Deutsche Grammophon records don't produce the thunder of the drums or reproduce adequately the low strings and bass voices.

Vanguard C-10070/1 has another good performance in which Abravanel conducts the Utah Symphony and University of Utah choruses with Bressler as soloist in the *Sanctus*.

Romeo and Juliet. Until now there were, besides Toscanini's definitive performance (see in Chapter 27), only the vastly inferior ones of Munch and Monteux; but now Philips PHS-2-909 offers Davis's excellent one with the London Symphony, which is reproduced with the more beautiful sound and greater clarity and distinctness of today. Nevertheless it is a performance to acquire only in addition to, not in place of, Toscanini's. For Toscanini's more animated and flexible tempos produce an even more effective *Love Scene* than Davis's; and his realization of *Last Agonies and Death of the Two Lovers* is more powerful than Davis's. Also, the extraordinary *Juliet's Funeral Procession* is spoiled in Davis's performance, as it is not in Toscanini's, by imbalance which in the first part causes the chorus's repeated *Jetez des fleurs!* on the note E to obliterate the orchestra's fugal march, and in the second part causes the chorus's repetition of the fugal march to obliterate the violins' groups of E's.

Royal Hunt and Storm from *The Trojans.* See under Overtures.

Symphonie fantastique. Davis's excellent performance with the London Symphony is on Philips 900-101;* Boulez's even clearer-textured one with that orchestra was briefly on CBS 32-B-10010 with the uninteresting *Lélio,* and presumably will be reissued alone. See also in Chapter 27: Argenta.

Te Deum. Philips SAL-3724 has Davis's effective performance with the London Symphony Orchestra and Chorus, a boys' choir, the dry-voiced and straining tenor Franco Tagliavini, and the organist Nicolas Knyaston.

(The) Trojans. At long last this great work is on records in its entirety (the later three of its five acts were recorded by Du-

cretet-Thomson years ago). Its greatness is different from that
of the *Love Scene* of *Romeo and Juliet* and the second and
third movements of *Harold in Italy:* of the incandescently
beautiful writing that overwhelms one in those early pieces
there is only one major example in *The Trojans*—the septet
in Act 4 concerned with the peace and enchantment of the
African night, the effect of whose exquisite vocal writing is
heightened by such orchestral details as the reiterated C of
the flute, the change from this to the alternation of C and D
flat, and every now and then the heavy punctuating beat on
the bass drum. There are other beautiful passages in the later
three acts concerned with the tragic involvement of Dido and
Aeneas; but much of the time, even in these acts, as in the
earlier two concerned with the fall of Troy, one hears only an
accomplished use of the Berlioz idiom in the service of the
text. And the greatness one is aware of here is that of the
arrestingly individual musical mind operating in, and command-
ing attention with, the use of the idiom with assured mastery
and complete adequacy to the text's every demand. Similar
mastery and adequacy in Davis's conducting, on Philips 6709-
002, makes this greatness of the work uninterruptedly evident
even at times when one is aware of Lindholm's tremolo-ridden
singing as Cassandra in the first two acts, or of the fact that
although Veasey and Vickers, the Dido and Aeneas of the later
three acts, sing beautifully in the quiet music of the first two,
their singing loses its beauty when they raise their voices in
anger and despair in Act 5. (The thing to do is to go from
side 9 of the Philips recording to Angel S-36695, which has
Baker's superb singing in the final scenes.) The other soloists
and the Covent Garden Orchestra and Chorus are good; and
the recording can be faulted only for not making audible the
powerful bass-drum beats that one hears punctuating the
phrases of the septet in the old Ducretet-Thomson performance.

Vocal Pieces. For *Sara la baigneuse, Méditation religieuse* and
La Mort d'Ophélie for chorus and orchestra see under *La Mort
de Cléopâtre.*

BIZET

Carmen. Angel S-3767 offers the opera in its original form with spoken dialogue, as it was first performed at the Opéra Comique, as against the version we hear, with the dialogue replaced by the recitatives of Guiraud; and it turns out that the dialogue adds a great deal to the dramatic effect. More important, the recording offers a performance superbly conducted by Frühbeck, in which Vickers's sensitive use of his lustrous voice would be reason enough for acquiring it, but Bumbry, in addition, does the best singing I have heard from her, the fine baritone Paskalis is the Escamillo, Freni is the Micaela, and the contributions of the lesser singers and the Paris Opera Orchestra and Chorus are excellent.

Of the version with recitatives Angel S-3613 offers the excellent performance conducted by Beecham, with De los Angeles, Gedda, Micheau, Blanc and the French National Radio Orchestra and Chorus.

See also in Chapter 27: Bjoerling, Slezak, Urlus. For the orchestral suite see in Chapter 27: Toscanini.

BLOCH

Quintet for Piano and Strings. Concert-Disc 252 has the performance by Glazer and the Fine Arts Quartet, which I haven't heard.

BOCCHERINI

Concertos for Cello. The genuine Concerto in B flat—not the Grützmacher fake that cellists continue to play—turns out to be an engaging minor work which Gendron performs well with the Lamoureux Orchestra under Casals on Philips 900-172 (with the genuine Haydn Concerto in D).

A better example of the individual operation of the Boccherini mind is the delightful Cello Concerto in D, which is performed not only with distinguished musical taste but with extraordinary grace and elegance by Natalia Gutman with the Moscow Conservatory Chamber Orchestra under Terian on Melodiya/Angel SR-40146 (with a less interesting Concerto in A minor by Vivaldi and a Tartini Concerto in A that has a fine slow movement).

Quartets Op. 58 No. 5, Op. 64 Nos. 1 and 2. Music Guild 123 has superb performances by the Carmirelli Quartet. Hope for a

possible reissue of the New Music Quartet's dazzling performances of four Boccherini quartets that were on Columbia ML-
5047. See also in Chapter 27: New Music Quartet; under MIS-
CELLANEOUS COLLECTIONS: Virtuosi di Roma.

Quintet Op. 37 No. 7. Members of the Academy of St. Martin-
in-the-Fields perform it on Argo ZRG-569 (with Mendelssohn's
Octet).

BRAHMS

Songs. I would expect Fischer-Dieskau's performances on Deutsche
Grammophon 138-011 to be excellent. See also in Chapter 27:
Lotte Lehmann; under MISCELLANEOUS COLLECTIONS: De los
Angeles, Ludwig, Schwarzkopf.

Symphonies. In addition to Toscanini's performances (see in
Chapter 27) there are good performances of No. 2 by von
Karajan with the Berlin Philharmonic on Deutsche Grammophon 138-925,* and by Kertesz with the Vienna Philharmonic
on London 6435.*

Variations on a Theme of Haydn. I can recommend no other
performance than Toscanini's (see in Chapter 27).

Variations on a Theme of Paganini. See in Chapter 27: Backhaus.
The Russian pianist Merzhanov's performance on Monitor
2013 is excellent except for a miscalculated tempo in Variation
10 of Book 1.

BRITTEN

Albert Herring. Parts of this opera offer brilliantly successful invention for the dramatic situation; other parts only what the
resourceful craftsman was able to produce to carry words and
action. London 1378* has the performance conducted effectively
by Britten with Pears in the title role.

(A) Midsummer Night's Dream. This work—with, from first to
last, real invention that works superbly for the situation and
words—is Britten's best; and on London 1385* he conducts an
excellent performance—with Harwood, Harper, Brannigan and
Pears, among others—in which the only flaw is the unattractive timbre of Deller's counter-tenor.

Serenade for Tenor, Horn and Strings. London 6398 has the per-
284

formance by Pears, Tuckwell and the London Symphony under Britten.

BYRD

Cantiones Sacrae. The fine motets by Byrd and Tallis in this jointly published collection are sung well on Oiseau-Lyre SOL-311/3 by the Cantores in Ecclesia under Michael Howard.

Mass for Four Voices. Argo 5362 has the excellent performance by the Choir of King's College, Cambridge, under Willcocks.

Collections. Bach Guild 557, *William Byrd and His Age,* had good performances by the counter-tenor Deller and the Wenzinger Consort of Viols. See under MISCELLANEOUS COLLECTIONS: Welch Chorale.

CHABRIER

Dix Pièces pittoresques for Piano. Except for the excessively fast tempo of *Idylle,* Ciccolini's performance on Angel S-36627 is excellent.

Collections. The *Suite pastorale, Marche joyeuse, Fête polonaise* and *España* are performed beautifully, but in insufficiently animated tempos, by L'Orchestre de la Suisse Romande under Ansermet on London 6438.*

CHERUBINI

Medea. This opera created a sensation in New York some years ago not merely with its unexpectedly impressive vocal and orchestral writing, but with Farrell's beautiful and eloquent singing in the title role. A few passages with that singing were on Columbia ML-5325. See under MISCELLANEOUS COLLECTIONS: Callas, Farrell. The performance with Gwyneth Jones on London 1389 is something to avoid; so is the Everest version of the performance with Callas that was on Mercury OL-3-104.

Requiem in C minor. The lovely choral writing in this work was another surprise when Toscanini broadcast the performance that was on Victor LM-2000 (see in Chapter 27).

Overtures. See in Chapter 27: Toscanini.

Chopin

Ballades. London 6422* has Ashkenazy's beautiful performances. See also under Collections: Cliburn.

Barcarolle. See in Chapter 27: Lipatti; and under Scherzos.

Concerto No. 1. The *New Yorker* reviewer who heard in Barenboim's performance of Beethoven's *Appassionata* Sonata the "extraordinary musical taste" and "infallible sense of form" of "one of the world's important artists of the keyboard" found Cliburn's performance of this concerto to be "a bit glib, with . . . no profound understanding of the Chopin style." Actually Barenboim's undisciplined performance of the *Appassionata* had revealed a total lack of the taste and intelligence and sense of form that made Cliburn's performance of the Chopin concerto that of a distinguished artist; and while Cliburn's grandly proclamatory style with the greater Chopin of this work and the sonatas was certainly not the traditional one the *New Yorker* reviewer was accustomed to, it just as certainly could not be described as "glib". It is now—recorded with the Philadelphia Orchestra under Ormandy—to be heard on Victor LSC-3147, with sound that is agreeable to the ear but a little peculiar in ways that are difficult to describe.

The finest of the performances in traditional style is Lipatti's (see in Chapter 27); and other fine ones are Pollini's with the Philharmonia under Kletzki on Seraphim S-60066, and Rubinstein's with the New Symphony of London under Skrowaczewski on Victor LSC-2575.*

Etudes. Philips World Series PHC-9115 has Harasiewicz's excellent performances, flawed by occasional excessive liberties with tempo.

Fantaisie. See under Collections: Cliburn.

Impromptus. Horszowski's performances are in Vox SVBX-5402, with the Concerto No. 1 and Nocturnes.

Mazurkas. Victor LSC-6177* has Rubinstein's performances.

Nocturnes. Rubinstein plays them, on Victor LSC-7050,* in the traditional mannered style I don't like; and in the finest two, Op. 27 No. 2 and Op. 48 No. 1, his impassioned playing of the opening pages disregards not only the character of the music but Chopin's explicit markings of *Lento sostenuto* for the first and *Lento* and *mezza voce* for the second.

Lipatti plays Op. 27 No. 2 as Chopin directs (see in Chapter 27). And see under Collections: Cliburn; under MISCELLANEOUS COLLECTIONS: Ashkenazy.

Polonaises. Philips World Series 9087 has Harasiewicz's performances of Opp. 26, 40, 44 and 53 and the Polonaise-Fantaisie Op. 61; Turnabout 35254/5 has Frankl's performances of all the Polonaises, including a few uninteresting products of Chopin's student years. See also under Collections: Cliburn.

Preludes Op. 28. I preferred the unmannered performances of Gulda that were on London LL-755 and until recently on imported Decca LXT-2837 (E) to Rubinstein's on Victor LM-1163.

Scherzos. Ashkenazy's performances are on London 6562, with the Barcarolle and the Prelude Op. 45. See also under Collections: Cliburn.

Sonatas. What was overwhelming, when Victor LSC-3053 appeared, was not only to hear the two sonatas as Cliburn performed them—with a sustained grandeur unprecedented in my experience (the prescribed *maestoso* of Rubinstein's beginning of Op. 58 is not maintained beyond the opening section), and with the new expressive dimension this gave them; it was also to hear the note-to-note operation of awesome musical powers in some of the greatest making of music on the piano I had ever heard.

Of the performances of Op. 58 in which the first movement is taken as though Chopin's direction were not *Allegro maestoso* but *Allegro appassionato,* the finest is Lipatti's (see in Chapter 27).

Sonata Op. 65 for Piano and Cello. This seldom-heard, beautiful work is performed with the right impassioned elegance by Ciccolini and Tortelier on Angel S-36591.

Waltzes. No other pianist has performed these pieces with the rhythmic subtlety and grace of Lipatti (see in Chapter 27).

Collections. One cannot imagine the introduction of Chopin's Ballade Op. 47 played more beautifully than it is by Ashkenazy; but when one plays Cliburn's performance of it on Victor LSC-2576 one is astounded to hear additional subtleties of inflection and tempo that testify to his extraordinary musical intelligence and taste. And I have never heard a performance of the Polonaise Op. 53 as distinguished in conception and as beautifully executed as Cliburn's on that record—from first to last an operation of disciplined mastery which holds the lilt and grace and plasticity within the limits of a perfectly proportioned and coherent shape that is achieved down to the least accompaniment note with absolute accuracy of tonal values and timing. And he operates in the same way in the other pieces on the record: the Fantaisie, Nocturne Op. 62 No. 1, Scherzo Op. 39, Waltz Op. 64 No. 2, Etudes Op. 10 No. 3 and Op. 25 No. 11.

COPLAND

Billy the Kid. Levine's performance with the Ballet Theater Orchestra is on Capitol HDR-21004, with the ballet score for *Rodeo* (and also with Bernstein's score for *Fancy Free* and bad ballet scores by William Schuman, Morton Gould and others).

In his performance of Copland's Suite from *Billy* with the Utah Symphony, on Music Guild MS-164 (originally on Westminster WST-14058), Abravanel omits the hauntingly beautiful passage following the *Celebration Dance* in Levine's performance, but adds the fine waltz for the *pas de deux,* also in Levine's performance, which Copland doesn't include in the Suite.

(The) Tender Land. Copland himself conducts the New York Philharmonic and good soloists in a large part of his finest score on Columbia CMS-6814.*

CORELLI

Concerti Grossi Op. 6. Angel S-36130 has Nos. 2, 6, 7 and 8 (*Christmas*), performed by the Virtuosi di Roma.

COUPERIN

Harpsichord Pieces. Malcolm's performances of the Ordres (suites) Nos. 8, 14 and 21 are on Argo ZRG-632.
Tenebrae Services (Leçons de Ténèbres). No. 1 was on Allegro 91,

later on Concord 4005, and most recently on Allegro LEG-9014, with tremendous expressive force from Cuénod's extraordinary singing. His voice is somewhat threadbare and rough in the later performance of all three on Westminster 9601.

Fischer-Dieskau's performances of all three, which I haven't heard, are on imported HMV ALP-2066 (mono) and ASD-615 (stereo) (E).

DEBUSSY

Estampes (*Pagodes, Soirée dans Grenade, Jardins sous la pluie*). Watch for a possible reissue of Rosen's performances of this work, *L'Isle joyeuse* and the two sets of *Images* on Epic LC-3945 and BC-1345, of which the latter reproduced the performances more adequately. And meanwhile see under MISCELLANE-OUS COLLECTIONS: Richter.

Etudes. These pieces, ostensibly exercising the hands in the playing of thirds, fourths, sixths and so on, exercise Debussy in the varieties of his fully developed style of writing for the piano; and some of the results—the Etudes concerned with thirds, octaves, eight fingers, chromatic steps—are as interesting pieces of music as the better-known ones with imaginative titles. Watch for a possible reissue of Rosen's excellent performance on Epic LC-3842 and BC-1242. Until then there is Gieseking's on Angel 35250.

Images for Orchestra (*Gigues, Ibéria, Rondes de printemps*). Not since the years of Toscanini and Cantelli have we heard orchestral performance with the technical and musical distinction of Boulez's performances of these pieces with the Cleveland Orchestra on Columbia MS-7362—and specifically such clarity and distinctness of the detail of Debussy's complex orchestral textures, such continuity of tension and shape in the progression. It is curious that Boulez ignores in the last movement of *Ibéria* the directions (e.g. *En cédant et plus libre*) for flexibility of tempo that Toscanini obeys in his performance; and Toscanini also performs the first movement with more flexibility of his more animated tempo—all of which makes his realizations of these two movements even more effective for me than Boulez's.

But whereas Toscanini obeys Debussy's metronome marking for the slow movement, Boulez takes a slower tempo in which he produces a more languorous realization of it that one may find even more attractive than Toscanini's lilting one.

Images for Piano (First Series: *Reflets dans l'eau, Homage à Rameau, Mouvement;* Second Series: *Cloches à travers les feuilles, Et la lune descend sur le temple qui fut, Poissons d'or*). Gieseking, on Angel 35065, plays these pieces and those of *Estampes* in an excessively delicate style which doesn't attain their occasional points of high sonority and splendor. The robust and brilliant sonorities of Rosen's performances were one of the excellences that make one hope for their reissue.

(La) Mer. The reprocessed recording of Boulez's performance with the New Philharmonia on Columbia MS-7362 produces the sufficient bass sound that the one first issued on CBS 32-11-0056 did not; and the performance ranks with Toscanini's and Cantelli's.

(L')Isle joyeuse. See under MISCELLANEOUS COLLECTIONS: Ashkenazy.

Nocturnes (Nuages, Fêtes, Sirènes). Performed well by Giulini with the Philharmonia on Angel S-35977.* See also in Chapter 27: Cantelli.

Prélude à l'Après-midi d'un faune. Performed by Boulez with *La Mer* on Columbia MS-7362. See also in Chapter 27: Cantelli.

DELIUS

Brigg Fair and *The Walk to the Paradise Gardens,* two of Delius's finest pieces, were on London 9066, excellently performed by Collins with the London Symphony. See in Chapter 27: Beecham.

DONIZETTI

Anna Bolena. This unfamiliar and early work surprises one with the impressive quality and freedom of its vocal and orchestral writing. In the performance conducted by Varviso on London 1436 the high range of Suliotis's voice is too unattractive to be expressively effective, but in its lower range her singing is dramatically powerful. Even with slightly tremulous and shrill high notes Horne produces the great singing of the performance; Alexander uses his fine tenor well; and Ghiaurov's rough-sounding bass can be accepted as being suited to his role.

Don Pasquale. Because of Oncina's unattractively hard, tight voice I advise against London 1260 and suggest instead the perform-ance with Valletti on imported Cetra LPC-1242 (I) or Cetra (Eurodisc) LPC-1242 (G) (avoid the Everest electronically al-tered version), or the earlier one with Schipa on imported Voce del Padrone QSO-53/5 (I).

(L')Elisir d'Amore. I recommend Seraphim 6001, with Carteri, Alva, Taddei, Panerai and the Orchestra and Chorus of La Scala con-ducted by Serafin; or London 1311, with Gueden, Di Stefano, Corena, Capecchi and the Orchestra and Chorus of the Maggio Musicale Fiorentino conducted by Molinari-Pradelli.

(La) Favorita. In the performance on Richmond 63510 Simionato's beautiful voice is clouded at times by strong vibrato, but Poggi's quavering voice is also unattractive in timbre. Bastianini and Hines are excellent; and the Orchestra and Chorus of the Maggio Musicale Fiorentino perform well under Erede.

Lucia di Lammermoor. Callas's early performance on Seraphim 6032 is the one to acquire, not her later one on Angel 3601, and not Sutherland's on London 1327 or any of the others.

Lucrezia Borgia. This unfamiliar work has impressive dramatic writing which attains its highest point of affecting expressive-ness in the concluding scene; but the aria of the dying Gennaro that impressed me as the finest piece in the opera at the concert performance with Caballé (which is available in an under-ground recording) is omitted in the performance with Caballé, Kraus, Verrett and Flagello conducted by Perlea on Victor LSC-6176.*

Roberto Devereux. This work is, to my ear, for the most part a routine exercise in the composer's style; and Sills's singing on Westminster 323 is unpleasantly tremulous and, at times, stri-dent, though spectacularly accurate in florid passages.

Collections. Caballé sings arias from *Lucrezia Borgia, Maria di Rohan* and *Roberto Devereux* on Victor LSC-2862* (with arias of Bellini).

Sills sings arias from *Lucia, Roberto Devereux* and *Rosa-monda d'Inghilterra* on Westminster 17143 (with arias of Bellini.)

291

See also in Chapter 27: Albanese, Bjoerling, Schipa; under
MISCELLANEOUS COLLECTIONS: *The Age of Bel Canto,* Evans,
Horne, Sutherland.

DOWLAND

*Lachrimae, or seaven Teares figured in seaven passionate Pavans,
with divers other Pavans, Galiards, and Almands.* There are
good performances by the Philomusica of London under Dart
on Oiseau-Lyre 50163; by Muller-Dombois and a quintet of
viols from the Schola Cantorum Basiliensis on VICS-1338;*
and by the Elizabethan Consort of Viols on Music Guild MS-872.
*Songs or Ayres of foure parts with Tablature for the Lute so
made, that all the parts together, or either of them severally,
may be sung to the Lute, Orpherian, or Viol de gambo.* Groups
of these lovely pieces are sung by the Golden Age Singers with
the lutenist Bream on Westminster 9602/3 and 9619. See also
under MISCELLANEOUS COLLECTIONS: Baker, Cuénod, *An Evening
of Elizabethan Verse and Its Music,* Pears.

DVOŘÁK

Carnival Overture. One of the composer's most attractive pieces;
see under *Slavonic Dances.*
Quintet Op. 97. Performed well by the Budapest Quartet and
Trampler on Columbia MS-6952* (with Beethoven's Quintet
Op. 29).
Quintet Op. 81 for Piano and Strings. Performed well by Curzon
and the Vienna Philharmonic Quartet on London 6357.*
(Avoid the gigantesque performance on Vanguard S-288.)
Slavonic Dances. Performed effectively by Szell with the Cleveland
Orchestra on Columbia M2S-726,* with the *Carnival* Overture.
By omitting the overture and the repeats in the dances Colum-
bia gets the dances onto a single record, MS-7208.
Symphonic Variations Op. 78. This seldom-played work—excel-
lently performed by Davis with the London Symphony on
Philips 900-196—provides an impressive demonstration of
Dvořák's spontaneous flow of lovely melodic, harmonic and
instrumental invention in a serious piece.

Symphonies. The engagingly melodious No. 8 (old No. 4) is performed well by Kubelik with the Berlin Philharmonic on Deutsche Grammophon 139-181,* and by Szell with the Cleveland Orchestra on Angel S-36043.

Of No. 9 (*New World*) I can recommend no other performance than Toscanini's (see in Chapter 27), whose freedom from the traditional distortions makes the work "as fresh and glistening as creation itself."

FAURÉ

Requiem. Best performed by Cluytens with the Paris Conservatory Concerts Orchestra, the Brasseur Chorus, De los Angeles and Fischer-Dieskau on Angel S-35974.*

FRANCK

Psyche. See in Chapter 27: Toscanini.

Sonata for Violin and Piano. What seems to be a good performance by Perlman and Ashkenazy is unclearly reproduced by London 6628; and while Stern's playing is admirably straightforward, in the performance on Columbia MS-6139,* Zakin's is excessively mannered. Grumiaux's performance with Hajdu, on imported Philips A-02236-L and SAL-3738 (stereo), should be good.

Variations symphoniques for Piano and Orchestra. Gieseking's fine performance with the Philharmonia under von Karajan was on the reverse side of Columbia ML-4536, which had the performance of Mozart's Concerto K.488 now on Odyssey 32-16-0371.

GABRIELI

Several of the magnificent pieces that Andrea and Giovanni Gabrieli wrote for performance by three or four choirs, brass, strings and organ in St. Marks, Venice, at the end of the sixteenth and the beginning of the seventeenth centuries, are on Angel S-36443, performed beautifully by the Ambrosian Singers and the instrumental groups under Denis Stevens.

GESUALDO

Columbia CKS-6318* has a number of this composer's madrigals
—whose strange and daring harmonic progressions make them
some of the most remarkable, powerful and moving music that
has come down to us—sung well by a vocal group under Craft;
two instrumental pieces, one played by Biggs on the organ,
the other by Rosenstiel on the harpsichord; and Stravinsky's
Monumentum pro Gesualdo, his masterly instrumental reworking of three madrigals, performed by an orchestra under his
direction.

Columbia MS-7441 offers Book VI of the madrigals in its entirety,
which should be listened to only a few at a time, not only
because of the powerful impact of each of the concentrated
pieces, but because Craft's vocal group this time, though it has
the impressive name The Singers of Venosa, includes a soprano
and tenor with obtrusive unattractive voices that make the
listening difficult.

Philips 839-789 has a number of madrigals on one side, and on
the other four Responsories, which exhibit less of the harmonic
strangeness of the madrigals. Or perhaps it is the difference in
the character of the performances, since even the madrigal
Moro, lasso from Book VI sounds like a different piece from
the one on the Columbia record: not only is the NCRC Vocal
Ensemble (Hilversum) conducted by Voorberg a larger group,
but its tone is richer and its style smoother.

See also under MISCELLANEOUS COLLECTIONS: Deller Consort.

GIBBONS

See under MISCELLANEOUS COLLECTIONS: Cuénod.

GLUCK

Orfeo ed Euridice. For the French *Orphée et Eurydice* of 1774
Gluck not only revised and expanded the Italian *Orfeo* of 1762
but transposed much of it so that Orpheus, originally sung by
a *castrato,* could be sung by a tenor. For a revival in 1859
Berlioz was commissioned to make the changes in key in the
French version that would enable a contralto to sing Orpheus;

and his version, sung in Italian, is the one we know. The performance of this version to acquire is the one on London 1285 with Horne's Orpheus, in spite of the deficiencies of Lorengar's singing as Eurydice; one to avoid is on Angel S-3717, with the harsh, tremulous and poorly phrased singing of Bumbry; another is on Victor LSC-6169, with the inadequate singing of Verrett.

The *castrato* voice was still a male voice; and that is a reason for preferring either the performance of the original Italian version with the eloquent singing of Fischer-Dieskau (and the enlivening conducting of Richter) on Deusche Grammophon 139-268/9; or the one of the French version on Philips World Series PHC-2-014, with the beautiful singing of Simoneau (and conducted well by Rosbaud).

See also in Chapter 27: Toscanini, Ferrier, Lemnitz; under MISCELLANEOUS COLLECTIONS: Berganza, Farrell, Horne, Schwarzkopf.

GRIFFES

Roman Sketches and Sonata for Piano. Lyrichord 105, with Hambro's excellent performances.

(The) White Peacock. This is one of the *Roman Sketches.*

HANDEL

Acis and Galatea. A good performance by Sutherland, Pears, Brannigan with the St. Anthony Singers and the Philomusica of London under Boult is on Oiseau-Lyre 60011/2; and Victrola VICS-6040 has Deller's spirited performance with Sheppard and other good soloists, the Deller Consort and the Stour Festival Chamber Orchestra.

Alcina. The work offers a profusion of fine arias in a context of boring recitative. Sutherland's singing, on London 1361, is an extreme of mannered crooning except in the arias in fast tempo which she sings in full voice with breathtaking accuracy and style in the florid passages. But there is superb singing by Sciutti, Berganza, Sinclair, Freni, Alva and Flagello, in a sensitive and spirited orchestral context provided by Bonynge with the London Symphony, and with Malcolm's richly inventive harpsichord accompaniment of the recitative.

Alexander's Feast. Performed well by Deller with Sheppard, Worthley, Bevan and the Oriana Choir and Orchestra on Vanguard S-282/3.*

(L')Allegro ed il Pensieroso. Willcocks conducts a performance on Oiseau-Lyre 60025/6* with especially lovely singing by Delman, Harwood and Watts and good contributions by the St. Anthony Singers and London Philomusica.

Chandos Anthems. They offer passages of Handel's fine writing for chorus and beautiful melodic writing. In the performances on Vanguard S-227/9 Mann sets good tempos; and life is imparted to the music by the singing of Boatwright, Bressler and the Rutgers University Collegium Musicum, and the playing of Raimondi and Krilov, among others.

Concerti Grossi Op. 6. Angel S-3647* has Menuhin's excellent performances with his Bath Festival Orchestra. (Avoid the performance on Victor LSC-6172.)

Concertos for Organ. The engaging works on Angel S-36599 and 36700 are performed well by Preston (on a remarkably clear-sounding organ) with Menuhin and his Festival Orchestra.

Dettingen Te Deum. Nonesuch H-1003 has an only moderately good performance; and I therefore recommend instead the excellent one by van der Horst with the Choir of the Netherlands Bach Society on imported Fonatana 894-049ZKY (G).

Dixit Dominus. This unfamiliar and superb early work is performed well on Vanguard S-249 by Wenzel with the Choir of the School for Choral Music, Halle, the Chamber Orchestra of Berlin and good soloists. (The sound needs additional bass.)

Israel in Egypt. Decca DXS-7178* has Waldman conducting the Musica Aeterna Orchestra and Chorus, Addison, Kopleff, Mc-Collum and Natale.

Jephtha. Handel's last oratorio is sung well by Grist, Forrester, Watts and Young with the Amor Artis Chorale and English Chamber Orchestra under Somary on Vanguard C-10077/9.

Julius Caesar. Sutherland's mannered singing in the excerpts on London 25876* makes it good to have on Victor LSC-6182* the New York City Opera's performance of the entire work, with

Treigle, Sills, Forrester and Wolff, conducted by Rudel. It is a very good performance, though not without flaws—the occasionally tremulous voices of Sills and Wolff, the occasionally excessive ornamenting of the repetitions in *da capo* arias.

Deutsche Grammophon 18-637 had excerpts excellently sung by Fischer-Dieskau and Seefried. And Fischer-Dieskau is excellent again in the complete work conducted effectively by Richter on Deutsche Grammophon 2711-009; but Troyanos's unpleasantly harsh voice is ruinous to Cleopatra's arias, which are the loveliest pieces in the opera.

Messiah. Of the several performances using a small chorus and orchestra like those of Handel's day and observing the conventions of Handelian performance—e.g. the double-dotting, the ornamentation of repeats in arias—it is Davis's on Philips PHS-3-992 that keeps the music most wonderfully alive and expressive with his tempos and inflection of phrase. He conducts the London Symphony Choir and Orchestra, Harper, Watts, Wakefield and Shirley-Quirk.

Ode for St. Cecilia's Day. Excellently performed by Willcocks with Cantelo, Partridge, the Choir of King's College, Cambridge, and the Academy of St. Martin-in-the-Fields on Argo ZRG-563. But I must add that the final number came off my record with almost no bass.

Royal Fireworks Music. The brilliant wind sonorities of the original becoming wearying; and one is grateful for the string sounds of the version excellently performed by Menuhin and his Festival Orchestra on Angel S-36604, with the Concerto in B flat for double woodwind choir, orchestra and organ.

Samson. One of Handel's finest works, excellently performed by Richter on Deutsche Grammophon ARC-198-461/4 with his Munich Bach Choir and Orchestra, Alexander Young, Arroyo, Stewart, Flagello and other soloists.

Semele. The excellent performance conducted by Lewis on Oiseau-Lyre 50098/100 has Vyvyan and Herbert singing with the New Symphony.

Solomon. Previously known to us as abridged, rearranged and reorchestrated by Beecham, the work is now to be heard in its original state, except for a few cuts, on Victor LSC-6187, sung well by Shirley-Quirk, Young, Endich and Brooks with the Vienna Jeunesse Chorus and Volksoper Orchestra under Stephen Simon.

Sonatas Op. 1 for Solo Instrument and Figured Bass. Nonesuch 71238 has the six intended specifically for violin—Nos. 3, 10, 12, 14 and the outstandingly fine and best-known 13 and 15—played well by Lautenbacher; Westminster 9064/6 all fifteen played well on the violin by Olevsky.

Suites for Harpsichord. Dart's performances of Nos. 1 to 4 on Oiseau-Lyre 50184 should be good. And see in Chapter 27: Landowska.

Water Music (Complete). Best performed by Menuhin with his Bath Festival Orchestra on Angel S-36173;* but Boulez conducts the less good Hague Philharmonic in an effective performance on Nonesuch 71127.*

Theodora. This unfamiliar oratorio has pages of beautiful solo and choral writing, and is sung well on Vanguard C-10050/2 by Harper, Forrester and Young with the Amor Artis Chorale and English Chamber Orchestra under Somary. (The sound needs additional bass.)

Collections. *I Know that my Redeemer Liveth* from *Messiah* is one of the arias Horne sings superbly on London 26067 (with arias of Bach).

I have heard no performance of *Total eclipse* from Samson as affecting as Richard Lewis's on Seraphim S-60028,* which has also his beautiful and moving performances of arias from *Acis and Galatea, Alexander's Feast, Jephtha, Joshua, Judas Maccabaeus* and *Semele.*

See also in Chapter 27: Baillie, Ferrier, Flagstad, Lilli Lehmann; under MISCELLANEOUS COLLECTIONS: *The Age of Bel Canto,* Berganza, De los Angeles, Domingo, Evans, Milnes, Price.

HAYDN

Andante and Variations in F minor for Piano. Demus's performance on imported Deutsche Grammophon SLPM-135-115 (E) should be good. (Rubinstein's on Victor LSC-2635 is not.)

Concerto Op. 21 for Harpsichord. A good performance by Igor

Kipnis with the London Strings under Marriner is on Columbia MS-7253 (with Mozart's Piano Concerto K.271, in which the harpsichord is ineffective).

An excellent performance on the piano by Devetzi with the Moscow Chamber Orchestra under Barshai is on Angel S-36238* (with Mozart's Concerto K.414).

(*The*) *Creation.* Of the several recently recorded performances the most effective in its realization of Haydn's extraordinary musical representation of chaos at the beginning, and the most musically sensitive throughout, is Jochum's with the Bavarian Radio Orchestra and Chorus, Giebel, Kmentt and Frick, on Philips PHS-2-903. See also in Chapter 27: Baillie.

Masses. Nos. 4 and 5, the early small-scale and engaging *Missa in honorem Sti Nicolai* and *Missa brevis Sti Joannis de Deo,* are performed well on Philips 900-134* by the Chorus Viennensis, Vienna Choir Boys, Vienna Dom Orchestra and soloists—the first under Furthmoser, the second under Grossmann.

No. 7, the *Missa in tempore belli* (*Paukenmesse*), is performed well on Deutsche Grammophon 138-881 by Kubelik with the Bavarian Radio Orchestra and Chorus and soloists who include Morison and Marjorie Thomas; and on Argo ZRG-634 by Guest with the Choir of St. John's College, Cambridge, Cantelo, Watts, Tear, McDaniel and the Academy of St. Martin-in-the-Fields.

No. 8, the *Missa Sancti Bernardi de Offida* (*Heiligmesse*), is performed well on Argo S-542 by Guest with the Choir of St. John's College, Cambridge, the Academy of St. Martin-in-the-Fields and a solo quartet comprising Cantelo, Minty, Partridge and Keyte.

No. 9, the *Missa Solemnis* (*Nelson Mass*), is performed well on Deutsche Grammophon 139-195* by Ferencsik with the Budapest Choir and Hungarian State Symphony, Stader, Hellman, Häfliger and von Halem; and on Nonesuch 71173 by Swarowsky with a Vienna State Opera orchestra and chorus, Stich-Randall, Casei, Equiluz and Simkowsky.

No. 10, the *Theresienmesse,* is performed superbly on Argo 5500* by Guest with the Choir of St. John's College, Cambridge, the Academy of St. Martin-in-the Fields, Spoorenberg, Greevy, Mitchison and Krause.

No. 11, the less familiar *Creation Mass,* is performed well on Argo ZRG-598 by Guest with the Choir of St. John's College, Cambridge, the Academy of St. Martin-in-the-Fields, Cantelo, Watts, Tear and Robinson.

No. 12, the *Harmonieumesse,* is performed well on Argo Z-515* by Guest with the Choir of St. John's College, Cambridge, the Academy of St. Martin-in-the-Fields, Spoorenberg, Watts, Young and Rouleau.

Quartets. Watch for another reappearance of the Schneider Quartet's performances for the Haydn Society, which pointed up the unpredictable and fascinating course of Haydn's lively, inventive mind as no other performances have done. The last time, 9083/5 had Op. 17; 9086/8 had Op. 20; 9017 and 9021 had Op. 33; 9089/91 had Op. 50; 9053, 9058 and 9065 had Op. 76; 9095 had Op. 77. In addition 9015 had Op. 33 No. 3, Op. 76 No. 2 and Op. 50 No. 6.

Watch also for a possible reissue of the Budapest Quartet's performances of the Quartets Op. 76 on Columbia SL-203 (ML-4922/4), which exhibited refinement of execution and style, as against the Schneider's more energetic, more sharply rhythmed, and therefore more enlivening inflection.

Of the performances available today the outstanding ones are the Quartetto Italiano's of the great Op. 76 No. 2, the fine Op. 64 No. 5 and the engaging Op. 3 No. 5 on imported Philips SAL-3591 (E).

An example of the Haydn operation in quartet-writing raised to incandescence, Op. 20 No. 5, is played well by the Allegri Quartet on Music Guild S-852,* with Op. 42 and Op. 3 No. 5.

The performances of the six of Op. 33 by the Weller Quartet on London 2214 should be good.

The Allegri Quartet's performances of the incandescent three of Op. 54 on Music Guild S-843* are good, as are its performances of the three of Op. 55 on Music Guild S-837.*

A good performance of Op. 76 No. 3 by the Drolc Quartet is on Seraphim S-60137, with Mozart's K.465. (Treble must be reduced to remove the distortion of the first violin's tone.)

(The) Seasons. Of recently recorded performances the best is Davis's with the BBC Symphony and Chorus, Harper, Davies and Shirley-Quirk on Philips PHS-3-911; and a good one is Goehr's

with the North German Radio Symphony and Chorus, Stich-Randall and other soloists on Nonesuch 73009, which I prefer to Böhm's on Deutsche Grammophon 139-254/6.

Sonatas for Piano. Watch for a possible reissue of Gould's performance of Peters No. 3 on Columbia ML-5274 (with Mozart's K.330), which electrified one's mind and held it fascinated with its sharply incisive shaping of the music and its continuity of tension. Balsam's blander and less effective performances are on Oiseau-Lyre S-273/5.*

Symphonies. Nos. 82 to 87 (*Paris*) are on Columbia D3S-769, excellently performed by Bernstein with the New York Philharmonic—which is to say, performed without his usual distorting italicizing.

Nos. 88 and 104, on Angel S-36346,* are performed well by Klemperer with the New Philharmonia.

Nos. 88 and 98 (corrected text) are on Deutsche Grammophon 138-823,* excellently performed by Jochum with the Berlin Philharmonic.

Nos. 94 (*Surprise*) and 99, on London STS-15085, are performed well by Krips with the Vienna Philharmonic.

Nos. 94 and 101 (*Clock*) are performed well on Deutsche Grammophon 138-782* by Richter with the Berlin Philharmonic; but in No. 101 Richter eliminates Haydn's little joke at the beginning of the Trio of the Minuet by correcting the incorrect harmony that Haydn carefully wrote in.

No. 95 is paced and shaped effectively, No. 101 is paced too slowly, by Reiner in his performances with a recording orchestra on Victor LSC-2742;* and he too eliminates Haydn's little joke in No. 101.

Nos. 96 and 97 are played beautifully by the Amsterdam Concertgebouw under van Beinum on imported Decca ACL-196 (E).

Nos. 100 (*Military*) and 102 are performed in matter-of-fact fashion by Klemperer with the New Philharmonia on Angel S-36364.*

And of No. 103 (*Drum Roll*) the best performance is Solti's with the London Philharmonic on imported Decca ACL-107.

See also in Chapter 27: Toscanini, Walter, Cantelli.

Trios. For piano trios see in Chapter 27: Casals, Goldberg.

The String Trios Op. 53 performed superbly by Grumiaux, Janzer and Czako on Philips 802-905 (with string trios of Schubert) offer writing in which one hears the same unpredictable play of Haydn's lively and inventive mind as in his quartets.

JANÁČEK

Sinfonietta. Performed well by Abbado with the London Symphony on London 6620 (with Hindemith's *Symphonic Metamorphoses on Themes of Weber*).

Slavonic Mass. Superbly performed on Deutsche Grammophon 138-954 by Kubelik with the Bavarian Radio Orchestra and Chorus, Bedrich Janáček, organist, and a solo quartet comprising Lear, Rössl-Majdan, Häfliger and Crass, who are superior to the soloists in Bernstein's performance.

LASSUS

The other excellent performances by Venhoda's Prague Madrigal Choir I have heard lead me to believe that the ones of the Mass *Ecce nunc benedicte Dominum* and other pieces on Nonesuch 71053 must be very good.

MAHLER

(Das) Lied von der Erde. The noteworthy feature of Kletzki's performance with the Philharmonia on Angel S-3607* is Fischer-Dieskau's singing of the songs usually sung by a contralto, which he makes sound as though they were intended to be sung only by him. I therefore prefer this performance—even with the unattractive tenor voice of Dickie—to any other, including Bernstein's whipped-up and italicized performance with the Vienna Philharmonic on London 26005, in which Fischer-Dieskau's singing includes not only new subtleties but occasional new overemphasis and excessive vehemence.

Songs. *Lieder eines fahrenden Gesellen* are sung best by Fischer-Dieskau on Angel 35522, with the superb orchestral context provided by Furtwängler with the Philharmonia.

Four of the songs to texts of Rückert, including the great *Ich bin der Welt abhanden gekommen,* are sung marvelously by Fischer-Dieskau with the Berlin Philharmonic under Böhm on Deutsche Grammophon 138-879 (with the excessively lugubrious *Kindertotenlieder*).

Songs to poems from *Des Knaben Wunderhorn* are sung well on Vanguard S-285* by Forrester and Rehfuss with the Vienna Festival Orchestra under Prohaska.

See also in Chapter 27: Ferrier; under MISCELLANEOUS COLLECTIONS: Ludwig.

Symphonies. Kubelik's excellent performance of No. 1 with the Bavarian Radio Symphony on Deutsche Grammophon 139-331 needs addition of bass.

No. 2 (*Resurrection*), on Angel S-3634, is conducted effectively by Klemperer and offers marvelous playing by the Philharmonia, with Schwarzkopf and Rössl-Majdan as soloists. See also in Chapter 27: Walter.

Much of No. 3 I find uninteresting; but its long slow finale is, I think, Mahler's most sublime utterance; and though Kubelik—conducting the Bavarian Radio Symphony and Chorus and Marjorie Thomas on Deutsche Grammophon 139-337/8—doesn't give this finale the sustained grandeur it has in Bernstein's performance on Columbia M2S-675 with the New York Philharmonic, Schola Cantorum and Lipton, one may decide that the charming second movement performed without Bernstein's arch distortions, and the beautiful fourth movement also performed more simply, outweigh the superiority of Bernstein's finale. Abravanel conducts an excellent performance on Vanguard C-10072/3 with the Utah Symphony and assisting choruses and alto soloist.

Of No. 4 the best performance is Kletzki's with the Philharmonia on Seraphim S-60105.

MENDELSSOHN

Concerto for Violin. Until Szigeti's incomparable performance (see in Chapter 27) is made available on a Seraphim reissue or an underground record, there is Stern's good performance with the Philadelphia Orchestra under Ormandy on Columbia MS-6062 (with the Tchaikovsky Concerto).

(*A*) *Midsummer Night's Dream* (Incidental Music). Kubelik's performance with the Bavarian Radio Symphony and Chorus on Deutsche Grammophon 138-959* is the only good one since Toscanini's (see in Chapter 27).

Octet for Strings. Columbia MS-6848* has an outstanding performance by Laredo, Schneider, Steinhardt and Dalley, violins, Tree and Rhodes, violas, and Parnas and Soyer, cellos (with Mozart's Concertone K.190). See also in Chapter 27: Toscanini.

Symphonies. Abbado conducts the London Symphony in an excellent performance of No. 3 (*Scotch*) on London 6587, with a performance of the delightful No. 4 (*Italian*) that can be faulted only for a second movement much slower than the *Andante con moto* Mendelssohn prescribes. For No. 4 see in Chapter 27: Cantelli, Toscanini, Koussevitzky.

MONTEVERDI

(*L'*)*Incoronazione di Poppea.* Angel S-3644* has an abridged version of an excellent Glyndebourne Festival performance conducted by Pritchard, with admirable singing by Laszlo, Lewis and the others except Bible, whose voice is almost all tremolo.

Madrigals. Vanguard S-297 has *Lagrime d'Amante al Sepolcro dell' Amata* (from Book VI) and *Lamento d'Arianna,* sung beautifully by the Deller Consort except for the unattractive countertenor of Deller that is prominent occasionally. See also under MISCELLANEOUS COLLECTIONS: Deller Consort.

Victrola VICS-1438 has the Deller Consort's performances of six madrigals and the piece *Tirsi e Clori* for five voices and instruments.

Of the *Madrigali guerrieri ed amorosi* (Book VIII), Nonesuch 71092 offers a long piece, *Il Ballo delle Ingrate,* and two short ones: *Non havea febo ancora,* with its moving middle section known as *Lamento della Ninfa,* and *Dolcissimo uscignolo.* And Nonesuch 71090 offers another long piece, *Il Combattimiento di Tancredi e Clorinda,* and five short ones: *Gira il nemico insidioso, Hor ch'el ciel e la terra,* a third piece not named on the record and album, *Altri canti di Marte,* and *Perché t'en fuggi o Fillide.* All these are performed beautifully by the singers and instrumentalists of the Società Cameristica di Lugano under Loehrer. Watch for a possible reissue of the

Deller Consort's performance of all the *madrigali amorosi* on Bach Guild 579.

Masses. The two *Masses for Four Voices* (1641 and 1651) are sung well by the Choir of St. John's College, Cambridge, under Guest on Argo 5494,* with two small pieces, *Laudate pueri* and *Ut queant laxis.*

(*L'*)*Orfeo*. The moving expressive recitative of this *favola in musica* is sung effectively by the soloists in the excellent performance with the Capella Antiqua and the Concentus Musicus of Vienna (including players of instruments of Monteverdi's time) conducted by Harnoncourt on Telefunken SKH-21.

Vespers of 1610 (*Vespro della Beata Vergine*) and *Magnificat.* Though the performance of this superb work on Telefunken S-9501/2 doesn't offer solo singing as beautiful as that of Ritchie, Morison and Lewis in the performance that was long available here—and is still listed as available in England—on Oiseau-Lyre 50021/2, its soloists are adequate, Jürgens's Monteverdi Chorus of Hamburg is excellent, and they are heard in the excitingly enlivened context provided by Harnoncourt's realization of Monteverdi's instrumental accompaniment in terms of the old instruments played by the Concentus Musicus of Vienna.

A second *Magnificat* for the *Vespers,* a simpler one for six voices and organ continuo, is sung well by the Choir of the Carmelite Priory under Malcolm on Oiseau-Lyre S-263,* with the 1651 *Mass for Four Voices.*

MORLEY

Vanguard S-157 has a number of fine pieces, sung beautifully by the Deller Consort (with madrigals of Wilbye). See also under MISCELLANEOUS COLLECTIONS: Cuénod, Deller Consort, *An Evening of Elizabethan Verse and Its Music,* Pears.

MOZART

Adagio and Fugue K.546. Performed well by Fricsay with the Berlin Radio Symphony on Deutsche Grammophon 136-398, with the Masonic Funeral Music K.477 (and Haydn's *Te Deum*).

Concerto K.191 for Bassoon. See in Chapter 27: Toscanini.

Concerto K.622 for Clarinet. De Peyer's performance with the London Symphony under Maag on London 6178* offers the most beautiful clarinet tone and phrasing I have heard in this work. One performance to avoid is Goodman's on VICS-1402.

Concertos K.412, 417, 447 and 495 for Horn. There is beautiful writing in all four; but K.447 is made the most impressive by the development section of the first movement, with its startling and dramatic shifts of key. Dennis Brain's performances on Angel 35092 are astounding in their extraordinarily supple tone and subtly detailed phrasing, and are provided with beautifully sensitive orchestral contexts by von Karajan with the Philharmonia.

Concertos for Piano. Ashkenazy's superb performance of K.271 with the London Symphony under Kertesz is on London 6501,* with K.246, a moderately engaging lesser work.

A good performance of K.450 by Frankl with the Württemberg Chamber Orchestra under Färber is on Turnabout 34027,* with K.413, a minor work.

Barenboim's performance of K.453 with the English Chamber Orchestra on Angel S-36513 shows him to be a crudely undisciplined musician who plays the piano badly, and as a conductor cannot achieve something as elementary as the balance of strings, woodwinds and brass necessary for clarity of texture in the playing of a chamber orchestra: right at the start the woodwind flutters that conclude the opening statement are made inaudible by the bassoons.

Rubinstein's only satisfying performance of Mozart is the one of K.466 with an orchestra under Wallenstein on Victor LSC-2635* (with Haydn's *Andante and Variations,* in which Rubinstein has the mistaken idea of playing the two alternating themes and their variations in different tempos).

The dramatic power and urgency which the first movement of K.466 calls for and Rubinstein's playing gives it is lacking in Ashkenazy's otherwise fine performance on London 6579, possibly because it is lacking in the orchestral context that Schmidt-Isserstadt provides with the London Symphony.

For K.467 see in Chapter 27: Lipatti, Gieseking.

In his performance of K.482 with the Vienna Chamber Orchestra under Angerer on Turnabout 34233 Brendel plays the first and last movements effectively, but in his fast tempo the great slow movement doesn't have the expressive effect it has in the prescribed *Andante*. See also in Chapter 27: Schnabel.

For K.488 see in Chapter 27: Gieseking, Schnabel.

I have never heard K.491 played with the powerful sculpturing of phrase, the energy in figurations and runs, the sustained tension and momentum of the performance by Gould with the CBC Symphony under Susskind that was on Columbia ML-5739. Watch for a possible reissue or underground release.

Watch also for a possible reissue of Fleisher's excellent performance of K.503 with the Cleveland Orchestra under Szell on Epic LC-3574 and BC-1025 (with a superb performance of Beethoven's Concerto No. 4). Barenboim's musically lifeless performance with the New Philharmonia under Klemperer is not an adequate replacement; but Cliburn's beautiful performance, if he ever records it, will be.

Concertos for Violin. The fine performances of K.216 and 219 by Grumiaux with the London Symphony under Davis that were on Philips 500-012 are listed as available on imported Philips 835-112AY (E).

Grumiaux's equally fine performance of K.218 with the London Symphony under Davis is on Philips 900-236, with the less interesting K.207. See also in Chapter 27: Goldberg, Szigeti.

Stern's excellent performance of K.216 with the Cleveland Orchestra under Szell is on Columbia MS-7062, with the Sinfonie Concertante K.364 for violin and viola (Trampler).

The excellence of the performance of K.219 on Pickwick S-4013 (with Bach's Concerto No. 1) is not only in Milstein's luminous tone and unaffected phrasing but in the wonderfully enlivened orchestral context that Blech creates around his playing with the superb Festival Orchestra.

Concertos for Miscellaneous Instruments. Watch for a possible reissue of the Perpignan Festival performance of the Sinfonie Concertante K.364 for violin and viola on Columbia ML-4564 with fine playing by Stern and Primrose and orchestral playing excitingly enlivened by Casals's conducting.

A superb performance of K.364 by Grumiaux and Pelliccia with the London Symphony under Davis is on Philips 900-130,* with the Violin Concerto K.211.

The Concertone K.190 for two violins and oboe is excellently performed by Laredo, Tree and Arner with the Marlboro Festival Orchestra under Schneider on Columbia MS-6848* (with Mendelssohn's Octet).

Dances. A group of engaging pieces in this genre—K.267, 462, 501 and 567—and a couple of marches are performed well by Boskovsky with the Vienna Mozart Ensemble on London 6412.*

Divertimentos. Of the engaging K.247 and 251 for winds and strings I prefer the better-paced, clearer-textured and musically enlivened performances by the small Collegium Aureum on Victrola VICS-1335* to those of the Berlin Philharmonic under von Karajan on Deutsche Grammophon 139-013.

For K.287 see in Chapter 27: Toscanini.

One of the finest of recent performances of K.563 for string trio is that of the Trio Italiano d'Archi on Deutsche Grammophon 139-150.* And excellent too is the one by Grumiaux, Janzer and Czako on Philips 900-173.

Masonic Music. Best known and most impressive is the Masonic Funeral Music K.477—a series of musical gestures of solemnity, grief and resignation, with occasional dramatic events provided by startling modulations—which is performed well by Fricsay and the Berlin Radio Symphony on Deutsche Grammophon 136-398, with the Adagio and Fugue K.546 (and Haydn's *Te Deum*).

London 26111 offers in addition the vocal pieces, performed well by the Edinburgh Festival Chorus, Krenn and Krause with the London Symphony under Kertesz. They sound at first like echoings of parts of *The Magic Flute;* but it is more accurate to say that those parts of *The Magic Flute* are in what can be called Mozart's Masonic style.

Masses. The excellent performance of K.317 (*Coronation*) by Markevitch with the Lamoureux Orchestra, Brasseur Choir, Stader, Dominguez, Häfliger and Roux that was on Deutsche Grammophon 18-631 and 136-511 is now available on imported 136-511 (G, F, I).

The *Mass in C minor* K.427 is performed effectively on Angel S-36205* by Gönnenwein with the Southwest German Chamber Orchestra, South German Madrigal Choir and soloists among whom the soprano Mathis is outstanding.

(Ein) musikalischer Spass. See in Chapter 27: Cantelli.

Operas. They begin with the ones Mozart wrote in his teens: the charming *Bastien und Bastienne,* excellently sung by Hollweg, Kmentt and Berry with the Vienna Symphony on Philips World Series 9024; *Ascanio in Alba,* which amazes one with the fifteen-year-old boy's completely assured handling of singers and orchestra in his own already fully achieved vocal and orchestral style in the charming pieces of this "dramatic serenade" for a ducal wedding, and which is sung well by Ligabue, Cundari and others with the Angelicum Orchestra of Milan and Polyphonic Chorus of Turin under Cillario on Victrola VICS-6126; the uninteresting *Lucio Silla,* performed competently on Victrola VICS-6117 by Cillario with a cast headed by Cossotto; and *Il Re Pastore,* of which the familiar aria *L'amerò, sarò costante* turns out to be the only piece in it of that magnitude, but the other arias are engagingly Mozartian, and of which Vaughan conducts a good performance on Victor LSC-7049* with Popp, Grist, Arlene Saunders, Alva, Monti and the Orchestra of Naples.

The major works of the fully matured Mozart begin with *Idomeneo,* of which the performance on Philips 3747/9 hasn't the great singers—Jurinac, Simoneau, Lewis—of the Glyndebourne performance conducted by Pritchard that was on Angel 3574 (and is now on imported World Record Club OH-210/3 [E]), but has good singers—Shirley, Davies, Rinaldi, Tinsley—and is superbly enlivened by Davis's conducting, as the Glyndebourne performance is not by Pritchard's.

The performance to acquire of *Die Entführung aus dem Serail* is still the one that was on Deutsche Grammophon 18-184/5 and is now on imported Heliodor 89756/7 (G), with Stader, Streich, Häfliger, Vantin, Greindl and the RIAS Symphony and Chorus conducted by Fricsay. The performance conducted effectively by Menuhin, recently issued on Angel S-3741, is sung inadequately in English; the others are flawed by poor singing or ineffective conducting.

The best recent performance of *The Marriage of Figaro* was

the one on Victor LSC-6408, with Tozzi, London, Della Casa, Peters, Elias and the Vienna State Opera Orchestra and Chorus conducted effectively by Leinsdorf: watch for a possible reissue on Victrola. Wórth acquiring is the performance that was on Epic SC-6022 and is now on imported Fontana SFL-14012/4 (E, G), which is paced rather slowly by Böhm—the result being a loss of animation and brilliance, but also certain gains: the exceptional clarity of the orchestral detail that is so rich in this work; the increased power of the Count's third-act aria; the increased effectiveness of the sublime *Contessa, perdono* passage at the end. And except for Berry's Figaro the singing is first-rate, with Jurinac and Schöffler outstanding as the Countess and Count and Streich an excellent Susanna. In the performance conducted by Böhm on Deutsche Grammophon 139-276/9 Mathis's Susanna is the one satisfying vocal performance—Janowitz's Countess being too bland, Fischer-Dieskau's Count too explosively vehement, Prey's Figaro too obviously that of a German. See also in Chapter 27: Glyndebourne Festival.

Outstanding among the performances of *Don Giovanni* is the one on Angel S-3605 conducted by Giulini, with Wächter, Taddei, Alva, Sutherland, Schwarzkopf, Sciutti and the Philharmonia Orchestra and Chorus. Sutherland's less attractive voice and more self-indulgently mannered singing spoil the performance on London 1434; the one conducted by Böhm on Deutsche Grammophon 139-260/3 has Fischer-Dieskau's impressive singing in the title role, but the unattractive voices of Nilsson, Arroyo and Grist and unsuitable voice of Schreier in the others; and I advise against the one conducted by Klemperer on Angel S-3700; but the 1955 performance reissued by Philips on World Series PHC-3-009 is worth acquiring—in spite of a poor Donna Anna and Leporello—for London's Don Giovanni, Jurinac's Donna Elvira, Simoneau's Don Ottavio and Sciutti's Zerlina. See also in Chapter 27: Glyndebourne Festival.

The performance of *Così Fan Tutte* to look for is the ear-ravishing one with Schwarzkopf, Merriman, Simoneau, Panerai, Bruscantini and the Philharmonia conducted by von Karajan that was on Angel 5322 and until recently on imported World Record Club OC-195/7 (E). In the one on Victor LSC-6416 Price sings well much of the time, but her voice sounds worn at times (for example in *Per pietà*); Shirley has to strain for the upper notes that are less attractive than the lower ones; and Troyanos's voice is a little harsh; but Milnes and Flagello are excellent, and Leinsdorf's pacing of the performance with the New Philharmonia is good. See also in Chapter 27: Glyndebourne Festival.

La Clemenza di Tito, which has never been staged here in my lifetime, turns out to have impressive melodic writing in addition to its excessive amount of recitative; and in the performance conducted effectively by Kertesz on London 1387 Krenn's secure delivery of Tito's climactic florid aria is breathtaking, and Berganza's Sesto is excellent, but Casula's voice is excessively tremulous and Popp's thin and acidulous.

The excellent *Magic Flute*—with Stader, Streich, Häfliger, Fischer-Dieskau, Greindl, the RIAS Symphony and choruses conducted by Fricsay—that was on Deutsche Grammophon 18-267/9 and briefly on Heliodor 25057 is now listed as available on imported Heliodor 89662/4 (G). And the 1955 performance conducted by Böhm, reissued on Richmond 63007, is worth having for Simoneau's Tamino, Gueden's Pamina and Lipp's Queen of the Night. The recent performances conducted by Böhm on Deutsche Grammophon 2709-017 and by Klemperer on Angel S-3651 I advise against. See also in Chapter 27: Beecham. (Toscanini's marvelous performance at the 1937 Salzburg Festival— with Novotna's Pamina, Roswaenge's Tamino, Domgraf-Fassbänder's Papageno and Kipnis's Sarastro is on an underground tape, and possibly on discs.)

London 25782 has Berganza's superb performances of Fiordiligi's arias and Dorabella's *E Amore un ladroncello* from *Così,* Cherubino's arias from *Figaro* and an aria from *Tito,* among other things.

Imported Heliodor 89817 (G) has Stader's beautiful performances of Ilia's arias from *Idomeneo,* Constanza's arias from *The Seraglio,* Pamina's *Ach, ich fühl's,* the Countess's arias from *Figaro* and Donna Elvira's arias from *Don Giovanni.*

Epic LC-3262 had Simoneau's ear-ravishing performances of Ottavio's arias from *Don Giovanni, Un' aura amorosa* from *Così* and an aria from *Tito,* among other things.

Argo SRG-524 has Spoorenberg's excellent performances of

two arias from *Idomeneo*, the lovely *L'amerò, sarò costante* from *Il Re Pastore* and *Et incarnatus est* from the *Mass in C minor*, and the less consequential cantata *Exsultate jubilate*.

Price's voice is unattractive-sounding and her deployment of it is unimpressive in the performances on Victor LSC-3113.

See also in Chapter 27: Hempel, Ivogün, Jurinac, Leider, Lilli and Lotte Lehmann, Onegin, Patzak, Pinza, Rethberg, Sayão, Schipa, Schumann, Slezak, Stabile, Steber, Urlus, Valletti, Wild-brunn; under MISCELLANEOUS COLLECTIONS: *The Age of Bel Canto,* Domingo, Evans, Ghiaurov, Horne, Price, Rothenberger, Schwarzkopf, Schreier, Sunderland, Tebaldi.

Piano Music (Complete). See in Chapter 27: Gieseking.

Quartets. In the Guarneri Quartet's performances of the Quartets K.589 and 590 on its first Victor record, LSC-2888, one heard playing on the highest level of instrumental virtuosity, tonal beauty, ensemble precision and musical understanding, but not without flaws in musical taste—the cellist's mannered statement of the second subject in the opening movement of K.589, his slide in the slow movement of K.590.

Such flaws are not heard in the playing of the other great American quartet of today, the Yale Quartet, and specifically its performance on Vanguard C-10019 of the Quartet K.421, the like of which in pacing, phrasing and articulation I haven't heard since the Budapest Quartet's performance thirty years ago. The record also has a fine performance of K.575. (Add bass for adequate cello sound; reduce treble for agreeable violin sound.)

The Yale K.421 surpasses in expressive power the performance by the great European group, the Quartetto Italiano, which op-erates with similar unfailing musical sensitiveness and taste in its performances of all six of Mozart's quartets dedicated to Haydn—K.387, 421, 428, 458 (*Hunt*), 464 and 465 (*Dissonant*)—on imported Philips SAL-3632/4 (E).

For the rest there are good performances by the Allegri Quar-tet of K.458 and 465 on Music Guild S-864 (add bass); this group's moderately good performance of K.499 on Music Guild S-866 (with Beethoven's Op. 18 No. 1); and a good one by the Drolc Quartet of K.465 on Seraphim S-60137 (with Haydn's Op. 76 No. 3) (reduce treble to remove the distortion of the first violin's tone).

Watch for a possible reissue of the Budapest Quartet's performances on Columbia SL-187 (ML-4726/8) and SL-228 (ML-5007/8).

Quartets for Miscellaneous Groups. The performance of the Quartet K.370 for oboe and strings by the Soloists of the Berlin Philharmonic on Deutsche Grammophon 138-996* (with the Quintet K.581 for clarinet and strings) has superbly phrased playing of the oboe part.

For the Quartet K.478 for piano and strings see in Chapter 27: Schnabel.

Quintets. See in Chapter 27: Budapest Quartet.

Quintets for Miscellaneous Groups. The performance of the Quintet K.581 for clarinet and strings by de Peyer and members of the Melos Ensemble on Angel S-36241* (with the Trio K.498 for clarinet, viola and piano) is made notable by de Peyer's extraordinary tone and phrasing.

The performance of the Quintet K.452 for piano and winds on London 6494 (with Beethoven's Quintet Op. 16) is made exciting by Ashkenazy's playing with the excellent London Wind Soloists.

Requiem. Kertesz's fine performance with the Vienna Philharmonic and State Opera Chorus, Ameling, Horne, Benelli and Franc on London 1157* is reproduced better than Davis's on Philips 900-160, and Davis's chorus is inferior.

Telefunken S-43059 has another good performance by Richter with his Munich Bach Choir and Orchestra, Stader, Töpper, van Kesteren and Kohn.

Rondo K.511 for Piano. See in Chapter 27: Schnabel. And Ashkenazy's performance is on London 6659 with those of the Sonatas K.310 and 576.

Sonatas for Piano. Cliburn's beautiful performance of K.330 is on Victor LSC-2931 (with Beethoven's Op. 81a).

Gould's electrifying performance of K.330 was on Columbia ML-5274 (with Haydn's Sonata Peters No. 3).

Columbia MS-7097 has Gould's performances of K.279, 280, 281, 282 and 283, MS-7274 his performances of K.284, 309 and 311, in which he largely ignores Mozart's directions for tempo, touch, dynamics and phrasing (for example in the poignantly expressive opening Adagio of K.282, which Gould's tempo and

313

touch convert into an Allegretto scherzando), tears through some of the Allegros in tempos that don't allow the music to be heard and grasped by the listener's mind, thumps out accompaniment figurations so that they predominate over the melody, arpeggiates what Mozart writes as solid chords, and otherwise damages performances which, when not so damaged, offer some of the most electrifying playing of instrument and music one can hear today.

Ashkenazy may have picked up from his friend Barenboim the practices he exhibits in K.310 and 576 on London 6659— of beginning a phrase with a force that he doesn't sustain to its end, and of contrasting force in one phrase with excessive delicacy in the next. But since he is an infinitely better musician than Barenboim his performances of the sonatas and the wonderful Rondo K.511 are fine ones in spite of those practices.

Eschenbach's performances of K.330 and 331 on Deutsche Grammophon 139-318, with the extraordinary Rondo K.511, and of K.332 and 333 on 138-949, articulate the pieces with delicacy and sensitiveness, but also with cohesive tension.

See also in Chapter 27: Schnabel, Lipatti.

Sonata K.448 for Two Pianos. London 6411 has the excellent performance by Ashkenazy and Frager.

Sonatas for Piano and Violin. Watch for a possible reissue of the Haskil-Grumiaux performances that were on Epic LC-3299 and 3602. Avoid the Szell-Druian performances on Columbia MS-7064 and the Szigeti performances on Vanguard S-262/7. See in Chapter 27: Goldberg, Szigeti.

Songs. Not all that Schwarzkopf sings exquisitely with Gieseking on Angel 35270 are as good as *Unglückliche Liebe, Abendempfindung, Der Zauberer, Das Veilchen, Das Lied der Trennung, An Chloë* and the delightfully humorous *Die Alte* which Schwarzkopf points up effectively.

Symphonies. Davis's excellent performances of K.200 and 504 (*Prague*) with the English Chamber Orchestra are on Oiseau-Lyre S-266.* His performance of K.201—which treats the first two movements with powerful expressive inflection, as against Cantelli's animation and grace—and his beautiful performance of K.543 with an excellent orchestra identified as the Sinfonia of London are on Victrola VICS-1378. His performance of K.338

with the Sinfonia of London is on VICS-1382, with the Oboe Concerto K.314 (Goossens); the one of K.425 (*Linz*) with the English Chamber Orchestra on Oiseau-Lyre 60049.

Casals's way with the last six symphonies on Columbia D3S-817 (MS-7381/3) is a combination of tempos slower than usual with powerful inflection and tension; and in K.425 and the finale of K.504 the tempos are too slow not only for Mozart's directions but for the music's effect. But in the earlier movements of K.504 and in the other symphonies the Casals way works with impressive effect, making the first movements of K.385 (*Haffner*), K.504 and K.551 (known as *Jupiter*) spacious and grand, the first movement of K.543 more powerfully expressive than usual in its lyricism, and the impassioned and dramatic first movement of K.550, the great G-minor, the most powerful and eloquent since Toscanini's. (Casals performs Mozart's first version of the G-minor, without the clarinets that he added in the version that is customarily performed.) And the performances gain by the playing of the outstanding musicians who make up Casals's orchestra at his festivals in Puerto Rico and Marlboro. K.504 and 551 are also on MS-7066; K.550 on MS-7262 (with a ponderously italicized Schubert *Unfinished Symphony*).

Giulini's excellent performances of K.550 and 551 with the New Philharmonia are on London 6479.

And Britten conducts the English Chamber Orchestra in a wonderfully enlivened performance of K.550 in which he makes several uncustomary repeats (e.g. the exposition of the second movement).

See also in Chapter 27: Toscanini.

Trios. The excellent performances of Jambor, Altay and Starker are listed as available on Period 1013. See also in Chapter 27: Goldberg.

Trio K.498 for Clarinet, Viola and Piano. Performed beautifully by de Peyer and members of the Melos Ensemble on Angel S-36241,* with the Quintet K.581 for clarinet and strings.

MUSORGSKY

Boris Godunov. Musorgsky's own work hasn't been available on records since the discontinuance of Victor LM-6063, which had parts of the 1956 Metropolitan Opera performance (in disturbingly poor English). But there is reason to expect a production of it at Covent Garden, which no doubt will be recorded.

Pictures at an Exhibition. Ashkenazy's performance of the original piano version on London 6559 is excellent except for a few details—the most important being the fussing with phrasing and tempo that spoils *Samuel Goldenberg.* Mehta's performance of the Ravel orchestration with the Los Angeles Philharmonic on the other side of the record is ineffective; and the performance to acquire is still Toscanini's.

Songs. The tremendous performance of *Songs and Dances of Death* by Vishnevskaya and Rostropovich that was on Philips 500-082 (mono) is now available only with inferior sound on World Series PHC-9138 (stereo) (with three good songs of Tchaikovsky and some uninteresting ones of Prokofiev). The six additional powerful songs of Musorgsky with orchestrated accompaniments that were on the mono record—*Cradle Song, The Magpie, Night, Little Star, The Ragamuffin, On the Dnieper*—are available on imported Philips SAL-3430 (E) (with a Markevitch performance of Stravinsky's *Symphony of Psalms*).

Capitol P-8310 had a beautiful performance of the *Sunless* cycle by Kurenko; Vanguard 1068 a good performance of *The Nursery* by Davrath.

See also under MISCELLANEOUS COLLECTIONS: Ghiaurov, Reizen.

PALESTRINA

Motets *Stabat Mater, Hodie Beata Virgo* and *Senex puerum portebat; Magnificat* and *Litaniae de Beata Virgine.* Sung well by the Choir of King's College, Cambridge, under Willcocks on Argo 5398.*

Motet and Mass *Veni Sponsa Christi.* Sung well by the Choir of St. John's College, Cambridge, under Guest on Argo ZRG-578, with several smaller pieces.

(The) Song of Songs. Watch for a Vanguard reissue of these 21 motets, to texts from *The Song of Solomon,* which seem to me the most beautiful and moving music by Palestrina that I have heard, and which were sung superbly by the Prague Madrigal

Choir under Venhoda on Bach Guild 647 (mono) and 5059* (stereo).

See also under MISCELLANEOUS COLLECTIONS: Wagner Chorale, Welch Chorale.

PROKOFIEV

Classical Symphony. See in Chapter 27: Koussevitzky.

Concerto No. 3 for Piano. In his superb performance with the Chicago Symphony under Hendl, on Victor LSC-2507, Cliburn sets deliberate tempos for the middle movement and the beginning of the finale that he makes effective with his unfailing sense for continuity and shape.

Concerto No. 1 for Violin. See in Chapter 27: Szigeti.

Columbia MS-6635 has Stern's excellent performance with the Philadelphia Orchestra under Ormandy.

(The) Prodigal Son. The Suite from this ballet score is performed well by Ansermet and L'Orchestre de la Suisse Romande on London 6538,* with the *Scythian Suite.*

Scythian Suite. The superb performance by Markevitch with the National Orchestra of the French Radio that was on Angel 35361 is now available on imported Music for Pleasure MFP-2080 (E).

Symphony No. 5. Performed well by Ansermet with L'Orchestre de la Suisse Romande on London 6406.*

PURCELL

Fantasias for Strings. See below in Collections.

Ode for St. Cecilia's Day. This fine piece, characteristic in the boldness of its harmonic progressions and in the florid vocal writing that Purcell makes so exciting, is performed effectively by Tippett with the Ambrosian Singers, excellent soloists and the Kalmar Chamber Orchestra on Vanguard S-286 (pseudostereo, but good sound).

Operas. For *Dido and Aeneas* see in Chapter 27: Flagstad.

Oiseau-Lyre 60047* has the excellent performance of *Dido and Aeneas* conducted by Anthony Lewis, with impressive singing by Baker and good singing and playing by the other soloists, the St. Anthony Singers and the English Chamber Orchestra.

The performance conducted by Barbirolli on Angel 36359 is one to avoid.

Oiseau-Lyre 50139/41 has an excellent performance of *The Fairy Queen,* conducted by Lewis, with Morison and Vyvyan, the St. Anthony Singers and the Boyd Neel Orchestra.

Oiseau-Lyre S-294* has a good performance of *The Indian Queen,* conducted by Mackerras, with Cantelo, Brown, Partridge, Keyte, Tear, the St. Anthony Singers and the English Chamber Orchestra.

Oiseau-Lyre 60008/9 has a good performance of *King Arthur,* conducted by Lewis, with some good singing by Morison among others, but some that isn't agreeable to the ear, and with a good chorus and orchestra.

Pavane and Chacony in G minor. See in Chapter 27: New Music Quartet.

Trio Sonatas. Nos. 1, 2, 4, 7, 8, 9 (the *Golden Sonata*) and 10 are performed well on Dover 5224 by the violinists Ciompi and Torkanovsky.

Vocal Music. Vanguard S-280 has the pieces that were on Bach Guild 570/1—lovely examples of simple melody like *Fairest Isle* and *I Attempt from Love's Sickness to Fly;* the beautiful duet *Close Thine Eyes;* and magnificent examples of Purcell's powerfully expressive florid writing like *I Love and I Must* and *Tell Me Some Pitying Angel*—excellently sung by Cantelo and Bevan, but less attractively by Deller.

Victrola VICS-1407 has the extraordinary *In Guilty Night* (*Saul and the Witch of Endor*) in addition to the *Te Deum, Jubilate Deo* and *Man that Is Born of Woman,* performed by the Deller Consort with the Stour Music Festival Choir and Orchestra.

Several other pieces are performed well by Oberlin and his associates of the New York Pro Musica Antiqua on Counterpoint 5519.

See also in Chapter 27: Baillie, Ferrier, Flagstad; under MIS-CELLANEOUS COLLECTIONS: Baker.

Collections. Angel 36270 had a group of fine instrumental pieces —several of the Fantasias for 4 or 5 strings, including the outstanding one *Upon One Note,* the Pavan No. 4 in G minor, and the Trio Sonatas in G minor and C—performed well by Menuhin and members of the Bath Festival Orchestra.

RAMEAU

Concerts en sextuor. This is the best-known arrangement for strings of the charming and lovely *Pièces de clavecin en concert,* and is performed well by the Paillard Chamber Orchestra on Musical Heritage 567 (1991 Broadway, New York 10023).

The original *Pièces de clavecin en concert* are performed well on Nonesuch 71063 by Veyron-Lacroix, harpsichord, with Rampal, flute, and Neilz, cello.

Harpsichord Pieces. I would expect Malcolm's performances on Argo 5491/2 to be excellent.

(Les) Indes galantes. The charming ballet music is performed well by the Collegium Aureum on Victrola VICS-1466.

Collections. The operatic excerpts performed well on Decca 9683 by singers and an instrumental group under Boulanger include music that is lovely and impressive.

RESPIGHI

Fountains of Rome and *Pines of Rome.* See in Chapter 27: Toscanini.

RIMSKY-KORSAKOV

Capriccio espagnol. See in Chapter 27: Argenta.

ROSSINI

(The) Barber of Seville. Angel 3638 has an outstanding performance conducted by Gui, with Bruscantini, De los Angeles and Alva.

Galliera achieves refinement and subtlety of phrasing and style in the performance on Angel 3559 with Gobbi, Alva and Callas, whose high notes are shrill and tremulous, but whose voice exerts its usual compulsion with the strange and beautiful timbre of its lower range, as her singing does with its powerful continuity in subtle expressive inflection of phrase.

(La) Cenerentola. The 1953 Glyndebourne Festival performance—
briefly available on Victor LHMV-600, now available on imported Voce del Padrone QSD-31/3 (I)—is made an extraordinary example of joint operation in operatic performance
by Gui's conducting, which I take to be responsible for the
style of the singing by Gabarain, Oncina, Bruscantini and the
rest, for the orchestra's sharp-witted phrasing, for the clarity
of the ensemble of voices and orchestra, for the sustained tension and exciting cumulative effect of the concerted numbers,
and possibly even for the remarkable accompanying of the
recitative by Balkwill.

The performance conducted by de Fabritiis on London 1376
has Simionato, with much of the bloom gone from her voice
but her style in melody and florid passages still a delight; and
it has Bruscantini's excellent Dandini; but the other singers are
mediocre.

(Le) Comte Ory. The similarly superb Glyndebourne Festival performance conducted by Gui that was on Angel 3565 is now
available on HMV (Odeon when imported) HQM-1073/4 (E).
Unfortunately the bloom is gone from Oncina's voice, and it
has a strong wobble in the high notes one fears he won't manage; but the rest of the singing is good.

(L')Italiana in Algeri. The superb performance conducted by
Giulini that was on Angel 3529, with an excellent cast headed
by Simionato and Valletti, is now available on imported Columbia QCX-10111/2 (I).

Except for the singing of Berganza the performance on London 1375 is poor.

William Tell. Available on imported Cetra (I) or Cetra-Eurodisc
(G) LPC-1232 is the performance with tight and hard singing
by the tenor Filippeschi but excellent singing by Carteri,
Taddei, Corena and others with the Turin Radio Orchestra
and Chorus. Avoid the poor-sounding Everest version.

Semiramide. In this work every character sings in every situation
in an extreme florid vocal style not for expressive effect but for
spectacular vocal display. And the singing of this music by
Sutherland and Horne on London 1383* is truly spectacular—
Horne's even more than Sutherland's because her voice has a
warmth and luster Sutherland's doesn't have, and her phrasing

is free of Sutherland's mannered moaning. Bonynge conducts the London Symphony effectively.

Arias. London 25106 has Berganza's fine performances with the London Symphony under Gibson.

Victor LSC-3015* has Caballé's excellent performances of arias from unfamiliar works which exhibit Rossini's early conventional writing in *Tancredi* (1812) and *Armida* (1817), the charming *Willow Song* from *Otello* (1816), the more distinguished melodic writing in *La Donna di Lago* (1819), the superb writing in *L'Assiedo di Corinto* (1826) and the *Stabat Mater*.

See also in Chapter 27: Ivogün, Pinza, Slezak, Supervia, Urlus; and under MISCELLANEOUS COLLECTIONS: *The Age of Bel Canto*, Callas, Horne, Milnes, Simionato, Sutherland, Tebaldi, Valletti.

Overtures. See in Chapter 27: Toscanini.

Giulini's performances with the original Philharmonia on Seraphim S-60138 (with overtures of Verdi) are good.

Sonatas for Strings. Of these charming works of Rossini's teens, in which it is astonishing to hear the operatic style of his maturity, Nos. 1 to 4 are performed excellently by I Solisti di Zagreb on Vanguard 2013.* Treble and bass had to be reduced in the mono version.

SCARLATTI

Sonatas. Valenti's early performances of the sonatas on Westminster 9317/8/9 are the ones to acquire for their verve and their pointing up of the detail of the delightful pieces. One wishes he had used a more delicate-toned harpsichord; but the volume can be reduced.

A number of fine performances by Sgrizzi are on Nonesuch 71094.

The excellent performances by Malcolm on a lovely-toned harpsichord that were on London LL-963 years ago are available on imported Decca ECS-542 (E).

See also in Chapter 27: Landowska.

SCHUBERT

Duets for Piano. The infrequently heard and beautiful Fantasie

Op. 103 and the engaging Rondo Op. 107 and *Marches carac-teristiques* are among the pieces performed well by Badura-Skoda and Demus on Deutsche Grammophon 139-107.*

Impromptus for Piano. Brendel's performances of both Op. 90 and Op. 142 are on Vox 512,390.

The best two of Op. 90, Nos. 1 and 3, are performed well, though a little over-expressively, by Nasedkin on Melodiya/Angel S-40145, with the Sonata Op. 53.

See also in Chapter 27: Schnabel, Lipatti.

Masses. The early small-scale Mass in G, with lovely lyrical writing that expresses what Tovey calls Schubert's "fragrant piety", is sung beautifully by the Shaw Chorale with undistinguished soloists on Victor LM-1784.

In striking contrast to the lyrical writing in much of the Mass in A flat is the somber, powerfully expressive passage beginning with *"Et incarnatus est"* in the *Credo*. Deutsche Grammophone 139-108* has a good performance conducted by Raitzinger, with the Regensburg Cathedral Chorus, the Bavarian Radio Symphony, Stader, Höffgen, Häfliger and Uhde.

The Mass in E flat, written in the last year of Schubert's life, has impressively forceful and dramatic passages as well as lovely lyrical ones, and is performed well on Decca 79422* by the Musica Aeterna Chorus and Orchestra and soloists under Waldman.

Moments musicaux. See in Chapter 27: Schnabel.

Octet Op. 166 for Strings and Winds. Performed beautifully— with marvelous playing of the prominent clarinet part by de Peyer—by the Melos Ensemble on Angel S-36529.

Quartets. Philips 900-139* has the Quartetto Italiano's superb performance of the *Death and the Maiden* Quartet and the *Quartettsatz.*

For Opp. 29 and 161 watch for possible reissues of the Budapest Quartet's performances.

Quintet Op. 114 (*Trout*) for Piano and Strings. The performance by Eschenbach and members of the Koeckert Quartet on Deutsche Grammophon 136-488* remains unequalled.

Quintet Op. 163 for Strings. Watch for a possible reissue or underground release of the performance by Stern, Schneider, Katims, Casals and Tortelier that was on Columbia ML-4714.

(*Die*) *schöne Müllerin*. See Songs.

Schwanengesang. See songs.

Sonatas for Piano. See in Chapter 27: Schnabel.

Rubinstein's performance of the posthumous Sonata in B flat on Victor LSC-3112 amazes one with how much he fails to perceive in the work he has loved and studied so long.

Vanguard 1157 had Brendel's excellent performances of the posthumous Sonata in C minor and uncompleted Sonata in C.

Dichter's performance of the posthumous Sonata in A on Victor LSC-3124 is made inadequate by its blandness.

London 6500* has Ashkenazy's masterly and beautiful performances of the Sonata Op. 143 and the Sonata Op. 120, better known but of slighter stature.

Monitor S-2109 has Kuerti's fine performance of the Sonata Op. 78. Peter Serkin's performance is one to avoid.

Nasedkin's excellent performance of the Sonata Op. 53 is on Melodiya/Angel S-40145, with the Impromptus Op. 90 Nos. 1 and 3, reproduced with too heavy bass and with buzzing in fortissimos.

Istomin's fine performance of Op. 53, reproduced better by Columbia MS-7443, has one flaw that he has taken over from Schnabel's performance: the pausing at the ends of phrases in the opening section of the second movement.

Sonata for Cello and Piano (*Arpeggione*). See in Chapter 27: Feuermann.

Sonatas for Violin and Piano. The charming early Sonata Op. 162 and even earlier Sonatinas Op. 137—of which No. 2, with its remarkable first movement, is superior to the other two— are on World Series S-9103, excellently performed by Grumiaux and Castagnone. See also in Chapter 27: Rachmaninov.

Songs. In Fischer-Dieskau's performance of *Die schöne Müllerin* on Angel S-3628* one hears the deployment of the superb voice with a sensitivity to the musical flow and to the sense of the words that makes his the most distinguished and affecting *Lieder*-singing of today.

Wondering why Fischer-Dieskau had recorded another performance of *Die Winterreise* on Deutsche Grammophon 139-201/2* so soon after the one on Angel S-3640,* I heard the reason in the very first piano chords from Demus, which though quiet had an incisiveness of attack and tone that contrasted with the blander playing of Moore in the Angel performance. And it became evident that Demus's marvelous playing—insufficiently audible behind the voice, unfortunately—stimulated the singer to greater expressiveness, and even to occasional excessive vehemence. See also in Chapter 27: Gerhardt, Hotter, Lotte Lehmann.

Angel S-36127* has Fischer-Dieskau's performances of the last songs of Schubert grouped under the title *Schwanengesang,* of which *Der Doppelgänger, Liebesbotschaft, In der Ferne, Abschied, Ihr Bild, Fischermädchen* and *Die Stadt* are outstanding.

Angel 35624 has Fischer-Dieskau's performances of familiar songs which include *Im Abendroth, Geheimes, Nachtviolen, Liebesbotchaft* and *Abschied,* and unfamiliar ones which include the impressive *Totengräber's Heimweh* and engaging *Der Einsame.*

Angel S-36341* has Fischer-Dieskau's performances of the well-known *Du bist die Ruh', Der Jüngling an der Quelle, Fischerweise, Des Fischers Liebesglück, An die Laute* and *Die Forelle,* with a few unfamiliar songs that are uninteresting.

Angel S-36342* has Fischer-Dieskau's performances of *Das Lied im Grünen, Litanei, Der Tod and das Mädchen, Auf dem Wasser zu singen* and *Das Heimweh,* among others.

Deutsche Grammophon 138-117* has Fischer-Dieskau's performances with Demus of songs to poems of Goethe, of which *Meeres Stille, Der Musensohn* and *Erster Verlust* are outstanding.

First Deutsche Grammophon 18-715, later Heliodor 25062, had Fischer-Dieskau's performances with Demus of a number of settings of texts on subjects of Greek antiquity, of which three were outstandingly impressive: *Lied eines Schiffers an die Dioskuren, Aus Heliopolis* and *Freiwilliges Versenken.*

The unfamiliar songs Fischer-Dieskau sings on Angel S-35656* I find uninteresting.

Most of the songs that the tenor Krenn sings on London 26063 are unfamiliar, many early, some surprisingly good, and all characteristic in what they communicate and how—except

Vom Mitleiden Mariae, whose spare, somber writing is like nothing I can recall in any other music of Schubert. The performances are made extraordinary by the quiet of Krenn's sensitively expressive deployment of his beautiful voice, which makes the occasional moments of intensity the more telling.

Schwarzkopf's early Schubert recital with the pianist Fischer on Angel 35022 offers *An die Musik, Das Lied im Grünen, Gretchen am Spinnrade, Nähe des Geliebten, Nachtviolen, An Sylvia* and *Auf dem Wasser zu singen,* among others, sung for the most part very beautifully.

Angel S-36462 has Christa Ludwig's excellent performances, with Geoffrey Parsons's enlivened accompaniments, of *Gretchen am Spinnrade, Erlkönig, Litanei, Der Tod und das Mädchen, An die Musik, Der Musensohn* and *Auf dem Wasser zu singen,* among others.

The performance of *Die schöne Müllerin* on London 5581 and 25155 some years ago—made outstanding by Britten's perceptive playing of the piano parts in support of the tenor Pears's sensitive inflection of a voice no longer fresh but agreeable, steady and flexible—is still available on imported Decca LXT-5574 and SXL-2200 (E).

The little that is left of Cuénod's unusual and expressively affecting tenor voice is enough for his musical intelligence to operate with in impressive performances, on Cambridge 1703, of *Der Jüngling und der Tod, Der Jüngling an der Quelle, Nachtviolen* and *Im Frühling,* among others.

On the other hand the late Fritz Wunderlich's performance of *Die schöne Müllerin* on Nonesuch 71211 is only a simple deployment of a beautiful tenor voice.

See also in Chapter 27: Bjoerling, Ferrier, Flagstad, Gerhardt, Lotte Lehmann, Schumann; and under MISCELLANEOUS COLLECTIONS: De los Angeles, Ludwig, Schwarzkopf.

Symphonies. See in Chapter 27: Toscanini, Cantelli.

In addition there are good performances of the *Unfinished Symphony* on London 6382,* and of the Symphony No. 9 on 6381,* by Kertesz with the Vienna Philharmonic.

Trios. The performance of Op. 100 by the Trio di Trieste on Deutsche Grammophon 139-106* is superb; and I would expect its performance of Op. 99—which was on Deutsche Grammophon 18-583, and is now available on imported 138-583 (G)—to be as good.

The playing of Stern, Rose and Istomin in Op. 99 on Columbia MS-6716* and Op. 100 on MS-7419 is very good, but not as fine as that of the Trio di Trieste.

See also in Chapter 27: Casals, Busch-Serkin Trio.

(Die) Winterreise. See Songs.

SCHUMANN

Carnaval. Novaes's excellent performance is on Turnabout 34164, with Papillons. See in Chapter 27: Rachmaninov.

Concerto for Piano. Lipatti's incandescent performance (see in Chapter 27) has never been equalled; but Cliburn's with the Chicago Symphony under Reiner on Victor LSC-2455* is a fine one; and Victor LSC-2997 offers Rubinstein's relaxed, spacious and beautiful-sounding playing in the beautiful orchestral context that Giulini provides with the Chicago Symphony.

Davidsbündlertänze. An excellent performance by Rosen was on Epic LC-3869 and BC-1269 (with a less good performance of Carnaval).

Dichterliebe. See Songs.

Etudes symphoniques. Ashkenazy's playing on London 6471* (with the Fantasia Op. 17) is now lyrical—and especially beautiful in the additional variations that are customarily omitted —and now impassioned, occasionally to the point of turbulent.

An excellent performance by Casadesus was on Columbia ML-5642.

Fantasia Op. 17. The superb performance by Curzon that was on London LL-1009 (with Kinderszenen), and later on imported Decca LXT-2933 (E), is now on imported Decca Eclipse ECS-568 (E).

Ashkenazy's playing in the opening movement, on London 6471* (with the Etudes symphoniques)—now impassioned, now lingeringly introspective—makes one aware of the movement's episodic character, yet manages to avoid discontinuity except at a couple of long pauses.

Fantasiestücke. Rubinstein's performance on Victor LSC-2669* (with *Carnaval*) suffers from occasional flamboyance.

Kinderszenen (Childhood Scenes). Curzon's beautiful performance is on imported Decca Eclipse ECS-568 (E).

Kreisleriana. The spontaneity and grace, tonal beauty and accurate execution of Rubinstein's performance on Victor LSC-3108 are a miraculous achievement by a man in his eighties. The remarkable piece *Vogel als Prophet* also is on the record.

Papillons. Novaes's fine, though mannered, performance is on Turnabout 34164 (with *Carnaval*).

Songs. Fischer-Dieskau and Demus operate marvelously together in the *Dichterliebe* cycle on Deutsche Grammophon 139-109;* but the singer's occasional excessive vehemence makes this performance less attractive than the one by the same artists that was on Decca 9930 and later on imported Deutsche Grammophon 18-370.

Angel S-36266* has Fischer-Dieskau's performance of the *Liederkreis* Op. 39, which includes several fine songs: *In der Fremde, Waldesgespräch, Mondnacht, Auf einer Burg,* another *In der Fremde,* and *Zwielicht.* I advise against the Ludwig-Berry performance on Deutsche Grammophon 139-386.

Of the settings of Heine poems that Fischer-Dieskau sings with Demus on Deutsche Grammophon 139-110,* I find only the familiar *Du bist wie eine Blume* and *Die Lotosblume* and the unfamiliar *Der Hans und die Grete* impressive. And some of the songs they perform on 139-326 are moderately interesting, the rest not even that.

See also in Chapter 27: Ferrier, Flagstad, Gerhardt, Lotte Lehmann; under MISCELLANEOUS COLLECTIONS: Schwarzkopf.

SHAPERO

Symphony for Classical Orchestra. An excellent performance of this fine piece conducted by Bernstein was on Columbia ML-4889.

SMETANA

(The) Bartered Bride. Kempe conducts an excellent performance

with Lorengar, Wunderlich, Mercker, Frick, the RIAS Chamber Chorus and the Bamberg Symphony on Angel S-3642.*
See also in Chapter 27: Jurinac.

(*The*) *Moldau.* See in Chapter 27: Toscanini.

STRAUSS

Orchestral Works. See in Chapter 27: Toscanini.

There was an excellent performance of *Don Quixote* by Szell with the Cleveland Orchestra and Fournier on Epic LC-3786 and BC-1135*; and there is a good one by Kempe with the Berlin Philharmonic and Tortelier on Seraphim S-60122.

Songs. Angel 35600 has Fischer-Dieskau's performances of *Traum durch die Dämmerung, Ständchen, Zueignung, Freundliche Vision, Ruhe meine Seele* and several less familiar songs, of which the best is *Wozu noch, Mädchen.*

On Angel S-36486 Fischer-Dieskau sings all of Opp. 10, 15 and 17, of which the familiar *Ständchen, Die Nacht* and *Zueignung* are the best, but several of the unfamiliar ones are enjoyable or interesting.

Caballé's ability to deploy her voice in sustained and beautifully inflected phrases produces superb performances of the songs she sings on Victor LSC-2956, which include *Traum durch die Dämmerung, Wiegenlied, Freundliche Vision, Befreit* and *Die Nacht.*

See also in Chapter 27: Bjoerling, Gerhardt, Lotte Lehmann, Schumann; under MISCELLANEOUS COLLECTIONS: Ludwig, Schwarz-kopf.

STRAVINSKY

Apollo (Apollon musagète). Stravinsky imparts to the performance with a recording orchestra, on Columbia MS-6646* (with *Orpheus*), the clarity, power and tension that make his performances of his works the best.

(*Le*) *Baiser de la fée.* The excellent. performance by Stravinsky with a recording orchestra that was on Columbia ML-6203 and MS-6803 is now listed as available here only with *Apollo, Orpheus* and *Pulcinella* on D3S-761, but is available alone on

imported CBS 72407 (E). Even better was his earlier performance with the superior Cleveland Orchestra on ML-5102.

Danses concertantes. A recent rehearing of Davis's performance
with the English Chamber Orchestra on Oiseau-Lyre 60050*
caused me to think better of it than originally.

Jeu de cartes. Stravinsky's superb performance with the Cleveland Orchestra is on Columbia CMS-6649,* with his re-orches-
tration of the *Bluebird pas de deux* from Tchaikovsky's *The
Sleeping Beauty.*

Victor LSC-2567 has a brilliant performance by the Boston
Symphony under Munch.

Davis's performance with the London Symphony on Philips
900-113* is unusual in the rather deliberate tempo of the first
deal, and in the beautifully fashioned detail.

Oedipus Rex. The earlier performance Stravinsky conducted on
Columbia ML-4644 had better soloists, chorus and orchestra
than the one he conducts on Columbia MS-6472,* which is in
turn more powerful than the otherwise good one conducted by
Davis on Angel S-35778.*

(L')Oiseau de feu. The entire score of the original ballet is performed by Stravinsky with a recording orchestra on Columbia
MS-6328* (on D3S-705* with *Petrushka* and *Le Sacre du printemps*).

Orpheus. Stravinsky's performance with the Chicago Symphony is
on Columbia MS-6646,* with *Apollo.*

Petrushka. Stravinsky's performance of the entire score with a
recording orchestra is on Columbia MS-6372* (on D3S-705*
with *L'Oiseau de feu* and *Le Sacre du printemps*).

Pulcinella. Stravinsky's performance of the entire score, not just
the instrumental suite, with a recording orchestra on Columbia
MS-6881* is excellent; but even better was his earlier performance with the superior Cleveland Orchestra on ML-4830.

(The) Rake's Progress. The performance Stravinsky conducts on
Columbia M3S-710* is excellent; but the earlier Metropolitan
Opera performance he conducted on SL-125 had one point of
enormous superiority in Harrell's singing as Shadow.

(Le) Sacre du printemps. Boulez's performance with the Cleveland
Orchestra on Columbia MS-7293 is like Stravinsky's with a
recording orchestra on MS-6319* in its power and tension, and

has in addition the beautiful and brilliant playing which this extraordinary conductor achieves with the virtuoso orchestra.

Symphony in Three Movements. Columbia MS-6331* has Stravinsky's performance with a recording orchestra.

Symphony of Psalms. Columbia MS-6548* has Stravinsky's performance with the CBC Symphony and Festival Singers of Toronto. His earlier performance on ML-4129, with less spacious and vivid recorded sound, had a little more power and tension in the first and last movements.

TALLIS

Cantiones Sacrae. The fine motets by Tallis and Byrd in this jointly published collection are sung well on Oiseau-Lyre SOL-311/3 by the Cantores in Ecclesia under Michael Howard.

The 40-part Motet *Spem in alium* is the most extraordinary of several beautiful and affecting pieces of vocal polyphony, including a few of the *Cantiones Sacrae,* that are sung well by the Choir of King's College, Cambridge, and the Cambridge Musical Society under Willcocks on Argo 5436.*

Lamentations of Jeremiah and several other fine pieces are sung well by the Choir of King's College under Willcocks on Argo 5479.*

TCHAIKOVSKY

Ballets. The entire beautiful score of *The Nutcracker* was performed most effectively by Irving with the New York City Ballet Orchestra on Kapp 5007. Of the currently available performances I would expect Ansermet's with L'Orchestre de la Suisse Romande on London 2203 to be good, judging by his performances of the other two ballet scores.

For the *Nutcracker Suite* see in Chapter 27: Toscanini.

The beautiful score of *The Sleeping Beauty* is paced most effectively, and cut least, in Ansermet's performance with L'Orchestre de la Suisse Romande on London 2304.*

The score of *Swan Lake* is performed, with some cuts, by Ansermet with L'Orchestre de la Suisse Romande on London 2204.* The small additional amount of music in the complete version on Melodiya/Angel S-4106 doesn't make the poor performance worth acquiring.

Concerto No. 2 for Piano. Of the available performances of this work—infrequently heard, but far superior to the ubiquitous No. 1 in substance and structure—I prefer Magalov's with the London Symphony under Davis on World Series 9007 to the less sensitive one of Graffman with the Philadelphia Orchestra under Ormandy on Columbia MS-6755.*

Concerto for Violin. I like best the quietly lyrical performance of Perlman with the Boston Symphony under Leinsdorf on Victor LSC-3014.* See also in Chapter 27: Hubermann.

Operas. In the Bolshoi Theater performance of *Eugene Onegin* on Melodiya/Angel 4115 Vishnevskaya's voice is unpleasant to the ear and incapable of expressive effect; the other female voices are also tremulous and unattractive; and though the male voices are good, the singing of the tenor Atlantov is too lachrymose. Moreover Rostropovich's conducting produces a performance which is sensitively phrased but lacks dramatic tension and propulsion. See in Chapter 27: Albanese.

The tremulous and shrill soprano voice of Milashkina and the hard, straining tenor of Andzhaparidzye impel me to advise against the current Bolshoi performance of *The Queen of Spades,* and to recommend instead the 1942 Bolshoi performance, reproduced with sound that is clear and agreeable, though with some high-frequency distortion, on Ultraphone 141/3 (Charles Consumer Service, 30 West 21 Street, New York 10010).

See in Chapter 27: Bjoerling, Jurinac, Sobinov; and under MISCELLANEOUS COLLECTIONS: Domingo, Farrell, Milnes.

Romeo and Juliet for Orchestra. See in Chapter 27: Toscanini and Cantelli. And Giulini's fine performance with the Philharmonia is on Angel S-35980,* with *Francesca da Rimini.*

Serenade for Strings. Performed well by Marriner with the Academy of St. Martin-in-the-Fields on Argo ZRG-584, with the inferior *Souvenir de Florence;* and by von Karajan with the Berlin Philharmonic on Deutsche Grammophon 139-030,* with the *Nutcracker Suite.*

Songs. See under MISCELLANEOUS COLLECTIONS: Tourel.

Suites for Orchestra. The Divertimento in No. 1 and the Theme and Variations in No. 3 are outstanding examples of the superb invention in some of the movements of these works, achieved with taste and precision in the use of the entire complex of musical line, color, texture and mass. They could be paced more effectively than by Dorati in the performances on Mercury SR-3-9018;* but I can't imagine them being played more beautifully than by the New Philharmonia in those performances.

No. 3 is performed well—except for a few oddities of tempo in the Theme and Variations—by Ansermet with L'Orchestre de la Suisse Romande on London 6543.*

Symphonies. The first three amaze one—No. 3 most of all—with occasional writing that could be the superb orchestral invention of Tchaikovsky's maturity; and I recommend Maazel's excellent performances with the Vienna Philharmonic on London 6426/ 7/8.*

With Maazel's equally fine performance of No. 4 with the Berlin Philharmonic on Deutsche Grammophon 18-789 not available, I recommend von Karajan's with that orchestra on Deutsche Grammophon 139-017. But watch for a possible recording by Davis.

Maazel's with the Vienna Philharmonic on London 6376, is the performance to acquire of No. 5.

For No. 6 (*Pathétique*) see in Chapter 27: Toscanini, Cantelli. And Maazel's performance with the Vienna Philharmonic on London 6409 is excellent.

For the *Manfred* Symphony see in Chapter 27: Toscanini. And an effective performance by Markevitch with the London Symphony is on Philips 900-110.*

Trio. Admirably performed by Rubinstein, Heifetz and Piatigorsky on Victor LM-1120.

Variations on a Rococo Theme. Rostropovich's impressive performance of this work, which has pages of superb Tchaikovskyan writing, with the Berlin Philharmonic under Karajan is on Deutsche Grammophon 139-044 (with Dvořák's Cello Concerto).

THOMSON

Four Saints in Three Acts. Victor LM-2756 has the 1947 performance of an abridgement by Thomson, conducted effectively by him, with excellent soloists (some from the cast of the historic 1934 stage production), chorus and orchestra.

VERDI

Operas. For *Aida, Un Ballo in Maschera, Falstaff, Otello* and *La Traviata* see in Chapter 27: Toscanini.

In addition, the *Aida* on London 1393 is worth having for the beauty and the musical sensitiveness and taste of Price's and Vickers's singing; an excellent *Falstaff* conducted by Solti, with Evans, Ligabue, Simionato, Freni and Elias, is on London 1395; another excellent *Falstaff* conducted by von Karajan, with Gobbi, Schwarzkopf, Barbieri, Moffo, Merriman, Panerai and Alva, is on Angel S-3552*; and a *La Traviata* on imported Cetra LPC-1246 (I) and Cetra-Eurodisc 70044XR (G) is worth having for the beautiful and expressively compelling singing of Callas early in her career (avoid the poor-sounding Everest version). The other currently available performances of these operas, and the ones of *Un Ballo in Maschera* and *Otello*, I advise against.

As for the operas not conducted by Toscanini, London 1432* has the performance to acquire—conducted by Solti, with Tebaldi, Bumbry, Bergonzi, Fischer-Dieskau, Ghiaurov and Talvela—of *Don Carlo,* which has pages that are among the incandescent achievements of Verdi's matured powers, notably the second-act duets of Carlo and the Queen, Rodrigo and the King, the entire scene beginning with the King's *Ella giammai m'amò,* and the tremendous orchestral introduction of the last act, leading to the Queen's *Tu che le vanità,* whose grandeur is heard nowhere else in Verdi.

The performance of *La Forza del Destino* to acquire is the one on Angel 3765 conducted by Gardelli, with Arroyo, Bergonzi, Cappucilli and Raimondi.

Schippers conducts Macbeth on London 1380* with a feeling for the Verdi style—i.e. an enlivening of the orchestral writing and an expansive treatment of the vocal melody—that Leinsdorf's conducting of the work on Victrola VICS-6121 doesn't exhibit. The London performance is therefore the one to acquire in spite of its cuts, and in spite of the superiority of

Rysanek's and Warren's singing in the Victrola performance to Nilsson's and Taddei's in the London.

Two performances of *Rigoletto* are outstanding: the one on Angel 3537 (mono), conducted by Serafin, with Gobbi in the title role, Di Stefano singing well in his mannered style, and Callas, her singing made unpleasant occasionally by the shrillness and wobble of her upper range, but exciting much of the time by the extraordinary timbre and expressive force of her middle and lower range, and by her unfailing sense for continuity of musical phrase and her power of expressive projection; and the one on Victor LM-6021 (mono) with Berger, Peerce and Warren.

Angel 3617 (mono) has a performance of *Simon Boccanegra,* conducted by Santini, with Gobbi, De los Angeles, Christoff and Campora.

Angel 3554 (mono) has a La Scala performance of *Il Trovatore* that is made outstanding by the playing of the orchestral part under von Karajan's direction. What I have said about Callas's and Di Stefano's singing in *Rigoletto* can be repeated here; and Panerai is excellent; but Barbieri's tempestuous singing produces unfocussed tones that are clouded by tremolo.

The *Il Trovatore* on Victor LM-6008 (mono) has superb singing by Bjoerling, Milanov and Warren. And of the two performances with Price I prefer the recent one on Victor LSC-6194, in spite of Mehta's too permissive conducting, because it has Bergonzi in place of Tucker, in addition to Cossotto and Milnes.

In the arias from *Nabucco, Ernani, Macbeth* and *Don Carlo* on Angel S-35763 again Callas's voice is unpleasantly shrill and wobbly in its upper range, beautiful and affecting in its lower range. And I must add that I find the tempo of the *Sleepwalking Scene* from *Macbeth* over-deliberate, and the expressive inflection in the early portion exaggerated to the point of hamming.

Caballé deploys her voice, on Victor LSC-2995,* in superbly shaped and dramatically expressive phrases in excerpts from unfamiliar early operas—*Un Giorno di Regno, I Due Foscari, Alzira, Attila, Aroldo, Il Corsaro, I Lombardi*—in which it is interesting to hear the Verdi powers operating impressively within the conventions of the style of the period.

One is astonished to hear the voice and art of Fischer- Dieskau that are overwhelming in German songs not working convincingly in the Verdi arias he sings on Seraphim 60014.

Victor LSC-2506* has Price's performances of Leonora's two arias from her first complete *Il Trovatore,* and her beautiful performances of Aida's two arias from *Aida;* VCS-7063 has these and in addition the *Sleepwalking Scene* from *Macbeth, Addio del passato* from *La Traviata,* the *Willow Song* and *Ave Maria* from *Otello* originally on LSC-2898 and 2968, and arias from the complete *Ernani* and *La Forza del Destino.* In some—*Aida, Macbeth* and the *Ave Maria*—the voice is ear-ravishing and is used with regard for continuity and shape of phrase; in others one hears occasional tremulousness, shrillness, and prolonging of notes with no concern for the resulting distortion of the phrase.

London 25082* has Tebaldi's lovely and expansive singing in excerpts from complete recordings of *La Forza del Destino, Il Trovatore* and *Otello.*

Ghiaurov's powerful bass voice, its earlier bloom and glow gone, is rough-sounding in the scenes from *Nabucco, I Vespri Siciliani* and *Simon Boccanegra* and Banquo's aria from *Macbeth,* on London 26146.

See also in Chapter 27: Bjoerling, Caruso, De Luca, Destinn, Gadski, Hempel, Homer, Kipnis, Kurz, Lemnitz, McCormack, Melba, Melchior, Milanov, Patzak, Piccaver, Pinza, Ponselle, Rethberg, Roswaenge, Sayão, Schipa, Sembrich, Stabile, Steber, Tauber, Urlus, Wildbrunn; and under MISCELLANEOUS COLLECTIONS: *The Age of Bel Canto,* Callas, Domingo, Evans, Farrell, Ghiaurov, Horne, Milnes, Rothenberger, Simionato, Sutherland, Tebaldi.

For overtures to the operas see in Chapter 27: Toscanini. And Giulini performs several of them well with the Philharmonia on Seraphim S-60138 (with Rossini overtures).

Choral Works. For the *Requiem* and *Te Deum* see in Chapter 27: Toscanini.

London 1275 has the one performance of the *Requiem* other

than Toscanini's whose pacing and shaping by Solti produce a satisfying statement of the work, with only a few flaws like the melodramatic accents on the chorus's whispered *"Dies irae"* and *"Rex tremendae majestatis"* and the crude slowing down for the last climax of the *Libera me*. With the Vienna Philharmonic and State Opera Chorus the performance offers superb singing by Horne and Talvela, good singing by the rather dry-voiced Pavarotti, and singing by Sutherland which is very fine in the earlier parts of the work that require the effortless sustained high notes that are the most attractive her voice produces. In the *Libera me* one hears a great deal of the unattractive lower range of her voice.

A *Te Deum* which one could think was Toscanini's is included in the *Four Sacred Pieces* that Giulini performs excellently with the Philharmonia Orchestra and Chorus on Angel S-36125.*

VICTORIA

Masses *O quam gloriosum* and *O magnum mysterium*. Sung well by the Choir of the Carmelite Priory, London, under McCarthy on Oiseau-Lyre S-270.*

Missa quarti toni, Motet *O vos omnes* and other pieces. Sung well, on Music Guild S-143,* by the Schola du Grand Scholasticat des Pères du Saint-Esprit du Chevilly under Deiss and the Chorale Sant-Jordi of Barcelona under Martorell.

Motet and Mass *O quam gloriosum* and other pieces. Sung well by the Choir of St. John's College, Cambridge, under Guest on Argo ZRG-620.

Requiem Mass for 6 Voices (1605), Responsory *Libera me* and Motets *Gaudent in coelis, O magnum mysterium, Ave Maria* and *Ascendens Christus*. Sung well by the Choir of St. John's College under Guest on Argo ZRG-570.

See also under MISCELLANEOUS COLLECTIONS: Welch Chorale, Wagner Chorale.

VIVALDI

(L')Estro Armonico. World Series PHC-3-017 has excellent performances of the twelve violin concertos by I Musici (increase treble and bass).

(*The*) *Four Seasons.* Angel S-35877* has fine performances of these four violin concertos by the Virtuosi di Roma; and I would expect the performances by I Musici on World Series 9104 to be as good.

Vocal Music. Victor LSC-2935* offers three fine pieces excellently performed: *Beatus vir* and a *Credo* by the Polyphonic Ensemble of Rome, a *Stabat Mater* by Verrett—all three with the Virtuosi di Roma under Fasano.

WAGNER

(*Die*) *Meistersinger.* The performance to acquire is the one conducted with animation and lyrical grace by Kempe, with excellent singing by Frantz, Grümmer, Schock and the others, and with beautiful playing by the Berlin Philharmonic. If no longer obtainable on Angel 3572 it is listed as available on HMV (imported as Odeon) HQM-1094/8 (E).

The performance on Richmond 65002 offers excellent singing by Schöffler, Gueden and the rest, but the excessively slow tempos of Knappertsbusch and poorly balanced recorded sound. The Bayreuth Festival performance on Seraphim 6030 I advise against.

Tristan und Isolde. See in Chapter 27: Furtwängler, Flagstad. In the performances on Deutsche Grammophon 2713-001 and London 1502 Nilsson's voice hasn't the beauty, and her singing hasn't the musical sensitiveness, of Flagstad's; the same is true of Windgassen's and Uhl's voices and singing as against Suthaus's; and neither Böhm's nor Solti's conducting achieves the relaxed, spacious, sensitive lyricism of Furtwängler's performance.

Collections of Excerpts. See in Chapter 27: Toscanini. On Angel S-36188* Klemperer's performances of the Prelude and Finale of *Tristan und Isolde* and the Funeral Music from *Die Götterdämmerung* with the Philharmonia approximate Toscanini's in tension and power, and the one of the Prelude to *Lohengrin* is more relaxed and comes off the record more beautiful in sound than Toscanini's.

Wesendonck Songs. See in Chapter 27: Flagstad. London 26147 has Horne's beautiful performance with the Royal Philharmonic under Lewis (with Mahler's *Kindertotenlieder*).

WALTON

Façade. This humorous setting of Edith Sitwell's poems seems to me Walton's most successful achievement as a composer. The music is more clearly audible behind the spoken poems in the old performance on Columbia CML-5241 than in the later one on London 4104.

WEBER

Arias from Operas. See in Chapter 27: Flagstad; under MISCELLANEOUS COLLECTIONS: *The Age of Bel Canto,* Farrell, Price, Sutherland.

Concerto No. 1 for Clarinet. De Peyer's unique tone and phrasing enhance the effect of the beautiful melodic writing in the performance with the New Philharmonia under Frühbeck on Angel S-36589, which offers also the engaging Concertino Op. 26.

Overtures. See in Chapter 27: Toscanini.

Sonatas for Piano. The grace and elegance of the writing in the lyrical Sonata No. 2 and parts of the dramatic No. 3 are admirably realized in Ciani's performances on Deutsche Grammophon 2530-026.

WILBYE

Vanguard S-157 has a number of lovely madrigals, sung beautifully by the Deller Consort (with pieces by Morley).

See also under MISCELLANEOUS COLLECTIONS: *An Evening of Elizabethan Verse and Its Music.*

WILLAERT

Motet *O crux splendidor*. This magnificent 16th-century work and several lovely secular pieces are sung beautifully by the Ambrosian Consort and Singers under Stevens on Odyssey 32-16-0202.

WOLF

Songs. The sixteen songs from the *Italian Song Book* that Fischer-

Dieskau sang on Decca 9632 are now available on imported Deutsche Grammophon 18-005 (I).

The *Spanish Song Book*, on Deutsche Grammophon 2707-035, has a large number of the songs that are interesting in their relation to the texts, a smaller number of the ones that are in addition moving or attractive as pieces of music—*Nun wandre, Maria, Die ihr schwebet, Ach, des Knaben Augen* and *Herr, was trägt der Boden hier,* of the religious songs; *In dem Schatten meiner Locken* and *Auf dem grünen Balkon,* of the secular ones. Fischer-Dieskau's singing is superb throughout; Schwarzkopf's is good in the religious songs, but mannered and affected in the secular ones.

Angel 35474 has Fischer-Dieskau's performances of a number of beautiful and affecting songs—*Phänomen, Anakreon's Grab, Verschwiegene Liebe, Lebe wohl, In der Frühe, Fussreise*—in addition to the *Harfenspieler* songs and *Cophtisches Lied* 1 and 2, which are interesting only in their relation to the texts.

The songs from the *Italian Song Book* on Philips 802-919, which Ameling sings beautifully except when she forces her soprano voice in climactic high notes, include a few that are superb pieces of music—the lovely *Nun lass uns Frieden schliessen* and *Auch kleine Dinge,* the ironic *Du sagst mir dass ich keine Fürstin sei, Du denkst mit einem Fädchen mich zu fangen* and *Ihr jungen Leute.*

See also in Chapter 27: Ferrier, Gerhardt, Hotter, Lotte Lehmann, Lemnitz, Schumann, Slezak; under MISCELLANEOUS COLLECTIONS: Ludwig, Schwarzkopf.

Quartets. Deutsche Grammophon 139-376 has the La Salle Quartet's excellent performance of the seldom-played Quartet in D minor that Wolf composed between the ages of eighteen and twenty-four, whose writing is remarkably individual, engaging and interesting, and also remarkably unrelated to what one hears in his songs.

RECORDED PERFORMANCES IN MISCELLANEOUS COLLECTIONS LISTED UNDER NAMES OF PERFORMERS OR TITLES OF RECORDS

(The) Age of Bel Canto. An assemblage, on London 1257,* of arias, duets and trios from familiar operas of Handel, Mozart, Weber, Rossini and Donizetti, and unfamiliar ones that include Donizetti's *Lucrezia Borgia*, Bellini's *La Straniera* and Verdi's *Attila*. The aria from *Attila* is one of several fine pieces; in addition there are a number of engaging ones, and a few that are uninteresting. Horne's singing is consistently first-rate; Sutherland's ranges from her superb performance in *Attila* to her mannered moaning in *La Straniera;* the tenor Conrad's is unattractive in tone and unimpressive in style.

Ashkenazy. London 6472* has beautifully shaped performances of Chopin's Nocturne Op. 62 No. 1 and Scherzo Op. 54 and Debussy's *L'Isle joyeuse* (with Ravel's *Gaspard de la nuit*).

Baker. Her unfailing musical intelligence and taste operate in the effortless deployment of her remarkably beautiful mezzo-soprano voice to produce the fine performances of old English songs by Dowland, Campion, Purcell and others on Angel S-36456 (with less interesting modern songs on the reverse side).

Berganza. London 25225 offers her stylistically impressive use of her fine mezzo-soprano voice in *Che puro ciel* and *Che farò* from Gluck's *Orfeo ed Euridice*, *Divinités du Styx* from his *Alceste, O del mio dolce ardor* from his *Elena ed Paride*, *Piangerò, la sorte mia* from Handel's *Julius Caesar*, and other 18th-century arias.

Callas. Imported Musidisc CE-5001 (F) has the recital that was on Cetra A-50175 years ago, with an early performance of *Qui la voce* from *I Puritani* in which one hears the extraordinary beauty of the voice she began with, and arias from *La Traviata* and *La Gioconda* with the reckless forcing whose cost to the voice is audible by the time of the Angel complete *I Puritani*.

Angel 35233 has her in good voice in exciting performances of arias from *The Barber of Seville, Dinorah, Lakmé, I Vespri Siciliani* and less consequential operas. And imported Columbia 33CX1540 (E) has impressive performances of arias from Cherubini's *Medea* and Spontini's *La Vestale* that were on Angel 35304 with arias from her recordings of *La Sonnambula* and *I Puritani*.

Cuénod. *Elizabethan Love Songs and Harpsichord Pieces,* on Lyrichord 37, includes two especially fine songs of Dowland, *Weep You No More, Sad Fountains* and *Sorrow, Stay,* and an extraordinary piece by Gibbons, *The Lord of Salisbury His Pavin.* Superb singing of his special kind by Cuénod, and good harpsichord performances by Chiasson.

English and French Songs of the 16th and 17th Centuries, on Westminster 9620, offers a number of pleasant French songs, several charming ones by Bartlett, Pilkington and Morley, and Dowland's *Flow, My Tears* and *I Saw My Lady Weep.*

Italian and Spanish Songs of the 16th and 17th Centuries, on Westminster 9611, also offers a number of fine songs.

Deller Consort. The madrigals on Vanguard 5031 include fine pieces by Monteverdi, Gesualdo, Morley and Tomkins.

Vanguard 5051 has Monteverdi's *Lagrime d' Amante al Sepolcro dell' Amata* and other fine pieces by Monteverdi, Marenzio and Gesualdo, among others.

De los Angeles. Capitol G-7155, *Five Centuries of Spanish Song,* had a number of fine songs from the Gothic, Renaissance and Baroque periods, which she made now moving, now delightful with her lovely voice, her musical taste, and her personal warmth and charm.

The Spanish songs of the Renaissance on Angel S-35888 are individually very fine, but collectively sound very much alike, and are therefore best listened to a few at a time. They are sung exquisitely to accompaniments on old instruments.

Her voice is unsuited to the concluding section of Schubert's *Der Tod und das Mädchen,* on Angel S-35971, but she does lovely singing in Scarlatti's *Le Violette,* Handel's *Oh! Had I Jubal's Lyre,* Schubert's *An die Musik* and *Wohin,* among other songs that are less interesting.

Domingo. His beautiful tenor voice is used with excellent taste, on Victor LSC-3083, in arias from Handel's *Julius Caesar,* Tchaikovsky's *Eugene Onegin* (in Russian), and *Don Giovanni, Luisa Miller* and *Simon Boccanegra,* among others.

Evans. London 25994* has impressive performances of *L'onore!* from *Falstaff,* the *Credo* from *Otello,* Pizarro's monologue from *Fidelio,* the *Catalogue Aria* from *Don Giovanni; Non più andrai* from *Figaro,* Papageno's first song from *The Magic Flute,* and a couple of Handel arias.

(An) Evening of Elizabethan Verse and Its Music, reissued on Odyssey 32-16-0171, has the verse spoken by Auden, the beautiful musical settings by Weelkes, Wilbye, Dowland, Morley and others sung by the New York Pro Musica Antiqua, which in 1954 included the counter-tenor Oberlin, whose marvelous voice is heard alone in two pieces, and Charles Bressler, whose fine tenor is heard in two others.

Farrell. Angel 35589 had performances of arias from *Alceste, Oberon, Ernani,* Tchiakovsky's *Jeanne d'Arc* and less consequential operas in which her voice and her way of using it placed her among the greats of our time.

Columbia ML-5408 had superb performances of arias from *Alceste, Fidelio, Der Freischütz,* Neris's aria from Cherubini's *Medea,* and Beethoven's *Ah, perfido!,* among other things.

Ghiaurov. The fresh, powerful voice is used impressively, on London 25769,* in *Ella giammai m'amò* from *Don Carlo,* the *Catalogue Aria* from *Don Giovanni,* and *Pimen's Narrative* from *Boris Godunov,* among other things.

History of Music in Sound. Each of the ten volumes is accompanied by a booklet with material from the corresponding volume of the Oxford University Press's *New Oxford History of Music.* Victor issued the volumes as follows:

Volume 1, *Ancient and Oriental Music,* on LM-6057
Volume 2, *Early Medieval Music up to 1300,* on LM-6015
Volume 3, *Ars Nova and the Renaissance,* on LM-6016
Volume 4, *The Age of Humanism,* on LM-6029
Volume 5, *Opera and Church Music,* on LM-6030
Volume 6, *The Growth of Instrumental Music,* on LM-6031
Volume 7, *The Symphonic Outlook,* on LM-6137
Volume 8, *The Age of Beethoven (1790-1830),* on LM-6146

Volume 9, *Romanticism (1830-90)*, on LM-6153
Volume 10, *Modern Music,* LM-6092

In his introduction to the booklet of Volume 2 Dom Anselm Hughes contends that the music "should not be regarded merely as a collection of interesting but dead museum pieces"; but I must report that among the pieces in this volume and on the first two sides of Volume 3 only very few have more than historic interest for me. But on the third and fourth sides of Volume 3 are pieces by Dufay, Ockeghem, Obrecht, Pierre de la Rue, Josquin, and their English contemporaries including Fayrfax and Taverner, that are lovely, charming and impressive to present-day ears. So with many of the pieces in Volume 4—the madrigals of Marenzio, Luzzaschi, Wilbye, Greaves, Weelkes; the French chansons; the church pieces of Victoria, de Monte, Palestrina, Lassus, Gallus, Tallis, Byrd, Gibbons, Morley (an especially beautiful *Agnus Dei*), Praetorius, Giovanni Gabrieli; the French, Spanish and English solo songs; a few of the instrumental pieces. And so with many of the pieces in Volume 5—the excerpts from operas of Cavalli, Cesti, Stradella, Alessandro Scarlatti, Handel, Logroscino, Lully, Rameau, Blow, Keiser; from oratorios of Carissimi and Marcello; from the church music of Rameau, Scarlatti, Pelham Humphrey, Greene, Schütz, Buxtehude and Bach. But except for a superb chorus from Handel's oratorio *Susanna,* the pieces in Volume 6 seem to me poorly chosen—i.e. not the most beautiful or impressive examples of the writing of Purcell, Domenico Scarlatti, the French harpsichordists, Vivaldi, Bach. And though Volume 7 has excerpts from operas of Gluck and Mozart and movements from instrumental works of Haydn and Carl Philipp Emanuel Bach that are musically impressive, it has other excerpts from operas of Dittersdorf and Grétry and movements from instrumental works of Boyce, Stamitz, Monn and Johann Christian Bach that have little but historic interest.

Volume 8 has excerpts from Cherubini's opera *Les Deux Journées,* Méhul's *Joseph,* Spontini's *La Vestale,* Spohr's *Jessonda,* Weber's *Euryanthe,* and Rossini's *Otello;* songs by Zumsteeg, Schubert and Loewe; chamber music by Spohr, Field and Prince Louis Ferdinand; piano pieces by Tomásek, Dussek, Clementi and Hummel.

Volume 9, which cannot provide complete documentation of its period, offers music that is presumed to be unfamiliar: passages from Meyerbeer's *Les Huguenots,* Berlioz's *Les Troyens,* Marschner's *Hans Heiling,* Smetana's *Libuse,* Glinka's *Ruslan and Ludmila* and Musorgsky's *Boris Godunov* (the original); songs by Schumann, Liszt, Franz, Cornelius, Wolf, Borodin, Musorgsky, Duparc, Chausson and Fauré; piano pieces by Liszt, Brahms and Grieg; chamber music by Mendelssohn, Schumann and Fauré.

Volume 10 offers partial documentation of impressionism with small pieces by Debussy and Falla; of late romanticism with pieces by Scriabin, Strauss, Reger, Schönberg and Berg; of the anti-romantic reaction with pieces by Satie, Bliss, Milhaud, Stravinsky, Bartók, Janáček and Hindemith; 12-note music with pieces by Schönberg and Dallapiccola; eclecticism with pieces by Roussel, Shostakovich, Copland, Rubbra and and Rawsthorne (the English origin of the project accounts for space being given to Bliss, Rubbra and Rawsthorne that is not given to Mahler, Prokofiev and Webern).

The performances are for the most part excellent.

Horne. The beautiful voice, the secure and accurate florid singing, the phrasing and style that created a sensation in a concert performance of *Semiramide* a few years ago are heard on London 25910* in arias from *Semiramide, La Cenerentola, L'Italiana in Algeri, Les Huguenots, Le Prophète, The Daughter of the Regiment* and *La Clemenza di Tito.*

On London 1263* the voice has less luster in its upper range, and produces a few growling low notes for dramatic effect, but is still extraordinary in its beauty, range, power and agility; and the use of it is magnificent most of the time in the performances of familiar and unfamiliar arias from *Orfeo ed Euridice, Fidelio, Le Prophète, The Barber of Seville, L'Italiana in Algeri, Tancredi, Otello* (Rossini's), *Semiramide,* Bellini's *I Capuleti ed i Montecchi,* Gounod's *Sapho,* and *Il Trovatore.*

See also *The Age of Bel Canto.*

Ludwig. Seraphim S-60034 has this remarkable singing actress's affecting performances of songs which include Schubert's *Fischerweise,* Brahms's *Sapphische Ode,* Wolf's *Gesang Weylas* and *Auf einer Wanderung,* Strauss's *Die Nacht,* and Mahler's *Ich bin der Welt abhanden gekommen* and *Des Antonius von Padua Fischpredikt.*

Milnes. His fine baritone voice is used well, on Victor LSC-3076, in arias from Handel's *Joshua,* Rossini's *William Tell,* Verdi's *Attila* and *La Forza del Destino,* and Tchaikovsky's *Queen of Spades* (in Russian), among others.

New York Pro Musica Antiqua. Oberlin and Bressler are heard in the performances on Decca 79406, *Elizabethan and Jacobean Ayres, Madrigals and Dances.* And see also *An Evening of Elizabethan Verse and Its Music.*

Pears. Victor LSC-3131 has his admirable performances, to lute accompaniments by Bream, of a number of Dowland's lovely and affecting songs—among them *I Saw My Lady Weep, Weep You No More, Shall I Sue, Sweet, Stay Awhile, Can She Excuse* —and charming songs by Morley, Rosseter and Ford.

Price. Her beautiful voice is occasionally afflicted with strong vibrato in the well-phrased performances of arias from *Dido and Aeneas, Figaro, L'Africaine, La Traviata* and *Otello,* and less consequential pieces, on Victor LSC-2898.*

On Victor LM-2968 the voice was ear-ravishing in Handel's *Care selva,* but tremulous and shrill in *Or sai chi l'onore* from *Don Giovanni* and the higher-ranging passages of the aria from *Der Freischütz;* and it had a hardness in the *Sleepwalking Scene* from *Macbeth* which it doesn't have on VCS-7063.

Reizen. Imported MK D-10435/6 (Four Continent Book Co., 156 Fifth Avenue, New York 10010) has this Russian bass's superb performances of Musorgsky's *The Seminarist, The Flea* and *Trepak* (the Rimsky-Korsakov falsification) in addition to songs of other Russian composers.

Richter. Deutsche Grammophon 138-849* has his exquisitely wrought performances of Debussy's *Estampes* and fine performances of Chopin's Polonaise-Fantaisie Op. 61 and Etudes Op. 10 Nos. 1 and 12, but an erratically paced Ballade Op. 52.

Rothenberger. Her beautiful soprano voice is heard on Seraphim S-60092 in admirable performances of *Martern aller Arten* from *The Seraglio, Ach, ich fühl's* from *The Magic Flute,* Marzelline's aria from *Fidelio,* Oscar's arias from *Un Ballo in Maschera,* and Violetta's first-act arias from *La Traviata,* among others.

345

Schreier. In the arias from *The Seraglio, The Magic Flute, Don Giovanni, Così Fan Tutte* and *La Clemenza di Tito* on London 26079 he uses with musical taste a fresh tenor voice that I find monotonous in its unvarying somewhat lachrymose timbre.

Schwarzkopf. Her performances of lovely and charming songs by Bach, Gluck, Mozart, Beethoven, Schubert, Schumann, Brahms, Wolf and Strauss that were on Angel 35023 are on imported Columbia 33CX1044 (E). They range from the exquisite sustained singing in Schubert's *Litanei*, Schumann's *Der Nussbaum* and Wolf's *Wiegenlied* to the excessively arch and staccato delivery of Schumann's *Aufträge*, the excessively dramatized delivery of Brahms's *Vergebliches Ständchen*.

Simionato. The beautiful mezzo-soprano voice, the superb style in ornamented melody, the brilliant bravura style in florid writing were highly impressive in the arias from *The Barber of Seville, La Cenerentola, Don Carlo* and Bellini's *I Capuleti ed i Montecchi* that were on London 5269.

Sutherland. Her earliest record, London 26111,* exhibits breath-taking ease, accuracy, tonal brilliance and style in florid passages and musical phrasing of melody in arias from *Lucia, Linda di Chamounix, Ernani* and *I Vespri Siciliani;* and this is true also of London 1214,* with arias from *The Seraglio, Norma, I Puritani, La Traviata, Otello* and less consequential operas.

The later London 25776* offers unfamiliar and interesting arias from Verdi's *I Masnadieri* and *Luisa Miller,* Rossini's *La Cambiale di Matrimonio* and Bellini's *Beatrice di Tenda,* with familiar ones from *Oberon, Dinorah, Le Cid* and *I Pagliacci*. And in these it offers her remarkable and at times spectacular control of a voice that is attractively bright only in its upper range; the impressive sense for shape of phrase and style that operates in her use of the voice part of the time; the mannerisms—the little moans, the little explosions of tone—that she indulges in at other times.

See also *The Age of Bel Canto*.

Tebaldi. What is on the still listed but unobtainable early London 5007 can be heard on imported Decca ACLN-299 (I): the fresh and lovely voice, occasionally a little tremulous and shrill, in arias from *Aida, Il Trovatore, Faust* (with a sustained note

346

in place of the trill at the beginning of the *Jewel Song*) and other operas.

Interesting, on London 25020,* is the simple phrasing in the Countess's arias from *Figaro,* and the increase not only in emotional warmth but in vocal beauty in *Selva opaca* from Rossini's *William Tell,* in which she evidently feels more at home than in the Mozart arias. The other pieces on the record are by Mascagni, Cilea, Catalani and Refice.

The much later London 25912 has arias from Verdi's *Giovanna d'Arco, Un Ballo in Maschera* and *Don Carlo,* in which her voice, even without its earlier bloom, is still a superb one that she deploys spaciously with impressive effect. The other pieces are by Mascagni, Cilea, Ponchielli and Puccini.

Tourel. Decca 9981 has fine performances of Tchaikovsky's *At the Ball, So Soon Forgotten, None but the Lonely Heart* and *When Spring Was in the Air,* among other Russian songs.

And the Russian songs she sings on Odyssey 32-16-0070* include several fine ones: Glinka's *Doubt* and *Elegy* and Tchaikovsky's *Lullaby* and *Pagadi* Op. 16 Nos. 1 and 2.

Wagner Chorale. Victoria's *Vere languoris,* Palestrina's *Super flumen Babylonis* and other pieces by these composers and Sweelinck, Josquin and Hassler are sung well on Angel S-36013.*

Welch Chorale. Lyrichord 52, *Motets of the 15th and 16th Centuries,* offers good performances of Palestrina's *Super flumen Babylonis,* Victoria's *Tantum ergo* and *Vere languoris,* Ingegneri's *Tenebrae factae sunt* and fine pieces by Dufay, Josquin, Dunstable, Byrd and others.

INDEX OF

MUSICAL PROCEDURES,

FORMS AND TERMS

GENERAL INDEX

INDEX OF PERFORMERS

INDEX OF PERFORMERS

NOTE

(March 1968)

When I revised certain chapters of the 1956 *Listener's Musical Companion* for the present version I overlooked the chapter on criticism, in which three passages required change. One is the statement on page 193 about Berlioz's letters: *Hector Berlioz: A Selection from His Letters* now offers a better selection than Barzun's and a more accurate translation by Humphrey Searle, including corrections of some of the mistranslations in Barzun's versions. The second is the statement on page 194 about the translations of Berlioz's *Evenings in the Orchestra*: the first translation by Roche did turn out to be preferable to Barzun's, which was not the new one he had contended was needed to replace Roche's, but was instead largely the same Roche translation with an occasional substitution of a Barzun word or phrase that as often as not was less good or less correct. And the third is the statement on page 196 about the editions of Shaw's music criticism: the contents of the Anchor paperback, *Shaw on Music*, are badly selected, arranged, titled and introduced by Eric Bentley; and one should read the original four volumes, which are still available in England and easy to obtain.

In addition I should mention that a selection from the three collections of Thomson's reviews and articles referred to on page 197, with additional later pieces, has been published in a Vintage paperback, *Music Reviewed*.

29

ADDITIONAL
RECORDED PERFORMANCES

Issued Through 1973

Performances of the Past

Beecham. Seraphim S-60165 has his performance of Berlioz's *Symphonie Fantastique* with the French National Radio Orchestra.

Bjoerling. His beautiful 1938 performances of *Cuius animam* from Rossini's *Stabat Mater, Ingemisco* from Verdi's *Requiem,* and *Ah, si, ben mio* from *Il Trovatore* are among the early performances on Seraphim 60168 (mono).

Budapest Quartet. The performances of Mozart's Quartets K.387, 421, 428, 458 (*Hunt*), 464 and 465 have been reissued on Odyssey Y3-31242 (mono).

Caruso. Seraphim 60146 (mono) has the very first European recordings of 1902-4; but one gets far better reproduction of the early Caruso voice from the first American recordings of 1904-6 on RCA VIC-1430 (mono).

De Luca. His beautiful singing is heard with Schipa's in the excerpts from *Rigoletto* on RCA VIC-1633 (mono), *Golden Age Rigoletto.*

Farrell. Her memorable singing in Cherubini's *Medea* is documented in the excerpts on Odyssey Y-32358 (stereo).

Ferrier. Her performances of Schubert and Wolf songs are now on Richmond 23184 (mono; reduce treble); and her performances of arias from works of Bach, Handel, Gluck and Mendelssohn on 23185.

Flagstad. The phenomenal early voice is heard in the duets with Melchior from Act 2 of *Tristan und Isolde* (with Flagstad singing Brangäne's warning), *Lohengrin* and *Parsifal* on RCA VIC-1681 (mono; reduce treble). And Seraphim 60145 (mono) has the *Tristan* duet (with Suthaus) and *Liebestod* from the performance of the opera conducted by Furtwängler.

Gadski. Her early singing in Verdi is further documented by the excerpts from *Aida* she recorded with Caruso, Homer and Amato, on RCA VIC-1623 (mono).

Gieseking. His incandescent pre-war performance of Mozart's Concerto K.271 is on Parnassus 7,* with the excellent pre-war performance of Beethoven's Concerto No. 1. And the extraordinary 1955 performance of Mozart's Concerto K.467 with Cantelli and the New York Philharmonic is on Opus MLG-70.*

Hofmann, Josef. The 1935 and 1938 performances on RCA VIC-1550 (mono) are offered as incomparably great examples of what some have contended is the correct style of playing Chopin (and other Romantic composers) that pianists of today are ignorant of. But I consider these wilfully mannered and distorted performances to be demonstrations of how the music should *not* be played, which is all they can teach to Cliburn, Ashkenazy and Pollini today.

Huberman. Rococo 2002 (mono; increase treble) has his superb performance of the Tchaikovsky Concerto.

Ivogün. Rococo 5328 (mono) has her performances of *Martern aller Arten* from Mozart's *Seraglio,* the Queen of the Night's arias from his *Magic Flute,* and the end of Act 1 of *La Traviata* (in German), with arias of Rossini and Donizetti in which she indulges in shocking exhibitionistic interpolations.

Kipnis. Seraphim 60163 (mono) has impressive performances of operatic excerpts which include the finale of *Die Walküre* and the *Catalogue Aria* from *Don Giovanni,* and songs of Wolf in which one can hear the German words are being sung by someone born in Russia.

Kreisler. Rococo 2006 (mono) has the first performance of the Beethoven Concerto he recorded in the twenties, in which one can hear the beautiful playing of his prime.

*Obtainable from Parnassus Records, P.O. Box 281, Phoenicia, N.Y. 12464.

Lipatti. London STS-15176 (pseudo-stereo) has his last public performance of the Schumann Concerto — a little grander and more meditative than the earlier one on the Odyssey record, but without the earlier one's incandescence. And Opus MLG-80 (mono) has his marvelously enlivening performance of Bach's D-minor Clavier Concerto.

Melchior. Seraphim IB-6086 (mono) has his performances of Wagner excerpts, including the final duet of Act 1 of *Die Walküre* with Lotte Lehmann and the second-act duet of *Tristan* with Leider; and also excerpts from *L'Africaine* and Verdi's *Otello* (in German). And RCA VIC-1681 (mono; reduce treble) has his performances with Flagstad of duets from *Tristan, Lohengrin* and *Parsifal*.

Pinza. To the Columbia performances of Mozart arias on the Odyssey record, Odyssey Y-31148 (mono) adds other Columbia performances of arias from *Don Giovanni, The Barber of Seville, Norma, Simon Boccanegra, Don Carlo* and the Rimsky version of *Boris Godunov*.

Ponselle. Odyssey Y-31150 has the performances of Verdi excerpts she recorded for Columbia in 1920-23, with disregard for shape of phrase that is more blatant than in the later performances on the Victrola record.

Rachmaninov. RCA VIC-1534 (mono) has his unbearably distorted performance of Chopin's Sonata Op. 35, but a beautiful shaping of the Nocturne Op. 15 No. 2 and excitingly incisive pointing up of details in the Waltzes that are played with enchanting grace.

Rehkemper. Parnassus 4 (mono) has his superb performance of Mahler's *Kindertotenlieder*, with Thorborg's of *Ich bin der Welt abhanden gekommen* and Zareska's of *Lieder eines fahrenden Gesellen*.

Rethberg. RCA VIC-1683 (mono; reduce treble drastically) has her historic performance of the *Ave Maria* from Verdi's *Otello*, and distinguished performances also of the *Willow Song*, the two arias from *Un Ballo in Maschera,* and arias and ensembles from *Aida*.

Sayão. Odyssey Y-31151 (mono) has her lovely singing in Cherubino's arias from *Figaro, Vedrai carino* from *Don Giovanni,* and the *King of Thule* and *Jewel Song* from *Faust*.

Schipa. See under De Luca.

Schnabel. His performances of Beethoven's Bagatelles Opp. 33 and 126, Variations Opp. 34 and 35 and *Diabelli Variations* are on Seraphim 6067 (mono); the ones of Beethoven's last five sonatas on 6066, with the rest of the sonatas on 6063/4/5. RCA VIC-1511 (mono) has his 1942 performance of Beethoven's Concerto No. 5 with the Chicago Symphony under Stock, reproduced with insufficient bass and a hum that is aggravated when bass is turned up. And a record with the performances of Mozart's Concertos K.482 and 488 can be obtained from International Piano Library, 215 West 91 Street, New York 10024.

Steber. Her great performance of Berlioz's *Les Nuits d'Eté* has been reissued on Odyssey Y-32360 (mono). And Y-31149 (mono) has the Verdi arias she recorded in 1950, with the duets from *Otello* with Vinay that were added in 1951.

Szigeti. Reissued on Columbia M6X-31513 (mono) are the uniquely great performances of the concertos of Brahms, Beethoven, Mozart (K.218), Prokofiev (No. 1), Mendelssohn and Bach (D minor), Handel's Sonata in D and Bach's G-minor Sonata for unaccompanied violin that Szigeti recorded in his prime; and with these the astounding performance of the Prelude to Bach's E-major Sonata that he recorded at the age of fifteen, and two of his performances with Schnabel at a Frick Collection concert in 1948 — the ones of Beethoven's Sonatas Opp. 24 and 96. For accurate sound of his playing, treble must be turned down drastically in the Frick performances; treble must be decreased and bass increased in the Bach D-minor; the 1908 Bach Prelude needs maximum treble, and a 5-kc cut-off which is needed also by the other concertos in addition to reduction of bass; and the Brahms Concerto needs reduction of treble.

Thorborg. See under Rehkemper.

Toscanini. A few of the performances with the BBC Symphony, apparently newly mastered, are on Seraphim 60150 (mono), with the sound of the Weber-Berlioz *Invitation to the Dance* still poor, but the sound of the Overtures to *The Magic Flute* and *La Scala di Seta* and the *Leonore* No. 1 now natural and clear (increase treble in all three; reduce bass in the last two).

RCA VIC-1521 (mono) has the superb orchestral context Toscanini provided with the NBC Symphony for Dorfmann's undistinguished playing in Beethoven's Piano Concerto No. 1. The poor sound of the 1941 performance of the Tchaikovsky Piano Concerto No. 1 with Horowitz on RCA VIC-1554 (mono) makes the 1943 performance on LM-2319 (mono) the one to acquire. The still unequalled performance of Beethoven's Ninth has been issued on the two sides of RCA VIC-1607 (mono). Underground records are now to be had of the 1937 Salzburg performances of *Falstaff*, *The Magic Flute* and *Die Meistersinger* (of the two available versions the one with an act of *Falstaff* on the last side has better sound); and of the 1940 Beethoven *Missa Solemnis* and Verdi *Requiem*.

In addition, RCA in England has been issuing — on records costing 99 English pence each — a *Toscanini Edition* with its own newly remastered versions of the NBC Symphony recordings. A reader has lent me AT-101 with Mendelssohn's *Italian* Symphony and Schubert's *Unfinished,* AT-108 with Rossini overtures, AT-111 with Debussy's *Ibéria* and *La Mer* and AT-112 with Berlioz's *Harold in Italy* (which was never reissued in American RCA's Victrola series); and I can report that the English remastering has produced sound which is more clearly and cleanly defined in quieter aural space than that of the American Victrolas — the Debussy pieces being amazingly improved not only in this respect but in the greater spaciousness of the sound that is so clearly and cleanly defined. The greater over-all attractiveness of the sound appears to have been achieved by a tipping of the balance away from the bass toward the treble; which necessitates, for my ears, a reduction of treble, and a stepping up of bass to restore adequate solidity down below (except in the first movement of the Schubert *Unfinished,* in which bass must be cut down). Other records in the series, which I haven't heard, are AT-102 with Schubert's Ninth, AT-104 with Tchaikovsky's *Pathétique,* AT-107 with Musorgsky's *Pictures at an Exhibition* and Ravel's *Daphnis and Chloë* Suite, AT-110 with Mozart's G-minor and *Jupiter* Symphonies, AT-114 with Dvořák's *New World* Symphony, AT-117 with Beethoven's Symphonies Nos. 1 and 2, AT-120 with

369

Haydn's Symphonies Nos. 94 and 101, AT-200 with Beethoven's *Missa Solemnis,* AT-202 with his *Fidelio,* AT-300 with *Un Ballo in Maschera,* AT-301 with *Falstaff,* AT-303 with *Aida.* My reader obtained his records from Henry Stave, 9 Dean Street, London W.1; and presumably they can be obtained also from Blackwell's, Broad Street, Oxford.

PERFORMANCES OF TODAY

BACH, CARL PHILIPP EMANUEL

Symphonies in D, E-flat, F and G. Deutsche Grammophon ARC-2533-050 has Richter's enlivening performances with his Munich Bach Orchestra.

BACH, JOHANN SEBASTIAN

Concertos. The performances of the *Brandenburg Concertos* by Anthony Newman and Friends on Columbia M2-31398 are unclear in texture; and I advise against them.

Marriner's performances of the *Brandenburg Concertos* with his Academy of St. Martin-in-the-Fields, on Philips 6700-045, give us the works approximately as Bach composed them originally in Weimar and Cöthen, without the changes he made when he copied them a few years later for the Margrave of Brandenburg. One basic difference was that, except for No. 1, they were written originally not as orchestral works but as chamber music for single players; and in addition there were differences in instruments. In the Marriner performance of No. 2 a treble recorder is used in place of the flute we have heard, and — since Bach specifies *"tromba o vero corno di caccia"* — a horn in place of the familiar trumpet; in No. 4 two high-ranging sopranino recorders are used as the approximation of the *"flauti d'echo"* specified by Bach, in place of the flutes or lower-ranging recorders we have heard. And in the first movement of No. 5 we hear the original harpsichord cadenza of 19 bars in place of the elaborate one of 65 bars that Bach substituted in the Brandenburg version. The horn in No. 2 works well; the sopranino recorders in No. 4 do not, for my ears. Marriner's pacing of the works, and the players' execution of them, are excellent, but in the end I prefer the Brandenburg versions as performed by Britten.

Philips 6500-119 has Grumiaux's excellent performance of the great D-minor Concerto for two violins with Koji Toyoda (with the uninteresting Concerto for oboe and violin and Vivaldi's fine Concerto Op. 3 No. 6).

Anthony Newman's insensitive performance of the great D-minor Clavier Concerto, on Columbia M-32300, is one to avoid.

Columbia M-30231 has a good performance of the *Italian Concerto* on the harpsichord by Igor Kipnis (with the English Suite No. 2 and other pieces).

Goldberg Variations. Anthony Newman's enlivening performance on Columbia M-30538 is preferable to Karl Richter's pedestrian one on Deutsche Grammophon 2707-057.

Mass in B Minor. London OSA-1287 has Münchinger's good performance, except for an unusually brisk opening chorus, with the Stuttgart Chamber Orchestra, Vienna Singakademie Chorus, Ameling, Minton, Watts, Krenn and Krause.

Sonatas for Violin and Harpsichord. The fine No. 3 — among the six on Vanguard VCS-10080 — is performed well by Buswell and Valenti except for an occasional discontinuity in tempo.

Suites for Orchestra. Argo ZRG-687/8 has excellent performances by Marriner with his Academy of St. Martin-in-the-Fields.

(The) Well-Tempered Clavier. The final Nos. 17 to 24 of Book 2 are performed by Gould on Columbia M-30537 with his eccentricities of tempo and touch.

BEETHOVEN

Concertos for Piano. To the Fleisher performances of all five reissued on Columbia M4X-30052, London CSA-2404 has added Ashkenazy's, which are made outstanding by their sensitivity and power, their feeling for continuity and proportion in shape, their disciplined use of the tonal resources of the piano. One

371

possible explanation of the overblown-sounding tuttis of the Chicago Symphony is Solti's excessive intensity and drive; another is the recording that causes the sound of piano and orchestra to recede into the distance when it is soft and to come near — too near for the tuttis — when it is loud.

Another sensitive ensemble collaboration by Bishop and Colin Davis (conducting the BBC Symphony this time) produces the excellent performance of No. 1 on Philips 6500-179. And Gould's performance of No. 1, unique in its excitingly enlivening style, has been reissued on Odyssey Y-30491.

Cliburn's grandly proclamatory playing in No. 3 with the Philadelphia Orchestra under Ormandy, on RCA LSC-3238, is in striking contrast with Radu Lupu's sensitive treatment of lyrical passages in the first movement, and greater animation and lightness in the finale, in the fine performance with the London Symphony under Foster on London CS-6715. Both are more impressive than the performance of Bishop with the BBC Symphony under Davis on Philips 6500-315.

Fidelio. The performance conducted by von Karajan on Angel S-3773 has little of the dramatic force of Toscanini's but is acceptably paced for the most part, and offers — in addition to the superb singing of Vickers — good singing by Dernesch, Donath, Ridderbusch, Kéléman and the others, and the beautiful playing of the Berlin Philharmonic.

Mass in C. Giulini's sensitively shaped performance with the New Philharmonia Orchestra and Chorus and soloists headed by Ameling, on Angel S-36775, is now the one to acquire.

Missa Solemnis. The greatest performance is still Toscanini's; but the one on Philips 6799-001 — in which Jochum conducts the Concertgebouw Orchestra, Netherlands Radio Chorus, Giebel, Höffgen, Haefliger and Ridderbusch — is excellent.

Quartets. The Yale Quartet's performances of Op. 130 on Vanguard VCS-10096 and Op. 135 and the Great Fugue Op. 133 on VCS-10097 are effective, but less so — i.e. more hurried, less relaxed, less sensitively phrased — than those of the Quartetto Italiano.

The La Salle Quartet not only concludes Op. 130 with the Great Fugue, on Deutsche Grammophon 2530-351, but, unlike the Quartetto Italiano, doesn't include on the record the finale that Beethoven substituted for the Great Fugue. That is reason enough to prefer the Quartetto Italiano recording; and in addition the Italiano performance is superior.

The Quartetto Italiano's performances of Opp. 74 *(Harp)* and 95, on Philips 6500-180, are superb. But its performances of Op. 18 Nos. 1 and 3, on 6500-181, seem to me excessively vehement.

Quintet Op. 29. An excellent performance by members of the Vienna Octet is on London CS-6674 (with the earlier and inconsequential Sextet Op. 81b for strings and horns).

Sonatas for Piano. The performances of all 32 by Claude Frank on RCA VICS-9000 are those of an excellent pianist and musician.

Cliburn's performance of Op. 57 *(Appassionata)*, on RCA LSC-4013, is like no other in the spacious grandeur of its impassioned character; and in it his extraordinary pianistic and musical powers operate under the control of the discipline that is the essential gift of the mature artist, revealing him again as one of the greatest musicians who have played the piano in this century. The record has also his impressive performances of Opp. 13 *(Pathétique)* and 27 No. 2 (known as *Moonlight*).

Gilels, on Deutsche Grammophon 2530-253, produces statements of Opp. 53 *(Waldstein)* and 101 which, except in big climaxes, lack the force and tension Beethoven's music should have even in *pianissimos.*

Gould's eccentricities of tempo and phrasing and touch make his performances of Op. 31 on Columbia M-32349 something to avoid.

Bishop's admirable performances of Op. 31 Nos. 2 and 3 are on Philips 6500-392.

Michelangeli's performance of Op. 7, on Deutsche Grammophon 2530-197, is uncharacteristically straightforward and effective, but — with its total of 31 minutes of playing on the record — expensive.

Symphonies. Someone accustomed to the intensity of the *Eroica* in Toscanini's performance may find Colin Davis's more relaxed and slower-moving performance with the BBC Symphony, on Philips 6500-141, unsatisfying; but I find it effective in its different way. (But the *Coriolan* Overture in Davis's slow tempo, on the same record, lacks the dramatic force it must have.)

Boulez's unprecedentedly slow tempos for the first and third movements of No. 5 — in his performance with the New Philharmonia on Columbia M-30085 — I find impossible to hear as valid.

Solti's performance of No. 9 with the Chicago Symphony, on London CSP-8, is on the whole effective; but the most effective is still Toscanini's.

Trios. Grumiaux and his associates offer outstanding performances of the engaging String Trios Op. 9 Nos. 1 and 3 on Philips 802-895.

Variations. London CS-6715, with Radu Lupu's fine performance of the Concerto No. 3, has also a performance of the 32 Variations in C minor which is excellent except for occasional discontinuities of tempo.

London CS-6727 has Curzon's excellent performance of the *Eroica* Variations (with Schubert's *Moments Musicaux*).

BELLINI

Norma. Caballé's singing, on RCA LSC-6202, is beautifully phrased and expressive, but will not satisfy anyone who knows Callas's performance on Seraphim 6037 (mono) (not the later performance on Angel S-3615).

Il Pirata. Though this early work doesn't attain the level of the ones that follow, it reveals Bellini as an accomplished practitioner of the style of his period who at times ennobles that style. The performance on Angel S-3772 offers Caballé's beautiful shaping of melody and her execution of florid passages with security and style. The others sing well, and Gavazenni conducts effectively.

BERLIOZ

Benvenuto Cellini. The masterly writing in this work can now be heard in the performance on Philips 6707-019 brilliantly conducted by Colin Davis, with the BBC Symphony, the Chorus of Covent Garden and an excellent solo group headed by Gedda.

(The) Damnation of Faust. Colin Davis, on Philips 6703-042, provides a superb orchestral context with the London Symphony for the excellent singing of Gedda (Faust), Veasey (Marguerite) and Bastin (Mephistopheles), and incandescent performances of the work's orchestral pieces. However, while the 1970 performance on Angel SCL-3758 is conducted less effectively by Prêtre, Gedda's singing in it gains by the more attractive quality of his younger voice, Baker's voice is more beautiful, and her employment of it more affecting, than Veasey's, and Bacquier's singing is better-sounding and expressively more effective than Bastin's.

(Les) Nuits d'Eté. The excellent performances on Philips 6500-009 — by Veasey, Armstrong, Patterson and Shirley-Quirk with the London Symphony under Davis — enable one to hear the songs sung by the different voices Berlioz intended.

Requiem. The performance on Philips 6700-019 in which Davis conducts the London Symphony Orchestra and Chorus is for the most part as effective as one would expect; but the *Offertorium* loses by being paced too slowly, and the *Sanctus* is damaged by the poor singing of the solo tenor. In addition one must be able to increase the bass substantially in playback if some of the thunderous climaxes of the *Tuba mirum* and *Lacrymosa* are to have adequate solidity down below, and if the string basses' quiet comments in these great sections are to be audible.

Collections. Boulez conducts the New York Philharmonic, on Columbia M-31799, in brilliant performances of the Overture to *Beatrice and Benedict* and *Roman Carnival* Overture, and performances of the Overture to *Benvenuto Cellini* and *Royal Hunt and Storm* from *The Trojans* in unusually fast tempos which lessen the effect of these two pieces.

BIZET

Carmen. Horne's singing in the title role and Maliponte's as Micaela are the only attractive features of the Metropolitan Opera performance of the original version with spoken dialogue, on Deutsche Grammophon 2709-043. I therefore recommend instead the performance of that version on Angel S-3767.

Variations Chromatiques for Piano. This strange and fascinating piece is played marvelously by Gould on Columbia M-32040 (with a questionable performance of Grieg's Sonata Op. 7).

BLOCH

The superb cellist Starker performs the brooding solo parts of *Schelomo* and *Voice in the Wilderness* with the Israel Philharmonic under Mehta, on London CS-6661.

BOCCHERINI

The Symphonies Op. 35 are performed well by Ephrikian with I Filarmonici di Bologna on Telefunken SKH-24.

BRAHMS

Symphony No. 4. Philips 6500-389 has an excellent performance by Haitink with the Concertgebouw Orchestra.

Variations on a Theme of Paganini. A good performance by John Lill is on Deutsche Grammophon 2530-059 (with the Piano Pieces Op. 76).

BYRD

Harpsichord Pieces. Gould's excitingly enlivening performances on his dry-sounding piano are on Columbia M-30825 (with pieces by Gibbons).

CAVALLI

La Calisto. This work by the best-known of the 17th-century composers of *dramma in musica* who followed Monteverdi is largely expressive *arioso* that leads to occasional melodic pieces which are very beautiful. Leppard, on Argo ZNF-11/12, conducts the Glyndebourne Festival performance of his realization of the score, in which the women — Baker, Cotrubas and Kubiak — sing impressively enough to induce one to accept the rough voice of Trama and the unattractive counter-tenor voice of Bowman.

CHOPIN

Etudes. Pollini's superb performances of all 24 of Opp. 10 and 25 are on Deutsche Grammophon 2530-291; and Kuerti's beautiful performances of Op. 25 on Monitor MCS-2133.

Mazurkas. They are performed well by Magaloff on London STS-15146/8.

Preludes. Freire's excellent performances on Columbia M-30486 are now the ones to acquire.

Collections. Ashkenazy's performance of the Sonata Op. 35 on London CS-6794 astounds one with its frenetic rushing of fast passages, disruption of the natural flow of melodic passages, and distortion of shape in the first two movements; and the Nocturnes Op. 15 exhibit the same defects. But the Mazurka Op. 59 No. 2 and Waltz Op. 18 are played enchantingly.

Watt's failure to maintain continuity in his changes of tempo in the Sonata Op. 35 and Fantaisie Op. 49, on Columbia M-32041, causes the performances to lack coherence.

COPLAND

Billy the Kid. The Suite (which doesn't include the waltz for the *pas de deux*) is performed effectively by Copland with the London Symphony on Columbia M-30114 (with excerpts from *Rodeo*).

CORELLI

Concerti Grossi Op. 6. All twelve are performed beautifully by Gracis with the Solisti dell' Orchestra Scarlatti on Deutsche Grammophon ARC-271-0011.

COUPERIN, FRANCOIS

Harpsichord Pieces. The Ordres Nos. 8, 11, 13 and 15 are performed, on Philips 6700-035, by the excellent harpsichordist Puyana on a Ruckers-Taskin instrument of Couperin's period.

377

Nonesuch H-71265 has the Ordre No. 26, with a number of pieces by Louis Couperin that I find more impressive than those of François, performed well by Albert Fuller on a modern Dowd harpsichord "inspired by . . . Taskin".

DEBUSSY

Images for Orchestra. Michael Tilson Thomas's superb performances with the Boston Symphony are on Deutsche Grammophon 2530-145.

Images for Piano. Deutsche Grammophon 2530-196 has Michelangeli's performances of the two sets (with *Children's Corner*).

Nocturnes. Boulez obtains beautiful playing from the New Philharmonia, on Columbia M-30483; but his tempo for *Fêtes* is too sluggish for the piece to achieve its festive character. The record also offers the less interesting *Printemps* and First Rhapsody for orchestra and solo clarinet (de Peyer).

Collections. Several of the best pieces for piano — *Reflets dans l'eau, La Soirée dans Grenade, Jardins sous la pluie, L'Isle joyeuse* — are on RCA LSC-3283, performed by Cliburn with an expansiveness of tempo and sonority, and a consequent largeness of shape and expressive content, that are not only different from what is usually heard but impressively effective.

DONIZETTI

Anna Bolena. In the performance on ABC/ATS-20015 Sills's voice much of the time is tremulous, edged, even strident, and not pleasant to listen to; and Verrett's has a metallic quality and strong vibrato; but there is fine singing by Burrows.

Lucia di Lammermoor. Sutherland's voice brightens after the opening scene, in the performance on London OSA-13103; but with her mannered deployment of it her singing cannot stand comparison with Callas's powerfully phrased singing in the 1953 performance on Seraphim 6032 (mono), which I recommend instead. Pavarotti's voice lacks ease of flow, but has acquired a little glow; and Milnes uses his beautiful voice admirably.

Maria Stuarda. Though not as powerful a work as *Lucrezia*

Borgia, it continues the interesting features of that earlier work — the occasional replacement of recitative by stretches of dramatically expressive *arioso,* the use of the orchestra to comment expressively on the vocal melody. In the performance on ABC/ATS-20010 Sills's voice is steady and agreeable when emotional intensity doesn't produce the flutter that clouds it and makes it strident. Eileen Farrell's voice, still beautiful in quiet moments, also becomes excessively tremulous with increased intensity. But the singing of Burrows and Quilico is excellent.

DOWLAND

Songs. See under MISCELLANEOUS COLLECTIONS: Pears.

DVOŘÁK

Legends Op. 59. These engagingly melodious pieces are performed well by Leppard with the London Philharmonic on Philips 6500-188.

Quintet Op. 81 for Piano and Strings. RCA LSC-3252 has the excellent performance of Rubinstein and the Guarneri Quartet.

Symphonies. It is interesting to hear how the Brahmsian details of the first two movements of No. 7 (formerly No. 2) are worked into the flow of engaging writing that is Dvořák's. Rowicki's excellent performance with the London Symphony is on Philips 6500-287.

The more impressive Symphony No. 8 (formerly No. 4) is performed well by Szell with the Cleveland Orchestra on Angel S-36043.

GESUALDO

Three fine motets, *Ave dulcissima Maria, O vos omnes* and *Hei mihi Domine,* and three madrigals, *Ecco morirò dunque* (its accompanying printed text incomplete), *Dolcissima mia vita* and *Moro lasso,* are sung beautifully by the Monteverdi Choir under Gardiner, on Argo ZRG-645 (with pieces by Monteverdi).

GIBBONS

Harpsichord Pieces. Gould's excitingly enlivening performances

379

on his dry-sounding piano are on Columbia M-30825 (with pieces by Byrd).

Vocal Pieces. A number, both sacred and secular, are sung by the Deller Consort on RCA VICS-1551.

GLUCK

Don Juan. The charming music for this ballet is performed well by Marriner with his Academy of St. Martin-in-the-Fields on London STS-15169.

HANDEL

Anthems for the Coronation of George II. These pleasant minor pieces are performed well by Menuhin with the Ambrosian Singers and his Festival Orchestra on Angel S-36741.

Concerti Grossi Op. 3. Less impressive than those of Op. 6, but pleasant to listen to, they are performed well by the Collegium Aureum on RCA VICS-6036.

Messiah. The performance on Vanguard C-10090/1/2 is conducted in routine fashion by Somary but has good singing by Margaret Price, Minton, Young, Diaz and the Amor Artis Chorale with the English Chamber Orchestra.

The performance on London 1396 I advise against because of the unattractive voices of Sutherland and Tourangeau and the unacceptably excessive ornamenting of vocal and instrumental parts.

Overtures. The unfamiliar ones to *Lotario, Esther, Admeto, Alcina, Orlando, Poro, Partenope* and *Ottone* offer characteristically engaging music and are performed well by Leppard with the English Chamber Orchestra on Philips 6599-053.

And the unfamiliar and similarly engaging ones to *Faramondo, Radamisto, Arminio, Deidamia* and *Scipio* are performed well by Bonynge with the English Chamber Orchestra on London CS-6711.

Royal Fireworks Music. Leppard's excellent performance with the English Chamber Orchestra is on Philips 6500-369, with three earlier concertos for winds and strings which use some of the substance of the *Fireworks Music* and *Water Music.*

Suites for Harpsichord. Nos. 1 to 4 are more attractive as performed by the late Thurston Dart on Oiseau-Lyre OLS-152
than as performed by Gould on Columbia M-31512.

Water Music. Leppard's performance with the English Chamber
Orchestra, on Philips 6500-047, is good, but is surpassed in
pacing and refinements of phrasing and instrumental execution by Menuhin's with his Bath Festival Orchestra. And this
performance of the entire superb work should be acquired,
rather than the good performance of excerpts by Kubelik with
the Berlin Philharmonic on Deutsche Grammophon 138-864
(with the *Royal Fireworks Music*).

HAYDN

Quartets. Deutsche Grammophon 2530-302 has the Amadeus
Quartet's graceless performances of the great Op. 54 Nos. 1
and 2.

Symphonies. Nos. 57 to 64 on London STS-15131/4 and Nos. 65 to
72 on STS-15135/8 offer only occasional interesting or impressive movements, and nothing like the incandescent operation of
Haydn's matured powers of invention and development in the
final Nos. 92 to 104. It is in Nos. 73 to 81, on STS-15182/5, that
one begins to hear the writing of a more accomplished composer
and a harmonic daring and rhythmic freedom which he will
carry to incandescence in the last series. Nos. 73, 77, 78 and 80
are especially good. STS-15229/34, beginning with No. 82, ends
with the great No. 92 *(Oxford)* of that last series, and offers in
between the fine Nos. 84, 86 and 88, with individual good
movements in the others. The Philharmonia Hungarica's playing under Dorati in all these is first-rate; and he paces and
shapes them well, except for his inability to conduct *adagio*
or *largo* as anything slower than *andante,* and *andante* as anything slower than *allegretto.*

The Dorati-Philharmonia Hungarica performances of Nos. 93
to 104 haven't yet appeared; but Deutsche Grammophon 2720-
064/10 meanwhile offers these works performed by the London
Philharmonic under Jochum, who conducts them admirably
except for occasional exaggeratedly fast tempos in which violin

passage-work is indistinct. This indistinctness results also from recording that causes the sound, when it is soft, to recede into the distance.

Except for his overaccentuation of the strong beats of the principal theme in the first movement of No. 94 *(Surprise)*, Casals's performances of this work and the less frequently played No. 95 with the Marlboro Festival Orchestra, on Columbia M-31130, are excellent.

No. 88 and the less interesting No. 89 are conducted in un-enlivening fashion by Böhm in the performances with the Vienna Philharmonic on Deutsche Grammophon 2530-343.

Trios. Of the rarely heard piano trios that offer additional examples of the incandescent operation of Haydn's last years, No. 25 (which Cortot, Thibaud and Casals recorded in the twenties), the outstanding No. 26, and No. 27 have been issued on Philips 6500-023, Nos. 29, 30 and 31 on 6500-400, and Nos. 21 and 23 and the outstanding No. 28 on 6500-401. The performances by the Beaux Arts Trio are excellent, except for the excessively fast tempo of the first movement of No. 28 that Haydn marked *Allegro moderato,* and the excessively slow tempo of its second movement that he marked *Allegretto.*

JANÁČEK

Choral Music. Nonesuch H-71288 has a number of character-istically powerful pieces for male chorus, sung well by the Moravian Teachers' Choir under Tučapsky.

Piano Music. In the early works which Firkusny plays well on Deutsche Grammophon 2707-055 one's interest is held by the idiosyncratic operation of the individual mind that produced the Sinfonietta and the *Slavonic Mass.* But the later operation of that mind in the Concertino and Capriccio for piano and orchestral groups — performed with members of the Bavarian Radio Symphony under Kubelik — I am unable to follow with understanding.

Sinfonietta. Ozawa performs it well with the Chicago Symphony on Angel S-36045, and Kubelik even better with the Bavarian Radio Symphony on Deutsche Grammophon 2530-075. But Kubelik couples it with an inferior work of Janáček, *Taras*

Bulba; whereas the Angel record offers the powerful and interesting Concerto for Orchestra of Lutoslawski.

LUTOSLAWSKI

See under Janáček.

MAHLER

(Das) Lied von der Erde. The performance Solti conducts with his nervous drive, on London OS-26292, has superb playing by the Chicago Symphony, beautiful singing by Minton, and singing by Kollo which is less agreeable to the ear. The performance to acquire is still Kletzki's with Fischer-Dieskau.

Lieder eines fahrenden Gesellen. Minton's performance with the Chicago Symphony under Solti, on London OS-26195, is very good, but is surpassed by Fischer-Dieskau's with the Philharmonia under Furtwängler on Angel 35522.

Symphonies. Horenstein's performance of No. 3 with the London Symphony, on Nonesuch H-73023, offers unaffected second and third movements that are preferable to the pretentious ones in Bernstein's performance, but an impassioned finale that is less effective than the one to which Bernstein gives the sustained grandeur it calls for.

Maazel's ineffectively fast tempos for the second and third movements of No. 4 make his performance with the Berlin Radio Orchestra, on Nonesuch H-71259, one to avoid.

MENDELSSOHN

Concerto for Violin. Grumiaux's performance with the New Philharmonia under Krenz, on Philips 6500-465, has the right impassioned elegance. The record also offers the 13-year-old Mendelssohn's deservedly unfamiliar Concerto in D minor.

MONTEVERDI

Madrigals. Philips 6703-035 offers the lovely pieces in the third book, and the ones in the fourth book, published eleven years later, whose harmonic writing begins to achieve the powerful

383

and dramatic expressiveness of the writing in the subsequent books. They are sung well, under Leppard's direction, by soloists who include Armstrong, Watts, Partridge, Tear and Keyte, and the Glyndebourne Chorus.

Philips 6799-006 offers the eighth, ninth and tenth books, of which we have had only selected pieces until now; and it is good to hear the unfamiliar ones even though not all are as fine as those we already know. The performances — with soloists who include Harper, Armstrong, Watts, Alva, Davies and Tear, and members of the Glyndebourne Chorus and Ambrosian Singers — are excellent.

Several pieces from the eighth book — *Hor ch' el ciel, Ardo avvampo, Altri canti di Marte* and the stage work *Ballo: Movete al mio bel suon* — and *Questi vaghi concenti* and *O ciechi ciechi* from other collections are performed well, on Argo ZRG-698, by the Heinrich Schütz Choir with vocal soloists and instrumentalists under Norrington's direction.

Zefiro torna, Era l'anima mia and *Ohimè se tanto amate,* and three motets, *Cantate Domino, Domine ne in furore tuo* and *Adoramus te,* are sung beautifully by the Monteverdi Choir under Gardiner, on Argo ZRG-645 (with pieces by Gesualdo).

MORLEY

First Booke of Ayres. The charming songs are sung well by Nigel Rogers with accompaniment of lute and viola, on Telefunken SAWT-9568.

MOZART

Choral Works. Colin Davis, on Philips 6500-271, conducts the London Symphony Orchestra and Chorus in superb performances of unfamiliar and familiar works. Unfamiliar are the *Vesperae Solennes de Confessore* K.339, of which the *Laudate Dominum* for solo soprano, beautifully sung by Kanawa, is only the most extensive and most affecting of the occasional fine solo passages; and the powerfully expressive *Kyrie* in D minor K.341. Familiar are the sublime *Ave verum* corpus K.618 and the brilliant showpiece for soprano, *Exsultate jubilate* K.165.

Concertos for Horn. All four are performed well by Civil with the Academy of St. Martin-in-the-Fields under Marriner, on Philips 6500-325; but the suppler tone and subtler inflection of the late Dennis Brain's performances on Angel 35092 (mono) make them the ones to acquire.

Concertos for Piano. In the performances of K.467 and 503 on Philips 6500-431 Colin Davis provides superb orchestral contexts for playing by Bishop that is unexpectedly inadequate in its lack of the sustained tension and force in quiet legato that is required in the enunciation of melody in Mozart's writing. The lack is evident in the occasional melodic phrases of the opening Allegro of K.467, and far more damaging to the long flow of quiet melody in the great Andante.

Brendel's nerveless playing — in the performances of K.459 and 488 with the Academy of St. Martin-in-the-Fields under Marriner, on Philips 6500-283 — shows little awareness of the marvelous happenings in the music.

Concertos for Violin. Zukerman's lovely-sounding but blandly phrased playing in K.218 and 219, on Columbia M-30055, is heard in sluggish, lifeless contexts provided by Barenboim with the English Chamber Orchestra.

Philips 6500-537 has Michelucci's fine performance of K.219 with I Musici, and I Musici's performances of Mozart's Adagio and Fugue in C and *Eine kleine Nachtmusik.*

Concertos for Miscellaneous Instruments. The excellent playing of Stern and Zukerman in the Sinfonie Concertante K.364, on Columbia M-31369, is heard in a crude orchestral context provided by Barenboim with the English Chamber Orchestra.

Divertimentos. K.334 for strings and horns is performed well by Marriner with his Academy of St. Martin-in-the-Fields, on Argo ZRG-705.

Masses. K.317 *(Coronation)* and the less familiar and less impressive K.257 are on Philips 6500-234, excellently performed by Colin Davis with the John Alldis Choir, soloists who include Donath and Davies, and the London Symphony.

On Philips 6500-235 Davis conducts a superb performance of the *Mass in C minor* K.427 with the London Symphony Orchestra and Chorus, but with soprano soloists, Donath and

385

Harper, who no longer are capable of the unstraining flow of beautiful vocal sound the music requires. I recommend instead the performance with Mathis and Erwin on Angel S-36205.

Operas. It is the impassioned performance of *Idomeneo* conducted by Davis that one must have; but one may want in addition the beautiful singing of Jurinac, Simoneau and Lewis in the blander 1956 Glyndebourne Festival performance reissued on Seraphim S-6070.

Davis conducts *The Marriage of Figaro* superbly on Philips 6707-014; but the very first voice one hears is that of a Figaro seemingly aged fifty; the next is the frayed voice of a no longer young Susanna; and the singing of the Cherubino, the Count and the Countess also are not equal to the demands of the vocal writing.

The much-needed good performance of *The Magic Flute,* on London OSA-1307, is conducted with animation and lightness by Solti, and has good singing by Lorengar, Deutekom, Burrows, Prey and Talvela.

Piano Music. Gilels's playing is smooth and nerveless in the works on Deutsche Grammophon 2530-061.

Quartets. The Quartetto Italiano offers beautiful performances of K.499 and 575 on Philips 6500-241, and K.589 and 590 on 6500-225.

Quintet K. 581 for Clarinet and Strings. The performance by Brymer and the Allegri Quartet, on Philips 6500-073, is very good; but de Peyer's more sensitive inflection of his more delicate tone makes his performance with the Melos Ensemble on Angel S-36241 the one to acquire.

Requiem. Böhm's ponderously slow pacing makes the performance on Deutsche Grammophon 2530-143 — with the Vienna Philharmonic and State Opera Chorus and soloists headed by Mathis — one to avoid.

Serenade K.361 for Winds. The accomplished wind-players of the Berlin Philharmonic under Böhm perform it admirably on Deutsche Grammophon 2530-136. And another good performance by the Netherlands Wind Ensemble under de Waart is on Philips 839-734. But both are surpassed, in tonal beauty and enlivening phrasing and style, by the earlier performance of the London Wind Quintet and Ensemble with Klemperer on Angel S-36247, which is available again after having been withdrawn for a time.

Sonatas for Piano. K.330, which Gould played superbly on a mono record ten years ago, is one of the four — with K.310, 332 and 333 — that he rips off on Columbia M-31073 at speeds which make the performances absurd and the music meaningless. And the eccentricities of tempo, touch and phrasing make his performances of K.331, 545 and 533/494, on Columbia M-32348, also ones to avoid.

Symphonies. Davis's latest performance of K.543 with the London Symphony on Philips 6500-559 is even more effective and beautiful-sounding than the one on RCA VICS-1378. The performance of the great G-minor on the same record begins with a strangely unimpassioned statement of the impassioned first movement; but the succeeding movements are allowed their eloquent expressiveness.

MUSORGSKY

Pictures at an Exhibition. Yeresko, on Melodiya/Angel 40162, offers the best performance of the original piano version, except that the concluding *Great Gate of Kiev* calls for climactic sonorities of more amplitude and weight.

Songs. The inflections of Luxon's singing and Willison's playing, in the superb performances on Argo ZRG-708, reveal how sensitized the writing for voice and piano is to the words of *Songs and Dances of Death,* the *Sunless* cycle, *The Flea* and *The Classic.* This is the first performance I recall of *The Flea* without Rimsky-Korsakov's revisions; and it provides another demonstration of how much better a composer Musorgsky was of his music than the man who insisted on rewriting it for him.

PALESTRINA

Masses. The *Missa Assumpta est Maria* and *Missa brevis* for 4 voices are on Argo ZRG-690, excellently sung by the Choir of St. John's College, Cambridge, under Guest's direction.

Motets. Vanguard has reissued *The Song of Songs* on Bach Guild HM-9SD.

PURCELL

Ceremonial Music. Argo ZRG-724 has some of the impressive music for festive occasions and funerals — the *Te Deum, Jubilate Deo, Funeral Sentences,* anthem *Remember Not Lord Our Offenses,* and three pieces for the burial of Queen Mary. They are performed beautifully by the Choir of St. John's College, Cambridge, the English Chamber Orchestra and others under Guest's direction.

Operas. Colin Davis, on Philips 6500-131, conducts a fine performance of *Dido and Aeneas,* with Veasey, Donath, Shirley-Quirk, the John Alldis Choir and the Academy of St. Martin-in-the-Fields.

In Britten's performance of his concert version of most of *The Fairy Queen,* on London OSA-1290, he conducts the music very effectively, but Vyvyan and Pears can no longer sing it as agreeably to the ear as they did in the early performance reissued on Oiseau-Lyre S-121/3E, which I therefore consider preferable.

Sacred Music. Telefunken SAWT-9558-B has some of the unfamiliar sacred vocal writing, sung well by the Choir of King's College, Cambridge, and soloists with the Leonhardt Consort under Willcocks's direction.

ROSSINI

(The) Barber of Seville. The performance on Deutsche Grammophon 2709-041 is made outstanding by the singing of Berganza and Alva, with its enchantingly swift and light and pointed-up delivery of florid passages (which Alva did not achieve in the earlier performance with De los Angeles); and by the similar pointed-up lightness, and withal the cohesive tension, of the orchestral context that Abbado provides with the London Symphony.

(La) Cenerentola. The similarly outstanding performance of this work with Berganza, Alva and Abbado, on Deutsche Gram-

388

mophon 2709-039, surpasses the 1953 performance conducted by Gui that I expected never to hear equalled.

Arias. London OS-26305 has Horne's superb performances of scenes with impressive writing from the unfamiliar *L'Assiedo di Corinto* and *La Donna del Lago*.

Sonatas for Strings. Philips 6500-243 has I Musici's excellent performances of Nos. 1 to 4.

SCHUBERT

Moments Musicaux. Curzon's beautiful performances are on London CS-6727 (with Beethoven's *Eroica* Variations).

Quartets. The Guarneri Quartet's beautiful performance of Op. 29, on RCA LSC-3285, is flawed by two details: in the first movement, after the *fortissimo* chord that is the climax of the development the Guarneri continues *fortissimo* instead of the *pianissimo* marked in the score; and in the Minuet, the return of the arresting three-note cello figure that began the movement, though marked *decrescendo*, is italicized tastelessly with swells.

Sonatas for Piano. Badura-Skoda, on RCA VICS-6128, reveals his lack of the musical powers required for effective realizations of the three great posthumous sonatas.

And Brendel's nerveless playing produces inadequate performances of the posthumous Sonata in B-flat on Philips 6500-285 and the one in A on 6500-284. But on 6500-415 he achieves effective realizations of the powerful first movement and wonderful finale of the one in C minor, with an Adagio one can accept even though it is slower than I think it should be. The record offers also good performances of Nos. 2, 3 and 4 of the Impromptus Op. 90, but an ineffectively metronomic one of the extraordinary No. 1.

London CS-6820 has Ashkenazy's beautiful performance of Op. 78; but I prefer the more animated tempos of Kuerti's performance on Monitor S-2109.

And London CS-6716 has Radu Lupu's beautiful performance of Op. 143, with the wonderful middle movement — which Ashkenazy plays very slowly — played *andante* and *alla breve* as Schubert directs.

Sonatas for Violin and Piano. Philips 6500-341 has the beautiful

389

performances of the Sonata Op. 162 and Sonatinas Op. 137 newly recorded by Grumiaux with Veyron-Lacroix.

Songs. Deutsche Grammophon 2720-059 has Fischer-Dieskau's newly recorded performances of *Die schöne Müllerin, Die Winterreise* and the songs published posthumously as *Schwanengesang*. His previous performance of *Die Winterreise*, on D. G. 2707-028, has Demus's incisive and enlivening playing of the piano part, which makes it superior and preferable to the new one with Moore's bland and unrhythmical playing. And though the voice is still remarkable and moving in the new performances of *Müllerin* and *Schwanengesang*, it no longer has the freshness and beauty it had in the early performances on Angel records; and his use of it now includes occasional excessive emphasis which the early performances were free of.

The Schubert settings of poems by Goethe that Fischer-Dieskau sings impressively on D. G. 2530-229 are early songs; but they include not only the uninteresting narrative song *Der Sänger* but the great *Erlkönig*, not only several moderately good songs but the fine second setting of *An den Mond*, lovely *Nähe des Geliebten* and great *Meeres Stille*.

The Schubert settings of texts of Friedrich Schiller that Fischer-Dieskau sings on D. G. 2530-306 I find mostly uninteresting — the exceptions being *Das Mädchen aus der Ferne, Das Geheimnis* and — most impressive in its matured writing — *Der Pilgrim*.

Most of the duets that Janet Baker and Fischer-Dieskau sing effectively on Deutsche Grammophon 2530-328 are settings of dramatic texts by Klopstock, Schiller and other poets, of which I find only the scene from Goethe's *Faust* musically impressive. And the all too brief Nocturne *Licht und Liebe* offers characteristically beautiful melodic writing.

For Krenn's performances see under MISCELLANEOUS COLLECTIONS.

SCHUMANN

Concerto for Piano. Bishop's performance with the BBC Symphony under Colin Davis, on Philips 6500-166 (with the Grieg Concerto), is good; but the definitive performance remains Lipatti's.

Davidsbündlertänze. Columbia M-32299 has the remarkably perceptive and beautiful-sounding performance of Perahia, with fine performances of the *Fantasiestücke* Op. 12.

Kreisleriana. Kuerti's excellent performance is on London STS-15255 (with the uninteresting Sonata Op. 14).

Songs. For Krenn's performances see under MISCELLANEOUS COLLECTIONS.

STRAVINSKY

Danses Concertantes. Columbia M-30516 has Stravinsky's performance with the Columbia Chamber Orchestra (with the Concerto in D for strings, the less consequential *Four Norwegian Moods* and the unattractive *Ode,* performed with other orchestras).

Petrushka. Boulez's performance, on Columbia M-31076, offers the rich sound of the New York Philharmonic; but the dry sound of the excellent recording orchestra in Stravinsky's own performance contributes to the power of that performance; and Boulez's hurrying of the fourth tableau deprives it of the power it has in Stravinsky's slower tempo.

(Le) Sacre du printemps. Michael Tilson Thomas's performance with the Boston Symphony, on Deutsche Grammophon 2530-252, is more animated than those of Boulez and Stravinsky, but highly effective in its own way, and more so than Colin Davis's with the London Symphony on Philips 6580-013.

TCHAIKOVSKY

Concertos for Piano. The long-needed performance of No. 2 is now provided by Zhukov and the Moscow Radio Symphony under Rozhdestvensky, on Melodiya/Angel SR-40097.

Operas. Joan's familiar aria proves to be the best of the excerpts from *The Maid of Orleans* performed on Melodiya/Angel 40156 by Russian soloists and the Moscow Radio Orchestra and Chorus. Arkhipova sings it with a voice that retains the impressiveness of its physical and expressive power even with the clouding vibrato that mars its beauty.

Songs. Though unfamiliar to the musical public that knows the instrumental music so well, they exhibit the musical invention and expressive power one hears in the ballet scores, orchestral suites and symphonies. And the ones on Argo ZRG-707 are excellently performed by Tear and Ledger.

Symphonies. Deutsche Grammophon 2530-078 has Thomas's superb performance of No. 1 with the Boston Symphony.

Barenboim's performance of No. 4 with the New York Philharmonic, on Columbia M-30572, is one to avoid. Another is Abbado's of No. 5 with the London Symphony, on Deutsche Grammophon 2530-198. And yet another is Maazel's of the *Manfred* Symphony with the Vienna Philharmonic, on London CS-6786.

Trio. The Beaux Arts Trio's performance on Philips 6500-132 is acceptable; but Rubinstein's playing makes the old one on RCA LM-1120 (mono) still the one to acquire.

VERDI

Aida. Price, Domingo and Milnes contribute beautiful singing to the performance conducted by Leinsdorf on RCA LSC-6198; but for a great performance of the work one must acquire Toscanini's.

Attila. In the performance on Philips 6700-056 Gardelli's conducting doesn't give the music the intensity and impact it can have; and the voices of Raimondi and Deutekom are inadequate for their roles; but the singing of Bergonzi and Milnes is excellent.

(Un) Ballo in Maschera. The deteriorated voice of Tebaldi and unattractively dry voice of Pavarotti make the performance on London OSA-1398 one to avoid.

Don Carlo. To the superb performance on London 1432 there has been added another superb one on Angel S-3774, conducted by Giulini, with Caballé, Domingo, Milnes, Raimondi, Verrett, Foiani and the Covent Garden Orchestra.

(I) Lombardi. Nothing in this unfamiliar work is as impressive as the trio that is all we have known until now. In the perform-

ance conducted by Gardelli on Philips 6703-032, Deutekom's voice is at times lovely but at other times unattractive; and Domingo and Raimondi are excellent.

Macbeth. The performance on London OSA-13102 — with dreadful singing by Souliotis, and explosively vehement singing much of the time by Fischer-Dieskau — is one to avoid.

Rigoletto. I continue to dislike the sound of Sutherland's mournful crooning in her lower range, in the performance on London OSA-13105; and I don't agree with Milnes's idea that effective singing of the title role requires a change of vocal color with every word. Pavarotti uses his ringing tenor well; and Bonynge conducts the work admirably.

VIVALDI

The Four Seasons. The best new performance is I Musici's on Philips 6500-017; very good too is Zukerman's with the English Chamber Orchestra on Columbia M-31798; but the *continuo* interpolations in Marriner's with the Academy of St. Martin-in-the-Fields, on Argo ZRG-654, I find excessive.

WAGNER

(Die) Meistersinger. The poor singing of Adam (Sachs), Kollo (Walther) and Donath (Eva) make the performance conducted by von Karajan, on Angel S-3776, one to avoid.

Tristan und Isolde. Seraphim 60145 (mono) has the Prelude, the second-act duet from *"O sink hernieder"* to the entrance of King Marke, part of the third-act duet of Tristan and Kurvenal, and Isolde's *Liebestod* from the unequalled performance with Flagstad and Suthaus conducted by Furtwängler.

The performance on Angel S-3777 is conducted well by von Karajan, and has good singers and the superb Berlin Philharmonic; but the only reason for acquiring it in addition to — not instead of — the Furtwängler performance is the singing of Vickers; and much of the time — notably in the second-act duet — he can barely be heard because of the recording that causes the sound, when it is soft, to recede into the distance.

Collections of Excerpts. Boulez's unusual retardations and accelerations in the performance of the Prelude to *Tristan* with the New York Philharmonic, on Columbia M-32296, I find unconvincing; but his slowed-down Prelude to *Die Meistersinger* is effective; and his *Faust Overture* is excellent. The record also has the Overture to *Tannhäuser*.

Wesendonck Songs. Colin Davis provides extraordinarily sensitive and beautiful orchestral contexts with the London Symphony, on Philips 6500-294, for singing by Nilsson that cannot transcend the unattractive timbre of her voice. The record also has excerpts from *Die Feen, Rienzi* and *Der fliegende Holländer.*

WEBER

Oberon. In addition to its well-known overture and aria *Ozean du Ungeheuer* the work has a number of fine pieces of music; but these occur at intervals in an enormous amount of spoken dialogue (German) of a preposterous play. In addition to Nilsson, whose voice I find unattractive in timbre, the performance on Deutsche Grammophon 2709-035 has Hamari, Domingo, Prey and the Bavarian Radio Symphony and Chorus under Kubelik.

Sonatas for Piano. Deutsche Grammophon 2530-026 provides an opportunity to hear the writing — in the lyrical Sonata No. 2 and parts of the dramatic No. 3 — that has a grace and elegance admirably realized in the performances by Ciani.

Symphony No. 1. Philips 6500-154, giving me my first hearing of this work that Weber wrote at the age of twenty-one, has enabled me to discover with pleasure its freshness of musical language and expressive content. Boettcher conducts the New Philharmonia in excellent performances of this symphony and Cherubini's in D.

WEELKES

A number of his madrigals, including the outstanding *Cease Sorrows Now* and *O Care Thou Wilt Despatch Me,* are sung by the excellent Wilbye Consort under Pears's direction, on London STS-15165.

WILBYE

A number of his madrigals are sung well — except for occasional exaggerated liveliness — by the Wilbye Consort under Pears's direction, on London STS-15162.

WOLF

The Mörike songs that Ameling sings on Philips 6500-128 include only a few of the best; and her lusterless voice makes her performances unattractive.

MISCELLANEOUS COLLECTIONS

(Julian) Bream Consort. RCA LSC-3195 now has the fine pieces by Dowland, Byrd, Morley and other Elizabethan composers originally on LDS-2656.

Bumbry. Her powerful voice is steady and used with dramatic eloquence which doesn't distort musical shape in arias from *Medea, Norma, Macbeth, La Forza del Destino* and *Don Carlo.*

Caballé. Deutsche Grammophon 2530-073 has her beautiful performances of *O beau pays* from *Les Huguenots,* the *King of Thule* and *Jewel Song* from *Faust,* Micaela's aria from *Carmen,* and less consequential French operatic arias.

RCA LSC-3209 has her beautifully phrased singing in the *Willow Song* and *Ave Maria* from Verdi's *Otello,* the second-act aria from *Un Ballo in Maschera,* and an aria from *Anna Bolena,* among other things.

Cliburn. RCA LSC-3185 has his superb performances of Chopin's Nocturne Op. 62 No. 2, Scherzo Op. 31 and Etude Op. 10 No. 12, and Debussy's *Reflets dans l'eau,* among other things.

Davis. Philips 6580-048 has his performances with the BBC Symphony of German overtures: one of Beethoven's *Coriolan* that is much too slow to achieve the piece's dramatic force; one of the Prelude to *Die Meistersinger* that Davis makes effective, in its slower than usual tempo, with his enlivening phrasing; and several good ones of the Overtures to *The Magic Flute, Der Freischütz,* Nicolai's *The Merry Wives of Windsor,* and Mendelssohn's *Hebrides.*

De los Angeles. What is left of her once lovely voice is an agree-able-sounding medium for charming performances of Spanish folksongs and Sephardic songs of Spanish Jews in exile, on Angel S-36716.

Domingo and Milnes. RCA LSC-3182 has their beautiful-sounding and well-phrased performances of duets from *I Vespri Siciliani, La Forza del Destino, Don Carlo, Otello* and *The Pearl Fishers.*

Freni. Vanguard VCS-10068 has her lovely performances of arias from Bellini's *La Sonnambula* and *I Capuleti ed i Montecchi,* Micaela's aria from *Carmen,* Nanetta's exquisite aria from the last scene of *Falstaff,* and less consequential pieces.

Ghiaurov. The bass voice that was so rich and smooth is now unpleasantly rough and harsh in the songs of Tchaikovsky, Glinka and Dargomizhsky on London OS-26249.

Katin. The recital reissued on London STS-15124 includes fine performances of Bach's *Chromatic Fantasy and Fugue,* Scar-latti's Sonatas L. 23 and 413, and Chopin's Berceuse (but an excessively mannered Waltz Op. 64 No. 2), among other things. To regain the original sound play the record not stereo but A+B, with treble reduced and bass stepped up.

Krenn. Some of the unfamiliar songs of Schubert and Schumann on OS-26216 are not as interesting as the familiar *Die Liebe hat gelogen* of Schubert and *Die Lotosblume* of Schumann; but all are sung beautifully.

Masters of Early English Keyboard Music. A large number of the pieces on Oiseau-Lyre OLS-114/8 are not by masters and not interesting; and there are uninteresting pieces as well as fine ones among those of Byrd, Tomkins, Bull, Gibbons and Farn-aby; but the ones by Bull on the last two sides are magnificent.

Pears. RCA LSC-3131 has a number of lovely and affecting songs of Dowland — including *I Saw My Lady Weep, Weep You No More, Shall I Sue, Sweet, Stay Awhile, Can She Excuse* — and charming songs by Morley, Rosseter and Ford, admirably sung to the lute accompaniments of Bream.

Price. Her upper range is unattractive in the arias from *Alceste, Don Giovanni, I Lombardi* and *Simon Boccanegra,* on RCA LSC-3163; but Micaela's aria from *Carmen, Du bist der Lenz* from *Die Walküre* and an aria from Offenbach's *La Perichole* are sung beautifully.

RCA LSC-3218 has superb performances of *Tu che le vanità* from *Don Carlo, Abscheulicher! wo eilst du hin?* from *Fidelio,* the finale of Act 1 of *La Traviata* (except for the concluding florid passages), and (in Russian) the *Letter Scene* from *Eugene Onegin* (in which her voice is at times disturbingly tremulous).

Simionato. Reissued on Richmond SR-33190 (pseudo-stereo) are the superb performances of arias from *The Barber of Seville, La Cenerentola, Don Carlo* and *I Capuleti ed i Montecchi,* with additional performances of arias from *Mignon, Carmen, Werther* and *Samson et Dalila.* (Reduce treble).

The Triumphs of Oriana. A dozen pieces by Morley, Wilbye, Weelkes and others from this collection are performed, on Argo ZRG-643, by the Purcell Chorus and Elizabethan Consort of Viols under Burgess.

Wunderlich. His beautiful voice is heard, on Seraphim S-60148, in excerpts, all in German, from *The Seraglio, Così Fan Tutte, Rigoletto, The Queen of Spades* and *The Bartered Bride,* among other things.

397

30

ADDITIONAL
RECORDED PERFORMANCES

1974 to April 1978

PERFORMANCES OF THE PAST

Argenta. Reissued on London STS-15266 is the outstanding performance of Tchaikovsky's Fourth with L'Orchestre de la Suisse
Romande; on STS-15020 the performance with the same orchestra of Debussy's *Images,* which includes the best of available
performances of the marvelous *Rondes de printemps.* Add bass
for adequate solidity; and reduce treble.

Backhaus. The performances of Chopin's Etudes Opp. 10 and 25
on the Bruno Walter Society's IGI-286* confirm my recollection
of a pianist with prodigious technical powers that produced the
figurations of the ones in fast tempo in completely straightforward fashion with astounding speed, ease and perfection, but
an uninteresting musician who inflicted appalling distortion of
phrase on the slow expressive ones.

Beecham. The performances of Mozart recorded with the London
Philharmonic from 1934 to 1940—which I listened to not on
Turnabout records but on imported World Records SHB.20
—include some that testify to Beecham's great gifts, but others
that offer instances of his quirkiness and perversity in tempo
and phrasing: the shocking arch inflection of bar 34 of the
Andante of the Symphony K.504, the excessively slow first

---

*The Bruno Walter Society's records are obtainable from DISCOCORP,
INC., P. O. Box 771, Berkeley, Calif. 94701.

movement of the Symphony K.201 and *Andante di molto* second movement of K.338 (described incorrectly as *Adagio di molto* on the record label), the jaunty opening of the great G-minor K.550. The sound required additional treble and bass, and a 5-kc. cut-off.

The performances with the Royal Philharmonic reissued on Odyssey records exhibit the beginnings of the stodgy and fussy playing of Beecham's last years.

Budapest Quartet. Additional reissues on Odyssey records include Beethoven's so-called middle quartets—the three of Op. 59 *(Rasumovsky)*, with Op. 74 *(Harp)* and Op. 95—on Y3-33316; the six of Haydn's Op. 76 on Y3-33324; and the three major quartets of Schubert on Y3-33320. The sound of the performances from the new records is finer in quality and more clearly and cleanly defined than the original sound; and Roisman's violin tone now has a body and glow it didn't have; but adequate cello sound requires additional bass; and I reduced treble slightly.

Cantelli. The Bruno Walter Society has issued on IGI-340 the performance of Verdi's *Requiem* in which Cantelli, in 1954, conducted the Boston Symphony, the New England Conservatory Chorus, and Herva Nelli, Claramae Turner, Eugene Conley and Nicola Moscona; and on IGI-326 the performance of Mozart's *Così Fan Tutte* that he conducted early in 1956 at the Piccolo Scala, with Schwarzkopf, Merriman, Sciutti, Alva, Panerai and Calabrese. They stand apart from all others as unique manifestations of individual genius, which no music-lover should miss, even though the sound of the *Requiem* is somewhat reduced in fullness and clarity (the brilliant sound of Verdi's *Te Deum,* also on IGI-340, requires reduction of treble), and the voices in *Così* are reproduced excellently but the orchestra's lower strings are only faintly audible.

Caruso. The performances following those of 1904-1906 that RCA reissued on ARM4-0302 enable one to hear the undiminished beauty of the voice (in contradiction of David Hamilton's statement in *The Times*) as it changed from the lyric tenor of the early years to the darker-timbred and more robust dramatic tenor of the later years; the undiminished ease with which it produced its outpouring of vocal splendor (again in contradiction of the *Times* reviewer); the somewhat lessened distortion inflicted on the musical phrase by this outpouring.

The result of the latest computerized reprocessing on CRM1-1749 is something to avoid.

Casals. His great pre-war performances of Beethoven's five cello sonatas are on imported Dacapo C-147-01538/9, and are available also with the famous Casals-Thibaud-Cortot performances of Haydn, Beethoven and Schubert trios on Spanish Odeon J-153-50136/40.

Della Casa. Reissued on London SR-33200 are her beautiful performances (in German) of Cleopatra's alluring arias from Handel's *Giulio Cesare,* recorded in the '50s (presumably mono), and her beautiful performances from later stereo recordings of Mozart's *Figaro, Don Giovanni* and *Così Fan Tutte.* Reduce treble.

De Sabata. London RS-62022 has his excellent performance with the London Philharmonic of Berlioz's *Roman Carnival* Overture, but a performance of Beethoven's *Eroica* whose slow tempos make the first movement and the beginning of the finale ineffective.

Gieseking. His extraordinary performance of Mozart's Concerto K.467 with the New York Philharmonic under Cantelli, described on p. 236, is now available in excellent sound on the Bruno Walter Society's IGI-349, whose reverse side offers a more characteristic—i.e. sensitively delicate—performance of the Concerto K.595 that is poorly reproduced.

The Bruno Walter Society's RR-411 has the performances of Mozart's Concerto K.271 and Beethoven's Concerto No. 1 that Gieseking recorded in the '30s with the Berlin State Opera Orchestra under Rosbaud. These too exhibit a vital energy that was unusual in his playing.

Kleiber, Erich. The performance of Beethoven's *Eroica* with the Vienna Philharmonic on London R-23202 (mono) is an excellent one except for the repeated exposition of the first movement, which had to be speeded up to fit on one 78-rpm record side.

The performances of Mozart's G-minor and Beethoven's Fifth with the London Philharmonic on London R-23232 are ineffective.

Lehman, Lotte. Performances of the '30s and '40s on the Bruno Walter Society's BWS-729 (mono) include one of the Finale of Wagner's *Tristan und Isolde* that lacks the spacious serenity it should have (and that follows an unbelievably bad performance of the Prelude by Monteux). *"Vissi d'arte"* from *Tosca* is sung more effectively; and in the German *Lieder* Lehmann employs her distinctively lovely voice in phrases shaped by her extraordinary powers of expressive projection.

London. His fine bass-baritone voice is heard, on Odyssey Y-32669 (mono), in excerpts from *Die Meistersinger, Rigoletto, Otello, Falstaff* and the Rimsky-Korsakov falsification of *Boris Godunov.*

Melchior. His best singing is heard in the European performances of the '20s on Seraphim 6086 (mono). RCA CRM3-0308 (mono) offers the performances he began to record here in 1937, when his voice had lost the glow of its prime but was still impressive—the Wagner excerpts with Flagstad, the songs of Strauss and Wolf that he phrases with admirable sensitiveness. The voice had lost a great deal more by 1941, when he sang with Traubel in Toscanini's performances of Wagner with the NBC Symphony; and his *forte* high notes are afflicted by high-frequency distortion from the record.

Muzio. Odyssey Y-32676 (mono) has lovely-sounding and simply phrased performances of arias of Handel, Gluck, Bellini and Verdi, among others, that she recorded between 1920 and 1923.

Rachmaninov. Of the five RCA albums containing all his recorded performances I recommend only ARM3-0295, which has the performances of Beethoven and Schubert sonatas with Kreisler.

Schnabel. In addition to the pre-war performances of Mozart's Concertos K.459 and 467 on imported World Record Club SH-142, there are now the post-war performances of K.466 and 491 on Turnabout THS-65 040 (mono), offering impressive examples of Schnabel's dealing with Mozart. The performances of Beethoven's Sonatas Opp. 109, 110 and 111 may be better reproduced by imported La Voix de son Maître VSM C 061-00.856M than by Seraphim 6066; the ones of Schubert's posthumous Sonatas in A and B-flat and his Op. 53 are on imported Electrola Dacapo C-147-01557/8; the ones of Schubert's Impromptus on 01339.

Comparing the performances of Beethoven's Sonatas Op. 109 and 111 that Schnabel recorded for Victor in 1942, and that have only now been issued by RCA on AVM1-1410 (mono), with the ones he recorded in the '30s on Seraphim 6066, one discovers how much the performances, by 1942, had lost of their earlier grace, their earlier continuity and perfection of proportion in the shaping of phrase, the relating of one phrase to the next, the building of the whole structure of a movement — to say nothing of the lessened accuracy of execution. But listened to by themselves they are, even with those losses, effective statements of the works.

The performances of Beethoven's five cello sonatas with Fournier are now on Seraphim 60117.

And the Bruno Walter Society's BWS-717 now has the performances of Mozart's Concerto K.482 with the New York Philharmonic under Walter and K.488 with the New York Philharmonic under Rodzinski that are mentioned on p. 246 and p. 368. In addition its SID-721 has a performance of Beethoven's Concerto No. 3 with an orchestra under Szell — the piano's sound, with treble reduced, good, but the orchestra's unpleasantly sharp — with a performance of Mozart's Sonata K.333.

Szigeti. The Bruno Walter Society's WSA-701 has a performance of Mozart's Concerto K.219 that is worth acquiring even though the record is noisy, the orchestra is poorly reproduced, and the reverse side has Berg's Violin Concerto.

Toscanini. Of the performances that he recorded with the Philadelphia Orchestra in the season of 1941-42 only the one of Schubert's Ninth was released in 1963, and the rest — of Mendelssohn's *Midsummer Night's Dream* music, Berlioz's *Queen Mab*, Tchaikovsky's *Pathétique* Symphony, Debussy's *La Mer* and *Ibéria* — have only now been issued, with the Schubert, on RCA CRM5-1900 (mono). In the notes for the Schubert in 1963 RCA ascribed the withholding of the recordings to the damage inflicted on them by faulty wartime processing — "mechanical [i.e. noisy] imperfections which neither the Maestro nor the company could accept," and which the restorative work of engineers using "new electronic transfer techniques" had now eliminated; and the annotator of the present volume writes that "the upper string partials" of the sound itself were obliterated. But in fact the test pressing of *La Mer* that I heard in 1942 produced beautiful sound and no disturbing noises that made the recording unacceptable to Toscanini (his delight with the first movement ended at the beginning of the second when he didn't hear a woodwind he expected to hear). It is the records issued now that produce occasional clicks and other noises which represent the deterioration of the metal masters; and the sound that the engineers have obtained from the masters now has less amplitude, depth and solidity than the sound from the test pressings of 1942. Nevertheless the records produce what one hears is marvelous playing of the orchestra under Toscanini, and his marvelous shaping of the music in his expansive style of that period. They offer, in fact, his last recorded performances in that earlier style, which are, as such, more effective, most of them, than the ones of the same pieces that he recorded later with the NBC Symphony. One can restore some of the solidity by turning up the bass; and the occasional noises can be endured as those of today's LP records are.

Reviewers could appear perceptive by taking the plausible line that Gershwin's *An American in Paris* — and in particular its blues — was music this Italian couldn't conduct effectively. But actually one is amazed to hear in the performance reissued on Victrola AVM1-1737 what — with his feeling for shape of phrase, his grace and rubato, in the playing of melody — Toscanini made of the piece and its blues.

RCA in England no longer produces the *Toscanini Edition* I describe on p. 369; but one can, and should, acquire the Victrola records of that edition produced by RCA in Germany. They are superior to the few Japanese pressings I have heard.

Tourel. Odyssey Y2-32880 (mono) has her lovely-sounding and beautifully phrased performances of Rossini arias (1946), arias from *Carmen* (1952), Musorgsky's *Songs and Dances of Death*

(1950) (regrettably the Rimsky-Korsakov falsification, with Bernstein's obtrusive piano accompaniments), and songs of Debussy, Ravel, Bizet, Satie and others.

Walter. The Bruno Walter Society's BWS-999 (mono) has two of Walter's best performances — the ones of Haydn's fine Symphony No. 86 with the London Symphony and incandescent Symphony No. 92 (*Oxford*) with the Paris Conservatory Concerts Orchestra that he recorded in 1938. Their one flaw is Walter's melting over the second subject of the opening movement of No. 86. The sound needs addition of treble.

Weingartner. EMI has issued in England RLS-717, *The Art of Felix Weingartner,* which makes it possible to hear, among other works, Beethoven's *Eroica* and Brahms's Second as they were performed by one of the legendary greats of this century, and to perceive now imperfections in performances that seemed perfect in the '30s.

Famous Wagner Interpreters, on Telefunken 6.48016, offers excerpts from the 1936 Bayreuth Festival performances of *Lohengrin* and *Die Walküre,* with the magnificent singing of the tenor Franz Völker and beautiful singing of the soprano Maria Müller, and *Siegfried,* with the impressive singing of the tenor Max Lorenz; and in addition a few performances recorded in 1933 in Berlin: Lorenz and the baritone Rudolf Bockelmann singing excerpts from *Tannhäuser;* Bockelmann singing "*Was duftet doch der Flieder*", and the superb tenor Roswaenge "*Am stillen Herd*" and the Prize Song from *Die Meistersinger.*

100 Years of Bayreuth, on Deutsche Grammophon 2721.115, offers only one performance — Nilsson's of the Finale of *Tristan und Isolde* — that was actually recorded in the Festival Theater. The rest were recorded elsewhere by singers who at some time sang in Bayreuth, beginning with Emmy Destinn's 1907 performance of Senta's Ballad from *Der fliegende Holländer.* Some great singers are heard in uninteresting music; but there are also Völker singing Lohengrin's Farewell to the Swan (1927); Margarete Klose Brangäne's Warning from *Tristan* (1954); Manowarda "*Was duftet doch der Flieder*" (1921), Hotter "*Wahn! Wahn!*" (1942), and Windgassen the Prize Song (1955) from *Die Meistersinger.*

PERFORMANCES OF TODAY

ALBENIZ

Of the two new performances of *Ibéria,* the one on Connoisseur
Society CS-2120 has Michel Block playing the piano beautifully
and the music sensitively, but exaggerating the rubato style of
the pieces (as de Larrocha does on London CSA-2235). I therefore prefer Ciccolini's performance on Seraphim SIB-6091.

BACH, JOHANN SEBASTIAN

Brandenburg Concertos. Leppard performs them well with the
English Chamber Orchestra on Philips 6747.166; but I prefer
Britten's more enlivening performances.
English Suites for Clavier. Gould plays them on the piano, on
Columbia M2-34578, in his arresting fashion, but not without
occasional disturbing eccentricities of touch or phrasing. The
music I find uninteresting.
Sonatas and Partitas for Violin (unaccompanied). Milstein's performances on Deutsche Grammophon 2709.047 are admirable;
but Szigeti's on Bach Guild 627 (mono) are made more impressive by his extra-dimensional musical insight and style.

BEETHOVEN

Bagatelles for Piano. Schabel's performances on Seraphim 6067
(mono) make Stephen Bishop's on Philips 6500.930 unsatisfying.
And Gould's on Columbia M-33165, which should be an exciting experience, are made unprofitable and irritating for the
most part by his perversities of tempo and touch.
Concertos for Piano. The musical sensitiveness and grace, the
beautiful playing of the piano, that one hears in the performances Rubinstein recorded in the '60s with the Boston Symphony under Leinsdorf are not to be heard in the ones on RCA
ARL5-1415 that he recorded recently with the London Philharmonic under Barenboim.

ADDITIONAL PERFORMANCES

The performance of No. 4 on Philips 6500.975 is, like the one of No. 5 a few years ago, made notable by the extraordinary integration of Bishop's sensitive playing with the beautiful playing of the BBC Symphony under Colin Davis.

Pollini plays impressively in the performance of No. 4 with the Vienna Philharmonic under Böhm, on Deutsche Grammophon 2530.791.

Concerto for Violin. Stern phrases the solo part admirably in the performance with the New York Philharmonic under Barenboim on Columbia M-33587. But for such solo playing in a superb orchestral context I suggest instead Grumiaux's performance with the marvelous Amsterdam Concertgebouw Orchestra under Colin Davis on Philips 6500.775.

Missa Solemnis. In the movements with changes of tempo Böhm — in the performance with chorus and orchestra of the Vienna State Opera and excellent soloists on Deutsche Grammophon 2707.080 — doesn't have Toscanini's feeling for the matching of tempos that will achieve continuity and coherence in the progression. Nor does he impart to the hushed orchestral prelude of the *Benedictus* the raptly mystical character that Toscanini gives it. Toscanini's, therefore, is still the performance to acquire.

Quartets. The Quartetto Italiano's performances of Op. 18 Nos. 2 and 4 on Philips 6500.646 are excellent, as are its performances of the three of Op. 59 on 6747.139, except for the too slow tempo of the opening movement of No. 1 and the excessive retardations near the end of its last movement.

London STS-15220 has the Weller Quartet's fine performances of Op. 74 *(Harp)* and Op. 95.

The La Salle Quartet's performance of Op. 132 on Deutsche Grammophon 2530.728 is tonally and musically undistinguished.

Sonatas for Piano. London CS-7028 has Ashkenazy's fine performance of the engaging Op. 2 No. 2, with the mechanical and uninteresting Op. 2 No. 3. CS-6821 has an excellent performance of Op. 10 No. 3, with a performance of Op. 57 *(Appassionata)* which may be the result of too much listening to Furtwängler: Ashkenazy plays the hushed opening statements of the first movement not in the prescribed *Allegro assai* tempo but as a slow introduction to the outburst in fast tempo a few moments later, and continues to shift back and forth between slow and fast thereafter, instead of maintaining, with subtle modifications, a basic tempo established at the beginning.

CS-6921 has Ashkenazy's superb performance of Op. 53 (*Waldstein*), whose Adagio for once is slow enough for it to achieve its profound expressiveness; but with a performance of Op. 81a (*Les Adieux*) in which its less profoundly expressive introduction to the first movement and *andante* second movement are played as though they were the Adagio of Op. 53. And one side of CS-7029 has Op. 101, of which the meditative opening movement is played very beautifully, but the march movement with what seems to me exaggerated accentuation; the other side a tremendous performance of Op. 109. (I attribute the occasionally percussive tone to the piano or the microphone placement.)

Stephen Bishop's performances of Opp. 110 and 111, on Phillips 6500.764, are those of an excellent pianist and musician; Ashkenazy's, on London CS-6845, those of an even better one, who plays with more perception of significant detail and clearer articulation (most strikingly in the fugal sections of the last movement of Op. 110) and achieves more cohesive and concise shape. I must add, however, that — possibly as another result of too much listening to Furtwängler — Ashkenazy's expansive slowing down of the *maestoso* introduction of Op. 111 is excessive and damaging to continuity of flow.

Pollini's performances of Opp. 109 and 110, on Deutsche Grammophon 2530.645, also are operations on the highest level of instrumental mastery and musical insight — a higher level than that of Lupu's sensitive performances of Op. 53 and Op. 27 No. 2 on London CS-6806, and of Emanuel Ax's well-conceived and executed performance of Op. 53 on RCA ARL1-2083, with the Variations Op. 35.

Lazar Berman's performances of Op. 57 and Op. 31 No. 3, on Columbia M-34218, are musically undistinguished and crude.

Sonatas for Violin and Piano. Fine performances of Op. 47 (*Kreutzer*) and Op. 12 No. 2 by Ashkenazy and Perlman are on London CS-6845.

And an excellent performance of Op. 47 by Solti (when he was still a pianist) and Kulenkampf is on London R-23214 (mono), with Mozart's Sonata K.454.

Symphonies. Of the recently recorded versions of the nine, Solti's, Kubelik's and Kempe's include performances of some of the works that are made ineffective by what seem to me errors in tempo and other defects; and only Haitink's, on Philips 6747.307, are well-conceived performances of all nine, which are well executed by the London Philharmonic, but would have been even better with the Amsterdam Concertgebouw. I suspect, moreover, that the Concertgebouw would have been recorded with more care, which would have produced clearer textures and more audible violins in big tuttis, and enabled one to hear the notes of the fast violin passages in bars 33 and 37 of the first movement of No. 2, the notes of the violins' opening theme in the finale of No. 8. Two details in No. 5 I cannot get myself to accept: the failure to make the prescribed pause between the two forceful opening statements of the first movement; and the disproportionately faster *più mosso* tempo at the beginning of the coda of the second movement.

Colin Davis produces with the BBC Symphony a first-rate performance of No. 4 on Philips 9500.032, and a good one of No. 6 (*Pastoral*) on 6500.463. In the performance of No. 5 on 6500.462 I can go along with the soberer first movement that moves less *con brio* than Toscanini's, but not the plodding Scherzo, which I find even less tolerable when it reappears in the buoyant finale. The *Allegretto scherzando* second movement and *Allegro vivace* finale of No. 8, on the same record, are also soberer than Toscanini's, but not excessively so. No. 7 is performed well on Philips 9500.219; but one cannot hear the descending sixteenth-notes of the theme of the finale.

Carlos Kleiber's performance of No. 5 with the Vienna Philharmonic, on Deutsche Grammophon 2530.516, is for the most part highly impressive, but is flawed, for me, by the disproportionately faster *più mosso* tempo of the coda of the second movement, the repetition of the exposition of the finale, the failure, in the development of the finale, to play the recurrence of the hushed passage from the preceding movement in its original tempo, and the exaggeration throughout of Beethoven's contrasts of loud and soft, which may be caused by recording that makes the sound recede into the distance as it becomes softer. Kleiber's performance of No. 7 on 2530.706 would be excellent in a hall; but the recording makes it a succession of extreme contrasts between close fortissimos and distant pianissimos.

Ozawa's performances of No. 3 (*Eroica*) on Philips 9500.002 and No. 9 on 6747.119 are musically inadequate and ineffective.

Trios. Except for the tempo of the first movement that is too fast for the right expressive effect, the Suk Trio's performance of Op. 97 (*Archduke*) on Vanguard SU-5 is superb.

Variations. Emanuel Ax's excellent performance of Op. 35 (*Eroica*) is on RCA ARL1-2083, with the Sonata Op. 53.

BELLINI

I Puritani. In the new performance on London OSA-13111 the peculiar timbre of Sutherland's middle and low range and her mannerisms of vocal production and phrasing make much of her singing unattractive; and Pavarotti's powerful tenor voice lacks the sensuous warmth and ease of flow required by the Bellini *cantilena*. I recommend instead the early mono performance with Callas that may still be available on imported QCX-10278/80 (Italy).

BERG

Wozzeck. Reissued on Odyssey Y2-33126 (mono) is the New York Philharmonic concert performance that Mitropoulos conducted effectively in 1951, with an outstanding cast headed by Mack Harrell in the title role and Eileen Farrell as Marie.

BERLIOZ

(The) Damnation of Faust. Ozawa, on Deutsche Grammophon 2709.048, paces the work well, and gets extraordinarily beauti-

ful playing from the Boston Symphony with the beautiful singing of Mathis, Burrows and McIntyre. But he doesn't get his singers to sing as expressively as Colin Davis does in his performance.

Harold in Italy. Until now Toscanini's performance was the only one to acquire; now, though it is still the one to acquire first, there is one to add to it: the excellent one by Colin Davis with the London Symphony on Philips 9500.026.

(Les) Nuits d'été. Though one should begin with Steber's great performance, one should add the exquisite performance by De los Angeles with the Boston Symphony under Munch, reissued on RCA AVM1-1412 (mono).

Requiem. Bernstein's performance on Columbia M2-34202 I advise against, suggesting Abravanel's on Vanguard records instead.

Romeo and Juliet. Ozawa's performance on Deutsche Grammophon 2707.089 — with the Boston Symphony, the New England Conservatory Chorus, Julia Hamari, Jean Dupouy and José van Dam — is a good one, except for the fast tempo that lessens the expressive effect of the great melody of the flute and English horn in the Love Scene. But Toscanini's performance is still the one to acquire first.

Symphonie fantastique. Colin Davis's new performance with the marvelous Concertgebouw Orchestra on Philips 6500.774 is the one to acquire — Solti's with the Chicago Symphony on London CS-6790 having an almost explosive nervous excitement that I find disturbing.

BIZET

Carmen. Solti, on London OSA-13115, conducts effectively the performance with Troyanos in the title role and Domingo as José, which — like the one excellently conducted by Frühbeck on Angel records — restores the original spoken dialogue in place of the recitatives inserted by Guiraud. But the superior singing of Bumbry and Vickers makes the Frühbeck performance preferable.

PERFORMANCES OF TODAY

BRAHMS

The Symphony No. 2 and *Variations on a Theme of Haydn* are performed beautifully by Haitink and the Amsterdam Concertgebouw Orchestra on Philips 6500.375.

London CS-6837 has the late Istvan Kertesz's excellent performance of the Symphony No. 3 with the Vienna Philharmonic, and the orchestra's effective performance of the *Variations on a Theme of Haydn* without him. In the performance of No. 4 on CS-6838 Kertesz doesn't maintain steady tempo in the first and last movements.

BRITTEN

The writing in *Death in Venice* doesn't convey the subtleties embodied in Mann's prose narrative and is of no musical interest in itself. The English Opera Group performance conducted by Steuart Bedford, on London OSA-13109, has the tenor Pears and baritone Shirley-Quirk as its principal singers.

BRUCKNER

Mass in E minor. The work, which has beautiful writing quite different from that of the symphonies, is performed well by the Bergedorfer Chamber Choir and wind-players of the Hamburg Philharmonic State Orchestra under Wormsbächer on Telefunken 6.41297 (with Schubert's *Gesänge zur Feier des heiligen Opfers der Messe*).

CHERUBINI

Quartets. My first hearing of these six works — provided by the excellent performances of the Melos Quartet of Stuttgart on Deutsche Grammophon 2710.018 — has left me amazed by the endlessly varied invention of a mind as lively as Haydn's in an idiom entirely his own.

CHOPIN

Ballades. A recording of performances by Cliburn is in preparation.

Barcarolle. See under MISCELLANEOUS COLLECTIONS: Cliburn.

Etudes. Ashkenazy's superb performances are on London CS-6844, with Op. 25 seemingly recorded on a more metallic-sounding piano than Op. 10.

Polonaises. Pollini's performances on Deutsche Grammophon 2530.791 are excellent; but the greatest recorded performance of Op. 53 is still Cliburn's.

Preludes. Pollini's performances on Deutsche Grammophon 2530.550 are powerfully declamatory; Perahia's on Columbia M-33507 sensitively and elegantly expressive. Perahia's may be closer to what Chopin imagined; but what Pollini's mind makes of the pieces is convincing and impressive.

Sonatas. Perahia's playing in Opp. 35 and 58, on Columbia M-32780, is very fine, but without the power and tension of Cliburn's. Nor is he aware of all that Cliburn shows his awareness of in the music — with, for example, what Cliburn has his left hand do in the middle section of the Scherzo of Op. 58.

Waltzes. Katin's performances on London STS-15305 are excellent; but Lipatti's on the Odyssey record or on Angel 3556 (mono) are still the ones to acquire first.

Collections. RCA ARL1-1569 has good performances by Emanuel Ax of the Polonaise-Fantaisie Op. 61, Andante Spianato and Grande Polonaise Op. 22, Nocturne Op. 62 No. 1 and Scherzo Op. 54, of which the best pieces are the first and the Andante of the second.

DEBUSSY

Estampes and *Images* for Piano. The robust and brilliant sonorities of Rosen's performances led me to recommend them on pp. 289 and 290; my later realization of their lack of plasticity and grace leads me to withdraw that recommendation. For Cliburn's performances of some of the pieces see p. 378 and under MISCELLANEOUS COLLECTIONS: Cliburn.

Etudes for Piano. Paul Jacobs's superb performances are on Nonesuch H-71322.

DONIZETTI

Gemma di Vergy. The concert performance of this unfamiliar work recorded on Columbia M3-34575 reveals Donizetti's powers operating with assurance to provide the dramatic action with expressively moving music. After a poor start Caballé's voice is agreeable except for the stridency of high notes in rapid florid passages; and it spins out beautifully shaped phrases in *cantilena.* The other principals sing well with the Schola Cantorum and the Opera Orchestra of New York under Queler's effective direction.

Maria Stuarda. It is sung, on London OSA-13117, by Sutherland, whose voice I find unattractive, Pavarotti, whose voice is agreeable in its lower range but becomes constricted and unattractive as it rises, and Tourangeau, whose voice is unattractive in its entire range, with the orchestra and chorus of the Teatro Communale in Bologna, and under the effective direction of Bonynge.

DOWLAND

Lachrimae. The Consort of Musicke that performs the work under Anthony Rooley on Oiseau-Lyre DSLO-517 uses mostly viols of Dowland's period, whose sound is more authentic but less pleasant than that of the modern strings and viols of the London Philomusica with which Thurston Dart performs the work on the earlier Oiseau-Lyre S-164E.

DVORAK

American Suite Op. 98B. The extraordinarily gifted Michael Tilson Thomas performs this unfamiliar and engaging piece with the Berlin Radio Symphony on Columbia M-34513. The reverse side has the less interesting *The American Flag* Op. 102, in which the orchestra is joined by vocalists.

Quartet Op. 96 *(American).* Performed superbly by the Guarneri Quartet on RCA ARL1-1791, with the less interesting String Quintet Op. 97.

Quintet Op. 81 for Piano and Strings. An incandescent performance by Stephen Bishop and four outstanding players of the

Berlin Philharmonic Octet is on Philips 6500.363, with a similar performance of the String Quintet Op. 97.

Serenade Op. 22 for Strings. An engaging early piece, performed by Marriner with the Academy of St. Martin-in-the-Fields on Argo ZRG-848 and by Leppard with the English Chamber Orchestra on Philips 9500.105, with Tchaikovsky's Serenade Op. 48 for Strings on the reverse side of each record. All performances are excellent; but I prefer Marriner's.

Slavonic Dances. Op. 46 has some of Dvořák's most attractive pieces; most of those in Op. 72 don't attain the level of the earlier ones. They are performed superbly by Kubelik with the Bavarian Radio Symphony — Op. 46 on Deutsche Grammophon 2430.466, Op. 72 on 2530.593. And I prefer these performances to Szell's more rigid ones with the Cleveland Orchestra on Odyssey Y2-33524.

Symphonies. No. 7 is performed effectively by Neumann with the Czech Philharmonic on Vanguard SU-7, but more brilliantly by the Concertgebouw Orchestra under Colin Davis on Philips 9500.132.

Neumann's performance of No. 8 with the Czech Philharmonic on Vanguard SU-2 is a good one, and is reproduced better than Walter's with an assembled orchestra on Odyssey Y-33231.

But No. 9 (*New World*), the finest, Neumann conducts stolidly on Vanguard SU-8; and Toscanini's is still the performance to acquire.

Trio Op. 90 (*Dumky*). A moderately interesting work, performed superbly by the Yuval Trio on Deutsche Gramophon 2430.594, with Smetana's Trio Op. 15.

FALLA

The Three-Cornered Hat. Boulez produces an excellent performance of this engaging ballet score with the New York Philharmonic and Jan De Gaetani, on Columbia M-33970, with Falla's uninteresting Harpsichord Concerto, performed by Igor Kipnis.

Seven Popular Spanish Songs. See under MISCELLANEOUS COLLECTIONS: Horne.

414

FAURE

Pelléas et Mélisande. The hauntingly lovely *Prélude* and exquisite *La Fileuse* and *Sicilienne* that Balanchine uses in his ballet *Emeralds* are performed beautifully by Andrew Davis with the New Philharmonia on Columbia M-34506, which offers also an excellent performance of Franck's Symphony.

Requiem. The performance on Philips 6500.969 — with Fournet conducting the Netherlands Radio Chorus, the Rotterdam Philharmonic, Ameling and Bernard Kruyzen — is good; but the Cluytens performance with De los Angeles and Fischer-Dieskau on Angel is better.

GERSHWIN

An American in Paris. An astounding experience, for me, was to hear what Michael Tilson Thomas did with this piece in his performance with the New York Philharmonic on Columbia XM-34205: not merely the grace and rubato with which he conducts the long blues section, but his lifting out into increased prominence and significance detail after detail of the long opening section. The reverse side has a skillful combination of the original Grofé orchestration of *Rhapsody in Blue* with the passages for piano extracted from Gershwin's own Duo-Art piano roll of his arrangement of the piece for solo piano.

GESUALDO

Madrigals. All six books of the 5-part madrigals are on Telefunken 76.35015; and one discovers that the familiar ones with the daring and strange harmonic progressions that achieve extraordinary expressive power are in the fifth and sixth books. What the earlier books offer is beautiful writing in the traditional style, with only a few pieces in the fourth book exhibiting the beginnings of his later idiosyncratic writing. Regrettably the records are not accompanied by the texts to which the music is so closely related, and which would be more useful than the biographical and historical notes. And though the Quintetto Vocale Italiano conducted by Ephrikian sings acceptably, its performances do not equal those that Robert Craft produces with his groups.

Reissued on Odyssey Y-32886 are Craft's performances of a number of fine pieces from the fourth and fifth books, with a few of Gesualdo's equally impressive sacred pieces, including the Responsory *Aestimatus sum.*

Responsoriae et alia ad Officium Sabbati Sancti. The responsories include *Aestimatus sum,* the *alia* a magnificent *Miserere;* and they are sung well by the Prague Madrigal Choir under Venhoda on Telefunken 6.41266.

GIBBONS

His fine madrigals and motets are sung on Oiseau-Lyre DSLO-512 by the Consort of Musick, one of whose sopranos has a disturbingly unattractive voice.

GLUCK

Iphigénie en Aulide. RCA ARL2-1104 offers a German performance of the version made by Wagner, who omitted some of Gluck's writing that he didn't approve of, provided the remaining arias and choruses of Gluck with instrumental preludes, postludes and transitions, replaced Gluck's conclusion with one by himself, revised Gluck's scoring, and substituted German for the original French — despite which one can perceive the high quality and moving expressiveness of the vocal writing Gluck achieved a dozen years after *Orfeo.* The performance conducted effectively by Kurt Eichhorn has not only superb singing by Fischer-Dieskau but good singing by Thomas Stewart, Ludovic Spies, Moffo (except for high notes she has to strain for) and Trudeliese Schmidt, with the excellent Bavarian Radio Chorus and Munich Radio Orchestra.

Janet Baker's beautiful mezzo-soprano voice and affecting expressiveness are heard, on Philips 9500.023, in the familiar *"Che puro ciel"* and *"Che farò"* from *Orfeo, "O del mio dolce dolor"* from *Paride ed Elena, "Divinités du Styx"* from *Alceste,* and unfamiliar arias from other operas.

HANDEL

Alexander's Feast. The performance on Vanguard HM-5051-SD of this enjoyable work that rises to an impressive conclusion is conducted well by Alfred Deller, and has excellent singing by Honor Sheppard, Worthley, Bevan and the Orianna Concert Choir.

Cantatas. The early *Agrippina Condotte a Morire* is sung well by Carole Bogard on Cambridge CC-2771, with arias from the opera *Agrippina.*

Janet Baker, on Phillips 6500.523, deploys her beautiful voice with her sense for shape of musical phrase and her expressive eloquence in the early *Lucrezia,* and in arias from Handel's later works, including the best-known *"Ombrai mai fu"* from *Serse* and *"Care selve"* from *Atalanta,* with Leppard conducting the English Chamber Orchestra.

Chandos Anthems. Two fine pieces, *I Will Magnify Thee* and *In the Lord Put I My Trust,* are performed well, on Argo ZRG-766, by Willcocks with the Choir of King's College, Cambridge, the Academy of St. Martin-in-the-Fields, a good tenor, Philip Langridge, and a less adequate soprano, Caroline Friend.

Concerti Grossi Op. 3. They are less impressive than those of Op. 6, but are pleasant to listen to, and are accompanied, on Philips 6700.050, by pieces that are outstanding: the familiar concerto grosso titled *Alexander's Feast,* and the unfamiliar Overtures in D and B-flat and Hornpipe in D. Leppard conducts the English Chamber Orchestra in excellent performances.

Israel in Egypt. Argo ZRG-817/8 has a good performance by Simon Preston with the Choir of Christ Church Cathedral, Oxford, a solo group, and the English Chamber Orchestra. The boy sopranos of the excellent male chorus are a little shrill, and the vocal timbre of the adult male solo alto is incongruous with the timbres of the other adult soloists.

Messiah. Leppard conducts a good performance, on RCA CRL3-1426, with Felicity Palmer, Watts, Davies, Shirley-Quirk and the English Chamber Orchestra and Chorus; but Colin Davis's performance is even better.

Saul. The rarely heard work turns out to offer for the most part pleasantly unimpressive writing, except for a few powerfully expressive passages — the chorus *"Envy! eldest born of hell!"* in Act 2, the Endor scene and mourning scenes in Act 3. It is performed well, on Deutsche Grammophon ARC-2710.014, by Mackerras with the Leeds Festival Chorus, the English Chamber Orchestra, Margaret Price, Sheila Armstrong, Davies, James Bowman (whose counter-tenor voice I find disturbingly unattractive) and McIntyre.

Semele. The work includes much attractive writing in addition to the well-known *"Oh sleep, why dost thou leave me?"* and *"Where'er you walk"*, and is sung well, on Vanguard VCS-10127/9, by Armstrong, Watts, Tear, Diaz and the Amor Artis Chorale with the English Chamber Orchestra under Somary.

Solomon. The performance conducted by Somary on Vanguard VSD-71204/6 is made outstanding by the singing of Armstrong and Diaz with the Amor Artis Chorale and English Chamber Orchestra.

Tamerlano. This unfamiliar work turns out to have a number of fine arias in a context of a large amount of recitative. It is performed, on Cambridge B-2902, in its entirety, with no changes in Handel's writing and with the vocal parts in their original ranges — which means that Tamerlano is sung by Gwendolyn Killebrew, who happens to have a mezzo-soprano voice whose timbre is suited to the vehement utterances of her role. The other principal roles are sung admirably by Alexander Young, Carole Bogard, Sofia Steffan and Joanna Simon; and John Moriarty conducts.

Water Music. Boulez's performance with the New York Philharmonic on Columbia M-33436 is an effective one, though made idiosyncratic by occasional unusual tempos and details of style that make me prefer Menuhin's with his Bath Festival Orchestra.

HAYDN

Cantatas. Philips 6500.660 has *Berenice che fai* and *Arianna a Naxos,* written for Haydn's concerts in London, superbly sung by Janet Baker, with arias from Mozart's *La Clemenza di Tito* and his songs *Abendempfindung* and *Das Veilchen.* Leppard conducts the English Chamber Orchestra for *Berenice* and the arias, and plays a *fortepiano* for *Arianna* and the songs.

Masses. The *Harmoniemesse* on Columbia M-33267 is less impressive than the other masses of Haydn's last years; and it is not helped by Bernstein's insensitive conducting of the New York Philharmonic, the Westminster Choir, Blegen, Von Stade, Riegel and Estes.

Operas. The public that has heard almost nothing of the operas Haydn wrote for the entertainment of Prince Nicolaus Esterhazy can now hear two of them — *La fedeltà premiata* on Philips 6707.028, and *La vera costanza* on 6703.077. They offer accomplished writing that is pleasant to listen to, culminating in finales similar to Mozart's but not their equal in quality and dramatic effect. Both are conducted admirably by Dorati; the excellent cast in *La fedeltà* includes Von Stade, Cotrubas and Alva; the other work has Jessye Norman at her best, which is extraordinarily beautiful, with Donath, and an excellent lyric tenor named Claes Ahnsjö, among others; and with them one hears the Suisse Romande Radio Chorus and Lausanne Chamber Orchestra.

Quartets. The six of Op. 50 on Deutsche Grammophon 2709.060 are given effectively enlivening performances by the Tokyo Quartet, such as the three of Op. 71 and the three of Op. 74 on London STS-15325/7 do not get from the Aeolian Quartet. For Op. 74 I suggest the Griller Quartet on Vanguard records.

The Cleveland Quartet's excellent performance of Op. 64 No. 5, on RCA ARL1-1409, is coupled with an excessively vehement one of Op. 74 No. 2.

Op. 74 No. 3 and Op. 76 No. 3 are performed effectively by the Alban Berg Quartet on Telefunken 6.41302.

The Amadeus Quartet, though not of virtuoso caliber, achieves acceptable performances of Op. 76 Nos. 1 and 4 on Deutsche Grammophon 2530.089.

Sonatas for Piano. A first volume of a series, London STS-15343/5, offers Landon Nos. 6, 10, 18, 33, 38, 39, 47, 50, 52 and 60 (Hoboken Nos. 10, 1, —, 20, 23, 24, 32, 37, 39 and 50), performed by John McCabe. In the progression from early to late — i.e. from before 1766 to the early 1790s — one hears, as in the parallel progression of the symphonies, an unimpressive beginning and an increasingly impressive manipulation of increasingly impressive substance; and the volume includes the Andante and Variations in F minor, composed in 1793, which stands out as unique not only in the beauty and expressiveness of the first section of the theme, but in what is done with it in the variations and the amazingly wide-ranging coda. McCabe points up the operation of the lively Haydn mind in the sonatas very effectively — which leaves one unprepared for his unenlivening and awkward dealing with the Andante.

Nonesuch H-71318 has Landon Nos. 53, 47, 31 and 61 (Hoboken Nos. 34, 32, 46 and 51); H-71328 has Landon Nos. 30, 32 and 50 (H. Nos. 19, 44 and 37) with the Andante and Variations in F minor. Gilbert Kalish's performances are fluent and sensitive — the sonatas calling for more pointing up of their liveliness, the Andante for more powerfully expressive treatment.

Symphonies. The early Nos. 20 to 35, on London STS-15257/62 offer an occasional lovely slow movement or charming minuet or finale, but no first movement with the incandescent operation of powers of invention and development that one hears in the final Nos. 93 to 104 on STS-15319/24. Dorati — in his performances with the Philharmonia Hungarica — continues to exhibit his inability to play slow movements in the slow tempos Haydn prescribes; and this time he astonishes one by changing a few notes of the authentic texts of Nos. 93 and 94 established in the Landon scores and exhibiting carelessness about rests and *fermatas*. These would be sufficient reason to acquire instead the performances of Nos. 93 to 104 by Jochum with the London Philharmonic, originally issued on Deutsche Grammophon 2720.064/10 and now being released on single records; and another reason is their superior orchestral playing.

Nos. 94 (*Surprise*) and 96 are on Philips 6580.124, admirably performed by Antonio de Almeida with the Orchestra Sinfonica di Roma.

Trios. The Beaux Arts Trio continues its series with Landon Nos. 32, 33 and 36 (Hoboken Nos. 18, 19 and 22) on Philips 6500.521; L. Nos. 34, 38 and 32 (H. Nos. 20, 24 and 32) on 6500.522; L. Nos. 29 and 27 (H. Nos. 15 and 14) on 9500.034;

and L. Nos. 26, 28 and 40 (H. Nos. 13, 16 and 17) on 9500.035. Variations. With the Mozart sonatas on London CS-7008 Alicia de Larrocha plays Haydn's great Andante and Variations in F minor, revealing an amazing lack of comprehension of the piece in the way she races through it. Kalish's well-paced performance on Nonesuch H-71328 is the one to acquire even though it lacks the powerful expressiveness the piece calls for.

JANACEK

Slavonic Mass (*Glagolitic Mass*). London OS-26338 has Kempe's excellent performance of this powerful work with the Royal Philharmonic, the Brighton Festival Chorus, Kubiak, Anne Collins, Tear and Wolfgang Schöne, of whom Tear hasn't the vocal power required by the declamatory writing he occasionally has to sing.

LASSUS

The vocal polyphony of the *Missa "Bell' amfitrit' altera"* is realized beautifully by the Choir of Christ Church Cathedral, Oxford, under Preston's direction on Argo ZRG-735, whose reverse side offers what I find to be the most impressive and affecting music of Lassus in my experience — the sixteen musical statements of his Penitential Psalm VII. And Preston conducts the same chorus, on ZRG-795, in the remarkably beautiful Motets *Omnes de Saba venient, Salve Regina mater misericordiae* and *Tui sunt coeli* and the Penitential Psalm V.

Deutsche Grammophon 2533.290 has the Penitential Psalms I and IV and Motets *Ave Regina coelorum, Salve Regina* and *O mors, quam amara est,* sung well by the Pro Cantione Antiqua, London, under Bruno Turner.

LUTOSLAWSKI

The powerful Concerto for Orchestra is performed well by Rowicki with the Warsaw National Philharmonic Symphony on Philips 6500.628, with two later pieces, *Funeral Music* and *Venetian Games,* that convey no expressive meaning to me.

MAHLER

(Das) Lied von der Erde. Haitink's performance with the superb Amsterdam Concertgebouw Orchestra, Janet Baker and the tenor James King, on Philips 650.831, is one of the best I can recall. But Fischer-Dieskau's singing makes the excellent Kletzki performance the one to acquire first.

Lieder eines fahrenden Gesellen. The performance to acquire is Fischer-Dieskau's earlier one with the Philharmonia Orchestra under Furtwängler on Seraphim 60272 (mono), with the *Kindertotenlieder.* But his later stereo performance with the Bavarian Radio Symphony under Kubelik, on Deutsche Grammophon 2530.630 (with uninteresting pieces by Martin), is also very fine.

Symphonies. James Levine, who conducts opera at the Metropolitan in masterly fashion, performs the Symphony No. 1 with the London Symphony on RCA ARL1-0894, No. 3 with the Chicago Symphony and Horne on ARL2-1757, and No. 4 with the Chicago Symphony and Blegen on ARL1-0895. He is completely successful in his dealing with No. 3, ending it with a superb statement of the final movement that is the grandest and most sublime of Mahler's utterances, and with No. 4, the most attractive of the symphonies (I must mention that the record doesn't reproduce the low notes of the string basses in bars 307-14 of the third movement). But his success with No. 1 is incomplete: he hears the second movement not as the lilting *Ländler* it is, but as the fast waltz it is not.

Bernstein's performance of No. 2 with the London Symphony, Armstrong and Baker, on Columbia M2T-32681, offers a prime example of his lack of discipline in the lilting Andante that should be played very simply, but whose flow he impedes and shape he distorts with his manipulation — the over-deliberate tempo that over-emphasizes the lilt, the over-expressive crescendos, retardations, pauses. It is a performance to avoid; and I suggest Klemperer's instead.

I recommend Klemperer's also in place of Mehta's with the Vienna Philharmonic, Cotrubas and Ludwig on London 2242, which reveals a lack of sense for proportion in changes of tempo that is damaging to the shape of the work.

MENDELSSOHN

Concerto for Violin. Ricci's performance with the somewhat brash-sounding Netherlands Radio Philharmonic, on London SPC-2116 (Phase 4), reveals his mastery of his instrument and his expressive warmth controlled by musical taste. The record offers also the Tchaikovsky Concerto.

(A) Midsummer Night's Dream (Incidental Music). Colin Davis produces, on Philips 9500.088, a beautiful-sounding performance with the Boston Symphony (which needs additional bass). The record also offers a similar performance of the Symphony No. 4 *(Italian)* whose *andante* second movement moves more slowly than the prescribed *con moto.*

Octet for Strings. An outstanding performance by I Musici is on Philips 6580.103, with the uninteresting early Symphonies Nos. 10 and 12 for strings.

Songs. Most of the unfamiliar ones that are sung beautifully by Peter Schreier on Deutsche Grammophon 2530.596 are uninteresting; but a few are pleasant to listen to, and one, *Neue Liebe,* is charmingly reminiscent of the music for *A Midsummer Night's Dream.*

Symphony No. 4 *(Italian).* See above under *A Midsummer Night's Dream.*

MEYERBEER

Le Prophète. This is the work not of a great composer but of a craftsman skilled in providing the varieties of music for the situations, action and spectacle of a Paris Opera "grand opera" —music that is effective for its every purpose, agreeable to listen to, and at times moving. It includes music for the spectacular singing that was one of the features of the "grand opera"; and in the performance on Columbia M4-34340 such singing is provided only by Horne, not by McCracken, whose voice becomes constricted and unattractive in its high range, and not by Scotto, whose every climactic high note is a strident scream. The Royal Philharmonic, the Ambrosian Opera Chorus and the conductor Lewis perform well.

MONTEVERDI

L'Incoronazione di Poppea. To the performance, authentic in text and style, issued on Cambridge 1901 some years ago Telefunken 6.35247 adds another conducted by Harnoncourt, whose Concentus Musicus provides the continuo accompaniment for the fine singing of the expressive recitative-like vocal parts by Donath, Soderstrom, Berberian and others. The roles are sung in their original vocal ranges — which is why Nero, originally written in the soprano range for a *castrato,* is sung by Soderstrom.

Vespers of 1610. The performance on Deutsche Grammophon 2710.017 is a very fine one in which Hanns-Martin Scheidt conducts the Regensburg Cathedral Choir, a small group of adult male soloists to whom are added a few boys from the Choir, and an instrumental group. The boys' voices are some of the most beautiful I can recall hearing, and make the second *Magnificat* a delight to the ear. The final record-side has the uninteresting Mass *In illo tempore.*

MOZART

Concerto for Clarinet K.622. The performance on Deutsche Grammophon 2530.411 has unusually fine playing of the solo part by Alfred Prinz — what is unusual being the sensitiveness comparable with De Peyer's in the inflection of a beautiful clarinet tone more delicate than De Peyer's. Böhm provides with the Vienna Philharmonic suitable contexts for this performance and the good one by Dietmar Zeman of Mozart's Bassoon Concerto K. 191.

Phillips 6500.378 has a performance of the Clarinet Concerto in which Brymer plays well, but not with the extraordinary tone and phrasing of De Peyer, and one of the Bassoon Concerto with good playing by Michael Chapman. Marriner conducts the Academy of St. Martin-in-the-Fields.

Concertos for Piano. Pollini, on Deutsche Grammophon 2530.716, plays the Concertos K.459 and 488 with a sensitiveness and grace which Böhm doesn't obtain from the Vienna Philharmonic.

The performances of the Concertos K.466 and 467 by Gulda with the Vienna Philharmonic under Abbado, on Deutsche Grammophon 2530.548, are good, except for the unattractively percussive sound of his playing and the slow tempo of the first movement of K.466 that lessens its dramatic urgency and power.

In the performance of the Concerto K.467 on London CS-6894 Uri Segal produces with the London Chamber Orchestra in the first movement a powerful introduction which prepares one for strong playing by the soloist, not for the delicate playing of Radu Lupu, and in the Andante a grand opening statement which prepares one for a similarly grand enunciation of the piano's long flow of melody, not for Lupu's dream-like pianissimo statement of it.

That Andante of K.467, played by Gilels in *allegretto* tempo and delicate lyrical style on Columbia/Melodiya M-33008, is not the overwhelmingly powerful utterance it becomes when played in the right *andante* tempo and with powerful sustained tension.

The tension that is lacking in that Gilels performance is lacking also in Brendel's playing in the Concertos K.466 and 491 on Philips 6500.533.

Judging by the lack of a sense for coherence and shape in the performance of the Concerto K.453 I advise against Peter Serkin's performances on RCA ARL3-0732 and on single records.

Perahia's understatement of the powerful opening movement of the Concerto K.491, on Columbia M-34219, is difficult to understand in the light of his strongly enlivened playing in K.449 on the reverse side.

In his performance of the Concerto K.503 with the Czech Philharmonic under Vlach, on Vanguard SU-11, Moravec doesn't always sustain to the end of a phrase the force with which he begins it. In addition the first movement is played too fast for it to achieve its prescribed *maestoso* character; the second movement too slowly for its prescribed *Andante*.

Ashkenazy's beautiful playing with the English Chamber Orchestra in the Concerto K.365 for two pianos, on London

CS-6937, enables the listener to perceive how heavy-handed and rhythmically sloppy Barenboim's playing is. The record has also the uninteresting Concerto K.242 for three pianos with Fou Ts'ong as the additional pianist.

Divertimento K.563 for String Trio. The occasional vehemence of the performance by Stern, Zukerman and Rose on Columbia M-33266 makes the Grumiaux Trio performance preferable.

Mass in C K.317 (*Coronation*). Kubelik's performance on Deutsche Grammophon 2530.356, with the Bavarian Radio Symphony Chorus and Orchestra, Mathis, Norma Procter, Donald Grobe and Shirley-Quirk, is a good one; but I prefer the pacing of the work by Colin Davis on the Philips record.

Operas. *The Abduction from the Seraglio* is paced and shaped well by Böhm, on Deutsche Grammophon 2709.051, in the performance with Arleen Auger, Reri Grist, Schreier, Harald Neukirch, Kurt Moll, and the Dresden State Orchestra and Chorus. Treble must be greatly reduced to obtain the normal sound of s and t and to lessen the stridency of Grist's high notes.

Solti's performance of *Così Fan Tutte,* on London OSA-1442, is admirable in its animated but not hard-driving pacing, its sensitive and plastically coherent shaping of the music, and has admirable singing by Lorengar, Berganza, Jane Berbié, Davies, Krause and Becquier, even with the lessened beauty and ease exhibited by Davies's voice and the no longer agreeable sound of Berganza's high notes. The orchestra is the London Philharmonic.

Even better is the *Così* on Philips 6707.025, with Colin Davis's superb conducting and the singing of Caballé, Baker, Cotrubas, Gedda and Richard Van Allan, which makes the harsh voice of Ganzarolli endurable. The orchestra and chorus are those of the Royal Opera House, Covent Garden.

The *Così* conducted by Böhm on Deutsche Grammophon 2709.059 I advise against.

Davis also conducts a superb *Don Giovanni* on Philips 6707.022, with Wixell's impressively effective singing in the title role, Burrows's ear-ravishing and beautifully phrased performances of Don Ottavio's arias, and the singing of the others

— Arroyo, Te Kanawa, Freni, Ganzarolli, Van Allan and Roni — that is agreeable-sounding and expressive.

The delightful overture and superb vocal writing of the two arias and trio of *The Impresario* testify to its having been composed in the same year as *Figaro*. Colin Davis, on Philips 9500.011, conducts an excellent performance with Cotrubas, Ruth Welting and the London Symphony. The reverse side has the uninteresting fragments of the uncompleted *Lo sposo deluso*.

Ameling's singing of arias from *Figaro, Don Giovanni* and *Così* and several concert arias to dramatic texts, on Philips 6500.544, is beautiful and flawlessly phrased; but her singing of these utterances of a number of different characters with a voice that never varies in timbre makes them sound like the utterances of one character. I must add that recorded performances of arias are rarely heard in orchestral contexts as beautifully played and musically sensitive as those De Waart provides with the English Chamber Orchestra.

Burrows, on Oiseau-Lyre DSLO-13, deploys his fine voice in arias from *Idomeneo, The Seraglio, Don Giovanni, Così* and *The Magic Flute* with London orchestras under Pritchard.

One is astonished by Frederica von Stade's performances of Mozart arias, on Philips 9500.098, which are successions of phrases that begin with an exaggerated pianissimo, erupt into an exaggerated fortissimo, and end with a return to exaggerated pianissimo. The record offers similar performances of arias from Rossini's operas.

Quartets. The six dedicated to Haydn — K.387, 421, 428, 458 (*Hunt*), 464 and 465 — are performed by the Quartetto Italiano, on Philips SC 71 AX301, with its perfection of tone, phrasing and ensemble, but with imperfections of tempo that make the Budapest Quartet's performances preferable. The sound needs reduction of treble.

The Guarneri Quartet's performances of K.387 and 421 on RCA ARL1-0761 and K.428 and 458 on 0762 offer the group's beautiful playing but exhibit its occasional insufficient animation and energy in the Minuet of K.421, the first movement of K.458, the pauses and slowing down in the Minuet of K.387.

The later ARL1-1153 has the remaining K.464 and 465, in which the tendency to slow down second subjects appears only in the first movement of K.464; but the changed recording team has produced damaging changes in the recorded sound, necessitating drastic reduction of treble. As against the intense expressiveness of these performances I prefer the more contained expressiveness and elegance of the Budapest Quartet.

The Quartets K.465 and 589 are performed well by the Tokyo Quartet on Deutsche Grammophon 2530.468.

The Weller Quartet's performances of the Quartets K.575 and 590 on London STS-15291 are very fine.

Quartet K.370 for Oboe and Strings. See below: Quintet K.581 for clarinet and strings.

Quintets. Telefunken 56.35017 presents a quartet of the first rank, the Danish Quartet, in long-needed performances, with an assisting violist, of the Quintets K.174, 406, 515, 516, 593 and 614 for strings — performances which exhibit, in addition to their excellences of tone and ensemble execution, an extraordinary sensitiveness to the music's every point of style, shape and expressiveness. To these are added the engaging Quintet K.407 for horn and strings, with remarkably fluent playing of the occasional florid passages for horn by Jacky Magnardi; the marvelous Quintet K.581 for clarinet and strings, with playing of the clarinet part by Guy Deplus that will not interest anyone familiar with De Peyer's performance with the Melos Ensemble; the Adagio and Fugue K.546 and *Eine kleine Nachtmusik*.

The distinguished violinist Grumiaux, who has led a string trio in fine performances, adds two players for superb performances of the String Quintets K.515 on Philips 6500.619, K.516 and 406 on 6500.620, and K.593 and 614 on 6500.621.

A very fine performance of the Quintet K.581 for clarinet and strings by Grumiaux and his associates with the clarinettist Pieterson is on Philips 6500.924, with the Quartet K.370 for oboe and strings, in which Pierlot's playing is surprisingly unimpressive.

Requiem. The performance conducted by Michel Corboz on RCA AGL1-1533 — with Ameling, Barbara Scherler, Louis Devos,

Roger Soyer and the chorus and orchestra of the Gulbenkian Foundation, Lisbon — is good; but Colin Davis's is better.

Serenades. The Serenade K.250 that Mozart composed for a wedding in the Haffner family amazes one with its prodigal flow of invention suited to both the festive and the solemn aspects of the occasion. De Waart's performance with the Dresden State Orchestra and Uto Ughi, solo violin, on Philips 6500.966, is excellent. And equally good is his performance with that orchestra of the Serenade K.320 (*Posthorn*), on Philips 6500.627.

The Serenade K.375 and even more impressive K.388 (which Mozart converted into the Quintet K.406 for strings) are performed well, on Deutsche Grammophon 2530.369, by the Vienna Philharmonic Wind Group.

Sonatas for Piano. Gould's misuse of the Fantasia K.475 and Sonatas K.457, 570 and 576 for the exercise of his eccentricities and perversities of touch, dynamics, phrasing and tempo, on Columbia M-33515, is something to avoid.

De Larrocha offers neat performances of the Sonatas K.330 and 311 and Fantasia K.297, on London CS-7008 (with Haydn's Andante and Variations in F minor), that are made to sound trivial by Cliburn's performance of K.330.

Sonatas for Piano and Violin. Szymon Goldberg no longer produces the beautiful violin tone of his earlier years, but exhibits his undiminished musical sensitiveness in the performances of the Sonatas K.303, 306, 376, 454 and 481 with Radu Lupu on London CS-2243, and their performances of K.296, 301, 302, 304, 305, 378 and 380 on CS-2244.

And an excellent performance of K.454 by Solti and Kulenkampf is on London R-23214 (mono), with Beethoven's Sonata Op. 47.

Symphonies. Fine performances of the Symphonies K.201 and 385 (*Haffner*) by Kertesz with the Vienna Philharmonic are on London CS-6830; and their performance of K.550, the great G-minor, is on CS-6931, with the early G-minor K.183. This coupling represents the persistent but erroneous idea that because they are in the same key the two have some essential relation — this in the face of the audible fact that there isn't a phrase in K.183 that resembles anything in K.550, and that what K.183 does resemble is some of the early and uninteresting symphonies of Haydn.

Marriner, on Philips 6500.162, conducts his Academy of St. Martin-in-the-Fields in a good performance of the first version of K.550, which uses flutes and oboes without the clarinets Mozart added in the revised version that is usually performed. It is good to have an opportunity to hear the first version and discover that the clarinets make the revised version the more poignant of the two, though the accompanying notes assert the contrary. The record also offers a good performance of K.385.

The performance of K.550 I recommend is Giulini's, which is coupled, on the London record, with K.551 (known as *Jupiter*).

K.551 is performed beautifully by the Boston Symphony under Jochum on Deutsche Grammophon 2530.357, with Schubert's *Unfinished* Symphony.

MUSORGSKY

Pictures at an Exhibition. A very good performance of Ravel's orchestral transcription by Giulini with the Chicago Symphony is on Deutsche Grammophon 2530.783, with Prokofiev's *Classical Symphony*.

In Tedd Joselson's performance of the original piano version, on RCA ARL1-2158 (with Prokofiev's *Visions fugitives*), all the Promenades are played too fast for their image of the viewer strolling from picture to picture; and the disregard of the prescribed markings of dynamics is damaging to some of the pieces. I suggest instead Yeresko's performance on the Melodiya/Angel record.

OCKEGHEM

The expressive and moving *Maria Motets* are sung well by the Prague Madrigalists under Venhoda on Telefunken 6.41878.

PERI

The expressive recitative-like arioso of the opera *Euridice* (1600) is sung well in the performance on Telefunken 6.35014 by the Coro Polifonico di Milano and I Solisti di Milano under Ephrikian.

PROKOFIEV

Classical Symphony. A beautiful-sounding performance — with a slower than usual opening movement — by Giulini and the Chicago Symphony is on Deutsche Grammophon 2530.783, with Musorgsky's *Pictures at an Exhibition.*

Concertos for Piano. Listening to Ashkenazy's superb performances with the London Symphony under Previn, on London CSA-2314, one hears that it is Prokofiev's early writing that is most attractive and impressive; and that of the three early concertos No. 3 is one of his finest works. Ashkenazy also plays with a small group the *Overture on Hebrew Themes,* and conducts an excellent performance of the *Classical Symphony.*

(The) Gambler. The vocal writing of this opera, another early work, is, like Peri's in *Euridice,* an expressive arioso, but in a modern idiom, and with Peri's mere instrumental *continuo* replaced by powerful orchestral writing that supports, reinforces and comments in the mordant Prokofiev manner. The performance conducted by Rozhdestvensky on Columbia/Melodiya M3-34579 offers the usual good male solo voices and in varying degrees unpleasant female voices of Russian opera performances, with the chorus and orchestra of the All-Union Radio.

Sonatas for Piano. The attractive early No. 2 and uninteresting later No. 8 are performed well by Tedd Joselson on RCA ARL1-1570.

Visions fugitives. These shadowy fragments employing Prokofiev's ways of writing for the piano are performed well by Tedd Joselson on RCA ARL1-2158, with a poor performance of Musorgsky's *Pictures at an Exhibition.*

War and Peace. I hear in this work a product of the resourceful craftsman of later years who could turn out music in any quantity, but with no expressive adequacy for the scenes of personal drama, and with the inflated patriotic rhetoric required in Soviet Russia for the scenes of war. The Bolshoi Theater performance conducted by Melik-Pashayev, on Columbia/Melodiya M4-33111, has tremulously shrill singing by Vishnevskaya but good singing by the baritone Kibalko and tenor Petrov.

PURCELL

Dido and Aeneas. Reissued on Vanguard HM-46-SD is the good performance conducted by Alfred Deller, with Sheppard, Watts, Bevan and the Oriana Concert Choir and Orchestra.

(The) Fairy Queen. The work is sung better by Sheppard, Bevan and some of the other soloists in the performance conducted by Deller on Vanguard SRV-311/2, than by Jennifer Vyvyan and Peter Pears in the performance conducted more effectively by Britten on Oiseau-Lyre S-121/3.

Ode for St. Cecilia's Day. The excellent performance of this fine piece conducted by Michael Tippett — with Cantelo, Brown, Bevan and others of the Deller Consort, and the Ambrosian Singers and Kalmar Chamber Orchestra — has been reissued on Bach Guild HM-33.

RIMSKY-KORSAKOV

May Night. This early opera (1878) is made enjoyable by its varied writing alternately for the two young lovers, the low-comedy characters out of Gogol, and the fantastic water-sprites. The performance conducted by Fedoseyev on Deutsche Grammophon 2709.063 has a good tenor, Konstantin Lisovsky, and a not too tremulous soprano, Ludmilla Sapagena, for the lovers, a soprano with a lovely small voice, Olga Pastushenko, for the maiden transformed into a water-sprite, good male singers for the comic characters, a woman whose voice is all tremolo for the comic sister-in-law, and the good chorus and orchestra of the Moscow Radio.

Rossini

Elisabetta d' Inghilterra. The amazingly precocious Rossini can, at the age of 25, write the serious music of this opera with assured competence, but not the dazzling incandescence of his writing for comedy in *The Barber of Seville* a year later. The performance conducted effectively by Masini, on Philips 6703.067, offers excellent singing by Caballé (except for occasional strident high notes in rapid florid passages), Carreras and Benelli with the London Symphony and Ambrosian Singers. The recording has Caballé, in a duet, sounding near with the other singer sounding some distance away.

Frederica von Stade's performances of Rossini arias on Philips 9500.098 are like those of Mozart arias on that record: successions of phrases that begin with an exaggerated pianissimo, erupt into an exaggerated fortissimo, and end with a return to exaggerated pianissimo.

Abbado's fine performances of Rossini overtures with the London Symphony on Deutsche Grammophon 2530.559 are recorded in a way that causes the sound, as it becomes softer, to recede into the distance, sometimes almost to the point of inaudibility.

Missa di Gloria. This unfamiliar work is, like the *Requiems* of Mozart and Verdi, an effective setting of the sacred text in the normal musical language and style of Rossini's other writing. It is performed well, on Philips 6500.612, by the BBC Singers, the soloists — Margherita Rinaldi, Ameral Gunson, Benelli, John Mitchinson, Jules Bastin — and the English Chamber Orchestra under Herbert Handt.

All six of the 12-year-old Rossini's charming Sonatas for two violins, cello and bass, his later Variations for clarinet and small orchestra, and the still later Serenade for small orchestra are performed well by I Solisti Veneti under Claudio Scimone on RCA AGL2-1339.

Scarlatti, Alessandro

The charming madrigals are sung well by the Monteverdi Choir of Hamburg on Deutsche Grammophon 2533.300.

Schubert

Masses. The lovely one in A-flat is performed well, on Nonesuch H-71335, by Dennis Russell Davies with the Carleton College Choir, Chamber Singers and Festival Chorale, Marlee Sabo, Jan De Gaetano, Paul Sperry, Leslie Guin and the St. Paul Chamber Orchestra.

And the one in E-flat, which has pages of extraordinary writing, is performed well, on Argo ZRG-825, by Guest with the Choir of St. John's College, Cambridge, Palmer, Watts, Keyte and the Academy of St. Martin-in-the-Fields.

Octet Op. 166 for Strings and Winds. This rarely performed work offers many pages of wonderful writing, and marvelous employment of the strings and winds in combination that is realized with extraordinary perfection in the ensemble performance, on RCA ARL1-1047, by the superb players: the Cleveland Quartet, Tuckwell (horn), Brymer (clarinet) and Martin Gatt (bassoon).

Quartet *Death and the Maiden*. The Guarneri Quartet, on RCA ARL1-1994, plays very beautifully, but without the animation, energy, passion and, in the finale, the overwhelming momentum of the Cleveland Quartet's performance on ARL1-0483.

Quintet Op. 114 *(Trout)* for Piano and Strings. The performance on RCA ARL1-1882 by Peter Serkin's Tashi and assisting players is straightforward and good, but is surpassed by the incandescently enlivening performance of the Köckert Quartet and Eschenbach.

Quintet Op. 163 for Strings. The excellences of the Weller Quartet's performance on London STS-15300 include flawless pacing, which makes it preferable to the performance by the Guarneri Quartet and Leonard Rose on RCA ARL1-1154, with its excessive slowing down of the second subject in the finale and a tempo that makes the impassioned middle section of the slow movement too fast in relation to the sublime opening section.

Sonatas for Piano. Pollini, on Deutsche Grammophon 2530.473, fails to realize the need of occasional accelerations of tempo in the first movement of the Sonata Op. 42, but manages to keep the movement from sounding stodgy in its too strictly maintained tempo. The record also has the uninteresting *Wanderer Fantasy*.

Ashkenazy's performance of Op. 53 on London CS-6961 is excellent.

Lupu, on London CS-6966, sets a flowing tempo that is better for the opening movement of Op. 78 than Ashkenazy's slower one; but in that slower tempo Ashkenazy plays with an expressive power that Lupu's performance doesn't have. And Ashkenazy continues this more expressively enlivening playing than Lupu's in the subsequent movements.

Eschenbach's faster than *molto moderato* tempo for the opening movement of the posthumous Sonata in B-flat, on Deutsche Grammophon 2530.477, deprives the music of the largeness of expressive content that requires the prescribed slower tempo; but his performance is musically sensitive and moves with continuity of tension and shape that Brendel's lacks; and so it is satisfying. But one should acquire the great Schnabel performance on imported records. And Curzon's brisk and rigid performance is one not to acquire.

The long-needed good performance of the posthumous Sonata in A is provided by Eschenbach on Deutsche Grammophon 2530.372.

Sonata for Arpeggione and Piano. An excellent performance by the cellist Lynn Harrell and James Levine is on RCA ARL1-1568, with the uninteresting Mendelssohn Sonata Op. 58.

Songs. The Fischer-Dieskau performance of *Die schöne Müllerin* on Deutsche Grammophon 2530.544 exhibits a saddening loss of the beauty his voice has in the earlier performance on Angel records.

Deutsche Grammophon 2530.528 offers superb singing by Christa Ludwig, with excellent playing by Irwin Cage, in *An den Mond* (D. 296), *Dass sie hier gewesen, Wehmut, So lass mich scheinen, Der Zwerg, Freudvoll und leidvoll, Das Mädchen, Wärst du bei mir im Lebenstal,* and others less interesting.

Symphonies. Haitink produces well-paced and shaped and beautiful-sounding performances with the Concertgebouw Orchestra of the Fifth and the *Unfinished* on Philips 9500.099, and the great Ninth on 9500.097.

Trios. Szerying's tone is not always agreeable in the performances of Opp. 99 and 100 with Rubinstein and Fournier on RCA ARL2-0731; and the works are performed more effectively by Stern, Rose and Istomin.

The Suk Trio's superb performance of Op. 99 is on Vanguard SU-6.

SCHUMANN

Concerto for Piano. Lupu's performance with the London Symphony under Previn, on London CS-6840, is excessively finicky; and the greatest performance is still Lipatti's on the Odyssey record (not the one on the London record), to which one can add Cliburn's.

Fantasia Op. 17. A superbly shaped performance by Pollini is on Deutsche Grammophon 2430.379, with the rarely heard Sonata Op. 11 that has occasional pages of highly effective writing for the piano.

Kreisleriana and *Humoreske*. London CS-6859 has Ashkenazy's admirably conceived and achieved performances of these works that offer pages of Schumann's effective writing for the piano and other pages that are boring.

Songs. The *Liederkreis* Op. 24 and *Myrthen* Op. 25 are sung well by Fischer-Dieskau, with enlivening playing by Eschenbach, on Deutsche Grammophon 2530.543.

Jessye Norman exhibits her vocal unevenness, and her singing has no expressive force, in the performance of the *Liederkreis* Op. 24 on Philips 9500.110, with the less valuable *Frauenliebe und Leben*.

SMETANA

Má Vlast. Ancerl's performance with the Czech Philharmonic on Vanguard SU-9/10 enables one to hear that the unfamiliar pieces in the cycle have only occasional effective moments, and the one entirely fine piece is the well-known *Vltava (Die Moldau)*.

Trio Op. 15. The Yuval Trio's superb performance is on Deutsche Grammophon 2530.594, with Dvořák's Trio Op. 90.

STRAVINSKY

Jeu de cartes. Stravinsky's own performance is clearer in texture and wittier than Abbado's with the London Symphony on Deutsche Grammophon 2530.537.

(Les) Noces. The first version, completed in 1917, for a large orchestra of woodwinds, brass, a few solo strings, piano, harpsichord, drums and other percussion — performed on Columbia M-33201 by Robert Craft with the Gregg Smith Singers and Orpheus Chamber Ensemble — reveals the basically percussive aural image that led Stravinsky to the 1919 version for various drums, other percussion, harmonium and pianola, of which Craft performs the first two tableaux on the record, and eventually to the final 1923 version for four pianos, drums and percussion, which should have been added on the record, rather than the unattractive *Symphonies for Wind Instruments* and uninteresting *Chant du Rossignal.* An English translation of the text is provided, but not the transliterated Russian that is essential for correlation of words with music.

Oedipus Rex. Stravinsky's earlier performance, which has been reissued on Odyssey Y-33789 (mono), is superior not only to his own later one on Columbia M-31129 but to Bernstein's new one on Columbia M-33999.

(L')Oiseau de feu. The original 1910 score employing an enormous orchestra is performed by Boulez with the New York Philharmonic on Columbia M-33508 and by Haitink with the London Philharmonic on Philips 6500.483; but though the tonal opulence of these performances is very attractive, I prefer Stravinsky's own realization of the score with an assembled orchestra.

Petrushka. One hears the tonal opulence of the original 1911 score in Haitink's performance with the London Philharmonic on Philips 6500.458; and the first three tableaux are paced effectively; but the last tableau is rushed through ineffectively; and I therefore suggest instead Stravinsky's own performance, in which he sets a better tempo for the last tableau and slows it down for a superbly effective Dance of the Coachmen and Grooms.

(Le) Sacre du printemps. Solti's animated pacing of the perform-

ance with the Chicago Symphony, on London CS-6885, damages the *Rondes printanières* that must be, as Stravinsky directs in the score, *sostenuto e pesante* for the right effect. Abbado's performance with the London Symphony on Deutsche Grammophon 2530.685 and Haitink's with the London Philharmonic on Philips 6500.482 are good, but without the overwhelming power and impact of Boulez's or Stravinsky's own performance.

TCHAIKOVSKY

Concerto for Violin. Ricci plays it with the somewhat brash-sounding Netherlands Radio Philharmonic, on London SPC-2116 (with the Mendelssohn Concerto), with expressive warmth controlled by musical taste; but there is a special pleasure in hearing the continence and elegance of Grumiaux's performance with the New Philharmonia under Jan Krenz, on Philips 9500.086.

Hamlet, Voyevode, Francesca da Rimini for Orchestra. The unfamiliar first two turn out to be less interesting than the familiar third, with its wonderfully evocative opening chords and the superb melodic invention of its central section concerned with Paolo and Francesca. Dorati's performances with the National Symphony on London CS-6841 are excellent.

(The) Nutcracker. Dorati's pacing of the work in the performance with the Amsterdam Concertgebouw Orchestra on Philips 6747.257 is too fast even for some of the animated passages, and damaging to two of the greatest passages in the score — those for the first-act forest scene and the second-act *pas de deux* of the Sugar Plum Fairy and Her Cavalier, which require slower tempos to achieve their musical grandeur. Previn's is the performance to acquire in preference even to Bonynge's good one on London 2239.

Operas. After performances of *Eugene Onegin* with the tremolo-ridden singing of Bolshoi Theater sopranos and mezzo-sopranos one welcomes the performance on London OSA-13112 with the agreeable-sounding singing of Kubiak, Hamari, Bernd Weikl, Burrows and Ghiaurov, and the admirably paced and shaped orchestral context that Solti provides with the orchestra of the Royal Opera, Covent Garden.

Columbia/Melodiya M4-33210 offers the Bolshoi Theater performance of *The Maid of Orleans,* which has melodic writing in the style of *Onegin,* and which suffers, in this performance, from the fact that the voice of its star, Arkhipova, is that of a mature woman, not of a young girl, and frequently reveals its age in tremulous stridency. Moreover the King's mistress is a soprano whose voice is all thin tremolo. But the male singers are good.

The Bolshoi performance of the later and greater *Pique Dame* (*The Queen of Spades*) on Columbia/Melodiya M3-33828 is flawed by the unattractive-sounding and tremulous singing of Milashkina in the role of Lisa; but the other principals sing well and Ermler conducts effectively.

Serenade Op. 48 for Strings. See Dvořák Serenade Op. 22.

Symphonies. No. 6 (*Pathétique*), on Deutsche Grammophon 2530.350, gets an admirably straightforward and effective performance by Abbado with the Vienna Philharmonic; but the performance of No. 4, on 2530.651, is spoiled by the traditional distorting excesses in tempo and change of tempo that also spoil Solti's with the Chicago Symphony on London CS-6983.

VERDI

Operas. Philips has been continuing its series of unfamiliar early works which reveal the unmistakable powers that do not yet achieve as impressive writing as they will later. Of these, *Un Giorno di Regno,* Verdi's one comic opera before *Falstaff,* and this one an attempt at the *opera buffa* of Rossini and Donizetti, surprises one with the writing that his gifts make effective and interesting. The performance Gardelli conducts on 6703.055 has beautiful singing by Carreras and Jessye Norman and effective singing by Cossotto and Wixell with the Royal Philharmonic and Ambrosian Singers. *I Masnadieri,* on 6703.064, has excellent singing by Caballé, Bergonzi, Cappucilli and Raimondi with the New Philharmonia and Ambrosian Singers under Gardelli. And *Il Corsaro,* on 6700.098, has Norman, Caballé and Carreras, again with the New Philharmonia and Ambrosian Singers under Gardelli.

Of the more familiar *Luisa Miller* the first two acts offer merely competent writing, except for the tenor aria *"Quando le sere al placido";* but the third has writing that is powerfully expressive and distinguished. The performance excellently conducted by Maag on London OSA-13114 has beautifully phrased singing by Caballé, superb singing by Milnes, and singing by Pavarotti that is agreeable-sounding in its lower range but constricted and unattractive as it rises, with the London Opera Chorus and the so-called National Philharmonic Orchestra.

Outstanding among the earlier works is *Macbeth;* and Deutsche Grammophon 2709.082 offers an outstanding performance in which Abbado produces with the orchestra of La Scala a superb context for the singing of the principals — Cappucilli, Verrett, Domingo, Ghiaurov — and the excellent La Scala chorus.

The very first phrases of the overture of the later *I Vespri Siciliani* seize one's mind with the power that operates throughout the work; and the performance superbly conducted by James Levine on RCA ARL4-0370 has excellent singing by Arroyo, Domingo, Milnes and Raimondi with the New Philharmonia and John Alldis Choir.

Also superbly conducted by Levine on RCA ARL4-1864 is *La Forza del Destino,* which is excellently sung by Leontyne Price, Domingo, Milnes, Cossotto, Giaiotti and Bacquier with the London Symphony and John Alldis Choir.

The beautiful second-act duet from *Un Ballo in Maschera* and first-act duet from *Otello* are sung well by Price and Domingo on RCA ARL1-0840 (with Puccini duets).

Philips 6580.171 has the baritone Wixell's impressive performances of arias from *Attila, Rigoletto, Il Trovatore, La Forza del Destino, Un Ballo in Maschera, Don Carlo, Otello* and *Falstaff.*

What one hears in Bergonzi's performances of arias on the three records of Philips 747.193 — the luster and ease of flow of his voice; the sensitiveness and feeling for shape of his phrasing; the grace and lilt of his style that is reminiscent of Schipa's — show him to have been the great singer of Verdi after Bjoerling.

Caballé's superb performances of arias from the early operas, originally on RCA LSC-2995, have been reissued with improved sound on AGL1-1283. Her recent performances of arias from the other operas on London OS-26424 are less good, spinning out phrases at excessive length.

The performance of *Il Trovatore* reissued on RCA AVM2-0699 (mono), with the beautiful singing of Milanov, Bjoerling and Warren, is one to acquire (reduce treble; increase bass). But the *Rigoletto* reissued on AVM2-0698, with Berger, Peerce and Warren, which is spoiled by electronic "enhancement", I advise against.

Quartet. This work of an accomplished composer experimenting with a new genre offers individual and attractive writing that is performed admirably by the English Chamber Orchestra under Zukerman on Columbia M-33415, with Rossini's charming Sonata No. 1 for violin, viola, cello and bass.

VIVALDI

(L')Estro armonico. Reissued on Bach Guild HM-37/9 are the excellent performances of the twelve violin concerti grossi by the Vienna State Opera Orchestra under Rossi.

(The) Four Seasons. The excellent performance by the violinist Yoshio Unno with the NHK String Ensemble is reissued on Odyssey Y-32884.

WAGNER

Lohengrin. Philips 6747.241 offers the excellent live performance recorded in the Bayreuth Festival Theater in 1962, with Sawallisch conducting, and Silya (her voice a little too slight and colorless for Elsa), Thomas, Vinay, Varnay and Franz Crass.

(Die) Meistersinger. The Bayreuth Festival 1974 performance on Philips 6747.167 is paced and shaped well by Varvisio and has the superb singing of Ridderbusch as Hans Sachs, but inadequate or poor singing in the other roles. And what one expected to be outstanding — the performance on Deutsche Grammophon 2713.011 with Fischer-Dieskau singing Sachs — is a great disappointment. The expressive intensification that another singer would achieve with a crescendo in the legato phrase Fischer-Dieskau achieves with an excessive change to

detached vehement barks. Of the other principals Domingo has a fine voice, but neither its timbre nor his German sounds quite right. And Jochum's pacing of the work lacks animation. However London OSA-1512 provides a performance that is excellently conducted by Solti and for the most part excellently sung by Norman Bailey (Sachs), Hannelore Bode (Eva, and astonishingly improved after her poor singing in the Bayreuth performance), Weikl (Beckmesser), Kurt Moll (Pogner), Hamari (Magdalene) and Adolf Dallapozza (David) with the Vienna Philharmonic and the chorus of the State Opera. With all these one accepts the Walther of René Kollo, who now phrases with a sensitiveness he lacked in the Karajan performance, but whose voice still hasn't the warmth and luster and ease of flow required by the successive versions of the Prize Song.

Excerpts. London CS-6860 offers Horst Stein's superb performances of the Overture to *Der fliegende Holländer,* Preludes to *Lohengrin* and *Die Meistersinger,* and Prelude and Finale of *Tristan und Isolde* with the Vienna Philharmonic. The first two require additional bass.

Very good too are Haitink's performances of the Preludes to *Lohengrin* and *Die Meistersinger* and Prelude and Finale of *Tristan* with the Concertgebouw on Philips 6500.932; but the Prelude to *Parsifal* needs a slower tempo.

The Prelude and Finale of *Tristan* and the Wesendonck Songs are performed well by Colin Davis and the London Symphony, on Philips 9500.031, with Jessye Norman, whose singing is now lovely, now not, and, to my ear, not expressive.

WOLF

Mörike Songs. The performances in the first volume of Fischer-Dieskau's new recording of the songs, Deutsche Grammophon 2709.053, reveal his voice's loss of tonal opulence, though not of its distinctive timbre; they reveal also an increase in the excessive italicizing of words that distorts the musical phrase; and the occasional explosive vehemence of his singing elicits explosions on the piano by Barenboim.

Deutsche Grammophon 2530.584 reproduces the concert in 1973 in which Fischer-Dieskau sang a number of the songs with the Russian pianist Richter. The voice is beautiful in quiet singing; but the occasional vehement outbursts are not agreeable to the ear; and Richter's playing, possibly because of microphone placement, is too obtrusive.

MISCELLANEOUS COLLECTIONS

Blegen. Columbia M-34518 offers her lovely singing in vocal pieces by Handel that include *"Care selve"* from *Atalanta* and *"Let the bright Seraphim"* from *Samson,* and excerpts from the less interesting *Su le Sponde del Tebro* of Alessandro Scarlatti, with Gerard Schwarz occasionally playing trumpet obbligato and performing a group of instrumental pieces by Handel, *A Sett of Aires,* in which he conducts the Columbia Chamber Ensemble.

Caballé. With the arias by Puccini, Mascagni, Giordano and the like, on London OS-26497, are *"Vieni! T'affretta!"* from Verdi's *Macbeth* and *"Tacea la notte"* from *Il Trovatore,* which are sung impressively except for the climactic high C in *"Tacea"* that is strident and not on pitch.

Carreras. His beautiful tenor voice is heard, on Philips 9500.203, in well-phrased performances of arias from unfamiliar operas by Donizetti and Bellini and works of Verdi.

Cliburn. RCA ARL1-1176 has his performance of Chopin's Barcarolle, a later and more cohesive performance of Debussy's *L'Isle joyeuse,* and performances of pieces by Schumann, Granados, Liszt, Rachmaninov and Ravel.

Domingo. He uses his fine tenor voice well, on RCA ARL1-10048, in arias from operas of Verdi, Bizet and Gounod and less consequential pieces.

Evans, Geraint. Reissued on London SR-33226 are excellent performances of arias from operas of Handel, Mozart, Beethoven, Donizetti, Verdi, Musorgsky and Britten.

Grumiaux. On Philips 6500.879 he brings his gift for sensitive and sustained phrasing to the melodic writing in a group of unfamiliar and engaging 18th-century violin sonatas by Leclair, Veracini, Vivaldi and Nardini.

Horne. An admirable performance with Martin Katz of Falla's *Seven Popular Spanish Songs* is on London OS-26301, with

443

performances of a few engaging songs by Nin, a few pleasantly melodious ones by Bizet, and Debussy's *Chansons de Bilitis,* which I find uninteresting.

Milnes. London OS-26366 offers his beautiful singing in arias from operas of Bellini, Donizetti and Verdi, in addition to a *"Largo al factotum"* from *The Barber of Seville* that is damaged by manifestations of excessive exuberance.

To his excellent singing in scenes from Verdi's *Macbeth* and *Luisa Miller and the aria "Eri tu"* from *Un Ballo in Maschera,* on RCA ARL1-0851, he adds a performance of an aria from *Euryanthe,* the least known but best of Weber's operas.

Pavarotti. The voice that becomes brassy and otherwise unattractive as it rises in its upper range is heard, on London OS-26510, in arias by Rossini, Donizetti and Verdi.

Von Stade. Her beautiful mezzo-soprano voice, on Columbia M-34206, is deployed in well-shaped phrases in arias from operas by Meyerbeer, Berlioz, Gounod, Thomas, Massenet and Offenbach.

PERFORMANCES ADDED
BEFORE THE BOOK WENT TO PRESS
BACH, CARL PHILIPP EMANUEL

His superb *Magnificat* is on Argo ZRG-853, excellently performed by the Choir of King's College, Cambridge, the Academy of St. Martin-in-the-Fields, Felicity Palmer, Helen Watts, Robert Tear and Stephen Roberts under Philip Ledger's direction.

BACH, JOHANN SEBASTIAN

The difference in sound between the baroque violin and bow with which Sergiu Luca plays the six Sonatas and Partitas for unaccompanied violin, and the modernized violin and bow used by Szigeti, is of less consequence than the difference between Luca's competent performances of the works on Nonesuch HC-73030 and Szigeti's overwhelmingly great ones, which Vanguard has reissued on HM-54/5/6 (mono).

BEETHOVEN

Even in the concert hall the first movement of the *Eroica* Symphony as Karajan performs it with the Berlin Philharmonic in Deutsche Grammophon 2740.172 would sound hurried to me, not only because of the fast tempo but because of the rigidity with which it is maintained—with not the slightest modification for the second subject or the dissonant climax of the development. And I would be troubled by that rigidity even of the acceptable tempo of the first movement of the Eighth. But in these and the other performances as they come off the records there is in addition what is done to them by the recording that makes loud passages sound as if played in the room in which one is listening, and soft ones sound as if played by another orchestra three or four rooms away. Thus Beethoven's contrasts of *fortissimo* and *pianissimo* are exaggerated to *ff and ppppp,* which is close to inaudible. And in fact the string basses' opening statements in the third movement of the Fifth *are* almost inaudible, as are their comments on the opening statements of the second movement of the Eighth. For someone interested in the nine symphonies as performed by Karajan with his extraordinary orchestra, the altered versions of them that come off the records will be frustrating.

Columbia has completed its reissue of the Budapest Quartet's great 1952 (mono) performances of the string quartets with Odyssey Y4-34644, which has the last five quartets and Great Fugue. (The bass knob must be turned up for sufficient cello sound.)

The beautiful performance of the Serenade Op. 8 for string trio that Szymon Goldberg, Paul Hindemith and Emanuel Feuermann recorded in the '30s has been reissued by the Bruno Walter Society on RR-459 (mono; with Hindemith's Trio No. 2).

Lynn Harrell and James Levine, on RCA ARL2-2241, play well together in the five Sonatas for cello and piano, but don't attain the spacious expressive power of the pre-war Casals performances on imported EMI-Electrola C 147-01538/9 (mono).

Ashkenazy continues his recording of the Sonatas for piano on London CS-7024 with excellent performances of the uninteresting Op. 10 No. 1, the more interesting Op. 10 No. 2, and the quiet and lovely Op. 28 *(Pastoral).*

The beautiful and moving Mass in C is on Argo ZRG-739 in an outstandingly fine performance conducted by George Guest, with the Choir of St. John's College, Cambridge, the Academy of St. Martin-in-the-Fields, Palmer, Watts, Tear and Christopher Keyte.

BERLIOZ

In the performance of the marvelous song cycle *Les Nuits d'Eté* on Columbia M-34563 Boulez provides superb orchestral contexts with the BBC Symphony for the unattractive-sounding singing of Minton and Burrows. Eleanor Steber's great performance on Odyssey Y-33287 (mono) is still the one to acquire.

BOCCHERINI

Philips 9500.305 offers the Quartetto Italiano's fine performances of the Quartet Op. 6 no. 1, which has perhaps the most extraordinarily lovely and affecting of Boccherini's slow movements, and two other products of his fascinatingly individual mind, the Quartets Op. 6 No. 3 and Op. 58 No. 2.

BRAHMS

All four symphonies and the Haydn Variations are performed well, except for an occasional excessively fast tempo, by Abravanel with the Utah Symphony on Vanguard VCS-10117/20.

In an otherwise effective performance of the Symphony No. 3 with the Chicago Symphony, on RCA ARL1-2097, James Levine slows down the coda of the second movement excessively, which changes its expressive significance for the worse. In his performance of the Symphony No. 4 with the same orchestra, on ARL1-2624, the first movement, marked *Allegro non troppo,* moves *troppo allegro* for it to achieve its proper expressive effect; and the *Andante moderato* second movement also is too fast.

Christa Ludwig, on Columbia M-34535, deploys her beautiful mezzo-soprano voice in well-shaped phrases with moving expressiveness in *Sapphische Ode, Immer leiser wird mein Schlum-*

mer, Feldeinsamkeit, Ständchen and other songs that include the *Zigeunerlieder,* with piano accompaniments by Leonard Bernstein.

BYRD

The powerfully expressive Masses for four and five voices are sung under Simon Preston's direction, on Argo ZRG-858, by the Choir of Christ Church Cathedral, Oxford, whose boys' voices are a little shrill.

CHOPIN

Deutsche Grammophon 2430.826 offers the beautiful playing of a new young Polish pianist, Krystian Zimerman, in the Andante spianato and Grande Polonaise Op. 22, Scherzo Op. 54 and other pieces, on a piano whose high notes are cold and die out too quickly.

London CS-7022 has Ashkenazy's fine performances of the Barcarolle, Polonaise-Fantaisie, and last Nocturnes, Waltzes and Mazurkas.

The reissue on Odyssey Y-34618 of Istomin's excellent performance of the Concerto No. 2 with the Philadelphia Orchestra under Ormandy enabled me to discover how much more beautiful this work is than hearings years ago led me to think. The record offers also Istomin's performance of Schumann's Concerto with an orchestra under Bruno Walter, in which the first movement sounds hurried.

DONIZETTI

The charming *L'Elisir d'Amore* is sung admirably, on Columbia M3-34585, by Cotrubas, Domingo, Wixell and Geraint Evans with the chorus and orchestra of the Royal Opera, Covent Garden, under Pritchard's direction.

The beautiful writing in *La Favorita,* which includes the tenor aria *"Spirto gentil"*, suffers, in the performance on London OSA-13113, from the worn, tremulous state of Cossotto's mezzo-soprano voice and the brassy, rasping tenor of Pavarotti.

ADDITIONAL PERFORMANCES

The performance of *Lucia di Lammermoor* conducted effectively by López Cobos, on Philips 6703.080, offers a newly corrected text that is sung well by Caballé, except for the occasional strident climactic high note, Carreras, Cappuccilli, Ricciarelli and Ramey with the ORF Orchestra and Chorus.

DOWLAND

The beautiful pieces in the *Second Booke of Songs* that are sung by the soprano or the bass of the Consort of Musicke, or by both, on Oiseau-Lyre DSLO-528/9, are made unenjoyable by the unattractive timbres of their voices; but this is not true of the ones sung by the tenor or by the entire quartet in which the soprano and bass are less prominently audible.

DVOŘÁK

The Symphonic Variations Op. 78, one of his best orchestral works, is on Deutsche Grammophon 2530.712 (with the uninteresting *Water Goblin* Op. 107 and *Noonday Witch* Op. 108), excellently performed by Kubelik with the Bavarian Radio Symphony.

The engagingly melodious *Legends* Op. 59 are on D.G. 2530.786, also excellently performed by Kubelik with the English Chamber Orchestra.

The engaging Piano Quintet Op. 81 is performed admirably by Emanuel Ax and the Cleveland Quartet on RCA ARL1-2240.

Stabat Mater, on D. G. 2707.099, has the defect of some other large-scale works of Dvořák's—that each section begins with an impressive idea that is dwelt on at what becomes excessive length. Kubelik produces an excellent performance with the Bavarian Radio Symphony and Chorus, Mathis, Anna Reynolds, Ochman and Shirley-Quirk.

GLINKA

The unfamiliar and fine songs on one side of Deutsche Grammophon 2530.725 (with songs by Rachmaninov on the reverse side) are sung by Vishnevskaya with expressive use of a voice that becomes harsh and tremulous in moments of intensity, and with admirable piano accompaniments by Rostropovich.

PERFORMANCES OF TODAY

HANDEL

The writing in *Belshazzar,* expressively adequate in the first act, comes to exciting life in the second. The work is performed well, on Telefunken 6.35326, by Harnoncourt with his Concentus Musicus, the Stockholm Chamber Choir, and soloists who include Palmer and Tear.

Judas Maccabaeus, though not on the level of the greatest works, is pleasant to listen to, and is sung well, on Archive 2710.021, by Palmer, Janet Baker, Davies, Shirley-Quirk and the Westminster School Choir with the English Chamber Orchestra under Mackerras's direction.

HAYDN

Colin Davis conducts the marvelous Concertgebouw Orchestra in the fine Symphony No. 88 and incandescent No. 99 on Philips 9500.138; and in another of the incandescent last symphonies, No. 103 *(Drum Roll)* and the less interesting No. 87 on 9500.323.

The Quartetto Italiano's beautiful performances of the Quartets Op. 76 No. 3 *(Emperor)* and No. 4 *(Sunrise)* are on Philips 9500.157.

The Beaux Arts Trio's excellent performances of the piano trios continue with the early Hob. No. 2 and late Nos. 6 and 8 on Philips 9500.325, and Nos. 7, 9 and the outstanding No. 12 on 9500.326.

Nonesuch H-71344 has Gilbert Kalish's sensitive performances of four piano sonatas: Hob. Nos. 36, 28, 41 and 49—the last a marvel of the Haydn operation of constant melodic, harmonic and rhythmic surprise.

Philips 6707.029 continues the series of Haydn's operas with *Orlando Paladino,* which again offers accomplished writing that is pleasant to hear, sung well by Arleen Augér, Ameling, Gwendolyn Killebrew, Claes Ahnsjö and Luxon with the Lausanne Chamber Orchestra under Dorati's direction.

JANÁČEK

The dramatic dialogue of *Katya Kabanova* proceeds in arioso with no expressive relation to the words or to the continuous

449

flow of powerful and often dissonant orchestral writing, except for a couple of passages sung by Katya at moments of great emotional intensity in which the arioso attains expressiveness. Søderstrøm's singing of this role is the outstanding achievement in the performance, on London OSA-12109, with Czech singers and the Vienna Philharmonic under Mackerras's direction.

MAHLER

The Symphony No. 2 is performed superbly, on Deutsche Grammophon 2707.094, by Abbado with the Chicago Symphony, Horne (who sings *Urlicht* with a beauty of vocal sound in sustained phrasing that is unique in my experience), Neblett and Margaret Hillis's chorus. The instrument called *Ruthe* in the score is omitted in the third movement; and the recording has soft passages receding into the distance, so that the brass or woodwinds occasionally sound as if they are placed in front of the violins.

Excellent performances of *Songs from "Des Knaben Wunderhorn"* by Jessye Norman and Shirley-Quirk with the Concertgebouw Orchestra under Haitink are on Philips 9500.316.

MENDELSSOHN

The engaging Symphony No. 3 *(Scotch)* and *Fingal's Cave* Overture are performed well by Comissiona with his Baltimore Symphony on Turnabout QTB-S-34604. Their equally good performance of Mendelssohn's most attractive symphony, No. 4 *(Italian)*, on 34643, is damaged by the obtrusively loud recorded sound of the kettledrums.

A finer performance of the *Italian* Symphony by the English Chamber Orchestra under Leppard is on RCA ARL1-2632, with the uninteresting Symphony No. 5 *(Reformation)*.

The Octet for strings is performed well by the Cleveland and Tokyo Quartets on RCA ARL1-2532.

MOZART

The spaciously grand *adagio* introduction to the Symphony K.504 *(Prague)*, as Britten performs it with the English Chamber Orchestra on London CS-6741, is overwhelming; and one continues to be overwhelmed by his treatment of what follows. The reverse side has a fine performance of Schubert's *Unfinished* Symphony.

Perahia's playing—in the performances of the Piano Concertos K.271 and 467 with the English Chamber Orchestra on Columbia M-34562—is made unsatisfying much of the time by his beginning a statement with a force that is not sustained but diminishes to a whispered conclusion. There is less of this damaging tendency in K.271 than in K.467.

The performances of the Piano Concertos K.503 and 595, on Deutsche Grammophon 2530.642, offer musically satisfying playing by Gulda with fine playing by the Vienna Philharmonic under Abbado.

Huberman's superb performance of the Violin Concerto K.216 with the Vienna Philharmonic under Dobrowen is excellently reproduced by the Bruno Walter Society's BWS-351 (mono); but though his playing in the Concerto K.218 is clear, the orchestra under Walter is reproduced very poorly.

De Peyer plays with more beautiful tone in his earlier performance of the Clarinet Quintet K.581 with the Melos Ensemble than in his new one with the Amadeus Quartet on Deutsche Grammophon 2530.720.

In the final volume of Sonatas for violin and piano, London CSA-2245, Szymon Goldberg again doesn't produce the beautiful tone of earlier years but plays with undiminished musical sensitiveness and admirable ensemble rapport with Radu Lupu.

The peculiarly altered and muffled sound with which they are reproduced by Bruno Walter Society RR-502 (mono) doesn't prevent one from hearing the impressiveness of Schnabel's 1943 performances of Mozart's Piano Sonata K.533 and Rondo K.494 and Beethoven's Bagatelles Op. 33, and the major portion of a 1944 performance of the great Andante of Mozart's Concerto K.453.

The performance of the *Requiem* reissued on Odyssey Y-34619 (mono)—with Bruno Walter conducting the New York Philharmonic, and beautiful singing by Seefried, Tourel, Simoneau, Warfield and the Westminster Choir—is a good one.

Philips 6703.079 makes it possible to discover the high quality of the unfamiliar *La Clemenza di Tito* in the excellent performance conducted by Colin Davis, with Janet Baker, Minton, Burrows, von Stade, Popp and the orchestra and chorus of the Royal Opera, Covent Garden.

The beautiful voices of Te Kanawa and von Stade, in the performance of *Così Fan Tutte* conducted by Alain Lombard on RCA ARL3-2629, are not matched, as this opera requires, by the voices of the tenor David Rendall and baritone Philippe Huttenlocher. The performance to acquire is still the one conducted by Colin Davis.

MUSORGSKY

Angel SX-3844 provides the first recorded performance of Musorgsky's own 1872 revision of his *Boris Godunov,* as distinguished from the Rimsky-Korsakov recomposition of the work that is still performed by most opera companies and has been recorded previously. The music is sung well by Talvela (Boris), Gedda (Dmitri), a number of Polish soloists and the Polish Radio Chorus of Krakow with the Polish National Radio Symphony; but its pacing by Semkow—now too fast, now too slow— is damaging to the work's significance and effect.

Musorgsky's more somber 1869 first version of Act 2 of *Boris* (with Shuisky's description of the murdered Tsarevich replaced by the expanded 1872 version) is on Columbia/Melodiya M-34569, sung by the impressive bass Shtokolov with soloists and orchestra of the Kirov Theater, Leningrad, under the effective direction of Eltsin. The reverse side has arias from operas by Glinka, Rimsky-Korsakov, Dargomyzhsky, Tchaikovsky and Rachmaninov.

Since the later *Khovantchina* was left with its final scene uncompleted and the earlier portions in disorder, someone had to put it in order and complete it; and Rimsky-Korsakov, who did this, also inflicted on it the same damaging "correction" as on *Boris*. But this doesn't prevent the distinctive character and power of Musorgsky's writing from being heard and exercising their overwhelming effect; and though the 1951 Bolshoi Theater performance on Bruno Walter Society RR-458 (mono) isn't accompanied by a libretto or a synopsis, the expressive arioso and orchestral writing hold one in their grip even with no knowledge of the action they are related to. The performance, conducted effectively by Nebolsin, has the superb bass Reizen as Dosifey, the impressive mezzo-soprano Maksakova as Marfa, and good singers in the other roles, except the tremulous soprano Kositzina as Emma.

PALESTRINA

The beautiful, but to my ears unchanging, vocal polyphony of the *Missa Aeterna Christi munera,* the *Oratio Jeremiae Prophetae* and the Motets *Sicut cervus desiderat, Super flumina Babylonis* and *O bone Jesu,* on Deutsche Grammophon 2533.322, is sung well by Pro Cantione Antiqua of London under Bruno Turner's direction.

SCHUBERT

The great posthumous Piano Sonata in A is performed well by Lupu on London CS-6996.

Grumiaux and Paul Crossley play beautifully together, on Philips 9500.394, in the charming early Sonata Op. 162 for violin and piano, and the even earlier Sonatinas Op. 137, of which No. 2, with its remarkable opening movement, is the best.

The Quartetto Italiano's tempo in the first movement of the Quartet Op. 29 is much too slow; and I recommend instaead the Budapest Quartet's performance in Odyssey Y3-33320 (mono).

SCHUMANN

A major work for piano, the Symphonic Etudes, and the engaging *Papillons* are on Columbia M-35439, excellently performed by Perahia.

STRAUSS

Reissued on London R-23241 (mono) is a performance of his orchestral masterpiece *Don Quixote* by Clemens Krauss with the Vienna Philharmonic and Pierre Fournier, of which the one flaw is the excessive slowing down of the impassioned climax of Variation 3 (near the end of side 1).

STRAVINSKY

James Levine, on RCA ARL1-2624, produces with the Chicago Symphony a performance of *Petrushka* that is paced almost exactly like Stravinsky's but makes the strands of the textures stand out not only more distinctly but with startlingly vivid orchestral coloring.

Colin Davis conducts the Concertgebouw Orchestra, on Philips 9500.323, in a powerful performance of *Le Sacre du Printemps* which, like Boulez's with the Cleveland Orchestra, offers the beautiful orchestral sound that Stravinsky's performance doesn't have.

TCHAIKOVSKY

Solti rips through the Symphony No. 6 *(Pathétique)* with his Chicago Symphony on London CS-7034; Ozawa, in his performance of No. 5 with the Boston Symphony on Deutsche Grammophon 2530.888, destroys coherence and shape with his exaggerated changes of tempo: and Yuri Ahranovitch's performance of the *Manfred* Symphony with the London Symphony, on D.G. 2530.878, is made ineffective by the pacing that disregards Tchaikovsky's directions.

An outstandingly fine performance of the opera *Pique Dame (The Queen of Spades)* on Deutsche Grammophon 2711.019 has effective conducting by Rostropovich, Vishnevskaya's agreeable-sounding and expressive Lisa, the Herman of Peter Gougaloff, whose tenor voice is lighter, more lyrical and more sensitively inflected than Atlantov's in the Bolshoi performance, Resnik's excellent Countess, Bernd Weikl's beautifully sung Yeletzky, good singing by the other soloists and the chorus of Radio France, playing by the Orchestre National de France which is vastly superior to that of the Bolshoi's orchestra, and recorded sound which also is superior to that of the Bolshoi performance.

The beautiful score for the ballet *Swan Lake* is performed well by Bonynge with the National Philharmonic on London CSA-2315.

THOMSON

The Mother of Us All, one of the very few American operas worth listening to (the others being Thomson's *Four Saints in Three Acts* and Copland's *The Tender Land*), is available on records at last on New World NW-288/9, performed by the Santa Fe Opera. Mignon Dunn is not the right singer for the central role of Susan B. Anthony, whose high notes are beyond Dunn's range of agreeable sound; but the other singers are good, and Leppard conducts effectively.

VERDI

Deutsche Grammophon 2709.071 offers the superb La Scala performance of *Simon Boccanegra* that Abbado conducted in Washington in 1976, with Cappuccilli in the title role, Ghiaurov as Fiesco and van Dam as Paolo, and made even better by the substitution of Freni as Amelia and Carreras as Gabriele.

Outstanding also is the performance of *La Traviata* on D.G. 2707.103, with Cotrubas, Domingo, Milnes and the orchestra and chorus of the Bavarian State Opera conducted by Carlos Kleiber. It is an operation strikingly similar to Toscanini's in the way the singers and players are, in the expressive plasticity of their singing and playing, held to the conductor's plastic and expressive shaping of the music—a shaping which, as it happens, is also, except for a few details, strikingly similar to Toscanini's in conception and in the realization of that conception in the progression of perfectly integrated singing and playing.

The *Il Trovatore* on London OSA-13124 has Sutherland and Pavarotti, whose voices I find unattractive, with the excellent singing of Horne and Wixell.

Philips 6700.105 makes it possible to hear the impressive writing in the early and unfamiliar *I Due Foscari,* excellently performed under Gardelli's direction by Carreras, Cappuccilli, Ricciarelli and Ramey with the ORF Orchestra and Chorus.

London has reissued on OSA-13122 the excellent performance of *La Forza del Destino* originally issued by RCA in the '60s, with Milanov, di Stefano, Warren, Tozzi, Elias and the chorus and orchestra of the Accademia di Santa Cecilia, Rome, under Previtali.

455

ADDITIONAL PERFORMANCES

Solti has again recorded the *Requiem,* this time on RCA ARL2-2476, with the Chicago Symphony and Chorus, Leontyne Price, Janet Baker, Luchetti and van Dam. The singing of Price and van Dam is excellent; but Luchetti's voice is less attractive, and the timbre of Baker's voice turns out to be obtrusively wrong for this music. In addition the exaggeration of contrasts of soft and loud is one of the manifestations of overexcitement and tension in the performance.

WAGNER

The early *Der fliegende Holländer* I find uninteresting; and the performance conducted by Solti on London OSA-13119 is a flawed one, with superb playing by the Chicago Symphony and good singing by Margaret Hillis's chorus, moderately good singing by Norman Bailey in the title role and Janis Martin as Senta, but singing by Talvela (Daland) that isn't agreeable to the ear, and singing by Kollo (Erik) that is even less so.

Martha Mödl and Wolfgang Windgassen in their prime are heard, on Telefunken 6.38020 (mono), in an excellent performance of the second-act duet of *Tristan und Isolde* (with the usual cut before *"O sink hernieder"* but none thereafter), with Brangäne's warnings sung well by Johanna Blätter. Rother's ineffective shaping of the Prelude is followed by Mödl's fine performance of the *Liebestod;* and another side has the long and boring first-act duet of Isolde and Brangäne. The recording subordinates Windgassen to Mödl in their duet.

COLLECTIONS

The English madrigals in honor of Queen Elizabeth that were assembled in 1601 under the title *The Triumph of Oriana* are sung admirably by the Pro Cantione Musicae under Ian Partridge on Archive 2533.347.

Vanguard's fine collection, *The English Madrigal School,* excellently sung by the Deller Consort, has been reissued on Bach Guild HM-57/58 (mono).

456